W9-DAW-520

The 100 Greatest
Literary Characters

The 100 Greatest Literary Characters

James Plath
Gail Sinclair
Kirk Curnutt

ROWMAN & LITTLEFIELD
Lanham • Boulder • New York • London

Published by Rowman & Littlefield
An imprint of The Rowman & Littlefield Publishing Group, Inc.
4501 Forbes Boulevard, Suite 200, Lanham, Maryland 20706
www.rowman.com

6 Tinworth Street, London, SE11 5AL, United Kingdom

Copyright © 2019 by The Rowman & Littlefield Publishing Group, Inc.

All rights reserved. No part of this book may be reproduced in any form or by any
electronic or mechanical means, including information storage and retrieval systems,
without written permission from the publisher, except by a reviewer who may quote
passages in a review.

British Library Cataloguing in Publication Information Available

Library of Congress Cataloging-in-Publication Data

Names: Plath, James, author. | Sinclair, Gail D., author. | Curnutt, Kirk, 1964– author.
Title: The 100 greatest literary characters / James Plath, Gail Sinclair, Kirk Curnutt.
Other titles: One hundred greatest literary characters
Description: Lanham : Rowman & Littlefield, [2019] | Includes bibliographical references
    and index.
Identifiers: LCCN 2018054443 (print) | LCCN 2018059165 (ebook) | ISBN 9781538103760
    (electronic) | ISBN 9781538103753 (cloth : alk. paper)
Subjects: LCSH: Fictitious characters. | American fiction—History and criticism. |
    English fiction—History and criticism.
Classification: LCC PS374.C43 (ebook) | LCC PS374.C43 .P54 2019 (print) | DDC
    808.8/027—dc23
LC record available at https://lccn.loc.gov/2018054443

For readers past, present, and future,
including our own next generation of readers:
our children and grandchildren

Contents

Acknowledgments

We wish to express our gratitude to our respective universities and support staff and to thank the 100 teachers, scholars, librarians, writers, editors, and book lovers who answered our "best characters" questionnaire—especially those who went beyond what was asked for: Edward Allen, Jackson R. Bryer, Donald J. Greiner, Brian Keener, Edward J. Manley, Larry Mazzeno, Susan Jaret McKinstry, Lorne Mook, Sharon Neal, Judith Newman, Kathleen O'Gorman, Carolyn Segal, Brian Steffen, Frederic Svoboda, Judith Valente, Martha Modena Vertreace-Doody, Frank Waterstraat, and Jim Zelenski. We are also grateful for the patience and support of our Rowman & Littlefield editor, Stephen Ryan.

Introduction

Writer John Gardner once remarked, "The first thing that makes a reader read a book is the characters." Behind every great book is a great character, and as Gabriel García Márquez reminds us, "In every novel, the character is a collage: a collage of different characters that you've known or heard about or read about." If the characters come alive, the novel comes alive. But among those great books and great characters, which ones stand out?

A Google advanced algorithm estimates that in modern history close to 130 million books have been published. Meanwhile, R. R. Bowker, the company that compiles a running list of books in print, estimates that in any given year there are approximately 275,000 classifiable books published, with some 43,000 of them likely to be fiction. Obviously, it's humanly impossible to read them all, and that alone makes it equally impossible to come up with a definitive list of "100 Greatest Fictional Characters in Literature." But if you lean heavily, as we did, in the direction of time-honored reader favorites, prototypes, and cultural influencers—characters who have become larger than their lives on the page—the task becomes slightly easier. We decided to prioritize those who have somehow entered the collective public consciousness, ones who were influential models for others to follow, and ones who have been so popular with readers that they have become significant, memorable, or even cherished. But to avoid an overly familiar list, we have also included characters who are so vibrant and alive that they deserve to be in such good company.

Because lists naturally reflect the knowledge gaps and inherent biases of their makers, we sought to compensate by consulting numerous reader- and industry-chosen lists and by polling 100 writers, professors, librarians, teachers, and book lovers—which, incidentally, is roughly twice the number that the now-defunct *Book* magazine polled when they created their frequently cited "100 Best Characters in Fiction" list. We coauthors specialize in American literature, so we were especially diligent in seeking suggestions from people outside the areas we know best. So there was indeed a method to our madness. We began the process by assembling a baseline list compiled from our research, read those recommended novels and short stories with which we were unfamiliar, then met to discuss the characters and agree on additional reading and research. More meetings led to a shorter list, and with three coauthors that list turned out to be a negotiated compromise. Along the way, we investigated new characters who came to our attention. In addition to the eighty-five characters we agreed upon, to move the book beyond the familiar we decided that each of us should get a handful of discretionary picks—strong fictional personalities that we think ought to be included.

We considered notables from literary and popular fiction and from children's literature, both classic and contemporary. In writing about the characters, we tried to describe them in such a way as to make clear why we think they belong in a volume such as this. As the author of *Empathy and the Novel* reminds us, "Fictional characters can become mental companions to last a lifetime, and relationships across generations can be built around affection for a character or a fictional world." There are fictional figures in this volume who *are* beloved across generations—even centuries—but to be included a character did not have to be lovable, heroic, or even likable. There are a great many in literature that are quite the opposite, yet there's something about them that makes them unforgettable.

Narrowing the number of characters to 100 proved challenging nonetheless, and there are a lot of deserving, memorable literary figures we had to omit. We deliberately tried to avoid picking multiple characters from single novels in order to create a broader list of books, and choosing a character within a single great novel proved yet another challenge. In the case of Huck Finn, for example, we could have just as easily gone with Jim, Huck's mentor, if it weren't for the fact that Huck has interactions with a great many more people that he also learns from. Tom Joad was enough of a folk hero that Woody Guthrie wrote a song about him, but Ma Joad is the backbone of the family. And what character is more memorable, Frankenstein's creature or the mad scientist who created him? Sometimes we went with the character without whom such a pairing would never have happened, but there were still tough calls every step of the way.

Our overall task was made only slightly easier by the fact that we were asked by the publisher to consider just fiction. If a character's first appearance was in a play, that person was ineligible, and the same with children's picture books, epic poems, comic books, and graphic novels. That's why there's no Odysseus, Beowulf, Don Juan, Lady Macbeth, Othello, or Willy Loman here, nor the Grinch, Batman, or Superman. Rowman & Littlefield hopes to publish separate volumes that will include such characters, and it's just as well. The book we have assembled is crowded enough with important, colorful, and absorbing characters.

But let's be clear: These are *our* 100 greatest fictional characters, and we understand perfectly well that readers will agree with some of our choices and question others. That's okay. After all, isn't it part of the nature and the fun of such lists? That's one reason why we decided to include not just the usual suspects but also lesser-known characters who are so psychologically complex or richly drawn that they deserve to be in a volume such as this. We hope you enjoy reading about these unique characters and that, in an age when so many other things vie for people's attentions, our list sparks a return to libraries and bookstores as much as it prompts debate.

BIBLIOGRAPHY

Keen, Suzanne. *Empathy and the Novel.* New York: Oxford University Press, 2007.

Parr, Ben. "Google: There Are 129,864,880 Books in the Entire World." Mashable. August 5, 2010. https://mashable.com/2010/08/05/number-of-books-in-the-world/#CNHJ1B2Aqmqy.

Wilkens, Matt. "How Many New Novels Are Published Each Year?" *MattWilkens.com* (blog). October 14, 2009. https://mattwilkens.com/2009/10/14/how-many-novels-are-published-each-year/.

A

CAPTAIN AHAB

First Appearance: *Moby-Dick*
Date of First Appearance: 1851
Author: Herman Melville (1819–1891)

I'll chase him round Good Hope, and round the Horn, and round the Norway Maelstrom, and round perdition's flames before I give him up.

Some only know him by his peg leg.

Others by the white scar that runs head to toe, the result of an unfortunate encounter with a lightning bolt. Still others by his entourage of harpooner henchmen with names like Fedallah, Daggoo, Tashtego, and Queequeg.

Mostly, readers know him because he's shorthand for any intense, self-destructive fixation. During their father-son presidencies, George H. W. and then George W. Bush both drew comparisons to him for declaring war on Saddam Hussein. In 1998 special counsel Kenneth Starr's inquiry into President Bill Clinton's extramarital dalliance with intern Monica Lewinsky inspired parallels to his mad pursuit. Even NFL quarterback Peyton Manning was said to resemble him for his relentlessly competitive approach to winning a Super Bowl.

Some days it seems everybody hunts a white whale.

"He," of course, is Captain Ahab, fifty-eight, a forty-year veteran of Nantucket whaling ostensibly leading the crew of the *Pequod* on a yearlong voyage in an industry that was by the mid-nineteenth century the fifth-largest sector of the American economy. Thirty-plus chapters into Herman Melville's *Moby-Dick*, after much speculation from our good-natured narrator, Ishmael—and only after the whaler has left port—the grizzled captain steps onto the quarterdeck to announce an entirely different mission: The *Pequod* will track down the "murderous monster" that "dismasted" him and wreak Ahab's revenge by making it spout "black blood."

And just like that, a novel that begins as a bawdy seaman's chantey (replete with fart jokes) transforms into a metaphysical inquiry into the limits of human knowledge in a hostile universe.

For most readers, deciding whether the "grand, ungodly, god-like man" driving the charge is a villain or a tragic hero is impossible. Ahab's refusal to bow to forces beyond his control inspires admiration, while his ability to impose his will on a ragtag ship of cannibals and Christians is a case study in totalitarian coercion. He's both a symbol of all-consuming ambition and a demagogic sociopath.

The word for Ahab's obsession is "monomania." The concept fascinated nineteenth-century Romantics intrigued by extreme forms of individualism that blurred the border between self-actualization and self-delusion. Melville discovered this theme through Nathaniel Hawthorne, whose protagonists often withdraw into dark brooding until they harden and turn inhumane. Had Melville not met Hawthorne in August 1850 while drafting a preliminary attempt at *Moby-Dick*, Ahab might have ended up a version of the cruel captains depicted in his earliest seafaring fiction, vicious men who abuse the labor of sailors, but not ones to sink into maelstroms of vindictive rage. Hawthorne was a moralist who cautioned that exorbitant gloom led to emotional sterility, but Melville believed in hurling oneself headlong into black thoughts, even if it wrecked a mind on the shoals of sacrilege . . .

Which is why *Moby-Dick* appears to cheer on Ahab's quest to conquer whatever force animates the white whale, even if—or especially if—it means committing heresy. Occasionally the captain wonders if his nemesis is driven by nothing but a dumb, predatory malice. He prefers to blame its evil, however, on that "unearthly, cozening, hidden lord and master, and cruel, remorseless emperor" who denies humanity control over its own existence yet refuses to protect it.

In other words, God.

Few characters interrogate "the Deity" as fiercely as Ahab. The captain calls him to the bar, demanding accountability for his absenteeism. Irate at his silence, the old man enacts diabolic sacraments, baptizing harpoon barbs in pagan blood in the name not of the Father but of the devil. Whether Ahab's blasphemy is symptomatic of his monomania or a declaration of independence from intellectual subservience to faith and creed is up to readers, though Melville made it pretty clear where he stood. "I have written a wicked book," he informed Hawthorne, "and feel spotless as the lamb."

Ahab's quarrel with God only partly explains his magnetism. While writing *Moby-Dick*, Melville absorbed oceans of philosophy, science, and global literature that he channeled directly back into the text, sometimes in the form of allusions, sometimes in passages wholesale cribbed from his sources. This encyclopedic ambition means for Ahab evoking a tradition of tragic heroes from the classical age through Shakespeare to the guilt-haunted Byronic rebels of the writer's own century. No matter how vivid his presence, Ahab is a palimpsest of other famous characters; he remains unique in literature in that he's both a man and an anthology of his antecedents. His list of predecessors begins with the heretical biblical king after which his "crazy, widowed" mother named him before she died in his infancy, dooming Ahab to live out a prophecy of evil. But he's also Oedipus and Narcissus, Prometheus, Satan from *Paradise Lost*, King Lear (with his very own fool, Pip, to question his self-destructive ire), Faust and Faustus, Napoleon, and Byron's Manfred, among others. The various idolatrous kings, fallen angels, and rebels Ahab embodies testify to how persistently myth and literature depict humans challenging their gods—and how persistently they dramatize the mortal costs of doing it.

Ahab's allusive dimension wouldn't resonate for readers if not for the final quality that makes him so memorable: his eloquence. Whether rousing his crew to commit to his suicidal mission, or dressing down Starbuck, the first mate who tries to rein him back to reason, or even in private moments of doubt, the captain orates more than he ever talks. His voice flows in cadenced tides, full of exclamations, apostrophes, and rhetorical questions inspired by the intricate poetry of the King James Bible, Shakespeare, and Milton. So spellbinding is Ahab's oratory that contemporary critics often compare him to Fascist demagogues who seize the bully pulpit to inflame the masses. Whether Melville would consider Ahab a foreshadowing of Hitler or Mussolini is questionable, but he clearly envisioned the captain as dangerously capable of hypnotizing his crew into submitting to his will—and, just perhaps, of entrancing readers' sympathies too.

Still, for all his grandiosity, it's Ahab's smaller moments that remind us of the pathos of his self-destruction. Heaping insult upon injury, Melville describes how the captain's first ivory peg leg snapped and speared him in the groin, nearly emasculating him—cause enough for an already crippled man not to emulate Job's patience. Then, too, the passing detail that Ahab is only recently married and the father of a young son he knows he abandons, just as he feels abandoned by God, adds an edge of self-recrimination that pure villains rarely possess. "The boy vivaciously wakes," says the captain, daydreaming of his family, trying to talk himself out of his chase, "and his mother tells him of me, of cannibal old me; how I am abroad upon the deep, but will yet come back to dance him again."

The old man will no more return than God will, however. In a book that accuses the Father of forsaking us, Ahab is a potent reminder that humanity shouldn't recapitulate that desertion and become our own worst orphan makers.

Bibliography

Moby-Dick; or, The Whale (1851)

—KC

ALADDIN

First Appearance: *The Thousand and One Nights*
Date of First Appearance: 1710
Author: Antoine Galland (1646–1715)

O Slave of the Lamp, I am hungry; and I wish thee to bring me something to eat, and let it be something good beyond imagination.

Mention Aladdin, and most people think of the 1992 Disney animated feature that spawned two sequels, six video games, several TV shows, a Broadway musical, and countless toys and collectibles. He's not original to Disney, though, nor does he trace back to the earliest tenth-century Persian and Arabian versions of *The Thousand and One Nights*—a beloved collection of folktales whose exact authorship is unknown. But we do know that he first appeared fully developed in "Ala-ed-Din and the Wonderful Lamp," one of two stories that French scholar Antoine Galland added around 1710 to his multivolume translation of the Middle Eastern stories.

With the so-called age of exploration already past, Galland's tale appealed as much to Europeans' nostalgic cravings for adventure and new discoveries as they spoke (and still appeal) to a universal desire to solve all problems with a simple rub of a lamp and its wish-granting genie. The narrator of *A Thousand and One Nights* may have the most interesting situation—Scheherazade must tell a story every night to keep from being executed—but it's the hero of one story, Aladdin, who emerges as the most engaging and fully realized character. He's captivated readers so much that his name and that Magic Lamp have been attached to countless diverse businesses and products—including a school, a bail bondsman, chinaware, drinkware, foodware, and Aladdin and Genie garage door openers.

Aladdin is an appealing character because he's a bit of a bad boy who reforms after the lamp brings him wealth—a positive case study for the transformative power of economic stability. Yet there's more. Not every wealthy person in this story—or in life—is generous, but Aladdin endears himself to the people by sharing his riches. Wherever he goes he has his servants throw gold coins to the people, no doubt remembering what it was like to be poor. He's no dummy either. Though initially happenstance gets him out of trouble, once he acquires the lamp he also finds a new confidence. He hangs out with a better crowd, trusts his instincts, and remains calm in the face of crises. Even when everything is taken from him, he still keeps his head and plots to get his bride and riches back again.

When the story begins, Aladdin is a ne'er-do-well living with his mother in a town somewhere in China, and perhaps Galland was able to write about him convincingly because he also grew up poor. One day Aladdin meets a scheming Moorish sorcerer who claims to be his uncle and takes Aladdin on a shopping spree, promising to make the boy a successful merchant. The next day his "uncle" asks him to walk with him, and when they reach a nearby mountain the Moor pulls out a box and "burnt it and muttered adjurations and said mysterious words, and straightway, amid murk and quaking and thunder, the earth opened." Sensing that Aladdin was about to run away, the Moor "smote him on the head, so that his teeth were almost knocked out, and he swooned and fell to the ground." Having discovered "by his science" that the greatest treasure in this cavern of riches—a Wonderful Lamp—could only be retrieved by a boy named Ala-ed-Din from a poor family belonging to that city of China called El-Kal'as, the sorcerer persuades Aladdin to go into that cave by giving him one of his magic rings as a talisman.

Told that he could take all the riches he could carry but that he must give the lamp to his "uncle," Aladdin has lived such a life of poverty that he cannot even imagine that any of the treasure is real. He bypasses the gold and instead gravitates toward trees he thinks are full of wonderful fruits. Seeing that they were instead gemstones, he automatically thinks they are glass or crystal, not the real thing, and since they're inedible he decides to gather some to "play with" later at home. His personality is also revealed when he refuses to hand over the lamp until the sorcerer reaches down to help him up the last steep step. His instincts tell him not to trust the man—though of course there was that little matter of the conk on the head. Enraged, the sorcerer leaves and the earth closes up again, sealing Aladdin inside. After spending three days in darkness crying and sobbing, Aladdin prays to God and testifies that "Mohammad is thy servant and apostle." Then, when he accidentally rubs the ring that the Moor had given him, a jinni (genie) suddenly appears and grants the boy's request to be transported to the surface world again.

Readers who are into trivia contests should know that Aladdin was not the one to discover the jinni in the lamp. That honor goes to Aladdin's mother, who tries to polish the lamp with a handful of sand before Aladdin can take it to the market to sell so they can buy food. And when his mother freezes in terror, then faints after a "jann of terrible aspect and vast stature came out of the lamp," Aladdin, remembering the Slave of the Ring, jumps right in and asks for something to eat—and not just anything. Rather brilliantly he asks (and will continue to ask) for things beyond human imagination and capability, so that his wish fulfillment is not limited by his own mind or ability. In the sixties, Aladdin would get a makeover as a woman in the hit TV series *I Dream of Jeannie*, with Barbara Eden causing all sorts of mischief for her "Aladdin," but in the original story it's Aladdin who has a mischievous streak.

When a crier decrees that all must clear the streets so the Sultan's daughter can bathe, else any who casts eyes upon her will be put to death, Aladdin takes the risk to see her naked and falls instantly in love, vowing to marry her. It's not all that simple, of course, and the rest of the tale is a roller-coaster ride. One minute Aladdin is rich, and the next he's poor; at times he's in the Sultan's good graces and confidently leading the Sultan's army in battle, and the next he's in chains because the magic was discovered. But through it all, Aladdin displays patience, wisdom, generosity, kindness, religious conviction, and cleverness. He matches wits with the Wezir and keeps the princess and the Wezir's son from consummating their marriage, and he impresses the Sultan with displays of wealth after that marriage is annulled and marries her himself. When happiness turns to sorrow after the Moor returns and transports the palace that magic had built and everything and everyone inside it to Africa, Aladdin uses his wits to get everything back, and he is loving and understanding when his wife tells how she gave away his lamp. Even then, Aladdin must fend off the Moor's revenge-seeking brother before they can live happily ever after. They *do*, of course, but it's not all magic— and maybe that's the point, after all.

Bibliography

The Thousand and One Nights (1704–1714, in English 1885–1888)

—JP

ALEX

First Appearance: *A Clockwork Orange*
Date of First Appearance: 1962
Author: Anthony Burgess (1917–1993)

There were three devotchkas sitting at the counter all together, but there were four of us malchicks and it was usually like one for all and all for one.

Fifteen-year-old Alex lives with his parents on the tenth floor of an apartment complex sometime in an unspecified future, and his room contains his prized possession: a stereo. Like most teens, Alex loves music, only his music of choice is classical—Beethoven especially—and Beethoven often makes him so passionate that he becomes sexually aggressive or violent. He plays Beethoven's Ninth while raping two ten-year-old girls he meets at a record store, and when his "droogs"—his gang of equally violent friends—revolts against his leadership and wants more of a democracy, all it takes is a passing car radio to set him off. "There was an auto ittying by . . . and I could just sloshy a bar or so of Ludwig van (it was the Violin Concerto, last movement), and I viddied right at once what to do." Drawing his knife, he cuts one of them and slashes another. End of challenge . . . for the time being.

Most writers would agree that it's hard enough to create an interesting character without also having to devise a language for the character to speak. But that's what Anthony Burgess did for the delinquent narrator of his 1962 dystopian novel *A Clockwork Orange*. For generations, teens have had their own set of slang terms, but Alex and his gang use an entire slang *language* they call "nadsat" (Russian for "teen"). That casual phonetic and Russian-based language makes his accounts of their ultraviolent delinquency all the more chilling.

"What gets into you all?" Alex's father wants to know. "You've got a good home here, good loving parents, you've got not too bad of a brain. Is there some devil that crawls inside you?"

Alex is called Little Alex by his father, but he refers to himself as Alexander the Large when he rapes those two girls after getting them drunk. He also calls himself Your Humble Narrator, though humility seems to be a trait that's fuzzily, if at all, present. We never learn his last name or even what his parents do for a living. We only know that Alex roams the streets at night in this future world. And we're not talking about shoplifting or smoking in the men's room. Alex and his gang aren't impoverished post-Dickensian orphans. For them, it's not about survival. It's recreation. It's a release of energy and hostility. Alex and his friends go to school during the daytime and return home to spend their nights punching, kicking, beating, raping, and torturing innocent people who just happen to be in the wrong place at the wrong time. They're not the only gang either. Delinquency and gangs are rampant—England's chief social problem. As Alex says, "The day was very different from the night. The night belonged to me and my droogs and all the rest of the nadsats."

These gangs don't look for trouble; they manufacture it. Instead of going to movies or another pastime, Alex and his droogs dress "in the heighth of fashion," wearing "waisty jackets without lapels," plus "off-white cravats which looked like whipped up kartoffel or spud" and "black very tight tights with the old jelly mould, as we called it, fitting on the crutch underneath the tights," with designs on them to draw attention to their crotches. Alex describes what seems like a routine for them: The teens leave their parents' houses and meet somewhere like the Korova Milkbar, where they order "milk-plus." After the drugs kick in, they look to satisfy their cravings for violence and sexual violence. Alex says they "found what we were pretty well looking for, a malenky ['little'] jest to start off the evening" who turns out to be a "schoolmaster type" that they assault. They take his books, they accuse him of reading pornography, and while one of them holds his hands they rip out his false teeth, crush them with their boots, punch him in the mouth, strip him down to his underwear, kick him in the stomach, and take what money he has. To avoid being caught and punished, they go to a bar and target a group of drunk old women to buy drinks for if they'll give them an alibi. Then they head out again, this time wearing masks of historical figures: Disraeli (Alex), Elvis Presley (Pete), Henry VIII (Georgie), and Percy Bysshe Shelley (Dim).

In one of the novel's key scenes made famous by the addition of a "Singin' in the Rain" homage in Stanley Kubrick's 1972 film version, Alex forces his way into the house of a writer working on a book called *A Clockwork Orange*, described as the "attempt to impose upon man, a creature of growth and capable of sweetness . . . laws and conditions appropriate to a mechanical creation." That high-minded view is brutally undercut by Alex and his droogs as they severely beat the writer, "making his litso all purple and dripping away like some very special sort of juicy fruit." Then, while one droog holds the writer's wife's hands, Alex says, "I ripped away at this and that and the other, the others going haw haw haw still, and real good horrorshow groodies they were that then exhibited their pink glazzies, O my brothers, while I untrussed and got ready for the plunge." They all take turns raping her. "Then there was like quiet and we were full of like hate, so we smashed what was left to be smashed."

Alex has been in and out of corrective schools since he was eleven, but when he takes a silver statue and "tolchocks" a wealthy "cat-lady" so hard he ends up killing her, that crazy scene with him fighting off her cats is followed by his droogs turning on him and leaving him for the police to find. As a result, Alex ends up in Staja (state jail), and the novel fast-forwards to the second year of his fourteen-year sentence. Here Alex's personality shifts as he strikes up a relationship with the chaplain (is he sincere?) and also submits to a new treatment he heard about that sets inmates up for early release. But the Ludovico Technique turns out to be a real "horrorshow," to use Alex's language, and he becomes a pawn in a sociopolitical experiment backed by the Minister of the Interior. Strapped to a chair that looks like it came from a dentist's office, Alex is forced to watch image after image of ultraviolence and torture until it sickens him.

With Alex we're never positive how much he's grown, how much he's acting, or how much he's been conditioned by shock treatments that essentially remove his free will to choose to be violent or not. It's when we see him paraded about like a freak-show curiosity at a public demonstration that we begin to feel something more than perverse fascination or repulsion. And when Alex says, in a final chapter that was removed from the American edition and film, that he has outgrown his delinquency and is ready to marry and start a family, incredulously, reluctantly, we want to believe him.

Bibliography

A Clockwork Orange (1962)

—JP

ALICE IN WONDERLAND

First Appearance: *Alice's Adventures in Wonderland*
Date of First Appearance: 1865
Author: Lewis Carroll (1832–1898)

When I used to read fairy tales I fancied that kind of thing never happened, and now here I am in the middle of one!

Literature is full of pilgrims in strange lands, but none more proper and innocent than Alice, and none stranger than the wonderland she discovers after falling down a rabbit hole. Alice's age is never mentioned in either of the two books in which she appears, but readers have assumed (and scholars confirmed) that this Victorian-era child is preadolescent, most likely seven years old, making her the youngest of the greatest fictional characters.

Alice's Adventures in Wonderland was published in England by Macmillan on November 26, 1865, written by Lewis Carroll, the pen name of Charles Lutwidge Dodgson, who taught at Christ Church, Oxford University. His inspiration for Alice was Alice Liddell, the daughter of Henry Liddell, the dean of Christ Church. As a passionate amateur photographer, Carroll often took Alice and her two sisters on outings so he could photograph them. And on July 4, 1862, he and the girls went on a boating trip with Reverend Robinson Duckworth, from Oxford to Godstow. To pass the time on the Thames, Carroll told a nonsensical story about a little girl named Alice and the fantastic creatures she encountered after chasing a talking white rabbit. The real Alice enjoyed the tale so much that she asked Carroll to write it down for her. He did, and the original manuscript he gave her, *Alice's Adventures under Ground*, is now at the British Library. But of course the world knows her story as *Alice's Adventures in Wonderland*, or *Alice in Wonderland* for short.

Carroll revised the story, adding a tea party scene and two characters—Mad Hatter and Cheshire Cat—that would become more famous than any from the original draft and doubling the manuscript's size. *Alice's Adventures in Wonderland* was instantly popular and has since been translated and republished in dozens of editions.

Children identified with Alice, for what youngster hasn't been bored or complained, as Alice did of the book her sister was reading alongside her, "What is the use of a book without pictures or conversations?" Throughout the first book and the 1871 sequel, *Through the Looking Glass & What Alice Found There*, set some six months later, Alice behaves like an average but proper child. Bored and in desperate need of diversion, she is imaginative enough to daydream the world she enters. In this fantastic place, where things make even less sense to her than her own world run by adults, she is trusting without seeming overly naïve, polite and well mannered yet also willing to stand up for herself, and wishing she were home again while also savoring the adventure. She's curious and inquisitive and, unlike the parents who produced children like her, far more open to experiencing strange customs and philosophies. For children learning their place in the world,

Alice is an inspirational character who displays a perfect balance of believable childlike vulnerability and a self-confidence and self-awareness that grows with every new dreamworld encounter.

The Alice books were popular with parents, too, because first and foremost Alice is obviously the product of a good upbringing, and her adventure in Wonderland makes her realize that there are "ever so many lessons to learn!" Mostly nonassertive, Alice is civil even in disputes and throws no tantrums. In Carroll's Wonderland, as it was for Jonathan Swift's Gulliver, it's the royalty—queens and duchesses—who pitch fits, acting like spoiled children. Meanwhile, the queens' soldiers, servants, and staff are dismissed as "just a pack of cards." For egalitarian-minded adults, such descriptions seemed a delicious satire—as much as a pointless "caucus race" the animals run, something that has now become a part of our vernacular, along with "grinning like a Cheshire Cat" and "falling down the rabbit hole."

But let's not downplay the adventures themselves. They aren't just fantastic— they're children's fantasies. What child wouldn't be enchanted to imagine him- or herself swimming with a mouse, as Alice did, or playing croquet with a flamingo for a mallet and a hedgehog for a ball, or walking through a mirror into yet another world with talking flowers, a conniving walrus, a lion, unicorn, and talking egg? How would it feel to be small as a mouse or big as a *house*? To children, their world seems too full of rules, but what would it be like if there *were* none? That too is explored. Children today know all about participation awards, and Alice hands out the first ones—a box of comfits (candies)—when she takes part in that caucus race, which has no rules and no winner and ends when Dodo capriciously says it's over.

The creatures in Wonderland range from the fantastic (talking animals) to the mythological (Gryphon) and scientifically extinct (Dodo). Although Alice's discussions with creatures like the Caterpillar may sound like nonsense, when he puffs on his hookah and asks, "Who are *you*?" Alice begins to wonder, because she feels so changed by her experiences. "But if I'm not the same, the next question is, Who in the world am I? Ah, *that's* the great puzzle!" And she begins thinking of children she knew and comparing herself to them to arrive at what might be *individual* about her—something all children invariably do.

Perhaps the most curious fact about Alice is that Carroll never physically describes her—something that seems deliberate, since elsewhere he writes, "If you don't know what a Gryphon is, look at the picture." Readers only learn from Alice that a friend's hair "goes in such long ringlets, and mine doesn't go in ringlets at all." Carroll left the visuals to artist John Tenniel, whose illustrations were an important part of the 1865 edition in which fair-skinned Alice has long blonde hair and wears a blue-and-white dress with a white apron front, white leggings, and black shoes.

That image of Alice was solidified in 1951 when Walt Disney created a full-length animated feature that has become the most popular of all the Hollywood adaptations, which began in 1903 with an eight-minute silent black-and-white short. Alice is considerably older in most of the live-action versions, ranging in age from ten and fourteen (in 1985 and 1999 TV movies) to age nineteen (1933 megastar movie featuring Charlotte Henry opposite Cary Grant, Gary Cooper, and W. C. Fields), twenty-one (Mia Wasikowska in Tim Burton's 2010 version), and twenty-two (Kristine DeBell starring in a 1976 porn version). Betty Boop, the Care Bears, Japanese anime, and Hanna-Barbera all offered their take on the *Alice in Wonderland* adventures. SyFy channel even pushed Alice down a wormhole 150 years into the future.

Elsewhere in pop culture, Jefferson Airplane's Grace Slick penned the psychedelic rock hit "White Rabbit," while John Lennon was partly inspired by Alice's adventures to create "I Am the Walrus." There are numerous video games, lunch boxes, clothing, toys, jewelry, watches, and, of course, the Mad Tea Party ride at Walt Disney theme parks. But you really know you've made it as a literary character when you have a syndrome named for you. British psychiatrist John Todd identified as "Alice in Wonderland syndrome" a condition where patients perceive objects as being larger or smaller than they are in actuality. And so this small girl remains large in the public consciousness.

Bibliography

Alice's Adventures in Wonderland (1865)
Through the Looking Glass & What Alice Found There (1871)

Works Cited

"'Alice's Adventures under Ground,' the Original Manuscript Version of *Alice's Adventures in Wonderland*." British Library. Accessed July 25, 2018. https://www.bl.uk/collection -items/alices-adventures-under-ground-the-original-manuscript-version-of-alices -adventures-in-wonderland.

Popova, Maria. "Meet the Girl Who Inspired 'Alice in Wonderland.'" *Atlantic*, July 5, 2012. https://www.theatlantic.com/entertainment/archive/2012/07/meet-the-girl-who -inspired-alice-in-wonderland/259474/.

—JP

HARRY "RABBIT" ANGSTROM

First Appearance: *Rabbit, Run*
Date of First Appearance: 1960
Author: John Updike (1932–2009)

If you're telling me I'm not mature, that's one thing I don't cry over since as far as I can make out it's the same thing as being dead.

Literature is full of heroes and antiheroes, but Harry "Rabbit" Angstrom is uniquely average—a flawed, irrepressible, and often unlikable human being who is still somehow so endearing to audiences worldwide that one novel couldn't contain him. Harry, a former high school basketball star who peaked too early and married too young, first appeared in *Rabbit, Run* (1960). Then John Updike did what no previous writer of literary fiction had attempted: He revisited his aging character, first with *Rabbit Redux* (1971), then *Rabbit Is Rich* (1981), and finally *Rab-*

bit at Rest (1990), tying up loose ends in a novella of lesser interest that functions as a postmortem—*Rabbit Remembered* (in *Licks of Love*, 2000). Cramming the novels full of American pop culture and history, Updike offered not only the story of an American everyman from early adulthood through his senior years, but also, as CNBC's Dick Cavett observed, "a splendid account of American life following the Second World War." Prize-winning British writer Ian McEwan went even further, calling it "the best contender for the Great American Novel."

When we first meet Harry, the only fictional character to appear in *two* Pulitzer Prize–winning novels (*Rabbit Is Rich*, *Rabbit at Rest*), he's a twenty-six-year-old who forces himself into a game of alley hoops that younger boys are playing. Harry, a composite based on two Shillington High School basketball players, is having a premature midlife crisis—one that comes from enjoying fame early but then lapsing into the mediocrity of everyday existence. He's convinced his alcoholic wife, Janice, got pregnant on purpose to force their marriage, and he's become so put off by her booziness that he leaves her twice during a second pregnancy. In *Rabbit, Run*, which Updike intended as a response to Jack Kerouac's counterculture novel *On the Road* (1957), there are consequences when the husband leaves home. Rabbit runs from his job selling kitchen gadgets, from his wife, from church, from extended family, and from expectations and obligations. He runs, first, to his old basketball coach, then to a chunky prostitute named Ruth, with whom he will have a child out of wedlock (we *think*) and who likes Rabbit for the same reason readers do: "You haven't given up. In your stupid way you're still fighting."

The BBC described the Rabbit novels as being "as much about the changing soul of the United States as about any individual character." That's especially true a decade later. In *Rabbit Redux*, after Janice moves out, an older Harry and his teenage son, Nelson, take in a runaway flower child and a black militant with a messianic complex. At a time when Huey Newton and the Black Panther Party were causing white America no small level of distress, and FBI director J. Edgar Hoover had pronounced them "the greatest threat to the internal security of the country," Harry was doing the unthinkable: He was engaging a black militant in conversation, trying to understand a different point of view. Through the conservative but inquisitive Harry, readers gained insights into the politicized drug- and sex-filled sixties that polarized the nation.

By *Rabbit Is Rich*, Harry, who had reconciled with Janice and has taken over her late father's auto dealership, finally achieves prosperity. His politics shift from Democrat to Republican, and seven years after Updike's death Harry will be cited as a predictor of the emerging Donald Trump supporters. But Harry is restless, still wanting more and not wanting to be left behind. In this third novel, which coincides with a "boom" period in America but also an energy crisis, the hypersexual Harry memorably makes love to his wife on a bed of gold Krugerrands and gets his comeuppance when he lusts after a wife in their circle of friends, only to be given another lover when the women agree to wife swapping.

Finally, in *Rabbit at Rest*, a fifty-five-year-old Harry is retired and living in Florida. Overweight, he's been told by his doctor to diet. Nelson and his wife, Pru, visit, and the day after Harry undergoes angioplasty Harry has sex with Pru, who says she hoped Nelson would become more like Harry instead of a drug abuser. Later she upsets everyone by confessing their tryst. Before he can smooth things over,

Harry has a heart attack and dies—fittingly, after playing basketball. "Enough" is the last word out of the mouth of "a mundane man facing the miraculous horror of his own end as indelible as any in our literature," observed an *Esquire* writer.

As NPR *Fresh Air* host Terry Gross noted, "Rabbit is a surprisingly complex character." He's unfaithful, impulse driven, prejudiced, and old-fashioned when it comes to women. But he is a seeker, a quester of truth. With a healthy libido and appetite for life, Rabbit, though in many ways a typical American male, nonetheless manages to see everyday objects and people in a more brilliant and illuminating light than the average person. He has never lost his childlike sense of wonder—a rare quality that draws people toward him. Harry may have lost his athletic ability and health, but he never loses his remarkable zest for life. As *Time* magazine described him in 2009, Rabbit remains a "sometimes appalling, but always authentic, American man"—so American that Rabbit dresses as Uncle Sam for the town parade and won't tolerate anyone badmouthing the U.S.

In a *New York Times Books* review, fellow novelist Joyce Carol Oates called the Rabbit novels "John Updike's surpassingly eloquent valentine to his country." It was a valentine that didn't translate well to the big screen, though. In 1970, independent filmmakers attempted an adaptation of *Rabbit, Run* starring James Caan as Rabbit, Carrie Snodgress as Janice, and Anjanette Comer as Ruth. But the film, distributed by Warner Bros., had difficulty capturing Harry's inner landscape, which is frankly what makes his character so fascinating. The book resonates because of Harry's interior monologues and Updike's exquisite descriptions, and those didn't transfer well to film. What's more, the premiere in Reading, Pennsylvania (renamed Brewer in the novels) was unenthusiastically received, so the studio canceled a planned wider release.

It's by virtue of the books alone that Harry "Rabbit" Angstrom has managed to remain in the public's consciousness. More than fifty editions of *Rabbit, Run* have been published since it was first released—not counting translations—and no one reads those books for any reason other than Harry. Essentially fictional biographies, their enduring popularity and critical acclaim is a testimony to the main character, whose status as a classic literary creation was reinforced in 2002 when *Book* magazine named Rabbit the #5 best character in fiction, behind Jay Gatsby, Holden Caulfield, Humbert Humbert, and Leopold Bloom. In his review of *Rabbit Angstrom: A Tetralogy*, Julian Barnes praised the collective series as "the greatest postwar American novel" and summarized why: "Harry is site-specific, slobbish, lust-driven, passive, patriotic, hard-hearted, prejudiced, puzzled, anxious. Yet familiarity renders him likable—for his humor, his doggedness, his candor, his curiosity, and his wrong-headed judgments."

Bibliography

Rabbit, Run (1960)
Rabbit Redux (1971)
Rabbit Is Rich (1981)
Rabbit at Rest (1990)
Rabbit Angstrom: A Tetralogy (1995)
Rabbit Remembered, in *Licks of Love: Short Stories and a Sequel* (2000)

Works Cited

Barnes, Julian. "Running Away." Review of *Rabbit Angstrom*, by John Updike. *Guardian*, October 16, 2009. https://www.theguardian.com/books/2009/oct/17/julian-barnes-john-updike-rabbit.

Gross, Terry. "Fresh Air with Terry Gross: John Updike *(Rabbit at Rest)*." In *John Updike's Pennsylvania Interviews*, edited by James Plath, 129–32. Bethlehem, PA: Lehigh University Press, 2016.

"John Updike: Prolific Author Who Captured the Spirit of Middle America and Is Best Known for His Harry 'Rabbit' Angstrom Series." *Telegraph*, January 27, 2009.

Junod, Tom. "The Miracle of John Updike." *Esquire*, January 28, 2009.

McElwee, Charles F., III. "Did John Updike Foresee the Trump Era?" *American Conservative*, December 19, 2016. Accessed July 24, 2018. https://www.theamericanconservative.com/articles/did-john-updike-foresee-the-trump-era/.

Oates, Joyce Carol. "So Young!" Review of *Rabbit at Rest*, by John Updike. *New York Times Books*, September 30, 1990, section 7, p. 1.

"Obituary: John Updike." BBC News, January 27, 2009.

"100 Best Characters in Fiction since 1900." NPR.org, from *Book* magazine, March/April 2002. Accessed July 22, 2018. https://www.npr.org/programs/totn/features/2002/mar/020319.characters.html.

Plath, James, ed. *Conversations with John Updike*. Jackson: University Press of Mississippi, 1994.

Schiff, James. "Inaugural John Updike Conference Returns 'Rabbit' to His Roots." Alvernia University news archive. Accessed July 24, 2018. https://sun.iwu.edu/~jplath/Conference_press_release.html.

Staskiewicz, Keith, and Isabella Biedenharn. "The United States of Books." *Entertainment Weekly*, September 4, 2015.

Time staff. "Top 10 John Updike Books." *Time*, January 27, 2009. Accessed July 22, 2018. http://entertainment.time.com/2009/01/28/top-10-john-updike-books/slide/all/.

—JP

BRETT ASHLEY

First Appearance: *The Sun Also Rises*
Date of First Appearance: 1926
Author: Ernest Hemingway (1899–1961)

Oh Jake . . . we could have had such a damned good time together.

Ernest Hemingway's lost generation protagonist Jake Barnes proclaims that Lady Brett Ashley is "damned good looking" and that she rocks curves "like the hull of a racing yacht," when she first appears in her tight sweater at one of those Parisian bars American expats loved to patronize in the 1920s. Admirers see Brett as the promised land, and they are pilgrims wanting to partake of the riches they hope she will impart. This is exactly the impression Brett wants to create with the "chaps" always surrounding her there or when she's being encircled by men just about anywhere. Brett is a player, and all the boys want to play. This includes Romero, the young bullfighter in the tight green toreador pants; the Jewish writer/ex-boxer Robert Cohn who follows her around like a lovesick puppy after their brief sexual affair; and it is especially true for Jake Barnes, whose war injury has robbed him of the ability for sexual consummation. Brett Ashley becomes a painful reminder of that trauma and its representation of the deeper wound the entire era sustained in the post–World War I aftermath of *The Sun Also Rises*.

Lady Brett bears an official British title through marriage, but many detractors argue that she might be less a proper lady and more of a tramp. Some critics, mostly men of a certain mid-twentieth-century mind-set, have called her a Circe, Siren, femme fatale, woman of loose morals, bitch, whore, nymphomaniac, "a lovely piece," and a wide range of unflattering descriptions because she doesn't behave the way they prescribe that ladies ought to. She's also been rescued from some of that criticism largely by more contemporary feminists who point out that she too is a war victim who suffers from what we now call post-traumatic stress syndrome. Having been a nurse, she could not have escaped the close-up horrors of war wrought on the bodies of wounded men she served as they flooded into makeshift triage centers and hospitals. Brett's history is also one of war trauma with three different personal chapters—her first love died in the war, her husband's emotional scars from his experiences caused trouble in their marriage, and Jake's battlefield injuries left him incapable of the sexual reciprocity she feels unable to live without even though she expresses sincere love for him.

Brett is certainly damaged. She confesses as much at many points, especially in conversations with Jake, but she is also intriguing as one of the thoroughly modern and newly self-possessed women who garnered so much attention in the 1920s and set the standard for what it meant to be a socially and sexually liberated woman. She's not a flapper girl of the American-grown F. Scott Fitzgerald type but is instead her own unique blend of masculine tweed and hair that's cut and brushed in a man's style and often topped with a fedora. She is a hard-drinking, physical-pleasure-seeking divorcée with a manly first name and a place at the bar with the boys, and yet in all of this Brett exudes highly charged female sensuality. Men want her. She is not afraid to go after them and makes no apologies for it; that is, with the exception of Romero, whom she takes as a lover but later relinquishes so she won't be "one of those bitches that ruins children."

Although Hemingway's novels all have male protagonists, one might argue that in *The Sun Also Rises* Brett is actually the centerpiece. Hemingway opens an early draft with the line "This is a novel about a lady." Following Fitzgerald's critical advice, he restructures the narrative, but in his heart, Brett remains its axis. She is the magnetized sun around which the male planets continue to orbit. At the Fiesta de San Fermín that kicks off the running of the bulls and the bullfight season in Pamplona, the celebratory crowd literally dances around Brett and then elevates her on a wine cask as the altarpiece of their bacchanalian revelry. She is the pagan goddess who is comfortable being worshipped but is afraid to enter a church, the house of worship where her charisma and sexual aura have no sway. Brett generates her own set of commandments, her internal moral compass as it were, that becomes what she has "instead of God," who perhaps has deserted the world, been killed in the war, or gotten lost in the chaos of the conflagration.

Stepping beyond the pages of *The Sun Also Rises*, Brett Ashley also has importance to the story behind the story. If readers are Hemingway aficionados to any degree, they are likely aware that the novel is a roman à clef. The action is so close to actual events surrounding a trip that Ernest, his wife Hadley, and a small group of their friends took in the summer of 1925 that Donald Ogden Stewart called the book "journalism" rather than fiction. As part of the entourage, he substantiated Hemingway's having hit the mark in fictionalizing the real-life model Lady Duff Twysden, who was also in attendance. Stewart confessed, "We were all in love with her. It was hard not to be. She played her cards so well." Twysden caused a bit of a row among the men fawning over her, including Hemingway, and pangs of jealous concern from Ernest's wife Hadley. An early possible title for the novel, "Two Lie Together," no doubt added to her consternation. Ironically, in the famous photo of the group sitting at an outdoor café, the real husband stealer is not Lady Duff but Pauline Pfeiffer, who sat at Hemingway's right and later became the second Mrs. Hemingway. In a book shedding light on this excursion's important and ultimately life-altering experience, Lesley Blume's *Everybody Behaves Badly*, with the subtitle's claim "The True Story behind Hemingway's Masterpiece," sums up the Pamplona trip as Hemingway's artistic palette for creating Brett Ashley and *The Sun Also Rises*.

What gives fictional characters lasting value, however, isn't that they come from real-life models so much as that they are true to life, can transcend time and place, and have plausible and transferrable currency for readers nearly 100 years later (or maybe still 100 more and beyond), as Lady Brett Ashley does. One might easily see her in the timeless jersey sweater, tweed skirt, and wearing no stockings as adoring men still surround her at Café Select, Le Dôme, or the La Rotonde on Paris's Boulevard Montparnasse. The updated Brett might be drinking a Moscow mule out of a chilled copper mug, a Long Island iced tea, or a chocolate espresso martini instead of absinthe or home-brewed Spanish Basque wine communally shared from a simple leather wineskin, but we would still recognize her and be awed by the charisma and self-assurance even if it is a facade, maybe especially because it is, to cover the loneliness, isolation, and sense of loss that comes from living a world less stable than it once seemed to be. Brett Ashley is Hemingway's thoroughly modern woman in his time as well as in our time.

Bibliography

The Sun Also Rises (1926)

Work Cited

Blume, Lesley M. M. *Everybody Behaves Badly: The True Story behind Hemingway's Masterpiece* The Sun Also Rises. Boston: Houghton Mifflin Harcourt, 2016.

—GS

B

GEORGE F. BABBITT

First Appearance: *Babbitt*
Date of First Appearance: 1922
Author: Sinclair Lewis (1885–1951)

This society stuff is like any other hobby; if you devote yourself to it, you get on.

Three years before Jay Gatsby pursued his own version of the American dream, George F. Babbitt was discovering that the dream isn't all it's cracked up to be. When we first meet him he's not rich; however, as a top-notch Realtor who helps clients buy and flip properties in order to make quick and outrageous profits, he's reached an enviable level of middle-class affluence. He has a wife, three children, a servant, and a five-year-old Dutch colonial house in an upscale suburban subdivision of Zenith (pop. 361,000), where every second house has a bedroom "precisely like his." The house has "the best of taste, the best of inexpensive rugs, a simple and laudable architecture, and the latest conveniences." Electricity in 1920 was still new enough that it too was a sign of affluence, as was the cigar lighter in his car that impressed clients. Babbitt has "enormous and poetic admiration, though very little understanding, of all mechanical devices. They were his symbols of truth and beauty," those gadgets—an outward, measurable sign of his success.

Babbitt considers himself sophisticated because he graduated from college, plays golf, smokes cigarettes, and takes a room with a private bath whenever he goes to Chicago. With a large head, thinning brown hair, and glasses, he's a "plump, smooth, efficient, up-to-the-minute and otherwise perfected modern" who, like other successful businessmen in his community, is expected to join at least one and preferably two or three businessmen's organizations. "It was the thing to do." Besides, lodge brothers often became customers, and it gave ordinary fellows the chance to acquire a title like "High Worthy Recording Scribe" or "Grand Hoogow." And, of course, "it permitted the swaddled American husband to stay away from home for one evening a week" when he could "shoot pool and talk man-talk and be obscene and valiant." Babbitt is a member of the Elks Lodge, Zenith Athletic Club, the local Realtors' association, and the Boosters' Club. Known for his oratory, he "spoke well—and often—at these orgies of commercial righteousness about the realtor's function as a seer of the future development of the community."

Critics were quick to compliment Sinclair Lewis for his creation of a believable flesh-and-blood character, but *Babbitt* is also a brilliant satire of the pre-Depression self-made man—someone who remains familiar to this day. As literary giant H. L. Mencken observed, Babbitt is a typical American businessman driven not by his own desires, but by what others in the community will think of him. A Republican precinct leader and mover and shaker in the local Presbyterian church, "his politics is communal politics, mob politics, herd politics; his religion is a public rite wholly without subjective significance," Mencken noted. The novel struck a nerve with Rotarian and Elks Lodge America, and some community organizations fought back against the image *Babbitt* conveyed by taking out radio and newspaper ads to tout the positive things that businessmen's organizations have done for the country. Eight years later, the controversy would inspire the Swedish Academy to make Lewis the first American to win the Nobel Prize in Literature. At the ceremony, Lewis was praised for his bold criticism of American institutions, his satirical eye, and his rich characters, with George F. Babbitt especially singled out.

For all the commotion, Babbitt is still a typical husband who complains about guest towels that can't be used and fusses over having to dress for dinner. He's also an average father: "affectionate, bullying, opinionated, ignorant, and rather wistful. Like most parents, he enjoyed the game of waiting till the victim was clearly wrong, then virtuously pouncing." Though he's a good provider, he resents the consumer-driven, keep-up-with-the-Joneses mentality of his family, who are suddenly nagging him to buy a sedan to replace the open car they drive—just because it's the latest status symbol—even though a part of him considers doing so, and for the same reason.

As a Realtor he's seen his share of (and "treasured") beautiful women, but he never "hazarded respectability by adventuring"—though lately he has been dreaming about a fairy girl, "so slim, so white, so eager." In his dreams, this presumably teenage girl's "dear and tranquil hand caressed his cheek"; with her he feels warmly loved in a way he no longer feels with his wife. The dreams are just the beginning of a growing restlessness that disrupts his life. Once excited about attending highbrow affairs, he now finds them tedious. He becomes annoyed by other couple's nagging complaints or predictable conversations. He lies about how entertaining parties are and finds an excuse to spend three weeks with a good friend in Maine, away from family and social obligations. And he satisfies a growing, suppressed urge to rebel against conformity by taking in a burlesque show and drinking so much Prohibition-era alcohol that he ends up singing out loud and arguing with a man who calls him a "bum singer." "Say!" Babbitt says. "I know what was the trouble! Somebody went and put alcohol in my booze last night."

People start to talk, but the reverend still asks him and two other pillars of society to elevate their Sunday school program from fourth to first in the city because, "there's no reason why we should take anybody's dust." Babbitt's solution? He institutes a "system of military ranks" in which he himself gets to be a colonel, and the Sunday school climbs into second place. For a time that success increases his standing at the Elks, Athletic Club, and Boosters, but soon his emerging "liberal" behavior hurts his business. His stenographer even quits to work for a more upstanding competitor. When Babbitt's good friend is imprisoned for shooting his wife, Babbitt is given some time alone to question his values while his wife and daughter head east for a spell. "What did he want? Wealth? Social position? Travel? Servants? Yes, but only incidentally." He does know that he wants his friend back again, "and from that he stumbled into the admission that he wanted the fairy girl—in the flesh." He yearns to be "one of those Bohemians you read about" and goes a little crazy, flirting with workers, servants, and other people's wives, then finally having an affair with one of his clients. That sets tongues wagging, but what pushes Babbitt even further off the social register is his response to a telephone worker strike that affects all the businesses in town. Though his colleagues call the protesters "bomb-throwing socialists" and dismiss the broadsides claiming they're not paid a livable wage as "all lies and fake figures," Babbitt interjects, "Oh rats, they look just about like you and me, and I certainly didn't notice any bombs." His liberal streak would be short-lived.

Eventually, "the independence seeped out of him and he walked the streets alone, afraid of men's cynical eyes and the incessant hiss of whispering." Babbitt finds the price of individualism to be too high, and he returns to the fold of conformity. He has a poignant reconciliation with his wife, and when he speaks again at the Boosters meeting, "he knew by the cheer that he was secure again and popular." So much for the myth of American individualism.

Bibliography

Babbitt (1922)

Works Cited

Mencken, H. L. "Portrait of an American Citizen." *Smart Set* 69 (October 1922).
The Sinclair Lewis Society. "FAQ 3: Why Did Sinclair Lewis Win the Nobel Prize?" Accessed October 17, 2018. https://english.illinoisstate.edu/sinclairlewis/sinclair_lewis/faq/faq3.shtml.

—JP

FRODO BAGGINS

First Appearance: *The Fellowship of the Ring: Being the First Part of the Lord of the Rings*
Date of First Appearance: 1954
Author: J. R. R. Tolkien (1892–1973)

You say the ring is dangerous, far more dangerous than I can guess. In what way?

"Frodo Lives!"

In the sixties that slogan appeared on buttons, T-shirts, bumper stickers, and backpacks, all because the counterculture movement embraced J. R. R. Tolkien's reluctant hero. In him, politicized hippies in America found an inspiration for their own epic task of trying to force cultural change and end an unpopular war in Vietnam. It wasn't *exactly* the same thing as inheriting a powerful ring, then traveling to a faraway land to destroy it and defeat the forces of evil. But it felt close. Like them, Frodo was just an ordinary person who found himself pushed by circumstances into putting himself on the line for the greater good.

Frodo Baggins is a short "stout little fellow with red cheeks," cleft chin, and the characteristic big feet of hobbits that have never worn shoes. He's also an orphan, and that makes him a perfect quester because he's not leaving any loved ones behind. As a relation of Bilbo Baggins, one of the only hobbits ever to travel beyond the Shire, he's heard his share of stories about Middle-earth. When Bilbo surprises everyone by disappearing after his 111th birthday, he leaves Bag End manor and all his belongings to Frodo, the eldest of his younger cousins whom he adopted as his heir. And Frodo takes possession of the ring left for him in an envelope the day he turns thirty-three—the age the Bible tells us Christ was when he embarked upon *his* mission.

In the novel, when the wizard Gandalf returns years later, it's to tell the hobbit he must leave at once. The Elven-ring, one of the Great Rings of Power, had been responsible for Cousin Bilbo's long life. But while the ring also has the power to make the wearer invisible, as Gandalf explains, any mortal who keeps one of the Great Rings "does not die, but he does not grow or obtain more life, he merely continues, until at last every minute is weariness." The ring that Frodo inherited is the Master-ring, the "One Ring to rule them all," which the Dark Lord Sauron lost many ages ago. The only way to keep Sauron from getting the ring that would help him enslave this entire fantasy world is for the ring-bearer to take the ring to Mount Doom in the land of Mordor and throw it back into the lava from which Sauron originally crafted it. The catch—besides Sauron's Black Riders seeking to destroy the ring-bearer and bring the ring back to their master—is that if the ring is worn or kept close to the ring-bearer's body, it can make him moody, distrustful, irrational, possessive, greedy, scheming, power hungry—even homicidal. Yet our meek hero willingly accepts the burden and continues to shoulder that burden, even as he can feel the ring's power and though it scares him.

Frodo is a refreshingly different kind of hero because he's not just reluctant— he's afraid. In fact, Frodo seems a timid fellow by nature, afraid to cross a certain farmer's land, for example, because he's terrified of him and his dogs. Having avoided that farm for years, he's anxious about crossing it to start his journey. Later, he's even tempted to put on the ring (which makes the wearer invisible) just to get out of an annoying, trivial situation. Besides lacking the hero's skills and temperament, Frodo also isn't the stand-alone champion we typically associate with heroic deeds. He needs (and gets) lots of help, so while the ring-bearer himself must be the one to destroy the ring, it really does take a team effort. Three hobbits accompany him on his journey, as well as Gandalf, a ranger they call Strider (who's really Aragorn, heir to a kingdom), a Captain of Gondor, a dwarf warrior, and an elven prince. They help Frodo but also oppose him at times when they've gotten too close to that ring. Early in the journey Frodo is seriously wounded by the Black Riders, and it's Strider/Aragorn who fights them off and takes him to a nearby elven refuge. Later, when Frodo and fellow hobbit Sam are separated from the rest and capture Gollum, who had possessed the ring before

Bilbo found it, Gollum betrays them and leads them into a cave where a giant spider injects Frodo with venom. With Frodo incapacitated and darned near lifeless, it's Sam who steps up and takes the lead, even finding the strength to carry Frodo for much of the time.

Frodo's heroism at first lies in what he's able to endure. Gandalf notices it when Frodo is first seriously wounded. "You were beginning to fade," he tells him. "But you have some strength in you, my dear hobbit!" Later, seriously wounded again, Frodo admits, "I am tired, weary, I haven't a hope left. But I have to go on trying to get to the Mountain, as long as I can move. The ring is enough. This extra weight is killing me. It must go." At times Frodo crawls when Sam is too tired to carry him, and when Gollum attacks in ambush in a last-ditch attempt to get his "precious" back again, Frodo fights back "with a fury that amazed Sam and Gollum also." Even as he gets close to accomplishing his mission, Frodo, affected by the ring, vows to keep it until it's wrestled from him, and afterward Frodo is "pale and worn, and yet himself again; and in his eyes there was peace now . . . his burden was taken away."

After the ring is destroyed and Frodo and the other hobbits are honored and presented with swords, they return to the Shire and find that a "chief" has taken over with his bands of Shirriffs bullying the hobbits and enforcing unfair rules. When the men tell Frodo they're going to arrest him for destroying a barrier and other infractions, he says, "Don't be absurd! I am going where I please, and in my own time." He adds, "Your day is over, and all other ruffians." A battle will later restore the Shire, but while Frodo leads, he does so without a sword in his hand. His "chief part had been to prevent the hobbits in their wrath at their losses, from slaying those of their enemies who threw down their weapons." He was, as the hippies would later appreciate, a pacifist at heart.

One of the best-selling novels ever, *The Lord of the Rings* has sold more than 150 million copies. Initially broken up into three installments at the publisher's behest, it was released in 1968 as a single volume that further popularized Tolkien and his characters. In 1999, Amazon.com customers voted *The Lord of the Rings* the Book of the Millennium, while in 2003 it was voted No. 1 in a BBC reader survey of the Top 200 Novels in the UK. There have been radio and theatrical adaptations, but Tolkien and his characters' pop-culture status was most reinforced by Peter Jackson's blockbuster movie trilogy, which starred Elijah Wood as a blue-eyed version of Frodo. Collectively the films earned thirty-seven Academy Award nominations and nineteen Oscars—including an unprecedented eleven nominations and eleven wins for the third climactic installment, *The Return of the King*.

Bibliography

The Fellowship of the Ring: Being the First Part of the Lord of the Rings (1954)
The Two Towers: Being the Second Part of the Lord of the Rings (1954)
The Return of the King: Being the Third Part of the Lord of the Rings (1955)
The Lord of the Rings (1968)
The Silmarillion (published posthumously, 1977)
Unfinished Tales (published posthumously, 1980)

—JP

LILY BART

First Appearance: *The House of Mirth*
Date of First Appearance: 1905
Author: Edith Wharton (1862–1937)

She was so evidently the victim of the civilization which had produced her, that the links of her bracelet seemed like manacles chaining her to her fate.

The old adage "Money makes the world go around" is truer than we would like it to be, especially for a good number of female literary characters, and this ends up being especially valid in Edith Wharton's *The House of Mirth*. As Virginia Woolf so eloquently summed up in her feminist text *A Room of One's Own* (1929), there are two essentials for female autonomy: having an independent space and sufficient funds to sustain oneself. Wharton's heroine Lily Bart is unable to obtain these two necessities and consequently becomes a tragic victim to her purse's lack of financial heft, her dependency upon a man to provide this, and the conflict between what she knows she needs but cannot stomach in order to survive. Lily will not succeed at the vocation in which she was born and well trained to flourish—marriage to the richest available man in New York's turn-of-the-century high society—and she will pay the ultimate price for her failure.

Wharton knew this society well, having grown up in the midst of its stifling elitism, and she created Lily Bart as a vivid example of the double standard under which women of that social realm are forced to operate or are often crushed. Men, if they aren't independently wealthy, have choices about how to sustain themselves. Lily's love interest, Lawrence Selden, has chosen law as a profession viewed slightly undesirable in this class but respectable enough for a gentleman without a sufficient trust fund, while her only acceptable path is marriage. Using their similar circumstances but examining them from opposite gender platforms, Wharton will frame the dilemma under which Lily must maneuver as she watches Selden survive unburdened by restrictions while she falls victim to them.

Lily Bart fully understands what is at stake. As her last name hints, she will be expected to barter her beauty, trained charm, and social panache to land the best marriage prospect, and this implies looking at dollar signs rather than focusing on the desired object of Cupid's arrows. Wharton builds the world of her not-so-mirthful symbolic house with a clear sense of what economist and sociologist Thorstein Veblen explains in his *The Theory of the Leisure Class* (1899) as this social stratum's practice of "conspicuous leisure," which inevitably also engages in "conspicuous consumption" to sustain such a lifestyle. Lily resides at the outskirts of this realm, having grown up with parents, now dead, who once had large enough means to establish themselves as members of the crème de la crème but whose coffers no longer possess sufficient funds to maintain a position for their daughter without an influx of outside funds; that is, a rich husband for Lily. She knows that to land a good prospect she will have to play society's game, following its rules by also being conspicuously idle and fashioned to compete as a desirable product on a high-end market where much is at stake.

Both Lily and Selden are utterly aware of the price for playing in this circle, and he notes to himself, "She must have cost a great deal to make, that a great many dull and ugly people must, in some way have been sacrificed to produce her." She is clearly a commodity for sale to the highest bidder as long as she retains the fine qualities a buyer might desire. One of Wharton's original titles, *A Moment's Ornament*, underscored this sense, but the assessment is obvious and becomes even more coarse as Selden discusses characteristics that "distinguish her from the herd of her sex." He emphasizes superficiality and describes Lily "as though a fine glaze of beauty and fastidiousness had been applied to vulgar clay." Her friend Carrie Fisher will astutely note later, "She had been fashioned to adorn and delight. . . . And was it her fault that the purely decorative mission is less easily and harmoniously fulfilled among social beings than in the world of nature? That it is apt to be hampered by material necessities or complicated by moral scruples?" Under such circumstances, Lily plays a game where failing to be victorious has many layers of consequence.

Knowing that Lily understands, accepts, and carries out her role in this milieu makes her an interesting character with ample area for a great novelist like Wharton to adorn the story. Lily almost literally becomes a shiny object in a storefront display window as she engages in the *tableaux vivants* or "living pictures" event her circle of acquaintances creates to replicate paintings done by old master artists. Lily chooses Joshua Reynolds's portrait of a woman, "Mrs. Lloyd," wearing a revealing gossamer gown as she carves her husband's name on a tree, a choice that speaks volumes about the woman as an objet d'art. Lily's re-creation generates a great deal of attention, but negatively so in both sexes' reactions. The women see her unscrupulously flaunting herself by revealing too much flesh, and the men view Lily as highly sexualized and therefore interesting for the wrong reasons. As she had earlier acknowledged, "I have to calculate and contrive, and retreat and advance, as if I were going through an intricate dance, where one misstep would throw me hopelessly out of time," and this slipup becomes the first significant rung in the descent of her reputation and ability to market herself at the level for which she is aiming, and at the age of twenty-nine, the clock is rapidly ticking.

Edith Wharton clearly sympathizes with Lily's plight, and in her memoir *A Backward Glance* (1934), she remarks that a "frivolous society can acquire dramatic significance only through what its frivolity destroys. Its tragic implication lies in its power of debasing people and ideals." This poisonous capacity and willingness to destroy Lily gain her sympathy from readers, compounded by the fact that "at heart, she despises the things she's trying for." What makes us finally compassionate rather than seeing her as a shallow gold digger is that she will pull herself back time and again from the brink of a chance to save herself in a well-placed marriage because it will not be a union of love.

When Lily's reputation has been ruined, she finds herself unsuited for any income-producing work and she takes a drug to induce sleep from which she does not wake. The question is whether her death is accidental or a suicide, but a previously undiscovered Wharton letter found a decade ago seems to be her definitive answer. In correspondence with a friend she writes, "I have a heroine to get rid of, and want some points on the best way of disposing of her." She continues by asking, "What soporific, or nerve-calming drug, would a nervous and worried young lady in the smart set be likely to take to, & what would be its effects if deliberately taken with the intent to kill herself?" Wharton's intent for Lily is clear, and we are left with yet another fictional female to mourn.

Bibliography

The House of Mirth (1905)

Works Cited

McGrath, Charles. "Wharton Letter Reopens a Mystery." *New York Times*, November 21, 2007.
Veblen, Thorstein. *The Theory of the Leisure Class: An Economic Study of Institutions.* New York: Macmillan, 1899.
Wharton, Edith. *A Backward Glance.* New York: D. Appleton, 1934.
Woolf, Virginia. *A Room of One's Own.* London: Hogarth, 1929.

—GS

BIG BROTHER

First Appearance: *Nineteen Eighty-Four*
Date of First Appearance: 1949
Author: George Orwell (1903–1950)

[Winston Smith] picked up the children's history book and looked at the portrait of Big Brother which formed its frontispiece. The hypnotic eyes gazed into his own. It was as though some huge force were pressing down upon you—something that penetrated inside your skull, battering against your brain, frightening you out of your beliefs, persuading you, almost, to deny the evidence of your senses. In the end the Party would announce that two and two made five, and you would have to believe it.

It feels safe to say that no other villain in literature has lent his name to a frivolous reality TV show in which generally unlikable people are forced to live with each other for the amusement of audiences tuning in from home. Yet that's exactly the fate of Big Brother, who began life as a fearsome symbol of totalitarian rule in George Orwell's *Nineteen Eighty-Four* but is more familiar today as the title of an entertainment franchise broadcast around the globe whose main appeal is voyeurism. At least in one sense, though, Big Brother's devolution makes sense: he has always been more of a concept than a person. Even before his alliterative name slipped into the vernacular as a code word for government surveillance—one of so many Orwell neologisms in this dystopian novel to do so that "Orwellian" itself became an adjective—the putative leader of the Party ruling Oceania existed in the novel as little more than a face. Granted, that face is blasted on huge screens, resembling either Hitler or Joseph Stalin with its black mustache and hair, but he never steps into a scene the way that other famous man behind the curtain, the Wizard of Oz, is forced to. Big Brother is an image, rather, one that stands for the worst abuses of propaganda by brainwashing the masses and dictating reality.

Big Brother's name is specifically mentioned only seventy-six times in this 328-page novel. Yet, much like the ominous slogan BIG BROTHER IS WATCH-ING YOU that is plastered everywhere throughout Airstrip One (the former Great Britain), his presence is inescapable. Even the everyman protagonist Winston Smith, a clerk in the Ministry of Truth who tries to maintain a skeptical distance from government dictums, finds himself swept up in the hysteria his image can provoke. In an early scene, Smith watches an anti-Semitic state denunciation of Emmanuel Goldstein, the so-called Enemy of the People, on a program called Two Minutes Hate. Smith is repulsed by the crowd jeering at Goldstein's image (especially by a child yelling, "Swine!"), but his hatred of Big Brother suddenly shifts to unexpected adoration as he sees the Party leader as invincible and fearless, the lone force able to stand up against "the hordes." The shift is a sign of how fluidly the animosity that Two Minutes Hate whips up can shift from target to target, and how expertly propaganda can shape the reactions even of resisters. Smith may not scream, "My Saviour!" at the screen as some in the crowd do, but he has to join in chanting Big Brother's name with it, or else his ambivalence will give away his true feelings. Yet even as he finds this ritual "sub-human," the "general delirium" that the Party's figurehead generates infects him against his will.

Orwell doesn't use the term "cult of personality" in *Nineteen Eighty-Four*, but that's clearly what he's cautioning against with "B-B," as he is affectionately known by worshippers. The heretical question that sows discord throughout the novel is whether a historical person named Big Brother actually exists—or if he ever did. In private moments, Smith tries to remember exactly when he first heard that name, but he can't call upon any knowledge outside official Party history. It insists that Big Brother has always been the "leader and guardian" of the revolution that installed "Ingsoc" (or English socialism) as the official state ideology some two decades earlier, but since Smith's job at the Ministry of Truth is to revise history by rewriting old articles from the *Times*, he knows not to trust official sources. It's suggested later that Big Brother is simply a controlling principle, a "guise" by which the Party engenders both fear and love, which individuals inspire more than faceless organizations. Much later, Smith is detained at the ironically titled Ministry of Love and interrogated by O'Brien, the Thought Police agent whose job is to trick potential subversives into revealing their disloyalty, and then torturing them to cure the "insanity" of not accepting Party dogma. Smith specifically asks if Big Brother exists in the same way he exists—in other words, as a real person. O'Brien's reply is chilling: "You don't exist."

It's worth asking why we've chosen Big Brother and not Smith as the novel's most memorable character. In stories of totalitarian oppression, readers' sympathies naturally go toward the freethinker who stands up for the sanctity of the individual. After his private denunciation of the cheering crowd, Smith purchases a diary and hides in a blind spot in his living quarters from Big Brother's omnipresent telescreen to record his opposition: DOWN WITH BIG

BROTHER. He soon commences an affair with another secret rebel, Julia, risking imprisonment because sex in Oceania for any other reason than procreation is illegal. Eventually, O'Brien invites the duo to study Goldstein's illegal tract, *The Theory and Practice of Oligarchical Collectivism*, and to join a subversive group called the Brotherhood, which is dedicated to leading a proletarian revolution to overthrow Ingsoc.

As it turns out, the invitation is a setup, and both Winston and Julia are tortured. Smith is thus less a hero than a victim of the system who is brutalized into submission. In the novel's most terrifying moment, O'Brien breaks him in Room 101, the chamber where everyone's worst nightmare is inflicted upon them. The torturer straps a mask attached to a cage of rats to Smith's face, leading a terrified Winston to denounce Julia, screaming, "Not me!" and begging that his torturer loosen the rats on her instead. Orwell wants us to understand that, despite what literature and myth may celebrate, there is no "last man," no unconquerable emissary of humanism to pin one's hopes for the future on. Nor is Smith a martyr. In our last glimpse of him, he sits in a café watching Big Brother announce Oceania's victory over its enemy, Eurasia, all thoughts of resistance wiped from his mind. He accepts the Party's insistence that $2 + 2 = 5$ and feels deep loyalty for Oceania's leader. "He loved Big Brother," the novel ends.

If not Smith then, why not O'Brien? In many ways, he is the most interesting character in *Nineteen Eighty-Four*. Most significantly, he is no ideologue. He bluntly tells Winston that the Party's only interest is power, not a set of ideals, for power is an end, not a means. The image of the future, he insists, is a boot stamping a face, and the only love will be blind loyalty to Big Brother. During the torture scenes, O'Brien also plays the role of a stern, punishing father figure, making Winston want to please him. The torturer also has an uncanny ability to read Winston's thoughts, knowing when he lies. He has studied humanity so he can destroy it.

Ultimately, though, calling O'Brien the most fascinating character betrays the torturer's own message that the individual is only a cell in a collective organism. Big Brother may only be the face of the organism, but existing as an abstraction allows him to exist everywhere. Besides, while the average person probably can't name Winston Smith's nemesis, everyone has heard of Big Brother—and not just because of the TV show. The name has become a convenient code word for our fears of the panopticon, the all-seeing state, and invasions into privacy.

What we don't admit enough—and what Orwell feared most—was how many among the masses are perfectly content with this omniscient sibling poking into the deepest, most individualistic corners of our mind.

Bibliography

Nineteen Eighty-Four (1949)

—KC

MARY KATHERINE BLACKWOOD

First Appearance: *We Have Always Lived in the Castle*
Date of First Appearance: 1962
Author: Shirley Jackson (1916–1965)

What place would be better for us than this? Who wants us outside? The world is full of terrible people.

"I dislike washing myself, and dogs, and noise. I like my sister Constance, and Richard Plantagenet, and *Amanita phalloides*, the death-cup mushroom," eighteen-year-old Mary Katherine Blackwood says, casually adding, "everyone else in my family is dead."

That's not *quite* true. Six years ago her mother, father, brother, and aunt all died at the dinner table after ingesting sugar that was laced with arsenic. Mary Katherine—Merricat for short—had been sent to her room without supper, as was often the case. Miraculously, Uncle Julian survived, and Merricat's older sister Constance, who took no sugar, was charged with murder. Though Constance did curious things like scrubbing the sugar bowl clean and telling police her family deserved to die, eventually she was acquitted in a trial that rocked the community. Now, Uncle Julian is in a wheelchair living in a room off the kitchen and writing his account of the "most sensational poisoning case of the century." He can't leave the house, and Constance is unwilling. But Merricat goes to town each week to bring back food and new library books, braving the children's chanted nursery-rhyme taunts each time:

> Merricat, said Connie, would you like a cup of tea?
> Oh no, said Merricat, you'll poison me.
> Merricat, said Connie, would you like to go to sleep?
> Down in the boneyard ten feet deep!

Merricat is extremely protective—and possessive—of her twenty-eight-year-old sister and wishes she could whisk her away from the villagers' cruel resentments. "I really only want a winged horse, anyway. We could fly you to the moon and back, my horse and I." Such fairy-tale overtones make their story seem almost fable-like. "When I was small I thought Constance was a fairy princess," Merricat says. "She was the most precious person in my world, always," and she remains such—so much that every Wednesday Merricat walks the perimeter of their property, mends any gaps in the fence, and checks to see if the gates are locked. A believer in rituals and superstitions, Merricat also creates "safeguards" to ward off anything, including unwanted change. She buries things all over the yard—a box of silver dollars near the creek, a doll and her baby teeth (thinking they might sprout one day into dragons) in the long field—and she nails a book to the tree in the pine woods, convinced that as long as they remained where she put them "nothing could get in to harm us."

We Have Always Lived in the Castle would be considered "southern gothic" if it weren't for the fact that author Shirley Jackson grew up in San Francisco, studied at Syracuse University, and settled in Vermont. But in her fiction, nothing is as tranquil or reasonable as it seems, and that goes double for Merricat, the narrator of this novel published just three years before the reclusive Jackson died of heart failure at the young age of forty-eight.

As a reviewer for the *Guardian* noted, "Merricat is a troubled young woman" who marks her days with "little OCD rituals." She's odd and eccentric, to be sure, but Merricat is also a rewardingly nuanced and subtle character whose menace unfolds so innocently, so gradually, and so matter-of-factly between the lines of her story that it's one of literature's more fascinating—enough for Stephen King to acknowledge it as an influence.

Merricat is always trying to remind herself to be kinder to Uncle Julian, whose room is just off the kitchen. Since the trial, Constance and Merricat weekly clean the whole house, but the only rooms the three of them ever use are the kitchen and back bedrooms. Outside, because the front of the house has a long lane that ends near the village and highway, the three family members tend to stay on the back lawn and adjacent vegetable garden that Constance tends, where no one in the village can see them.

Merricat tells us that Constance "always touched foodstuffs with quiet respect," but adds that she herself was not allowed to help prepare food or gather mushrooms, though she did carry vegetables in from the garden or apples from the old trees. Likewise, she was not allowed to wash the dishes, but she could carry them. The list of what Merricat is "allowed" or "not allowed" to do is long enough to suggest that not all is perfectly normal with her. Is it post-traumatic stress syndrome? Was she like this before the family tragedy? Later, when Constance's best friend comes to visit and brings another person with her, Merricat gets quietly upset: "I'll send them away. She knows better than this." At first we wonder how fragile Constance is, until the women leave and Constance gently tells her little sister, "Kind of a weak first step. It's going to be fine, Merricat." More clues, dropped like a trail of bread crumbs, lead us to realize that Merricat is the bigger concern.

Is she a danger to herself or others? One episode suggests so. When Merricat finds a nest of baby snakes near the creek and kills them because, she says, "I dislike snakes and Constance had never asked me not to," readers get a full sense of the innocent menace she represents. Like a fairy-tale witch, Merricat devises "three powerful words, words of strong protection" that, if never spoken aloud, no change would come: "Melody," "Gloucester," and "Pegasus." But after the book she had nailed to a tree falls down, soon afterward their cousin, Charles, comes and asserts himself, displacing Merricat by taking over the grocery shopping. "You'll have to find something else for her to do, Connie," he says, but Merricat's response is to begin reciting the properties of the *Amanita phalloides* ("You stop that," he says) and ends with her concluding, "Death occurs between five and ten days after eating" ("I don't think that's very funny"). Later, when he suggests that she will be the one who is gone a month from now, Merricat goes into her father's old room and hammers "with a shoe at the mirror" until it cracks. After Charles unearths her box of silver dollars, it annoys her that he didn't even bother to fill in the hole again. "'Don't blame *me*,' I said to the hole; I would have to find something else to bury here and I wished it could be Charles."

This modern fairy tale ends when Merricat sets the upstairs on fire to destroy the value of the house, thinking then Charles might leave. The villagers gather, some shouting, "Let it burn." After the fire is doused, an angry mob throws rocks at the house and enters, breaking things as they go and sending the two sisters running upstairs to hide. Later, guilty villagers will leave food at the front door, but one mother tells her boy to stay clear of the house. "The ladies don't like little boys. . . . They'd hold you down and make you eat candy full of poison." With the fire having burned out the roof, Merricat seems happy. "Our house was a castle, turreted and open to the sky." And she muses, "I wonder if I *could* eat a child if I had the chance."

Bibliography

We Have Always Lived in the Castle (1962)

Work Cited

Barnett, David. "*We Have Always Lived in the Castle* by Shirley Jackson—A House of Ordinary Horror." *Guardian*, December 21, 2015. https://www.theguardian.com/books/2015/dec/21/we-have-always-lived-in-the-castle-by-shirley-jackson-a-house-of-ordinary-horror.

—JP

MOLLY BLOOM

First Appearance: *Ulysses*
Date of First Appearance: 1922
Author: James Joyce (1882–1941)

He said the day we were lying among the rhododendrons on Howth head in the grey tweed suit and his straw hat the day I got him to propose to me yes first I gave him the bit of seedcake out of my mouth and it was leapyear like now yes 16 years ago my God after that long kiss I near lost my breath yes he said I was a flower of the mountain yes so we are flowers all a womans body yes.

Not many characters can be boiled down to a single word, but Molly Bloom, the thirty-four-year-old, opera-singer wife of Leopold Bloom in James Joyce's *Ulysses*, can: *Yes.*

That affirmation begins and ends her spotlight chapter, which closes Joyce's modernist landmark. Molly is the novel's earth goddess, the embodiment of fleshly pleasure who stands in contrast to the sterile intellectualism of her husband and *Ulysses*'s third central character, Stephen Dedalus. The irony is that while Molly is associated with the body, she exists mostly in the ruminations of other characters who greatly misread her and in her own whirlpooling thoughts about love and marriage, the quintessential example of "stream of consciousness" narration. Physically, she is present only twice in the text, first when Leopold Bloom's odyssey begins in chapter 4 ("Calypso") and then when he returns home to 7 Eccles Street in the penultimate chapter 17 ("Ithaca"). Nevertheless, her presence challenges other characters' reductive ideas of women's sexuality by testifying to the complexity of femininity.

Not that Molly is pure as snow. *Ulysses* retells Homer's *Odyssey* by drawing ironic parallels between the warrior-king's epic adventures after the Trojan War and the minutiae of modern life on a single day (June 16, 1904) in Dublin, Ireland. Leopold Bloom is a mock-heroic everyman, with Dedalus an adoptive version of Odysseus's son, Telemachus. Molly is Penelope, the king's loyal wife who resists the advances of suitors when her husband is presumed dead. Only Molly isn't loyal: June 4 is the day she commits adultery with concert promoter Hugh "Blazes" Boylan, who rather ungenerously leaves behind incriminating crumbs in the Blooms' marital sheets.

Whether Boylan is Molly's first dalliance is unclear. Because Bloom itemizes a list of romantic rivals for her affection, critics have claimed she's had as many as twenty-six lovers; others insist that Boylan is her first, possibly her second. Either way, Molly commits adultery to snap Leopold back to passion after exactly ten years, five months, and eighteen days without consummating their intimacy, dating back to the death of their son, Rudy, who lived only eleven days. (The Blooms' surviving child, Milly, is fifteen and an aspiring photographer.)

Mrs. Bloom is no intellectual. She misinterprets metempsychosis as "met him pike hoses," prompting her to ask Leopold, "Met him where?" Yet Molly has a streetwise awareness of men's foibles. Awakened in the early hours of June 5 when her husband stumbles into their bed to kiss the "plump mellow yellow smellow melons of her rump," she suspects from his request for breakfast in bed that he's orgasmed during his peregrinations. (He has indeed—by masturbating.) Because her thoughts are associational instead of linear, she bounces from thinking of her volatile romp with Boylan to memories of past suitors, whether the tenor Bartell d'Arcy or Lieutenant Gardner, who died in the Boer War. A train whistle leads her mind to her childhood on Gibraltar and a love letter she received from Lieutenant Mulvey. She compares her childhood to her daughter's, expressing jealousy over Milly's beauty, which Molly is losing. The sudden start of her period reassures her Boylan didn't impregnate her that afternoon. She regrets her advertising-salesman husband's shaky finances and defends him against the condescension of others who think he's dull. Molly also considers an affair with Dedalus. Thinking of buying flowers to prepare for a visit from her husband's surrogate son segues into memories of the day Bloom proposed to her at Howth Head, calling her his "flower of the mountain": "I put my arms around him yes and drew him down to me so he could feel my breasts all perfume yes and his heart was going like mad and yes I said yes I will Yes."

Readers familiar with Joyce's biography often assume Molly is his tribute to Nora Barnacle, his partner for nearly forty years. (The pair weren't legally married until 1931, by which point they had raised two surviving children.) *Ulysses* takes place on the exact day the pair first shared sexual contact—and, at the risk of being too explicit, June 16, 1904, commemorates the most significant hand job in literary history. The raunchier thoughts that drift through Molly's mind also echo the startlingly scatological love letters Joyce and Nora traded in 1909 when he left their expatriate home in Trieste to seek a publisher for his epochal story collection *Dubliners* (1914).

Several differences separate Nora and Molly, though: Molly is half-Spanish, born on Gibraltar, and Nora wasn't a singer. Nor, Nora insisted, was she as fat as Molly, who at 160 pounds fears turning matronly. Yet in one crucial way Nora inspired her counterpart. Her letters to Joyce eschewed punctuation and capitalization, resembling one long sentence. Her husband melded her style with the extreme form of interior monologue known as stream of consciousness, in which a character's random thoughts are presented in all their swirling, unedited immediacy. A challenging read, Molly's monologue runs eight paragraphs, with a period only at the end of the fourth and eighth to create a sense of balance and proportion.

Many commentators hailed Joyce for accurately representing women's minds, but Nora demurred—as have latter-day feminists, who consider Molly a man's vision of a woman. The charge seems undeniable given his description of the five-minute orgasm Boylan gives her, which makes her want to shout obscenities, "like fuck or shit or anything," or in her dismissal of other women as "a dreadful lot of bitches." Joyce didn't help his case by declaring that as the "*clou*" or axis of the novel Molly's monologue was built around four cardinal points: "the female breasts, arse, womb, and cunt." So much for the female brain!

Representative or not, Molly's lewd language was one reason *Ulysses* was banned in America until 1933. That year U.S. District Court judge John M. Woolsey ruled the book's intent was literary, not lascivious, a decision upheld by his appeals court counterpart, Augustus Hand, who described Molly's soliloquy as "pitiful and tragic, rather than lustful." That's certainly been the judgment of fans, who are drawn more to those ebullient yeses than to Mrs. Bloom's willingness to let her husband "stick his tongue 7 miles up my hole" to satisfy his derriere obsession. Homages to *Ulysses*'s concluding lines are countless. Most notably, British songstress Kate Bush's 1989 hit song "The Sensual World" borrows Molly's imagery for a lilting paean to desire. (Originally, Bush requested permission to sing the final passage, but Joyce's estate refused until 2011, when the songwriter rerecorded the melody with the original text as "Flower of the Mountain.")

Especially because modernist literature tends toward bleak despair, Molly's yeses are a rare but powerful affirmation of the uplift of romance.

Bibliography

Ulysses (1922)

—KC

JAMES BOND

First Appearance: *Casino Royale*
Date of First Appearance: 1953
Author: Ian Fleming (1908–1964)

The only secret side of the business is the addresses of these people.

"Bond, James Bond."

That's how Britain's top postwar secret agent introduces himself, though after appearing in twenty-four internationally distributed blockbuster films he's a character who needs no introduction. Even people who haven't read the books or seen the movies seem to know that James Bond, a.k.a. Agent 007, is a suave womanizer, a resourceful escape artist, an expert gambler, a wine and spirits connoisseur, a fast-driving lover of expensive sports cars, and a cool-under-pressure man of action who likes his martinis shaken and doesn't mind if the women who stir him happen to be working for the opposition.

The world's most famous spy was created on January 15, 1952, by Ian Fleming, who pounded away at his typewriter in the living room of his "Goldeneye" Jamaica estate and finished his first Bond novel, *Casino Royale*, a little more than two months later. According to biographer Andrew Lycett, 007 was a composite based on naval attachés and spies whom Commander Fleming encountered while working a desk job for naval intelligence. Over a fourteen-year period he wrote twelve Bond novels, which collectively sold more than 100 million and were subsequently made into films played by seven different actors: Sean Connery (six films, 1962–1971, plus an independently produced 1983 remake), George Lazenby (one film, 1969), Roger Moore (seven films, 1973–1985), Timothy Dalton (two films, 1987–1989), Pierce Brosnan (four films, 1995–2002), and Daniel Craig (four films, 2006–2015). Fans usually don't count a poorly received 1967 parody starring David Niven.

Fleming originally intended Bond to be a dull man, much like himself, so he gave him what he told the *New Yorker* was "the dullest name I ever heard"—the name of an American ornithologist who wrote the definitive field guide to Caribbean birds, a book owned by avid bird-watcher Fleming. But he also gave his alter ego some of the traits that he lacked, such as a job in the field, superior fighting skills, and an easy directness with women. Bond was based on Fleming's knowledge of the spy school near Guildford and the exploits of an agent-friend in Bucharest, which in 1940 was "the spy capital of Central Europe," according to his biographer. Described by the beautiful Vesper Lynd as "very good looking," Bond reminded her of Hoagy Carmichael, "but there is something cold and ruthless in his . . ." An explosion cuts her off in midsentence, though readers get the point. Bond is ruggedly handsome. Nothing rattles him, not even a bomb. He's tough and can endure all manner of torture. Sophisticated as well, in *Casino Royale* he smokes a special blend of Morland cigarettes and drinks dry martinis. Fleming even gives the recipe: "Three measures of Gordons, one of vodka, half a measure of Kina Lillet. Shake it until it's ice cold, then add a large thin slice of lemon peel."

Fleming gave readers a comprehensive look at his secret agent in *From Russia with Love*, taken from a SMERSH file on Bond: dark, clean-cut face with a three-inch scar showing whitely down the sunburned skin of the right cheek; black hair, firm jaw, slim build; all-round athlete; knows judo; high tolerance of pain; expert pistol shot, boxer, knife thrower; speaks English, French, and German; and carries a .25 Beretta automatic holstered under his left arm. His vices? Smokes heavily; drinks, but not to excess; and women. *Not thought to accept bribes.* In an era of double agents and Red Scare paranoia, that last detail was not insignificant. Bond had integrity, and his vices were manly ones, not flaws of character. Everything he did was high stakes, whether it involved nuclear weapons, a game of baccarat, vehicular chases, or flirtations with femmes fatales.

It would be a mistake to call James Bond the first spy—that was Johnny Fedora, who appeared in the 1951 novel *Secret Ministry*—but not unreasonable to call him the prototype for every spy novel to follow. Bond's character was dynamic, especially showcased within a now-familiar formula: exotic locations, Bond "girls," cat-and-mouse games with agents and evil masterminds, unique henchmen who invariably fight or torture Bond, deadly gadgets provided by Q Branch, frequent partnerships with CIA agent Felix Leiter, and a tongue-in-cheek cynical tone that made Bond the perfect hero for an unsettling post–World War II world. ("I can't let them get away with it. These are killers. They'll be off killing someone else tomorrow. . . . Besides, they ruined my shirt!")

Bond was uniquely *of* his time, but he also allowed readers to escape the stress of living in a world dominated by two nuclear superpowers—one reason, perhaps, why President Kennedy and his brother Bobby were fans. Bond, whose code name refers to the World War I German diplomatic code cracked by Blinker Hall, personified strength, cunning, and calmness. At a time when fear was driving people to build backyard bomb shelters and Sen. Joseph McCarthy was ferreting out alleged Communists and Soviet spies in Hollywood, Bond was the cool hero people needed to believe was working behind the scenes to keep everyone safe—even if his opponents were often independent criminal organizations looking to incite war between the U.S. and USSR in order to emerge as the dominant world power.

Like the western heroes John Wayne popularized after the Second World War, Bond was a man's man, even appearing in *Playboy* magazine ("The Hildebrand Rarity," March 1960). Yet his brand of sexism ("Women were for recreation. On a job, they got in the way and fogged things up with sex and hurt feelings and all the emotional baggage they carried around") was also embraced by women of the time, perhaps because it was a small price to pay for the kind of strength that he projected. Bond appeared in the women's magazine *Cosmopolitan* as well ("Quantum of Solace," May 1959)—something almost mind-boggling, given that "Bond saw luck as a woman, to be softly wooed or brutally ravaged" and in the seventh novel beds a lesbian who explains that before him she "never met a man before."

In fiction, Bond wasn't just a "real man." He was also a real human, more so than the cinematic counterpart audiences first encountered in *Dr. No* (1962). In the *Casino Royale* novel, for example, after witnessing the chaotic aftermath of a bomb blast, "Bond felt himself starting to vomit." Later, after being tortured for days, he worries that he might not be able to sexually "rise" to the next occasion. In the movies, Bond is cool both inside and out; while the Bond of the novels keeps his composure, inside he's often seething, as when the villainous Goldfinger successfully negotiates a sand trap in a high-stakes game. The movie Bond is an iron man, but the Bond of the novels sometimes needs Benzedrine to keep going. It's the superhuman movie Bond that pop culture has toasted with James Bond's 007 Special Blend beer/malt liquor and celebrated with merchandise of all kinds.

The Bond books have been translated into twelve languages, and since Fleming's 1964 death his estate has enlisted seven different writers to continue the Bond and related series. And with MGM continuing to churn out Bond films, this Cold War hero remains hot as ever.

Bibliography

Casino Royale (Jonathan Cape, 1953)
Live and Let Die (Jonathan Cape, 1954)
Moonraker (Jonathan Cape, 1955)

Diamonds Are Forever (Jonathan Cape, 1956)
From Russia with Love (Jonathan Cape, 1957)
Dr. No (Jonathan Cape, 1958)
Goldfinger (Jonathan Cape, 1959)
"Quantum of Solace" (*Cosmopolitan*, May 1959)
"From a View to a Kill" (*Daily Express*, September 21–25, 1959)
"The Hildebrand Rarity" (*Playboy*, March 1960)
"The Double Take" (a.k.a. "Risico," *Daily Express*, April 11–15, 1960)
For Your Eyes Only (Jonathan Cape, 1960)
Thunderball (Jonathan Cape, 1961)
The Spy Who Loved Me (Jonathan Cape, 1962)
On Her Majesty's Secret Service (Jonathan Cape, 1963)
"007 in New York" (*New York Herald Tribune*, October 1963)
"The Property of a Lady" (*Playboy*, January 1964)
You Only Live Twice (Jonathan Cape, 1964)
The Man with the Golden Gun (Jonathan Cape, 1965)
Octopussy and the Living Daylights (Jonathan Cape, 1966)

Works Cited

Hellman, Geoffrey T. "Talk of the Town: Bond's Creator." *New Yorker*, April 21, 1962, 32.
Lycett, Andrew. *Ian Fleming*. New York: St. Martin's, 1995.

—JP

PHILBERT BONO

First Appearance: *The Powwow Highway*
Date of First Appearance: 1979
Author: David Seals (1947–2017)

We are making with a raiding party to New Mexico to rescue a maiden from the savages.
Wanna come?

Everyone in Lame Deer, the agency village of the Northern Cheyenne in Montana, knew the old Buick had many owners before Philbert Bono's cousin traded it to him in 1978 for two ounces of marijuana and an old horse saddle. But with Philbert riding his "war pony," the rusted-out car that can't go over forty-five miles per hour on the freeway becomes a part of tribal legend, along with Philbert himself.

As film critic Roger Ebert wrote after seeing the 1989 film version of David Seals's *The Powwow Highway*, "Anyone who can name his 1964 Buick 'Protector' and talk to it like a pony has a philosophy we can learn from." Ebert added, "One of the reasons we go to movies is to meet people we have not met before. It will be a long time before I forget [Gary] Farmer, who disappears into the Philbert role so completely we almost think he is this simple, openhearted man" beneath whose simplicity lurks "a serene profundity." It's not just the actor, of course. Philbert Bono—whose name means "good nut"—is strong comic-heroic character.

At six foot four, Philbert is a "great giant of an Indian" who wears his waist-long black hair tied "in a single greasy braid." Aside from a down vest and two beaded barrettes, he dresses all in denim. Philbert was born fat, and at thirty-three he's still fat. Readers meet him long after the childhood taunts and rejections he endured at Mission School, where he technically never passed beyond first grade. They might have shipped him off to a school for the mentally handicapped, except that his mother knew he wasn't "mental" and so did the whole town. He was just "stupid," and the kids called him "Crackers" because of it.

Philbert would be a sympathetic character without that backstory, as it's hard not to appreciate a man who sees a war pony in a beat-up Buick and approaches life as Philbert does. As the narrator explains, "Philbert had conquered failure with doggedness. He plowed through poverty with thoughts of wealth. He overcame depression by simply denying its existence." Powered by beer, marijuana, and junk food, Philbert gravitates toward good times with friends. He's *not* a seeker, we're told, because he's happy in his own skin and has a childlike innocence, a basic goodness, an ultrapositive mind-set, and an earnest desire to learn the old ways of the Cheyenne—even if the rest of the tribe thinks he's marching to the beat of a sadly outdated drummer. That's made perfectly clear when he goes to see tribal elder Aunt Harriet to obtain wisdom, and she's more interested in her television "stories" than in telling the stories of her people. As he leaves disappointed, she calls out to him ("Hey Fat Philbert") and shares a quote her grandmother heard from an uncle, who had heard it from Dull Knife: "Keep your pony out of my garden." Then she cackles. It may be a joke and utter nonsense to her, but to Philbert, whose Indian name is Whirlwind, the old ways are something to ponder, just as throughout the novel he contemplates the magic-but-tragic history of his people and other Plains tribes.

Not bright, not athletic, but genial and helpful as all hell? Those are the qualities of a sidekick, not a hero, and readers expect Philbert to settle into a sidekick's role when Cheyenne golden boy Buddy Red Bow hops into Philbert's Buick and tells him that his sister, Bonnie Red Bow, has been arrested on a drug charge. They need to drive to Santa Fe to post bail and get her out of New Mexico, and he's got gas money—money the tribe gave him to buy breeding bulls. For Buddy, a Vietnam War veteran and previously active member of the American Indian Movement, it's a simple drive-there-and-back shell game: write out a check for Bonnie's bail, then write a different check for the bulls, and by the time that first check bounces they will have transported Bonnie safely across state lines. It doesn't happen that way because Philbert is the *hero* and he has a more spiritual journey in mind, starting with gathering power before going on a "war party." Philbert is earnest about living as the Old Ones did, though he's such an unlikely Cheyenne to lead a war party that one of the spirits of the Old Ones who watch from a sacred mountain near Fort Robinson, where many Native Americans were imprisoned or killed, remarks, "Not exactly the second coming, but who's counting?" Another Old One quips, "Could have been worse."

Philbert may be comic, but he's serious in his pursuit of a communal spiritual renewal, beginning with himself. He feels a growing determination to keep the old ways alive because he sees value in them. He prays after acquiring Protector, and he has a vision as his ancestors once did—though, in true comic-hero fashion, that vision comes after downing a case of beer and smoking an ounce of marijuana. Yet throughout the novel Philbert is taken increasingly more seriously as he becomes focused on the old ways and becomes himself transformed. Others notice, especially Buddy, who joins Philbert when he wades into a river to chant before they begin their journey to Santa Fe. On the road, when Buddy is sleeping, instead of following the signs for Santa Fe, Philbert impulsively detours toward Bear Butte, the sacred mountain of the Cheyenne, because he felt called to the Black Hills by "some great power" and "it was heavy shit, like the Ten Commandments." Along the way Philbert will continue to detour in the direction of sites that are sacred to the American Indian, gathering such tokens for his sacred medicine bundle as small rocks that he finds in his pocket or stuck to him after visiting a site. Whether he's singing the truths of Bear Butte at a powwow dance (after which the dancers "exploded in an involuntary unity"), attacking a snowplow that buried his Protector and the Indians inside it, or, in a later novel, crashing a police roadblock, Philbert isn't just fat . . . he carries weight.

Children love Philbert for the stories he tells them and the way he plays with them on their level—a natural-born tribal storyteller—but for Philbert those stories aren't relics. They're keys to a meaningful present. He *becomes* Wihio the trickster, creator of the universe, when he saves the day by wandering into the basement of the Santa Fe police station and filling his pockets with seized currency, then tying a rope from the bars of the jail to Protector's bumper and breaking Bonnie free, Old West–style.

Hailed as an underground classic, *The Powwow Highway* was published in a limited edition in 1979 by a small press but quickly went into multiple printings and then a mass-market paperback release after the film came out. Though Seals—a writer, actor, American Indian activist, and founder of the Bear Butte Council—died in 2017, his alter ego lives on as a testimony that you *can* get there from here, if your heart is pure and you trust in the powers that gave you life.

Bibliography

The Powwow Highway (1979)
Sweet Medicine (1992)

Work Cited

Ebert, Roger. "Powwow Highway." Review of *The Powwow Highway*, by David Seals. RogertEbert.com. April 28, 1989. https://www.rogerebert.com/reviews/powwow-highway-1989.

—JP

EMMA BOVARY

First Appearance: *Madame Bovary*
Date of First Appearance: 1857
Author: Gustave Flaubert (1821–1880)

Love must come suddenly, with great outbursts and lightnings—a hurricane of the skies, which falls upon life, revolutionizes it, roots up the will like a leaf, and sweeps the whole heart into the abyss.

Of the sisterhood of nineteenth-century heroines destroyed by their desire to love passionately—Anna Karenina, Tess Durbeyfield, Edna Pontellier, among others—Emma Bovary has always been the most divisive. As the provincial wife of a kind but unambitious country doctor, she cultivates florid ideas of love by reading tawdry romances. After two disappointing extramarital affairs that don't live up to the promise of her books, she tries to satisfy her longings with a wild spending spree, stocking up on a wealth of luxury items that can't begin to satisfy her insatiable yearning. Upon sinking her family into ruinous debt, she kills herself by eating arsenic. The conflation of love and acquisition makes her a wickedly satirical embodiment of the bourgeoisie's gluttonous consumer hungers, a symbol of the trashy materialism of the middle class. Her gruesome suicide, which leaves her corpse oozing black liquid, is described so explicitly that it seems invasive, an almost clinical debunking of her self-absorbed illusions and petty vanities.

Yet her author also famously declared, "Madame Bovary, c'est moi," suggesting how much Flaubert projected his own Romanticism into Emma's unrequited desires. His identification with the character calls attention to the empathy the novel appears to encourage for this adulterous wife by refusing to judge her with the outright condemnations that writers of the time interjected into their fiction. "I do not want my book to contain a *single* subjective reaction, not a single reflection by the author," Flaubert insisted when writing the novel. "Nowhere in my book must the author express his emotions or his opinions." While contemporaries portrayed their doomed romantics as pitiable victims, *Madame Bovary* gives audiences the space to either hate or love its titular character. What makes Emma memorable is how often she provokes readers to one or the other extreme; reactions to her rarely take the middle ground. People either hate her, or they are her.

Flaubert subtitled the book *Mœurs de province* ("Customs of the Province," but usually translated as "Scenes from Provincial Life") and dramatized Madame Bovary's tragedy through three central locations. Part 1 mostly takes place in the small town of Tostes, where Charles Bovary assumes the post of a "health officer"—a far less prestigious position than that of a doctor—and on a remote farm meets Emma Rouault, a young woman educated in a convent but now stuck tending to her aged father. When Charles's older wife suddenly passes away, he and Emma marry, but the new Madame Bovary quickly finds marriage as tedious as rural housekeeping. After a chance invitation to attend an aristocratic ball, Emma grows sick from discontent with her unglamorous environs. To make her happy, Charles relocates the family, which now includes a daughter, to the village of Yonville-l'Abbaye, whose tastes are typified by the opportunistic pharmacist Homais.

In part 2, Emma grows infatuated with the naïve law student Léon Dupuis, who flees to Paris for fear of acting on his attraction to a married woman. In his absence Madame Bovary succumbs to the charms of the unrepentant womanizer Rodolphe Boulanger, who seduces her (at a county fair, no less) only to reject her when she grows needy. Emma once again falls into a deep depression, which Charles attempts to cure by taking her to an opera in the larger city of Rouen. There Emma is by chance reunited with Léon, who has grown worldlier and more assertive since leaving Yonville.

After consummating their mutual attraction during a scandalous six-hour cab ride in part 3, the pair embark on a flagrant affair. Illicit excitement soon turns routine, however, and Emma discovers that adultery contains "all the platitudes of marriage." In her disillusionment, she falls prey to the merchant Lheureux, who takes advantage of her not sexually but financially by encouraging her to buy furniture and clothes on credit. When both Léon and Rodolphe reject her pleas to borrow money to pay her debts—and after her various male admirers in Yonville turn her down (though one offers a loan in return for sex)—she commits suicide to escape her shame. Her death devastates Charles and dooms Berthe, their daughter, to life as a mill worker. As if to confirm that only the cynical and duplicitous survive, Flaubert's final line reveals that Homais has been awarded the medal of the Legion of Honor, France's highest civic award. Ostensibly the long-coveted honor is for public service, but the conniving apothecary actually receives it for helping the local prefect win election. The message is simple: The world is not for romantics.

In dramatizing Emma's desires, Flaubert delved so deeply into her thoughts that he foregrounded a narrative technique that previous writers had used intuitively without bothering to name it. Known today as *discours indirect libre* (free indirect discourse), the device presents a character's unspoken feelings without attribution tags such as "she thought that," achieving an immediacy that fuses the voice of the character and narrator and renders authorial intent ambiguous. To quote the novel's most notorious example, when Emma first sleeps with Rodolphe, Flaubert writes, "So at last she was to know those joys of love, that fever of happiness of which she had despaired! She was entering upon marvels where all would be passion, ecstasy, delirium." In such moments it's unclear whether Flaubert paraphrases Emma's thoughts in his own words or whether he himself believes that she is "entering upon marvels," not just condoning but celebrating her passion and ecstasy. Depending on how the reader interprets it, the passage is sincere, or it's ironic; free indirect discourse effectively serves as a mirror that reflects to audiences either the sympathy or the moral judgment with which they react to Emma's thoughts.

Flaubert's refusal to censure his heroine for committing adultery landed *Madame Bovary* in an obscenity trial in 1857. The prosecutor, Ernest Pinard, even quoted the line cited above, declaring, "Who can condemn the woman in the book? Nobody. . . . Would you condemn her in the name of the author's conscience? I do not know what the author's conscience thinks." The rigorous objectivity or "impersonality" achieved both through free indirect discourse and the writer's devotion to *le mot juste* (the right word) made Flaubert a god to later generations of aestheticians, many of whom had nothing in common with Emma Bovary. Even Ezra Pound—a poet not exactly known for romantic ardor—idolized the author of *Madame Bovary*: "His true Penelope [muse] was Flaubert," Pound wrote in his poetic declaration of independence, *Hugh Selwyn Mauberley* (1920).

As for Emma herself, she endures as a Rosetta stone for our mixed feelings about sentimentality, passion, and all those messy emotional wants that tend to embarrass us. Judging Madame Bovary is easy. Yet anyone who has stumbled into an affair or even grown infatuated with another person, daydreaming of what love and gratification they might lavish on us, will recognize in her our own susceptibility to constant craving. If Madame Bovary isn't us, then we are likely either dullards like Charles or schemers like Homais the grandstanding glad-hander.

And that means that while life might be safer and saner, it would be a lot less romantic, too.

Bibliography

Madame Bovary (1857)

—KC

JEAN BRODIE

First Appearance: *The Prime of Miss Jean Brodie*
Date of First Appearance: 1961
Author: Muriel Spark (1918–2006)

I have frequently told you . . . that my prime has truly begun. One's prime is elusive. You little girls, when you grow up, must be on the alert to recognize your prime at whatever time of your life it may occur. You must then live it to the full.

Muriel Spark's *The Prime of Miss Jean Brodie* belongs to a persistent if overlooked genre about teachers' effect on student lives. Whether in novels such as James Hilton's *Goodbye, Mr. Chips* (1934), E. R. Braithwaite's *To Sir, with Love* (1959), Bel Kaufman's *Up the Down Staircase* (1964), Pat Conroy's memoir *The Water Is Wide* (1972), or in movies like *Dead Poets Society* (1989) and *Mona Lisa Smile* (2003), these narratives pit flamboyant, unconventional educators against small-minded administrators and parents who fear that any subject unique or rebellious—like literature!—will subvert middle-class values.

Spark's short, crystalline novel is the rare example that critiques the pedagogues rather than the petty bureaucrats. To wit: Not many other teachers in this genre sing Mussolini's praises or spend their holidays admiring Hitler's good work in Germany. Set in Spark's native Edinburgh, Scotland, in the 1930s when some Europeans were indeed infatuated with Fascist strongmen, the novel asks whether the sway charismatic teachers hold over young minds is healthy. The book makes it clear Miss Brodie is a self-absorbed quack, but it also treats her tragically, offering her as a tribute to all the lonely people who live vicariously through art and other people.

At first, Miss Brodie seems like every humanities-leaning student's dream teacher. She believes art and religion are more valuable than science and math. She skips lesson plans to recount tears-inducing stories about the fiancé she lost in the Great War. She insists that education is about "leading out" or developing talents already inside students instead of stuffing them full of bland facts.

Yet Miss Brodie also plays favorites. She gathers around her a group she insists is exceptional—the "crème de la crème," she boasts—though none of her girls seems particularly extraordinary. Other students dismiss "the Brodie set" as snobs who undermine the collective spirit at the Marcia Blaine School for Girls.

Among Miss Brodie's chosen few, Sandy Stranger provides the narrative consciousness through which readers slowly recognize the magnetic teacher's flaws. Through strategically placed flashbacks we see how Miss Brodie made Sandy and her other pet students dependent on her approval. Spark also flashes forward to the 1940s and 1950s to reveal how in adulthood the girls regard their teacher. Sandy equates Miss Brodie with the theological limitations of Calvinism, which insists that God in his omnipotence selects for salvation those he blesses out of nothing more than favoritism, providing no opportunity to earn grace. The teacher's callousness is evident in her treatment of the so-called dimmest of the set, Mary Macgregor, who suffers her abuse in silence. Even after Mary dies in a hotel fire at twenty-four, entirely unprepared to face an emergency, Miss Brodie can find nothing nice to say about her.

Another girl, Joyce Emily Hammond, is so beguiled by her teacher's romantic vision of Fascism she runs away to fight in the Spanish Civil War and is promptly killed in a train attack. Even after World War II, the worst Miss Brodie can say about Hitler is that he "was rather naughty." While other girls such as Eunice Gardiner look back at her as a harmless eccentric, Sandy struggles with the complex resentment she harbors toward the woman. It remains unresolved even after Miss Brodie dies from cancer at fifty-six, alone in a retirement home, and after Sandy joins a convent and transforms herself into Sister Helena of the Transfiguration.

The brilliance of Spark's plot lies in the way her skipping back and forth in time reveals major plot twists while building suspense over the motives behind crucial character actions. We discover halfway through the story, almost offhandedly, that Sandy is the member of the set who betrays Miss Brodie in 1939 to the school's headmistress, Miss Mackay, costing the teacher her job. Ostensibly, the reason for the firing is Miss Brodie's Fascist sympathies, which by the outset of World War II are considered seditious. But not until far deeper in the book are the true reasons revealed. As the girls grow up, they discover Miss Brodie is in love with their art teacher, Teddy Lloyd. Because Teddy is married, she transfers her attention to the music teacher, Gordon Lowther, who is cowed by the knowledge he is the far less interesting choice.

When Mr. Lowther unexpectedly throws Miss Brodie over for a woman as dull as he is, the spinster attempts to engineer a vicarious love affair between Teddy and the beautiful but dispassionate Rose, with Sandy as her confidant. Mr. Lloyd paints portrait after portrait of the two girls, but Miss Brodie's features creep into the imagery, suggesting his longing for her. Sandy soon seduces Teddy, though not out of jealousy of Rose. Her affair is a simple act of rebellion against her mentor, an attempt to prove the limits of Miss Brodie's omnipotence. When the teacher seems unperturbed by her pupil's assertion of will, Sandy reports her politics to Miss Mackay. Only years later when another of the now-grown girls visits her at her convent does the woman now known as Sister Helena discover that Miss Brodie told other members of the set before her death that she suspected Sandy was the culprit.

Part of what makes *The Prime of Miss Jean Brodie* so intriguing is Spark's refusal to clarify Sandy's feelings toward her teacher. Sister Helena's repeated insistence that the girls didn't owe Miss Brodie their absolute loyalty seems evasive. Her reasons for entering the convent are ambiguous enough to wonder whether she is serving an unconscious penance for her actions or hiding behind religion to escape responsibility for them. Yet in the end the character who captures the popular imagination is not the novel's Judas figure but its victim. Most former students have a Miss Brodie in their lives, a teacher who once seemed larger than life but who with time and reflection shrinks in grandeur in front of our eyes until we recognize the power they wielded over us substituted for the unfulfilled parts of their lives. The pathos of the novel lies in the emphasis on that word "prime": The more Miss Brodie asserts she is in hers, the more we realize she has never really had one.

The Prime of Miss Jean Brodie was adapted into a moderately successful London play in 1966 that enjoyed a Broadway run two years later. Its script became the basis for a hit 1969 film that won Maggie Smith her first Academy Award for Best Actress. The movie remains highly regarded thanks to Smith's commanding performance, but it sacrifices Spark's flash-forwards for straightforward chronology, diluting the suspense (and softening Sandy, played by Pamela Franklin). The novel's Miss Brodie is kookier and more clueless in her hauteur—the kind of influence we look back upon later in life and wonder, "How were we ever so young we fell for that?"

Bibliography

The Prime of Miss Jean Brodie (1961)

—KC

AURELIANO BUENDÍA

First Appearance: *Cien Años de Soledad—One Hundred Years of Solitude*
Date of First Appearance: in Spanish (1967), in English (1970)
Author: Gabriel García Márquez (1927–2014)

Look at this mess we've found ourselves in, all because we invited a gringo *to eat a banana.*

If one book can be described as the novel of crossover moving Gabriel García Márquez from a popular Latin American writer to a man of international acclaim and from less notoriety to literary stardom, it would be *One Hundred Years of Solitude*. This tour-de-force tome is largely responsible for Márquez receiving the Nobel Prize in Literature in 1982 and making the family name of Buendía as identifiable as any other among fictional characters. It also does not hurt that there was an inordinate number of Buendías over the course of 100 years with names so nearly indistinguishable from each other that a genealogy chart is necessary to keep them separate. Thankfully, Márquez provides this helpful tool at the front of the book, but even so, keeping track is no easy task as we read through the hundreds of pages illuminating the family's history-filled century. To use Aureliano Buendía as an example, he has one son Aureliano José with a woman in his hometown of Macondo, Colombia, seventeen other sons all named Aureliano conceived by seventeen different women during his years away at war, a great-nephew Aureliano Segundo, and yet two more Aurelianos in another generation. Márquez marks a century of complexity in the Buendía family's strange journey and in the original Aureliano, who is equally a complicated man complexly evoked in this epic novel.

One Hundred Years of Solitude begins with a statement about Aureliano Buendía rather than introducing his father José Arcadio, whose journey to and in the founding of Macondo actually sets in place the rest of the story's action. In a passage noted as one of the great opening lines in fiction, Márquez writes, "Many years later, as he faced the firing squad, Colonel Aureliano Buendía was to remember that distant afternoon when his father took him to discover ice." The duality of his personality—the steely coldness of facing death with calm resolve and the nostalgia of an experience shared with his father—are melded here into a singular significant point. Beyond relevance to a particular flash in time, Márquez brilliantly uses this scene to make a statement about the circularity of history and memory and the ability to bring them together at crucial moments, and insignificant ones for that matter. He does so, perhaps, to emphasize Aureliano's centrality in the family alongside his grander participation in the national history—the inner essential circle's connection to the larger sphere. Márquez also acknowledged in his Nobel acceptance speech the grandness of life and human tenacity in saying, "To oppression, plundering and abandonment, we respond with life. Neither floods nor plagues, famines nor cataclysms, nor even the eternal wars of century upon century, have been able to subdue the persistent advantage of life over death." Aureliano, and frankly most of his family, show this to be true through the family's intrepid endurance.

Aureliano Buendía, called Colonel Aureliano Buendía through most of the book, begins life as an intelligent, shy, and reticent child who even in the womb was said to have cried. He also exhibits an ability to see the future, including his intended but aborted death by firing squad, and such visions may explain his desire to sequester himself both in his youth and when he returns from war. As a boy, he takes up goldsmithing and spends endless hours melting gold coins, shaping the metal into fish with scales, inserting small jewels for eyes, and then selling the pieces for more gold coins to repeat the cycle. Later when he comes back from two decades of combat, he will continue this activity as an avocation to calm his nerves and a means of isolating himself from others. The reclusive side of Aureliano shows a personality differing from the battle-fierce warrior who led more than thirty rebellions during the course of the Colombian war, except that even during those years he develops the eccentric practice of marking a chalk circle around himself to keep others out of his personal space, perhaps for fear of his safety, but just as likely because of the fear of his isolation being breeched.

Even so, Aureliano also sought solace in his loneliness, but his failure to intuitively understand what true connection entails creates more trauma through his choice for a wife. Oddly, and creepily, he chooses a nine-year-old girl named Remedios, whom he may believe to be the remedy for his cloistered life. He must wait several years before she can physically become a wife, and even when she reaches puberty at around the age of twelve, she is clearly still emotionally a young girl who knows nothing about being a spouse or a companion. She retains her dolls as the intimate objects of connection in the marriage, and she dies early of some unclear internal illness, likely a pregnancy wrought on a girl too young to carry a child to full term. Beyond what our sensibilities see as an unsavory sexual coupling, Aureliano's choice marks another of his failures to crack "the hard shell of his solitude" and connect on a satisfying level with those around him.

Aureliano becomes both more deeply introspective and nostalgic as he ages, yet also increasingly emotionally distant. Márquez writes of him, "He was preserved against imminent old age by a vitality that had something to do with the coldness of his insides," but in an effort to flee from "the chill that was to accompany him until death, he sought a last refuge in Macondo in the warmth of his oldest memories." In this way, he tries to keep painful memories at bay while paradoxically embracing feelings that bring back a warmth from the past. Like his father, he will die in the yard outside the family home, only to be found later, rather than in his bed surrounded by family, but they will at least be near.

The Buendía family tree is complicated, each member is uniquely inimitable, and every life is one of interior solitariness in some fashion or another. For Márquez, Aureliano Buendía is the amalgamation of this and the intersection of familial and national past, present, and future with its grand cycles, complex genealogy, and complicated interwoven plots. Márquez greatly admired William Faulkner's work of a similar nature and theme, and he took to heart Faulkner's phrase "The past is never dead. It's not even past." *One Hundred Years of Solitude* substantiates that belief in his own work. He incorporates a strong sense of realism blended with the Latin American concept of magical realism that is his heritage and part of the stories his grandmother told to him, and from her, he learned for his own tales that "what I had to do was believe in them myself and write them with the same expression with which my grandmother told them: with a brick face." He succeeded.

Bibliography

One Hundred Years of Solitude (1967)

Work Cited

Márquez, Gabriel García. Interview by Peter H. Stone. "Gabriel García Márquez: The Art of Fiction No. 69." *Paris Review*, 82 (Winter 1981).

—GS

NATHANIEL "NATTY" BUMPPO

First Appearance: *The Pioneers, or The Sources of the Susquehanna*
Date of First Appearance: 1823
Author: James Fenimore Cooper (1789–1851)

Should we distrust the man because his manners are not our manners, and that his skin is dark?

In the 1992 film adaptation of James Fenimore Cooper's novel *The Last of the Mohicans*, actor Daniel Day-Lewis cries out, "I will find you" as a British colonel's daughter is captured by a hostile Indian tribe who then escape with her into the vast American wilderness. Day-Lewis's presence looms large on the screen and amplifies the great white hunter persona that was immensely popular in American frontier folklore, and frankly still is. Cooper no doubt had in mind Daniel Boone (1734–1820), Davy Crockett (1786–1836), and other real-life woodsmen folk heroes representing the rugged pioneer spirit and embodying the skills of a soon-to-be dying breed. The story captures this idealized figure and era and is part of a novel series collectively titled the Leatherstocking Tales, chronicling the path of protagonist Nathaniel "Natty" Bumppo, best known as Hawkeye, as his life parallels the gradual demise of the American frontier.

Cooper's central character goes by many names throughout his journey—Hawkeye, Pathfinder, Deerslayer, Trapper, Leather-stocking, and Long Rifle—each related to a specific role in the volume in which he appears. At his prime, he is described as being "six feet tall in his moccasins, thin and wiry," with amazing physical strength and endurance. Hawkeye cuts an impressive path with his dexterity in the woods, and he is a fearless hunter, crack shot with a long rifle, an expert scout and trapper, a fierce warrior, and a man who is able to meld into the world of the Indians he admires and white settlers and military often at odds with them. Hawkeye, though white, has been mostly raised among the Indians, but as a man with a foot in those often adversarial worlds, he must straddle a treacherous path. Both sides see him as a man of honor and one whom they can trust.

Hawkeye is simpatico with friendly Indian tribes, particularly the Delawares who serve as a synecdoche of what the future holds for the Indian race. The elder chief Chingachgook watches as his only son Uncas is killed in battle and knows that the tribe will become extinct upon his own death. The demise of the frontiersman is also Hawkeye's future, along with the vanishing of the frontier itself, and he must journey far from where he had begun as a young man in upstate New York in order to go past the edges of civilization. He will die on the prairies of the Midwest as a symbolic last man of his frontier breed, though he in some way anticipates the rugged men of the Wild West that follow.

In spite of criticism that Cooper's writing style was cumbersome, his dialogue awkward, and plots slowly paced, his hero was hailed as a pathfinder and a trailblazer, not just of the forest, but of his time as well; Hawkeye was viewed as the nineteenth-century literary equivalent of today's rock stars.

Famed artist N. C. Wyeth lent his artistic talent to illustrating the 1919 deluxe edition of the book that became essential reading for American boys. An international audience also clambered to know more about the frontier that had long vanished on their continents, and they were especially interested in tales about its indigenous population and the woodsman who both battled and befriended them. Europeans found that these tales linked to their own interest and idealization of the romanticized, uncivilized man who by living simply outside of society remains untethered to, and thus uncorrupted by, its evil influence. *The Deerslayer*'s opening borrowed from Lord Byron's *Childe Harold's Pilgrimage* suggests, "There is a pleasure in the pathless woods," and America's vast forestland, viewed as a New World Eden with Hawkeye as the guide to its mysteries, held great fascination for them. D. H. Lawrence would describe the world Cooper had created through artistic terms as "some of the loveliest, most glamorous pictures in all literature."

That American frontiersman, even though his demise follows the conquest of the West, lends some of his qualities to the new pioneers of the twentieth century, and he had borrowed some of his characteristics from the past. "The Thrilling Detective Website" notes in particular that "Cooper's *Leatherstocking Tales* form a major link between the chivalric tradition of the Arthurian legends as a woodsy sort of King Arthur trying to keep a heavily forested Camelot from the extinction he knows is coming, and the myth of the American frontiersman/private eye as knight (cf: Marlowe, Chandler, Archer, etc., etc., etc.)." By adjusting the geography and replacing the vast, dangerous forests with "the new urban wilderness of the mean streets," one can make the leap from Hawkeye, commander of the woods, to Hawkeye, private eye, a man whose skills for survival in a violent world are much the same: a mastery of his weaponry, an ability to track people through a forest of clues, and a willingness to put personal safety on the line to save victims in danger.

Hawkeye has also permeated pop culture in a number of notable ways. He was featured in at least seven films, television shows, or series, including the popular Day-Lewis movie. Hawkeye has also brought his skill as a hunter and warrior to the Classics Illustrated and Marvel comic book versions of *The Last of the Mohicans*, where an adventure-seeking audience who might have missed him in Cooper's books could be added to his list of fans. And even a comic book remix has been brought further up to speed with the Natty Bumppo–inspired Hawkeye in the Avengers series "Tales of Suspense #57" as a "reluctant villain" battling Iron Man. Though he has certainly evolved in appearance from Cooper's frontiersman, he bears the name and his bow and arrows harken back to the forest more than a cityscape. Hawkeye's immediate popularity in this genre soon moved Stan Lee and artist Don Heck to make him a permanent member of the Avenger team. Meanwhile, in the 1968 book by Richard Hooker, *MASH: A Novel about Three Army Doctors*, and film and TV series it inspired, the main character Hawkeye Pierce reveals that he got his nickname from Cooper's Hawkeye in *The Last of the Mohicans*—the only book his father had ever read. And finally, without stretching our imaginations too far, we can see strong traces of Hawkeye as Luke Skywalker trading in the long rifle for a lightsaber.

Cooper's idealized pioneer Hawkeye remains a beloved archetype who reminds us of the doctrine of nature and the value of a self-sustained individual. His adventures may ultimately be a dirge for a lost way of life, but they also bring us closer to understanding the need to restore man's harmony with nature as a spiritual salve for the troubled soul. We see his close communication with the so-called noble savage populating the American continent of old as a harkening back to a more Edenic oneness with our primordial past. That, and Hawkeye is just one supermacho dude in buckskin whose romping through the vast forests brings back to life a distant memory that had been left in a well-worn book in need of dusting off.

Bibliography

The Pioneers, or The Sources of the Susquehanna (1823)
The Last of the Mohicans: A Narrative of 1757 (1826)
The Prairie: A Tale (1827)
The Pathfinder, or The Inland Sea (1840)
The Deerslayer, or The First War Path (1841)

Works Cited

Lawrence, D. H. *Studies in Classic American Literature.* New York: Thomas Seltzer, 1923.
Mann, Michael, dir. *The Last of the Mohicans.* Twentieth Century Fox, 1992.
"Natty 'Hawkeye' Bumppo." The Thrilling Detective. Accessed October 2, 2018. http://www.thrillingdetective.com/bumppo.html.

—GS

C

CACCIATO

First Appearance: "Going After Cacciato" in *Ploughshares*
Date of First Appearance: Spring 1976
Author: Tim O'Brien (1946–)

Cacciato smiled. . . . The smile was immaculate. A baby's smile, beguiling and meaningless. "Hi," he said.

Naming the most memorable warrior/soldier in literature is a daunting task. One might go old school and cite Achilles, the great Greek swordsman who takes out Hector in Homer's *Iliad* and in a rage drags his corpse around the walls of Troy, disrespecting his enemy's corpse. Or one might cite Beowulf, the hero of the Geats who slaughters Grendel, that monster's mother, *and* a dragon before his own demise. Perhaps even King Arthur or Gawain of Round Table fame.

Those legendary figures symbolize the glory of war, though, and modern readers are likelier to look to more complex psychological depictions of battle. Some might nominate Henry Fleming, the young private of Stephen Crane's *The Red Badge of Courage* (1895), who heals his shame for deserting a Civil War battle by returning to his Union regiment to serve as an unarmed flag bearer. Or they might vote for Frederic Henry, the American fighting for Italy in the Great War in Ernest Hemingway's *A Farewell to Arms* (1929), who escapes a humiliating retreat to run away to Switzerland with his pregnant lover. Given how deeply the Vietnam War still haunts the American psyche fifty years on, readers might look for a veteran of that doomed conflict. There's no shortage of candidates: the title character of David Rabe's *The Basic Training of Pavlo Hummel* (1971), the lone-wolf Marine Ray Hicks in Robert Stone's *Dog Soldiers* (1974), perhaps even the original Rambo in David Morrell's *First Blood* (1972) before Sylvester Stallone movies turned him into a cartoon. An even more unconventional choice might be the entire fictional Alpha Company that Tim O'Brien depicts in his seminal short-story cycle *The Things They Carried* (1990).

Most soldiers in Vietnam fiction are depicted as everymen, neither supermen nor cowards but men weighing the moral costs of serving in an unjust war. Because these soldiers are representative figures, our vote ultimately goes to the more enigmatic title character of O'Brien's 1978 National Book Award–winning novel *Going After Cacciato*. With several chapters first published as short stories—including the opening section, which appeared in *Ploughshares* in 1976—*Cacciato* is frequently hailed as the greatest Vietnam War novel for its rendering of the surreal experience of coping with combat. That surrealism begins and ends with the fact that O'Brien's rather opaque private—whose name in Italian means "hunted"—is at once real and a figment of the imagination.

In 1968 (a year before O'Brien's own army service in the war) Private Cacciato announces to fellow members of Third Squad, First Platoon, Alpha Company, First Battalion of the Forty-Sixth Infantry that he's deserting to walk 8,600 miles to Paris. After he disappears, Third Squad tracks him to the Laos border. As the men fire flares preparing to rush the hill where Cacciato camps, the main protagonist, Paul Berlin, suffers a breakdown, discharging his M-16 wildly and fouling his pants before blacking out. Never learning whether his quarry was captured or killed, Paul later imagines chasing the deserter all the way to the *ville lumière*, he and his squad engaged in ever-more fantastic adventures as they cross from Laos to India, Afghanistan, Iran, and finally into Europe. As Berlin's way of overcoming the trauma of war, the fantasy is a form of healing that allows him to deal with his overwhelming fear. In the words of the Siegfried Sassoon quote that serves as the novel's epigraph, "Soldiers are dreamers."

Going After Cacciato alternates between three distinct narrative strands. The dream sequence, which unfolds over twenty of the forty-six chapters, projects Third Squad forward in time from October 1968 to April 1969. The story of the men's pursuit is imagined on a single night (November 20, 1968) during which Berlin stands guard duty over the South China Sea in the Quang Ngai Province. On this night, Paul ruminates on the nature of war and the need for storytelling in ten chapters titled "The Observation Post." The third series recounts Berlin's time in country since his arrival the previous June; its sixteen chapters depict the casualties of Third Squad, such as Billy Boy Watkins, who dies of fright stepping on a land mine, and Bernie Lynn, killed dragging the body of Frenchie Tucker from the elaborate tunnel system where the Vietcong hide. The losses are reported with journalistic clarity, itemizing with a grisly precision wounds, triage, and corpses, facts without a larger sense of meaning. By contrast, the "road to Paris" vignettes are amalgams of Hollywood movies, western folktales, and travel-guide vistas. In Laos, the team picks up a Vietnamese girl, Sarkin Aung Wen, with whom Berlin later plans to settle into a Paris apartment, deciding not to return to the war. In another moment, the soldiers fall into a tunnel, *Alice in Wonderland*–like, and are confronted by an old man, Li Van Hgoc, who has been sentenced to guarding the subterranean passageways for deserting the North Vietnamese army. When passing through Tehran, they witness an Iranian soldier distracted by a buzzing fly try to maintain his dignity as he's about to be beheaded for going AWOL. Along their journey, at least three Third Squad men abandon the mission. Clearly, Berlin uses his fantasy to grapple with the morality of desertion.

Cacciato makes cameo appearances in the dream sequence. One soldier, Stink Harris, nearly captures him but is wounded. In Mandalay the squad spots him dressed as a priest; when Berlin tries to arrest him, Cacciato's fellow clerics run interference. They discover the deserter in the newspaper, boarding a train to Kabul, or spy him in an outdoor market in Paris. When Paul follows him to an old hotel, Cacciato sits in bed peeling carrots, friendly and entirely fearless. Throughout the novel, he is described as dumb as "a month-old oyster fart," a near simpleton and a baby, but really he represents a clean conscience: He feels no shame for quitting the war, and, unlike the other men, he's not been corrupted by it. (In the factual chapters, he's the one man in the squad who doesn't support fragging their lieutenant, Sidney Martin, who orders them into suicide missions in the tunnels.) Cacciato is nearly Christlike in his equanimity. The question is whether Berlin is his Judas.

In the novel's final chapter, Paul imagines kicking open the hotel door to arrest Cacciato, his fear causing him to fire his M-16 again out of control. His mind immediately snaps back to the real moment he regained consciousness on the hill where the men stormed the deserter's camp. O'Brien implies that in his blackout Berlin may have shot Cacciato dead, though the possibility is only hinted at. Perhaps to protect Paul, or maybe to perpetuate a communal lie, the squad assures him that Cacciato got away. The novel ends with Berlin asking his lieutenant if it's likely the escapee reached Paris. "Miserable odds," the officer answers, but "maybe so."

Cacciato may be a deserter, but he represents what all soldiers want: to believe they have the choice to leave war—and to leave behind the trauma of having fought it too.

Bibliography

Going After Cacciato (1978)

—KC

HOLDEN CAULFIELD

First Appearance: "I'm Crazy" in *Collier's*
Date of First Appearance: December 22, 1945
Author: J. D. Salinger (1919–2010)

I don't give a damn, except that I get bored sometimes when people tell me to act my age. Sometimes I act a lot older than I am—I really do—but people never notice it. People never notice anything.

Is there a kid in literature who's a bigger pain in the ass than Holden Caulfield?

Not if you're among the dozens of school boards, libraries, and worrywart parents who since 1951 have tried to ban J. D. Salinger's *The Catcher in the Rye*. Adults have censored Holden for glamorizing apathy, for flunking out of school, and even for saying "goddamn" 251 times. He's been both accused of being a Communist plot to undermine American optimism and implicated in the murder of a Beatle. Worst of all, he's to blame for countless derivative young adult novels that celebrate the teenager as the standard bearer of idealism and dismiss anyone over thirty as a hypocritical sellout.

For millions of readers who identify with his disaffection, though, Holden is our greatest literary reminder to question adulthood. Before him, fictional youth grew up because it was expected of them. (Huck Finn is a notable exception.) The very name of the genre dedicated to adolescents, the bildungsroman, or the "novel of development," demanded they mature. There were certainly casualties along the way—suicides like the hero of Willa Cather's "Paul's Case" (1912) or Quentin Compson in *The Sound and the Fury* (1929)—but by and large youth accepted that the bittersweet reward for losing their innocence was adulthood's hard-won wisdom. In his opening salvo (seemingly addressed to a psychologist treating him after a mental breakdown), Holden dismisses this sentimental piety as "that *David Copperfield* kind of crap." To him, growing up makes you a "phony," an insult he hurls roughly three dozen times.

The Catcher in the Rye follows the sixteen-year-old over a New York City weekend during which he sports a red hunting cap that signals his nonconformity. Doffing it exposes a circle of prematurely gray hair, an ironic symbol of the stress of adolescence. Searching for authentic, meaningful experience, Holden mostly discovers humiliation. Twice he's beaten up, first by a classmate at the third elite prep school he's failed out of who doesn't understand he's still mourning the death of his brother Allie years earlier—a major source of Holden's depression—then by a pimp after he decides not to lose his virginity to a prostitute. A complacent date named Sally Hayes rejects his offer to run away to live in the woods; taxicab drivers think he's a smart aleck for asking where the ducks in Central Park go during winter. Eventually, Holden sneaks home to visit the one person whose opinion he values, his ten-year-old sister, Phoebe, who grills him about why he can't care about anything. Borrowing from a Robert Burns poem, Holden confesses his only ambition is to safeguard children from falling from cliff edges hidden by tall fields where they play, an image of that fabled fall from innocence into experience: He wants to be the catcher in the rye.

Salinger was barely twenty-two when he created Holden for a 1941 story called "Slight Rebellion off Madison." World War II, where the author saw combat on D-day and at the Battle of the Bulge, delayed its publication for five years. By the time the *New Yorker* printed it, a version of Holden and Phoebe's conversation called "I'm Crazy" had already appeared in *Collier's*. The accompanying illustration suggests how far cultural conceptions of the awkward age had to evolve before Holden could emerge as the patron saint of aggrieved adolescence; far from a surly teenager, he looks like a cherubic schoolboy. In these formative stories Holden likewise seems less idealistic than churlishly entitled. Only when Salinger shifted from third to first person did teenage discontentment attain gravitas. Neither precocious nor precious, Holden speaks in a voice that's wounded, indignant, defensive, and fumblingly inarticulate. If Herman Melville once wrote that great apostates declare, "NO! in Thunder," Holden made it de rigueur for rebels without a cause to proclaim, "I don't know."

Holden's conversation with Phoebe sits at the idealistic heart of *Catcher*. A later exchange with the only adult the boy respects offers its most practical wisdom. Surprised when his former pupil arrives uninvited at his doorstep, Mr. Antolini warns the teenager that he will destroy himself without making a dent in the system he detests. With compassion and patience, he counsels Holden to fight winnable battles with humility. Mr. Antolini's presence reminds us that as much as for adolescents, *The Catcher in the Rye* is written for adults charged with protecting them. The book urges elders to take youth's alienation seriously and assure them they can cope.

Unfortunately, Holden decides his mentor has a sexual interest in him and runs away without pondering the advice. Salinger never clarifies whether Mr. Antolini is a predator; most readers believe Holden misinterprets his concern. The twist is necessary for the theme, for if Salinger resolved Holden's conflict, teenage angst could be minimized as that proverbial "passing phase" young people supposedly grow out of. Instead it falls to Phoebe to save her brother. When Holden announces his plan to run away to California, Phoebe insists she will join him, not wanting to lose another brother. Holden realizes that far from protecting her innocence he's pushing her over the emotional edge, causing her grief and worry, and he agrees to seek help. The novel then flashes forward a year, ending with Holden in treatment, a hint of maturity behind his sarcasm as he addresses "you," the psychologist treating his breakdown, but really all adults. If we want young people to grow up, *Catcher* implies, it's up to elders to create a world worth inheriting.

Holden became a literary icon because he speaks both to and for a demographic whose emotional well-being gauges the state of society. Authorities who tried to suppress him only burnished his authority, making his "slight rebellion" seem more dangerous, and therefore more desirable, to younger readers. More recently, critics have enumerated the flaws that make Holden an imperfect spokesman for teens: He's too privileged, too contemptuous of popular culture, too white even to represent the experience of all adolescents. His intoxicating voice can also be dangerous. When Mark David Chapman murdered former Beatle John Lennon on December 8, 1980, holding a copy of the novel inscribed "From Holden Caulfield / To Holden Caulfield / This is my statement," *Catcher* fans had to reckon with the solipsistic superiority Holden can confer upon the disaffected. In his delusion, Chapman convinced himself that Lennon was a phony whose music misled a generation, and only by killing the rock star could he save future youth from falling for idols. Resisting Holden just a little—reading him as Mr. Antolini does—is necessary so we don't assume our alienation makes us better than the placidly content Sally Hayeses surrounding us.

Despite that caveat, Holden remains the teenager adults want to believe embodies the coming-of-age process: Disillusioned but not nihilistic, a truth seeker instead of complacent settler, annoying but not irredeemable, he protests society's failings so that the future might promise meaningful values worth growing up for.

Bibliography

"I'm Crazy" (*Collier's*, 1945)
"Slight Rebellion off Madison" (*New Yorker*, 1946)
The Catcher in the Rye (1951)

—KC

CELIE

First Appearance: *The Color Purple*
Date of First Appearance: 1982
Author: Alice Walker (1944–)

Everything want to be loved. Us sing and dance and holler, just trying to be loved.

Zora Neale Hurston once wrote that black women are "de mule uh de world" below white men and women and on a rung further still below black men. Put succinctly, they are the bottom of the heap when it comes to receiving power, riches, respect, or much of anything valuable the world might have to offer or to refuse. Alice Walker's Celie in *The Color Purple* certainly bears this out in dramatic and heart-wrenching fashion. Instead of the usual slave narrative, Walker tells the story of subtler but also more insidious abuse within the most intimate unit of the black family. Beaten, raped, and impregnated twice by her father, whom she later learns is her stepfather (not that this revelation makes it much less heinous), robbed of her sister and her two children, and bereft of any other source of kindness, Celie turns to God in an interesting and unusual way. Rather than simply praying to a disembodied male entity in the sky, the barely literate Celie chooses to write him letters. The power of her simple epistles and the quiet but ultimately defiant spirit rising up from those pages also lifts her to the rank of a remarkable character in spite of the lowly position from which she sends her cry to be acknowledged and loved.

Celie's story begins at fourteen with her first letter, an idea that comes from a threat her stepfather poses as the only refuge available to a poor black girl. He warns her, "You better not never tell nobody but God." With no escape from him in a home and a world that also offer no solace, God becomes the silent entity to whom Celie addresses her simple but poignant correspondence. But the post office route only goes one way, and no reciprocal dispatches float back to her from a supreme male on high. Later, when with Celie's help her sister Nettie escapes to Africa, letters are again Celie's only means of communication, but that address also seems to be at the silent end of a one-way postal line. Her isolation and abandonment from anything but misery is complete.

The Color Purple is Celie's story, and Walker invests the book with two narrative tracks that impact who she is and how she relates to her world. The early words of anguish emphasize Celie's male relationships, which have always been violent. She acts to protect Nettie from being her father's next sexual abuse victim and then from the man to whom he marries off Celie. Though this man's first name is Albert, Walker allows Celie a modicum of dominion with her reference to him only as Mr. _____. He holds the power to beat and abuse her, but she strips him of a name and a place in her interior world, the only space Celie can own. When she discovers he kept hidden from her letters Nettie had been sending from Africa, Celie finally finds her voice and the strength to rebel. She defiantly claims, "I'm poor, I'm black, I may be ugly and can't cook, a voice say to everything listening. But I'm here." And the choir says, "Amen, Sister!" She isn't just speaking to Mr.

_____. She's telling the universe that she has arrived as a force who will no longer be silent, and not just with Mr._____, but with all the Misters who cross her path.

The second and more valuable narrative track is Celie's relationship with women. For most of her life Nettie has been the only person Celie loves or from whom she has received love. That connection provides her innate power to safeguard her sister, but in order to protect herself Celie must rely on other women who serve as spirit guides, most importantly Shug Avery who is Mr. _____'s mistress. While nursing Shug back to health after Mr. _____ brings her home in terrible condition, Celie eventually develops a friendship with Shug and then finds sexual fulfillment with her. Of even more value, she receives love and her first taste of joie de vivre. Shug demonstrates an organic spirituality and belief that God isn't just a heavenly, more positive iteration of the abusive males she has experienced, but one who wants humans to appreciate joy and beauty in the world. She tells Celie, "It pisses God off if you walk by the color purple in a field somewhere and don't notice it," and she preaches that a powerful God-force comes from within, not from some building where people pray.

Appropriately, one of Celie's first acts after declaring selfhood is to reconnect with Nettie and to move out of Mr. _____'s house and begin earning her own living designing and sewing men's pants for women. The symbolism of this act is unmistakable and important to Walker because it epitomizes a supremacy wrenched out of the marginalization and invisibility women like Celie have previously known. She hails Celie's liberation and appropriation of the color purple with its emblematic qualities of power, royalty, strength, dignity, and resplendent nature, and Walker associates those characteristics with a representative feminism she calls African American womanism. The strength Celie derives from the women around her reflects Walker's own sisterhood with her literary godmother Zora Neale Hurston, whose seminal work *Their Eyes Were Watching God* several decades earlier had provided a guidepost for female autonomy and sexuality. Walker rescued the novel and its author from relative obscurity, even honoring Hurston's unmarked grave with a headstone, and she was rewarded in return with literary inspiration.

The novel's blatant messages are not without strong controversy. On the one hand, Celie does not mince words, so graphic sexual language, violent abuse, and a lesbian relationship simply become part of the fabric of her life she discloses to God. This starkness kept the book out of some classrooms, but the strongest resistance came from black men who felt Walker played into the white stereotypes of black men as sexually violent and dangerous. Filmmaker Spike Lee was among the prominent voices to criticize what he felt was unfair internal racism. And though the work is centered almost exclusively in the black community, Walker depicts whites mostly as stereotyped racists as well. On the opposite end of the spectrum, black women and feminists of all races sang the novel's praises for its liberation of black females.

Despite the serious criticism from some camps, *The Color Purple*'s publication in 1982 won Alice Walker immediate praise, and she became the first African American woman to be awarded both the Pulitzer Prize and the National Book Award in 1983. Famed director Steven Spielberg made her novel into a successful 1985 movie, which received eleven Academy Award nominations, though no wins. Oprah Winfrey, who played Sophia in the film, also coproduced with Quincy Jones a Broadway musical version running from 2005 to 2008 with eleven Tony nominations, and another award-winning revival ran from 2015 to 2016. With stars like Whoopi Goldberg and later Jennifer Hudson playing the lead role, Oprah as Sophia, and Danny Glover as Mr. _____, the novel's success put Alice Walker, *The Color Purple*, and Miss Celie on the map for all time.

Bibliography

The Color Purple (1982)

Work Cited

Hurston, Zora Neale. *Their Eyes Were Watching God*. Philadelphia: J. B. Lippincott, 1937.

—GS

CHARLOTTE

First Appearance: *Charlotte's Web*
Date of First Appearance: 1952
Author: E. B. White (1899–1985)

Never hurry and never worry!

Charlotte's Web begins with a child's simple but probing question: "Where's Papa going with that axe?" Even city-dwelling carnivores know the answer and perhaps cringe at their complicity while hiding a stack of breakfast bacon behind the morning's paper. The circle of life for most farm animals ends at someone's table unless, like the White House's traditional pardoning of the Thanksgiving turkey, something intercedes to stop the carnage. For a little runt of a pet pig named Wilbur, his salvation comes from a surprising source, an *Araneus cavaticus*, better known as a simple barn spider named Charlotte A. Cavitica, Charlotte for short. Even arachnophobes can't help finding charm in this anthropomorphized creature who shows her "humanity" by talking, spelling, and cleverly outmanipulating human behavior to save a good-natured pig even though she dies in the end, as we all do—but alone and at the fairgrounds, which really isn't fair for our hero Charlotte, the little spider that could, and did, teach us the value of true self-sacrificing friendship.

The story behind E. B. White's *Charlotte's Web* is almost as charming as the famous children's tale itself. Actually, it's two anecdotes: one about a pig and the other about a spider. In "Death of a Pig," a piece White had written for his day job at the *New Yorker*, he confesses that a porcine resident of his farm in Maine was destined for slaughter when it abruptly became ill and died short of its scheduled murder. White laments the loss of the animal he tried to nurse back to health that "had evidently become precious" to him even though his original intent was to be its executioner. He had also taken note of an intricately crafted web hanging in the barn the pig had occupied and the spider's absence after depositing a woven silken pouch there. White's innate curiosity persuaded him to carry the egg sack to his New York apartment where the next generation of arachnids hatched and made themselves *arachnids non gratae* with the housekeeper, forcing White to remove the offspring to their geography of origin. With the barnyard backdrop back in place, he put the pig and the spider events together, and the rest is history.

Charlotte as the central character of White's tale is fascinating for several reasons. First among them is White's choice to elevate almost to the status of sainthood a creepy crawler prone to send chills down the spines of many and propel them scrambling in the opposite direction. Charlotte is the furthest removed from kinship with the barnyard's other talking menagerie, the lowest on a hierarchy of multilegged creatures there, and she makes no bones about her nature. She does what spiders do: She eats other living beings, which sounds a bit close to one of the stronger underlying themes about meat-eating guilt. She understands the cycle of life and her role as one who devours flesh and blood (if insects can be said to have flesh), but Charlotte convincingly argues that she is a merciful killer assisting in the management of the food chain even though she also interrupts it to save another species' flesh and blood for no apparent reason other than that it is a good thing to do for cross-species friendship.

Charlotte is also interesting because though she is the furthest removed from kinship with the other talking menagerie and the lowest on the hierarchy of non-humans there, she serves as the voice of reason from the spiderweb above, a sort of Mother Teresa to the barnyard crew. Her first words in the book are "Do you want a friend, Wilbur?" when she sees the lonely pig suffering, and it is Charlotte who concocts the plan to save Wilbur when she hears of his imminent demise. She keeps the other animals calm, compels them to work for the good of the cause, and in general saves the day and the pig with her plan to elevate him with five words—"SOME PIG" . . . "TERRIFIC" . . . "RADIANT" . . . "HUMBLE"—cleverly timed and woven into her web to attract human attention and sympathy. And while delaying Wilbur's mortality presumably to its natural end, she also fully embraces her own, but not before contributing to life's ongoing process by laying 514 eggs, three of which will continue as Wilbur's future confidants.

Charlotte may be most fascinating for the actions her tale has caused humans to take, not just in the story, but for real people whose responses have at times been peculiarly reactive. In 2003 a school in England banned *Charlotte's Web* because pork discussion might be offensive to Muslims even though technically Charlotte was saving the pork from others eating it, and even when the Muslim community said not to worry, no offense taken. A group of Kansas parents in 2006 felt highlighting talking beings other than humans was sacrilegious and that death was no subject matter for children. (Have they seen what happened to Bambi's mother?) The children's book world is still waiting for a ban because Wilbur likes to play in the barnyard poo pile!

White took earlier criticism for his spider-glorifying tale and its potential affront to children's sensibilities with a tongue-in-cheek response when he revealed his intention to follow Charlotte's popularity with "a new book about a boa constrictor and a litter of hyenas. The boa constrictor swallows the babies one by one, and the mother hyena dies laughing." Kind of makes you want to read more of White's work, doesn't it? What he took seriously, however, was the necessity for Charlotte to die, even though he could not read that passage without emotion, evidenced by his seventeen tries at a taped reading before getting through it without his voice faltering with emotion.

White's love of life and the special soft spot for the vulnerable "sub-human" creatures that surrounded him on his beloved farm retreat elevated his imagination not just with Charlotte and Wilbur's case, but in two other popular children's tales he wrote—*Stuart Little*, about a mouse-like boy born to a human family, and *The Trumpet of the Swan*, about a bird without a voice that learns to communicate through a musical instrument. Whatever elements make talking animals interesting, sacrilege or not, White tapped into the phenomenon as ancient as Aesop's fables and a staple of children's tales, making his own *Charlotte's Web* one of the most successful of them all. Like virtually all other literature of lasting merit, the book has sold millions of copies, has been translated into many languages, and has won the hearts of generations of children, even with the sad demise of its charming Charlotte.

What White has successfully done in *Charlotte's Web* is to make a silk purse out of a sow's ear with Wilbur, and to use a lowly spider named Charlotte to teach the valuable qualities humanity would be better for demonstrating to each other. White had perhaps anticipated Charlotte with a portion of a poem written earlier to his wife—a fitting end to this piece.

> Thus I, gone forth, as spiders do,
> In spider's web a truth discerning,
> Attach one silken strand to you
> For my returning.

Bibliography

Charlotte's Web (1952)

Work Cited

White, E. B. "The Death of a Pig." *100 Years of Atlantic Stories*, January 1948.

—GS

BENJY COMPSON

First Appearance: *The Sound and the Fury*
Date of First Appearance: 1929
Author: William Faulkner (1897–1962)

Caddy held me and I could hear us all, and the darkness, and something I could smell. And then I could see the windows, where the trees were buzzing. Then the dark began to go in smooth, bright shapes, like it always does, even when Caddy says that I have been asleep.

In 1928 William Faulkner was thirty, unemployed, and living with his parents. The publisher of his first two novels had just rejected his third. With nothing to lose, he started a fourth book, indifferent to what editors or readers might think because he never expected it to be published. The result was an uncompromisingly experimental portrait of a fallen southern family, *The Sound and the Fury*, which revolutionized point of view and the way time unfolds in fiction. The narrator of its opening section, a thirty-three-year-old man-child named Benjy Compson, also changed how literature depicts the cognitively disabled. Neither a monster nor a buffoonish imbecile, Benjy is a figure of extreme innocence, personifying the terror of not knowing how to make sense of the modern world. Unable to tell past from present or even speak out loud, he is isolated without any means of coping. He may just be Western literature's most vulnerable character ever.

Faulkner's initial inspiration for Benjy was Edwin Chandler, a neighbor in Oxford, Mississippi, often picked on because of his Down's syndrome. Faulkner wasn't interested in medical accuracy or in advocating for improved treatment of the mentally challenged, though. He was intrigued by the artistic possibilities of conveying a radically unconventional perspective. The novel opens with Benjy watching men hit a ball and move a flag; only when they yell "caddie"—the nickname of his long-lost sister, Candace, exiled from the Compson family seventeen years earlier for getting pregnant before marriage—do readers realize he doesn't know the men are playing golf. Faulkner renders the simplest of experiences harrowingly unfamiliar, forcing us to share Benjy's bewilderment as he witnesses actions that seem random because he cannot grasp their purpose.

Another key element of Benjy's characterization is his sense of time—or his lack of it. Because he can't comprehend the concept of chronology, he experiences memories in the present moment, dooming him to suffer repeatedly the abandonment he felt when Caddy fled their family. Faulkner provides a few tools to help readers distinguish different scenes from the fall from innocence that shatters the Compsons, most notably italicized passages that signal shifting time frames. The author even toyed with the possibility of using different-colored ink to mark various moments of family history, but printing costs were prohibitive. (Not until 2012 would a publisher attempt the idea; the resulting edition cost $345.) It's not even clear how many time frames we pass through. Faulkner claimed eight periods, but subsequent critics have discerned as many as sixteen. Ultimately, the inability to determine an exact number demonstrates the effectiveness of *The Sound and the Fury*'s experiment with nonlinear narration: As a measure of experience, the novel insists, time confuses more than it clarifies.

Despite Faulkner's stylistic pyrotechnics, the abuse Benjy has suffered throughout his life is painfully clear. His mother originally named him Maury to honor her brother—a shifty character who doesn't deserve the tribute—but changed it when she realized her youngest child was abnormal. More horrifically, the Compsons castrated Benjy at some point after Caddy's departure after he mistook a passing schoolgirl for his sister and his reaching out for her was interpreted as an attempted rape. His bitter caretaker/brother Jason calls him "the Great American Gelding." Other characters dismiss him as "baby," a "damned looney," and even "a big foolish dog." Only the Compsons' African American housekeeper, Dilsey Gibson, shows him compassion, though she cannot protect him from Jason's bullying. Taking him to Sunday services, Dilsey can only believe Benjy will be rewarded for his suffering in the afterlife.

In creating Benjy, Faulkner basically fused two parallel literary traditions. The first was the isolato, a figure of extreme alienation who protests the world's loss of humanitarian values—in this case, the loss of Caddy's love and protection. The related tradition is known as the "holy fool," or the term Faulkner used when describing Benjy, the "idiot." These are characters like Shakespeare's jesters and clowns, Melville's Pip in *Moby-Dick*, or Dostoevsky's Prince Myshkin in *The Idiot* who oppose the tyranny of reason by embodying the "madness" of seeing the world in an idiosyncratic way. Holy fools are known for garrulity and digression, their "babbling" breaking norms of syntax to speak intuitive wisdoms. As a mute, though, Benjy can only emit moans and bellows, dramatizing the powerlessness of language to connect people. As an epigraph to *The Sound and the Fury*, Faulkner borrowed a passage from Shakespeare's *Macbeth* to suggest how Benjy's inability to communicate symbolizes the ultimate meaninglessness of existence: "Life's but a walking shadow . . . a tale / Told by an idiot, full of sound and fury, / Signifying nothing." The novel underscores this bleak vision by drawing ironic parallels between Benjy and Christ. Turning thirty-three on Holy Saturday, 1928, the emasculated lamb has no power to redeem his family, the South, or the modern world.

As another mark of innovation, *The Sound and the Fury* follows Benjy's section with his two brothers telling their versions of Caddy's shunning: First, Benjy's older brother Quentin, who commits suicide in 1910 out of guilt over his incestuous desire to protect her purity, and then Jason, who embezzles the child support the unfairly ostracized mother has for years sent her family to raise her illegitimate daughter. Ultimately, though, it's Benjy who remains the novel's most touching voice. Because the pathos of his utter helplessness is such a product of Faulkner's technique, adaptations have never come close to dramatizing his disorientation as movingly as the novel does. In Martin Ritt's 1958 movie version, Jack Warden portrays Benjy as a lurking menace, while James Franco's depiction in his 2014 self-directed film relies on twitches and tics, his showy mannerisms made all the more unwatchable thanks to a prosthetic set of crooked teeth. Only the New York theatrical company Elevator Repair Service has found a convincing way to represent Benjy in the flesh in its 2008 and 2015 productions, and only then through a mixture of pantomime, wall projections, and Faulkner's own words read aloud. Benjy has enjoyed a far more successful legacy in literature. Daniel Keyes's *Flowers for Algernon* (1966) and Mark Haddon's *The Curious Incident of the Dog in the Night-Time* (2003) are just two well-known novels inspired by Faulkner's experimentation whose developmentally challenged protagonists are depicted humanely while they narrate in stylistically innovative ways.

Later Faulkner writings reveal that life never improves for Benjy. A 1946 appendix to the novel reports that Jason commits him to the state insane asylum to get rid of him; when Benjy returns home in *The Mansion* (1959), he accidentally dies in a fire (just as Edwin Chandler did) that burns down the Compson house. His grim fate is further proof of what Benjy Compson represents: He is twentieth-century humanity, neutered and speechless, at the mercy of forces it can't begin to fathom, much less control.

Bibliography

The Sound and the Fury (1929)
The Mansion (1959)

Works Cited

Faulkner, William. "1699–1945. Appendix. The Compsons." In *The Portable Faulkner*, edited by Malcolm Cowley. New York: Viking Press, 1946.
———. *The Sound and the Fury (April Seventh, 1928)*, play. Elevator Repair Service (2008, 2015).
Haddon, Mark. *The Curious Incident of the Dog in the Night-Time*. New York: Doubleday, 2003.
Keyes, Daniel. *Flowers for Algernon*. New York: Harcourt, Brace & World, 1966.

—KC

DON VITO CORLEONE

First Appearance: *The Godfather*
Date of First Appearance: 1969
Author: Mario Puzo (1920–1999)

I'll make him an offer he can't refuse.

On the day of his daughter's wedding, by custom, supplicants come to ask "Godfather" Don Corleone for favors. Among them is his entertainer godson who wants a big part in a film that a Hollywood producer has refused him. Not to worry, Godfather tells him. "I'll make him an offer he can't refuse." That line, spoken with only slight variation by Marlon Brando in the 1972 film adaptation of Mario Puzo's best-selling novel, was memorable enough to merit a No. 2 ranking on the American Film Institute's Top 100 Movie Quotes of All Time. It was also a line often mimicked after Brando played the Godfather with a distinctively husky whisper that he based on real mob boss Frank Costello.

If ever a fictional character was completely taken over by an actor in a film adaptation, it's Don Corleone. Puzo said that while he originally heard the voice of his mother ("a wonderful, handsome woman, but a fairly ruthless person") whenever the Godfather spoke, after Paramount released *The Godfather* in 1972 all he heard afterward was Brando's raspy voice. But Puzo, who cowrote the screenplays for *The Godfather* and two sequels, said he "always had Brando in mind" when he was writing the novel. So was the Don a composite of Puzo's mother, Brando, and Costello? It would appear so—along with "olive oil king" Don Joe Profaci and Carlo Gambino, a mobster who had children and a home life.

Before Tony Soprano and his family there was Vito Corleone, the first in-depth fictional character to give readers a glimpse into the world of Italian American organized crime in America. *The Godfather* remained on the *New York Times* Best Seller List for sixty-seven weeks, selling 9 million copies the first two years and adding terms like *Cosa Nostra* and *consigliore* to the popular lexicon. Though Puzo said he wrote the characters based solely on research, actual "wise guys" later said they saw themselves and their world in his descriptions. The action takes place in Hell's Kitchen on the west side of Manhattan, where Puzo was born and the fictional Corleone settled after his father was killed by the Sicilian Mafia and his mother sent him to America for his own safety. Vito wisely refused to state his last name (Andolini), so the immigration official named him for the village he came from.

In the novel—which expanded into three films—"Don Corleone was a man to whom everybody came for help, and never were they disappointed." All that was required was that they proclaim their "friendship," and "it was understood, it was mere good manners, to proclaim that you were in his debt and that he had the right to call upon you at any time to redeem your debt by some small service." Though Corleone deals in olive oil and, later, illicit booze and prostitution, his real trade is psychology. He reads people as if he were studying the New York Stock Exchange prices, and he's so highly analytical that his hunches are really calculations. With that Hollywood producer, for example, he asks the *consigliore* who met with him if the man has "real balls" and hears, "You're asking if he is a Sicilian. No." Days later the *consigliore* receives instructions from his Don, and the producer awakens to find the severed head of his prized $600,000 racehorse in his bed. In one shockingly bloody instant he gets the message that despite his wealth, power, and White House and FBI connections, "an obscure importer of olive oil would have him killed"—all because he wouldn't give a movie role to his godson. That scene, along with the shower scene from *Psycho*, became one of the most iconic shocker moments in movie history. Puzo's novel and Francis Ford Coppola's blockbuster trilogy quickly became a part of American pop culture. The 1972 film earned eleven Oscar nominations, winning Best Actor, Best Picture, and Best Adapted Screenplay, while the sequels received eighteen nominations and six Oscars, including Best Picture and Best Adapted Screenplay.

With a national chain (Godfather's Pizza) and a host of independent restaurants named for him, it's safe to say that Don Corleone is at the center of the public's fascination with the novel. In Corleone, Puzo reinforced stereotypes and also shattered them. As a writer for *Smithsonian* magazine observed, the novel and films "Italianized" America and reinforced the mythic status of the immigrant's journey. While the novel depicted mobsters engaged in criminal activities, under-lying everything was the strong sense of family and values. Out of love, Vito's mother had sent him to America, and that same scenario repeats when a gang war escalates and Vito sends one son to Las Vegas partly for his own safety and exiles another to Sicily after the boy kills the men responsible for an attack on Vito that left him hospitalized. Later, when Vito calls a meeting of all the heads of the crime families and says, "The time is past for guns and killings and massacres. We have to be cunning like the business people," it's not hard to appreciate the parallel Puzo implies: All businessmen can be ruthless.

What makes Corleone an ultimately sympathetic character is that apart from "business" he has a strong moral code and doesn't seek underworld glory. He comes to the U.S. as an adolescent, marries a sixteen-year-old Sicilian immigrant two years later, and starts having babies. Dirt poor and working at Abbandando's grocery, he watches a man named Fanucci collect tribute from the grocer and other businesses. One day Corleone does a neighbor a favor by hiding a bundle for him. Later, thinking the man is repaying him, Vito helps him carry a rug intended for Vito's apartment, only to realize they're burglarizing the place. From there it's a short leap to agreeing to be the driver for a silk dress heist, and when Fanucci tries to take his "tribute," to take him out of the picture. After that, the neighborhood respects him, especially when he refuses to take over Fanucci's protection racket. Soon the requests begin. A widow evicted because of a dog needs his help. Store owners come to him for protection from hoodlums. Then the rumors begin—that Vito is connected to the Sicilian Mafia, when it's really just "business."

Corleone never threatens, always preferring irresistible logic and making sure his people are taken care of. Corleone makes himself "protector of the Italian families" in his ever-expanding neighborhood, and when a gang war begins it's because Corleone refuses to get into something as damaging to the community as drugs. He may have whacked two of Al Capone's men to send a message, and he may have orchestrated the final retaliation for a rival family's killing of his son, but he has scruples. Vito believes that a "man who is not a father to his children can never be a real man," and he dies, ironically, while playing with his grandson in the garden after having survived the mob wars. As he falls, it's hard not to think of him earlier holding his friend's hand after the man had requested that his Godfather save him from death.

But there's only so much a Godfather can do.

Bibliography

The Godfather (1969)

Works Cited

Ferranti, Seth. "Meet the Unconventional Mafia Boss Who Inspired 'Godfather' Don Corleone." *Vice*, June 18, 2018. https://www.vice.com/en_us/article/nekm3z/who-is-don-vito-corleone-godfather-based-on-frank-costello.

Gambino, Megan. "What Is the Godfather Effect?" *Smithsonian*, January 31, 2012. https://www.smithsonianmag.com/arts-culture/what-is-the-godfather-effect-83473971/.

Gussow, Mel. "Mario Puzo, Author Who Made 'The Godfather' a World Addiction, Is Dead at 78." *New York Times*, July 3, 1999. https://www.nytimes.com/1999/07/03/movies/mario-puzo-author-who-made-the-godfather-a-world-addiction-is-dead-at-78.html.

—JP

JANIE CRAWFORD

First Appearance: *Their Eyes Were Watching God*
Date of First Appearance: 1937
Author: Zora Neale Hurston (1891–1960)

Ships at a distance have every man's wish on board.

The title for Zora Neale Hurston's *Their Eyes Were Watching God* references a deity who reigns over darker-skinned children shunned as less than equals. They possess the same passions and dreams as seemingly favored light-skinned sons and daughters enjoy, but it would appear that the God to whom they lift their gaze bestows blessings with much less frequency upon them. Expressing her dismissal of racism, Hurston writes in disbelief, "How *can* any deny themselves the pleasure of my company!" and her fictional trailblazer Janie Crawford reflects a similar defiance. Janie casts off expectation by taking the reins of her own fate and rejecting her grandmother's belief that a black woman's lot is to be the most put upon among God's creation. Janie becomes the first central female of color in an American novel, the first of more to follow who take on the aura Toni Morrison later describes for her own fictional "bodacious black Eves." These women follow Janie in taking a bite of the tempting apple the original Eve would proudly have them relish.

Janie begins her journey as a second-generation descendant of slaves and with a servant's future, but she possesses an inner drive to escape the heritage Nanny has come to accept and project on her. She resents the mule-like treatment of expected servitude, if not to whites then to Mr. Logan Killicks (Killjoy), the older man to whom her grandmother marries her off for financial stability. Nanny's primary objective is to safeguard Janie economically, but the forces that compel the teenager are stronger than either the old or the young woman can control. In subtle poetic fashion early in the novel, Hurston establishes Janie's sensuality as a central force she both seeks and exudes. From her dawning awareness begun as a teen while watching the buzzing bees in search of pollen's "golden dust," Janie runs toward self-actualization and the promise of love's equanimity.

Janie's second husband Joe Starks takes her to Hurston's Eatonville, Florida, the first incorporated black community in America, and sets her up in a financially comfortable life as his wife and first lady of the mayor he becomes. Marriage to Logan Killicks dampens Janie's sensuality, and the constraints of Starks's expectation that she be a trophy wife and not a real life's partner spawn an even longer and more painful suffocation of her personal liberation and sexual fulfillment. Janie eventually musters the gumption to repay that robbery by denigrating Joe's manhood as he lies ill and awaits death. This is not an endearing moment for her, but it is the point at which Janie fully frees herself to become her own woman.

Hurston unabashedly pushes the envelope when highlighting Janie's search for sensual satisfaction, and in doing so she presents the quest as a positive driving force rather than a negative one. The novel's opening scene, chronologically the ending point of Janie's journey, provides the highly sexualized description of her return to Eatonville. Janie is now a forty-year-old woman rejecting the traditional head rag to let her hair swing freely down the back of the men's overalls she is wearing, perhaps because she knows they emphasize "firm buttocks like she had grape fruits in her hip pockets," and "pugnacious breasts trying to bore holes in her shirt." Pretty hot stuff for the pre–civil rights 1930s. Janie is returning from having run away with a younger man named Tea Cake, a potential grifter perhaps only after her money, but a man with whom she doesn't mind working all day in the muck fields of the Everglades so they can be together then through the hot evenings—double entendre fully intended.

Hurston is very intentional in making both Janie and the story of her love sizzle, but not without criticism. In Janie's return as the woman with the audacity to claim herself, the men ogle her with lust, the "porch" (community) sits in judgment, and nobody can "talk for looking" as she unabashedly walks past them on her way home. They cannot comprehend her abdication as queen of a well-apportioned throne and the kingdom of Eatonville, her reckless relinquishing of everything stable to satisfy desire. As Janie shares the tale to her best friend Pheoby, she provides details about her time with Tea Cake that the community strains to know: a devastating hurricane, a rabid dog bite, Janie's committing murder for self-protection against her rabies-infested lover, her acquittal and ultimate return home in sexy vagabond clothing. Though she may have become the black sheep criticized by the flock, she returns triumphantly as a clearly love-fulfilled independent woman.

In some ways, Eatonville's "porch" condemnation of Janie Crawford reflects Hurston's own rebuke from fellow Harlem Renaissance writers. Richard Wright, Ralph Ellison, and Alain Locke, among others, felt they were the literary protectorate of their race, and Hurston was a detractor. Wright, in particular, believed that her portrayal of Janie pandered to a white audience's love of the minstrel show designed for laughs at blacks' expense. Beyond the novel's steamy if not seamy sexuality, some felt her strong use of dialect offered denigrating folkism rather than realistic lyricism, and the *New York Times*' support of the novel likely fed the intraracial blame game pointed at Hurston. She, in turn, labeled her black critics the "niggerati" for what she saw as their own form of pandering to white literary modes. Whatever forces were at play, the novel slipped into obscurity until Alice Walker resurrected it in a literary rebirth Hurston could not have foreseen at the time of her death.

To some extent, Janie Crawford's story represents the reverse trajectory of what was to become Hurston's own tragic arc, but the tale is more remarkable because of that reversal. While Janie rose to financial comfort and self-confidence, Zora moved from a strong self-concept early on to her death a few decades later as an unknown domestic servant. Alice Walker's tracing of that decline in her 1975 *Ms. Magazine* piece "In Search of Zora Neale Hurston" brought the then little-known author and her work back to light. She attested to the worth of *Their Eyes Were Watching God* and expressed deep sadness that its author had lain in an unmarked pauper's grave, a neglect she rectified with a headstone tribute, "A Genius of the South." That marker and the more than 1 million copies of the novel sold since 1990 in some measure help make up for the long lack of recognition.

Neither Zora nor Janie could hope for better prophets than the lineup of current stars who have hitched their wagons to the legacy of strong black women, both fictional and real, to follow. Maya Angelou and Oprah Winfrey have added their names to Alice Walker's and Toni Morrison's as women who embrace the adage to "jump at de sun" that Zora gleaned from her mother's advice. While the details of Hurston's decline place a sad punctuation mark on the end of a life that had begun with such promise, her literary afterlife provides a second chance for the spirit of the vibrant author who would certainly be jumping with joy at her legacy now.

Bibliography

Their Eyes Were Watching God (1937)

Works Cited

Hurston, Zora Neale. "How It Feels to Be Colored Me." *The World Tomorrow*, May 1928.
Morrison, Toni. *Paradise*. New York: Penguin, 1999.
Walker, Alice. "In Search of Zora Neale Hurston." *Ms. Magazine*, March 1975.

—GS

D

CLARISSA DALLOWAY

First Appearance: *The Voyage Out*
Date of First Appearance: 1915
Author: Virginia Woolf (1882–1941)

It might be possible that the world itself is without meaning.

"Mrs. Dalloway said she would buy the flowers herself." This is the opening line of Virginia Woolf's novel *Mrs. Dalloway*, and in itself the sentence and the situation are unremarkable. Purchasing flowers isn't a life-altering bucket list activity or one worthy to inspire a book's actions and the thousands of words that will describe them. Yet here it is, in some ways signaling a new literary era of ordinary experience as a fiction-worthy topic. As Woolf struggled intellectually with women's place in literature, she felt that what male history had left obscure and unrecorded deserved its due. Though she might rail against women seen as mere domestic objects, she also valued their role and paid tribute to them in her focus on the female experience. In doing so, Woolf certainly claimed her place as a pillar of modern feminism, and her character Clarissa Dalloway is worthy to be remembered in that oeuvre. By tracing Mrs. Dalloway through the course of only one day, we get enough detail to imply the scope of her life in full, and that's a pretty remarkable feat for a few waking hours on a not-particularly-extraordinary day.

The novel was actually called *The Hours* in an early draft and divided into twelve sections representing blocks of waking activity and thought. The first of these two is easy to follow. Woolf traces her protagonist's movement as she first prepares for and then hosts a party, thus the reason for purchasing flowers at the novel's opening. That simple sentence provides a second detail later understood as well. Mrs. Dalloway is of the privileged class who has household servants to manage the peremptory chores, so her taking on this task, and noting it, has significance in her sense of worth and also has an important function for Woolf's authorial purpose. As Clarissa walks home from the flower shop, she will begin a stream-of-consciousness memory recall triggered by what happens around her. The flowers remind her of an important episode when she was eighteen and kissed a girl and met the man she would marry, the backfiring of a car triggers feelings about the war, hearing an old beau is in town causes her to wonder how her life might have been different if she had married him, and the many random memories that flood through her mind unbeknownst to others as she goes about the surface tasks of the day will elucidate what makes Clarissa tick, what troubles her, and what brings her joy. By the end of this one day's passage symbolically noted by Big Ben's chiming the passing hours, we will know Clarissa much more thoroughly from those memories floating through her internal musings.

Making so much of a twenty-four-hour calendar marking, even if it is one that has a party attended by Britain's prime minister, seems "much ado about nothing," but for Clarissa, "she always had the feeling that it was very, very dangerous to live even one day." On the surface, this seems just hyperbole, but when looked at introspectively as Clarissa does, any day has the possibility to experience or to recall life-altering moments. At her party she will hear of a young ex-soldier Septimus Warren Smith who earlier that afternoon had taken his own life. As readers, we have been following that story when we're not peeking in on Clarissa's thoughts, so we already know this, but what we become privy to is how Clarissa feels about it. Initially angry that such unsavory news intrudes upon her party, she begins to internalize the preciousness of holding on to or letting go of life, and having the ability to make that choice provides a comforting sense of power.

Several times in the course of her day Clarissa repeats a line taken from a song in *Cymbeline*, one of Shakespeare's lesser-known plays. "Fear no more, the heat o' the sun" references the peace found in the grave, the idea that in death one will be finished with life's toils and sorrows. But she also celebrates the joyous moments that are triggered too. The fresh morning air brings back a day in young adulthood when she cried out, "What a lark! What a plunge!" as she opened the doors and the country air came flooding in. She quotes *Othello*'s Desdemona at another point of ecstasy when she feels "if it were now to die 'twere now to be most happy." Clarissa notes the composite nature life exudes every day and on this particular day, which ends triumphantly with the line, "For there she was," reappearing at her party after contemplating whether to continue to be or not only a short time earlier. She represents in a significant way Woolf's own musing about suicide. In *Mrs. Dalloway*, she fashions Clarissa as a positive foil to Smith's suicide, one who chooses not to commit the act, but she also celebrates his brave victory, the self-possession of embracing death on his own terms as Woolf eventually does by drowning herself on March 28, 1941.

Death with a capital "D" is the overarching quandary Clarissa struggles with at the end of her day in June, but she also ponders the essential components that make up living—what it means to be a lover, a wife, a mother, a woman, an unextraordinary human being who leaves no remarkable stamp on the world, but "there she was" nonetheless, and through it all "doing good for the sake of goodness." This existential philosophy simplistically stated provides the core value Clarissa will cling to through this one day and the days that repeat themselves until they don't. In doing so, she is simultaneously stoic and heroic in the quiet way representing the internal world that we inhabit, the one that more fully reveals the self than its external manifestations have done.

Woolf was influenced by James Joyce's earlier novel *Ulysses* with the focus on a single day for its protagonist Leopold Bloom, and in turn *Mrs. Dalloway*'s single day directly inspired Michael Cunningham's 1999 Pulitzer Prize–winning novel *The Hours*, made into a highly acclaimed film by the same name (2002). Cunningham brilliantly creates three additional single days—a day in the life of Virginia Woolf, the one in which she kills herself; a day in the 1950s where a housewife is reading *Mrs. Dalloway*, baking a birthday cake for her husband, and contemplating her own sphere as a wife and mother; and a day in the late twentieth century with another Clarissa who is hosting a party that evening for her friend, who kills himself earlier in the afternoon. Like Woolf's protagonist, this Clarissa's day begins as she "carries her armload of flowers out into Spring Street."

Mrs. Dalloway is on both a grand and a small scale an examination of life and death, and Clarissa becomes a quiet emissary of that contemplation as she realizes there is "something, after all, priceless." She is memorable for the struggle and for the realization that paradoxically, both life and death are gems of inestimable value.

Bibliography

Mrs. Dalloway (1925)

Work Cited

Cunningham, Michael. *The Hours*. New York: Picador, 1998.

—GS

MR. DARCY

First Appearance: *Pride and Prejudice*
Date of First Appearance: 1813
Author: Jane Austen (1775–1817)

It is a truth universally acknowledged, that a single man in possession of a good fortune, must be in want of a wife.

And we might add a quote of our own:

It is a truth universally acknowledged, that a single man in possession of a good fortune, will have no dearth of interested prospects.

Jane Austen set the stage of idealized romance for all time when she wrote *Pride and Prejudice*. And if keeping in step with the book's male protagonist isn't enough, there is the BBC's 1995 television miniseries spin on the wet T-shirt look with Colin Firth as Mr. Darcy sporting a drenched and clinging shirt as he emerges from an impromptu swim in an idyllic country pond. The popularity of this image, and the larger-than-life statue replicating it that now resides in an English lake, speaks to the flip side of the male gaze, the sexual aura surrounding the female worship of Austen's überdesirable male and the fact that interest in hot romance is alive and well. Austen's Mr. Fitzwilliam Darcy unknowingly sets the bar for all would-be husband prospects to follow. The scores of books too numerous to mention, literally hundreds of Facebook groups with names like "I Refuse to Settle for Anything Less Than Mr. Darcy," and every romantic comedy male lead since then—Mark Darcy in the *Bridget Jones's Diary* series (incidentally played by Colin Firth as the modern Mr. Darcy as well as the Austen version), Disney's *Beauty and the Beast*, *Sex and the City*'s Mr. Big, and just about every Hallmark movie and Sandra Bullock film male lead—are all Mr. Darcys in updated clothing.

So, what are the qualities women find irresistible in this preeminent bachelor with an attitude of privilege and superiority? A few points are obvious. Mr. Darcy is tall, handsome, rich, presents a "noble mien," has a beautiful English estate, and is exceedingly eligible. Who wouldn't be interested in those qualifications? But that's too easy for Austen's carefully constructed plots and complicated characters. To throw more pepper into the pot, early in the novel he's also arrogant, an elitist, and a bit of a surly gent. In first seeing Elizabeth "Lizzy" Bennet, he says, "She is tolerable, but not handsome enough to tempt *me*." One makes excuses, however, because "one cannot wonder that so very fine a young man, with family, fortune, everything in his favour, should think highly of himself." Indeed, he does.

Mr. Darcy presents a challenge for the young ladies hoping to land a highly desirable match, and this makes the chase all the more interesting even if women of that period aren't supposed to be the prowler, they are supposed to be the prey. The man who is hard to catch is all the more alluring because of the huntress's quest to bag her big game trophy. But Austen doesn't stop there because, again, such a scenario would be too easy. She adds the brilliant second tier that moves her romance from an interesting tête-à-tête to an epic drama whose pattern is endlessly duplicated in stories women love to love and men love to mock and ridicule (at least if other men are watching them). Elizabeth Bennet isn't interested in Mr. Darcy, and this literary tension is the perfect setup to make the story such a romantic tease.

To Mr. Darcy's credit and added to what we come to adore about him, in spite of an initial failure to see Lizzy as physically attractive, he finds her intellectually engaging and an equal conversational sparring partner. At some point Mr. Darcy realizes he doesn't want an empty-headed trophy wife who looks beautiful at his side but otherwise bores him, and he opens up to the belief that Miss Bennet might be a good match. In the slow burn that is first a mental courtship before a physical one, the readers follow with eager anticipation as Mr. Darcy eventually comes around to valuing the qualities for which women want to be appreciated—their wit, wisdom, and charm rather than a perfect face and figure.

For all his gentleman's training, however, Mr. Darcy fails miserably in applying romantic persuasion, and in taking on the pomposity the "Fitzwilliam" name projects, he lays out his case for marriage to Elizabeth by saying, "Could you expect me to rejoice in the inferiority of your connections?—to congratulate myself on the hope of relations, whose condition in life is so decidedly beneath my own?" It is hard to imagine she didn't jump at the chance to marry him on the spot. Instead, Lizzy jabs back by saying he did not behave in a "gentlemanlike manner," which of course turns the tables. She has suddenly become the conquest that has eluded him and is now all the more valuable because of it.

Mr. Darcy moves from being an insensitive jerk to a romantic dreamboat largely because he wakes up, feels ashamed of his insensitive behavior, and changes. Marriage proposal number two shows marked improvement when he humbly confesses, "The recollection of what I then said, of my conduct, my manners, my expressions during the whole of it, is now, and has been many months, inexpressibly painful to me." As one critic puts it, "He is a *bad boy* who changes for the heroine of the story," or because of her. Either way, we love it that a good woman can rescue a man who needs help discovering the qualities that make him worthy to be saved. This is a win-win—the female lover's ego is pumped up because she alone has the power to inspire the transformation; plus she wins the guy who is still tall, handsome, and rich, but now he's also charming and head over heels in love with only her.

Mr. Darcy as romantic role model is so ingrained in our culture that he has now ventured into the pop and countercultural realms. A pseudopsychological description of something called "The Mr. Darcy Effect" has become a thing. Just Google it and see how many articles come up discussing what a prominent force this is at least in our imaginary longings. And for women wishing to polish up on their desirable wife qualities, the "Marrying Mr. Darcy" board game is available. The Courtship phase helps them with their skills so that in the Proposal stage they can win the most desirable man. Really, we wouldn't make this up! And along those lines of merging into the ridiculous, Mr. Darcy has even found his way into a *Mr. Darcy, Vampyre* novel and as the great protector against a zombie apocalypse in *Pride and Prejudice and Zombies*. A Dark Jane Austen Book Club exists as well and proudly boasts of being avid Austen readers who also enjoy "the occasional bloody mayhem thrown in for good measure." The possibilities are boundless.

First Impressions was an early title for *Pride and Prejudice*, and *Lasting Impressions* could become its subtitle. Mr. Darcy, exemplar of all that is desirable in the perfect man, has taken his place in history as the object of female desire and the swoon-worthy catch at the end of the marriage fishing pole.

Bibliography

Pride and Prejudice (1813)

Work Cited

Church, Clare. "Let's Stop Romanticizing Mr. Darcy When There Are Way Better Options in Literature." *Mary Sue*, April 16, 2018.

—GS

PILATE DEAD

First Appearance: *Song of Solomon*
Date of First Appearance: 1977
Author: Toni Morrison (1931–)

I wish I'd a knowed more people. I would of loved 'em all.

"Sometimes a writer imagines characters who threaten, who are able to take the book over," Toni Morrison once told an interviewer. "To prevent that, the writer has to exercise some kind of control. Pilate in *Song of Solomon* was that kind of character. She was a very large character and loomed very large in the book. So I wouldn't let her say too much."

Yet Pilate Dead (the family surname a result of a clerical mistake by a drunken Yankee in the Union Army) looms larger than life in this Depression-era novel, Morrison's third. Pilate isn't just a survivor—she thrives, despite being motherless since birth, orphaned at age 12, estranged from her only brother and his family for most of her life, and abandoned, shunned, even feared everywhere she's forced to wander because she was born without a navel. The ultimate outsider, Pilate willfully helps others who are marginalized or on the cusp.

When the Swedish Academy awarded Morrison the 1993 Nobel Prize in Literature, they cited three novels, among them *Song of Solomon*, Morrison's 1977 story of a young black man trying to find his place in the world. The main character, Macon Dead III, called "Milkman," has three would-be guides and indoctrinators: his father, Macon II, a well-heeled property owner who wants to teach him how to prosper as he did in a white world; Guitar, an angry young black man who joins a homegrown terrorist group and tries to radicalize Milkman; and Pilate, the aunt his father forbids him from seeing.

"*Solomon* seemed to be very much a male story about the rites of passage, and that required a feeling of lore," Morrison told another interviewer. Pilate is the "carrier" of family lore and cultural myth. When she sings "O Sugarman done fly away" on the sidewalk as a crowd gathers, it has generational weight—though readers later discover that when her dead father came to her and said, "Sing, Sing," he was actually speaking the name of the mother she never knew. Yet, singing, "which she did beautifully, relieved her gloom immediately," and everyone else's, one suspects. It certainly had that effect on Milkman.

In announcing *Song of Solomon* as an Oprah's Book Club selection twenty years after its initial publication, Oprah Winfrey called Pilate "the one person in the family who is open, unfettered, whole: the exiled one," the "unkempt, mystical, bootlegging Aunt Pilate." When readers first meet her, Pilate is wearing a raggedy old knit cap and unlaced men's shoes, using an old quilt for a cloak. At the same time a crowd assembles to watch a black insurance agent fly off the roof of Mercy Hospital, as promised, inside that hospital Pilate's nephew is being born. As birth and death conflate, she sings a song that feels connected to the very beginning of the African and African American experience, a song about flying, about going home—one of the novel's main themes. In a young Milkman's eyes, Pilate was "ugly, dirty, poor, and drunk, the queer aunt whom his sixth-grade schoolmates teased him about." But though she made her living as a bootlegger, Pilate never drank the wine she sold, and as Milkman approaches manhood his views of her change—especially as she becomes his "pilot," directing him to seek a rich family history rather than the gold he and Macon II and Guitar pursue.

Like all mythic characters, Pilate has a mystical beginning. Her mother died during childbirth and the midwife thought the baby dead inside. Then Pilate emerged "struggling out of the womb without help . . . dragging her own cord and afterbirth." As a character, Pilate is colorful without seeming quirky or contrived. She wears a single earring—a brass snuffbox containing a piece of paper on which her father wrote her name—and she keeps her "inheritance" in a green sack that hangs from the ceiling of her narrow one-story house with no gas or electricity, water drawn from a well, and a basement that seemed to be "rising rather than settling." Pilate, whose name was chosen randomly from the Bible—a family tradition—can quote the Bible "chapter and verse," and she does not fear death because she "spoke often to the dead"—especially her father, whom she and brother Macon saw blown to pieces because he refused to leave the land he was cheated out of. Wherever she moves she carries with her the bones she believes are from an old man that her six-year-old brother—Milkman's father—murdered in half fear, half revenge within months of watching their father killed.

During her brief and only period of schooling, Pilate's favorite subject was geography, which she found useful during "twenty-some-odd years" of wandering. Just as she eventually decides to openly embrace and display her smooth belly, she becomes determined that the lack of a navel will no longer define and isolate her. Pilate cuts her hair and asks herself, "When am I happy and when am I sad and what is the difference? What do I need to know to stay alive? What is true in the world?" After giving birth to a daughter, Reba, she moves to Michigan to be near her brother and his family, and eventually Reba will have a daughter and Pilate will be the matriarch of their little family.

Readers are told that palm oil flows through Pilate's veins, and she laughs but never smiles. A natural healer, she also has a darker mystical side, creating a love potion to make her brother attracted to the wife he no longer wants to touch because he thinks she was too "friendly" with her father, the only black doctor in their Michigan town. And when Macon finds out about the baby and wants to get rid of it, Pilate uses a voodoo doll to restrain him. In this way, she was responsible for saving Milkman's life, just as she would do so later in the novel when Milkman is fully grown.

According to her daughter, Reba, Pilate can go months without food, "like a lizard." Pilate "never bothered anybody, was helpful to everybody," but also believed to "have the power to step out of her skin, set a bush afire from fifty yards, and turn a man into a ripe rutabaga." Though a "tall black tree" and gentle by nature, Pilate was capable of fierceness. She could hold her own among "quarreling drunks and fighting women." She uses a knife to threaten a man who was abusing her daughter, and later breaks a bottle over Milkman's head because his leaving for so long caused her granddaughter, who was in love with Milkman, to wither away and die.

In reviewing the novel for the *New York Times*, Reynolds Price called Pilate "bizarre and anarchic." Literature is full of Christ and anti-Christ figures, but Pilate stands alone as a strong female character ironically named for the biblical governor of Judea best known for his weakness: washing his hands of the decision to crucify Christ and leaving it up to the crowd. Morrison's "Pilate-figure" saves someone's life not once, but twice.

Bibliography

Song of Solomon (1977)

Works Cited

McKay, Nellie. "An Interview with Toni Morrison." In *Conversations with Toni Morrison*, edited by Danille Taylor-Guthrie, 138–55. Jackson: University Press of Mississippi, 1994.
Price, Reynolds. "The Adventures of Macon Dead." *New York Times*, September 11, 1977. https://www.kirkusreviews.com/book-reviews/toni-morrison/song-of-solomon/.
"*Song of Solomon* by Toni Morrison." *Kirkus Reviews*, September 1, 1977. https://www.kirkusreviews.com/book-reviews/toni-morrison/song-of-solomon/.
"*Song of Solomon* by Toni Morrison." Oprah.com. October 18, 1996. https://www.oprah.com/oprahsbookclub/about-toni-morrisons-book-song-of-solomon/all.

—JP

REBECCA DE WINTER

First Appearance: *Rebecca*
Date of First Appearance: 1938
Author: Daphne du Maurier (1907–1989)

I am very different from that self who drove to Manderley for the first time, hopeful and eager, handicapped by a rather desperate gaucherie and filled with an intense desire to please. . . . What must I have seemed like after Rebecca?

It's a charismatic character indeed who can dominate a novel without ever appearing in a single scene. Yet that's exactly what the titular heroine of Daphne du Maurier's gothic romance *Rebecca* does. Dead before the story begins, Rebecca haunts this modern-day rewrite of *Jane Eyre* even more than Bertha Mason, the original madwoman in the attic, does Charlotte Brontë's 1847 classic. Like the first Mrs. Rochester, the first Mrs. Maxim de Winter holds the secret to mysteries that a naïve young successor must unravel from behind the locked doors of an eerie British manor. But while Bertha suffers from inherited insanity, Rebecca exemplifies a distinctly modern condition: She was an emasculating bitch. Or so her husband would have us believe.

The idea for *Rebecca* arose from insecurities the prolific du Maurier, barely thirty but already the author of three novels, suffered in the mid-1930s. Her husband, Frederick "Boy" Brown, known as Tommy, had once been engaged to a mercurial woman named Jan Ricardo, and du Maurier found herself haunted by the possibility that he still held a torch for her. The author also grew up feeling neglected by her actor father, Sir Gerald du Maurier. Famous as the first man to play Captain Hook onstage, he preferred showering his attention on young actresses rather than his daughter. Suffering an inferiority complex, du Maurier fixated on the theme of jealousy and produced a narrative that allowed her to vicariously vanquish rivals for both men. In doing so, she single-handedly revitalized the genre of gothic romance that had died out after the one-two punch of *Jane Eye* and Emily Brontë's *Wuthering Heights* in the late 1840s. Setting the novel, like most of her works, in her native Cornwall, du Maurier infused the landscape of southwest England with a foggy ominousness while exposing the manors of the rich as hotbeds of sexual domination, bribery, and murder.

The novel begins with one of the most famous lines in literature: "Last night I dreamt I went to Manderley again." As the unnamed narrator reveals, she and her husband have been displaced by the loss of their estate to the impersonal Hotel Cote d'Azur in Monte Carlo, though she reveals the circumstances only gradually, creating intense suspense. In her early twenties, she explains, she met a grieving widower twice her age named George Fortescue Maximilian "Maxim" de Winter who convinced her to quit her job as the secretary to a stuffy American, Mrs. Van Hopper, to marry him. The couple no sooner arrives at Manderley than the woman discovers she can't compete with the memory of Maxim's first wife. The housekeeper, the dour Mrs. Danvers, reminds her constantly than she's no substitute for Rebecca.

Even worse, Maxim seems obsessed with his loss. Brooding at cliff edges, staring into the sea where his first wife drowned, he's a contemporary version of the Byronic hero. Although emotionally aloof, he insists on his second wife's total obedience, to the point the narrator compares herself to the family dog at their feet. "These things are not discussed," Maxim insists when she pries into his anguish. "They are forbidden."

Much of the novel's suspense arises from the narrator's struggle to assimilate into life at Manderley, which is still stocked full of Rebecca's possessions. The second Mrs. de Winter can't put on a raincoat without finding a handkerchief monogramed with a taunting "R. de W." in its pocket. A nightgown left on a closet nail is also monogrammed, and books inscribed with her signature fill the manor. The new Mrs. de W. feels pressured in two simultaneous ways. Maxim infantilizes her, treating her like a daughter until she fears Mrs. Danvers; when she accidentally breaks a china cup of Rebecca's, for example, she hides the pieces. Yet the narrator also feels her identity melding with Rebecca's, as if the setting itself coerced her to assume her predecessor's personality. Mrs. Danvers is the main villain of this effort, engineering humiliation after humiliation for the new wife. She even tricks the narrator into unknowingly wearing a dress of Rebecca's to a ball, embarrassing Maxim. At another point the old housekeeper nearly pushes her out of a window telling her she's not fit. As Mrs. Danvers insists, Rebecca had a lion's courage and a man's aggression. She lived for no one but herself.

Just when the narrator appears most defeated, however, du Maurier stages a remarkable twist. Thanks to the chance discovery of a sunken boat carrying

Rebecca's body, Maxim confesses that he never loved his first wife. Rebecca was cruel and unfaithful, driving him to madness. When she boasted of being pregnant with another man's child, de Winter shot her and sunk the vessel with her corpse aboard.

Far from horrifying the narrator, the news empowers her: Realizing that Maxim hated Rebecca, she can now trust that he only feels passion for her. Together, the pair endure an inquest that rules Rebecca's death a suicide, then a subsequent blackmail attempt by Jack Favell, the dead woman's cousin, who claims the child Rebecca carried when killed was his. Du Maurier drops a deus ex machina to free the couple: Rebecca's London doctor appears to report that she had cancer and only six months to live anyway, making the murder a mercy killing. Moreover, thanks to a uterine deformity, she couldn't conceive children, foiling Favell's plot. The news drives Mrs. Danvers to madness, and she burns Manderley to the ground.

The lingering question of the novel is who the real Rebecca de Winter was. Was she the conniving, malignant seductress who tricked Maxim into murdering her as a final deceit? Or was she a woman who defied patriarchal expectations until her husband, like the folkloric Bluebeard, dispatched her through the ultimate act of control? The novel never provides a clear picture of Rebecca, leaving readers poring over clues and offering conflicting interpretations as they debate the degree to which the narrator's account is reliable. As du Maurier's own son once pointed out, "Everybody else [in the story] thought the sun shone out of her ass. . . . There's never a bad word about Rebecca except from Max." What isn't ambiguous is that the new Mrs. de Winter gains power in her marriage through her role in covering up her husband's crime. By the end of the novel, she has accomplished exactly what Rebecca never could, making Maxim subservient to her.

Rebecca was a massive best seller on both sides of the Atlantic in the late 1930s, selling 40,000 copies in one month in the UK and 400,000 in the U.S. The novel remains a cultural touchstone, and not just because of the classic Alfred Hitchcock adaptation in 1940 (though Hitchcock had to water down the moral ambiguity, dispatching Rebecca with an accidental fall instead of a bullet from her husband). Du Maurier herself wrote a stage version (her short story "The Birds" also inspired a later Hitchcock classic), and an opera was staged in 1983. A musical version of *Rebecca* played in Europe and Asia to great acclaim in 2006–2009 and was scheduled to premiere on Broadway in 2012 before financing fell through.

Perhaps the greatest sign of the novel's enduring appeal is that since the 1990s no fewer than four novels have retold the story to explore its gender dynamics for contemporary readers: Susan Hill's *Mrs. de Winter* (1993), Maureen Freely's *The Other Rebecca* (1996), Sally Beauman's *Rebecca's Tale* (2001), and Cassandra King's *Moonrise* (2013). As these homages reveal, du Maurier's classic raises endlessly debatable questions about marriage and women's freedom that send us back to Manderley and to Rebecca time and time again.

Bibliography

Rebecca (1938)

—KC

DRACULA

First Appearance: *Dracula*
Date of First Appearance: 1897
Author: Bram Stoker (1847–1912)

I never drink . . . wine.

Your friend,
Dracula

Seriously? It's hard not to smile a few pages into Bram Stoker's novel when you read the count's signature on a note left at a Transylvania hotel for a lawyer he had hired. Dracula is so infamous now that it seems nothing short of crazy someone could see that name and not run the opposite direction—especially after the hotel proprietor and his wife looked at each other "in a frightened sort of way" and, when asked what they know about Count Dracula and his castle, "both crossed themselves and refused to speak further."

Dracula himself may as well have swooped in and said, "I vant to suck your blood"—a line that never appears in the book, incidentally. But Count Dracula has become such a campy part of pop culture that everyone *thinks* he said it. Since debuting in Stoker's 1897 novel, Dracula the Un-dead (a term Stoker popularized) has appeared in close to twenty stage adaptations, almost as many musicals, a dozen radio shows, a handful of ballets and operas, and more than 200 films. It's the films, of course, that have made him most famous—some of them action oriented (*Van Helsing*), some dramatic (*Bram Stoker's Dracula*), some tongue in cheek (*Love at First Bite, Dracula: Dead and Loving It*), some revisionist (*Blacula*), and some just plain ridiculous (*Batman Fights Dracula, Billy the Kid vs. Dracula*). Bela Lugosi established the titular role in Universal's 1931 classic monster movie, then reprised it for the popular *Abbott and Costello Meet Frankenstein* (1948) and several other films and TV productions. Christopher Lee brought the character to life with longer fangs for another generation in ten releases from Hammer Films, and the public's fascination with vampires has grown, like those teeth, ever since—all because of Dracula, who has become fun scary and nonthreatening enough that he even inspired a children's breakfast cereal ("Count Chocula") and a *Sesame Street* character (the Count) who teaches preschoolers how to count. Meanwhile, Bran Castle, the only fortress in Transylvania that matches Stoker's description, has claimed the title of "Dracula's Castle" (though Stoker never visited), and his character's popularity is confirmed by the nearly half million tourists that visit the site each year.

John Polidori was the first to incorporate the vampire of superstition and folklore into fiction with his 1819 publication *The Vampyre*, but it was Stoker's novel that provided an expanded description and solidified characteristics that would be copied over the next century and a quarter: the transformation into a bat, the mind control, the inability to see his reflection in a mirror, the all-black attire, the sleeping in coffins, the turning of victims into vampires, and the repulsion by garlic or crucifix. All the vampire books and entertainments to follow—including

Interview with the Vampire, the *Twilight* and *Vampire Diaries* series, and cult TV classics like *Buffy the Vampire Slayer, True Blood,* and *Dark Shadows*—owe Stoker a debt of gratitude. It was Stoker who got the public to see vampires not as vague one-dimensional objects of folklore, but as fascinating almost-humans with qualities and emotional capabilities that made Dracula and other vampires seem more real and plausible. Stoker further reinforced the possibility of their existence by using a storytelling structure using "journal entries" and letters from lawyer Jonathan Harker, his fiancée Mina, and their friend Dr. Seward—along with newspaper clippings and a "sound recording" by Seward's colleague, Dr. Van Helsing. Together they function as eyewitness accounts, which in 1897 would have made Dracula incredibly chilling.

What's most fascinating about Dracula for modern readers is that things don't always come easily for him. For a member of the nobility he really works for it, a lunch-pail kind of guy. Lacking a staff (they're either dead or fellow vampires hidden away) he has to do everything himself. After Harker catches him making up his room and setting the dinner table himself, he realizes that Dracula was also probably the carriage driver. And when Dracula holds Harker a "veritable prisoner"—all doors are locked, the windows overlook a 1,000-foot drop, and outside are wolves Dracula seems to control—he gets Harker to write postdated letters he dictates, then crawls out of his window *face-first* down the side of the castle and into town to mail them, so as not to arouse suspicion over Harker's absence. It's all pretty tiring, apparently—as is trying to find a new minion in London, which he does by flying into the room of a serial killer being held in a mental hospital. It takes repeated trips and a bit of stealth and tiring mind control to pull off the killer's escape, and it can't be effortless transforming himself out of mist to stand alongside Mina and Harker, who had finally escaped. After putting Harker into a deep coma, Dracula warns, "If you make a sound I shall take him and dash his brains out before your very eyes," and with a "mocking smile" he adds, "First, a little refreshment to reward my exertions. You may as well be quiet; it is not the first time, or the second, that your veins have appeased my thirst!"

What the Count says is often worthy of an exclamation mark. "Patience!" he shouts at his three vampire brides when he catches them licking their lips over a fresh blood supply. He's a dramatic fellow whom Mina describes as "a tall, thin man, all in black," with "waxen face; the high Aquiline nose" and red eyes and "parted red lips, with the sharp white teeth showing between." And when he is sated, his face is "bloated" and "blood-stained and fixed with a grin of malice."

A calculating schemer, Dracula enlists a string of lawyers to help him purchase properties in London so he can presumably seek victims outside of Transylvania, where it's becoming harder to lure people to his castle. A guest must enter of his or her own free will. That's one of the conditions of being a vampire, and another more famous condition is that the vampire must be killed with a wooden stake to the heart—though ultimately that's not how Harker and the others bring him down before he can turn poor Mina into one of his vampire brides. With a band of gypsies also armed and wanting to attack Dracula, Harker finally delivers a fatal blow with a "great bowie knife"—an oversized American blade named for Jim Bowie of Alamo fame. One suspects that future accounts went with the wooden stake because they're easier to come by.

What made Dracula originally unique are now such clichés that what seems fresher are the mundane details of his life—like the all-night conversations he has about myriad subjects in his extensive library with intended victim Harker—or elements of Stoker's vampire legend that Hollywood didn't pick up, like a sacred wafer of Communion as a defense against the vampire. Then again, a cross is more instantly recognizable as a protection than an envelope. What ultimately haunts more than Dracula himself are the stinging words that one of the vampire brides levels—"You yourself never loved; you never love!"—and the Count's response, "Yes, I too can love."

Bibliography

Dracula (1897)
Dracula the Un-dead ("the official sequel" written by Stoker's great-grandnephew Dacre Stoker with Ian Holt, 2009)

Work Cited

Insider, Ro. "Nearly Half a Million Foreign Tourists Come to Central Romania to Visit Dracula's Castle." *Romania Insider*, January 21, 2017. https://www.romania-insider.com/nearly-half-a-million-foreign-tourists-visit-draculas-castle-in-romania/.

—JP

TESS DURBEYFIELD

First Appearance: *Tess of the D'Urbervilles*
Date of First Appearance: 1891
Author: Thomas Hardy (1840–1928)

"It was to be." There lay the pity of it.

Thomas Hardy's 1891 novel comes along several decades after publication of the Grimm brothers' fairy-tale collection and is a sort of Victorian antithesis to the happily-ever-after stories of women finding love and economic protection in a well-placed marriage. *Tess of the D'Urbervilles* is not destined to be one of those tales. Hardy's maiden is not rescued by a handsome prince; she is instead destroyed first by a fake one and then by another man who in failing to be her savior intensifies her death spiral. Tess Durbeyfield is indeed a memorable character who, as noted critic Irving Howe writes, "lives beyond the final pages of the book as a permanent citizen of the imagination," largely because her innocence, which, instead of commending her to good fortune, condemns her to a tragic end. She is doomed in spite of our hope to the contrary, and we can only watch helplessly as the cruel twists of her destiny send Tess down the path to one of the most heartbreaking endings in fiction.

As the novel opens, Tess is a fresh-faced sixteen-year-old participating in the annual rite of spring festival and wearing the traditional white dress meant to symbolize virginity. She seems unaware of her budding womanhood on full display, what Hardy later describes as her "pouted-up deep red mouth," and "a luxuriance of aspect, a fullness of growth, which made her appear more of a woman than she really was." Tess's parents are not so naïve, however, and conspire to use their daughter's sexual appeal to an advantage after discovering that the surname Durbeyfield descends from an ancient noble line, and a family not too distant from them bears the ancestral pedigree. They send Tess to the D'Urbervilles in the hope of gaining some financial benefit, but in lieu of honest gentility and familial generosity, Tess finds a nouveau riche family who had usurped the name to generate the appearance of status, and the man who undoes her, or at least the first one who does.

As we might expect in a novel emphasizing the imbalance of gender and economic power, Tess becomes the sexual target of Alec Stoke-D'Urberville, the heir to the family fortune and a self-proclaimed "damn bad fellow." She is unaccustomed to anyone as slick as this mustachioed Mephistopheles, so Tess misjudges his sexual overture and only acknowledges afterward, "I didn't understand your meaning until it was too late." Her failure to understand will be Tess's Achilles heel over the course of the novel. Alec's seduction/rape—left somewhat ambiguous by Hardy—results in Tess's shift from the pure woman identified in the novel's subtitle to a fallen woman, never mind that she didn't tumble of her own accord but was pushed. Her shame is accentuated by the tangible proof she cannot hide from the world after returning to her parents' dairy farm to bear a child, name him Sorrow, and then when the baby dies shortly thereafter, bury him. Tess implores her mother to explain, "Why didn't you tell me there was danger in men-folk? Why didn't you warn me?"

Why indeed, though Tess's painful enlightenment does not seem to cure her vulnerability; it only serves to accentuate it. Her failure to properly assess situations and appropriately calculate her response occurs time and again, misstep after misstep, as she chooses badly or fails to proactively protect herself in spite of experiences that might have taught her to be cautious. If we fault Tess for anything, it is this failure to learn and to act in self-preservation. We secretly yearn to step into the pages of the novel and say, "Have you learned nothing, baby girl?" The reality is she still fails to understand that society demands chastity of women but excuses its lack in males—the age-old idea that boys are going sow their seed, but the garden is to blame for the planting. Tess will find no solace in such a world as Hardy has placed her. He well knows it is a novelist's cruel trick to make us love best those made to suffer most, and he intends for both Tess and his readers to feel this pain.

Ironically, Tess's greatest woe comes in the form of a harp-playing angel, but not the heaven-sent type dispatched to her rescue. The person Tess sees as her redeemer is the second man to undo her and this time in an even more devastating way. Alec D'Urberville had made her an object of sexual pleasure. Angel Clare makes her an object of feminine virtue. He puts her on a pedestal and projects his own perception of the divine female on her. In Angel's imagination Tess is "no longer the milkmaid, but a visionary essence of woman—a whole sex condensed into one typical form." He requires nothing less of Tess than to be a paragon of virtue, and his failure to love her for better or for worse as the marriage vow promises is the knife that cuts deepest. Angel's self-flagellating, self-pitying wedding night confession about losing his virginity to a prostitute shows he is no saint, but he fails to see that his sin of choice bears more stain than Tess's forced loss of purity. In passing judgment, he proves he is a hypocrite as well as a louse, and after her own disclosure, followed by Angel's declaration that she is "dead" to him, his immediate abandonment leaves her to be buffeted once again by fate's unremitting fury.

Hardy's ending will achieve three things—retribution for Tess's sins for those who insist on justice for her crimes, a tragic ending for those who expect one from a good Victorian novel, and immortality for his character whose passions and innocence play against her in every turn and in every heartrending way. Tess's effort to obtain Angel's forgiveness by killing the man who had first taken her innocence sets the stage for the ending's high drama, and her apprehension at the famed English site of Stonehenge provides the striking visual that filmmaker Roman Polanski capitalizes on in his 1979 movie simply called *Tess*. The site of ancient ritual markedly underscores society's adherence to the past and its rigid mores. Tess must be hanged because she has sinned against them. Happily, Polanski saves us the trauma of seeing her lifeless body dangling at the end of the rope, and instead simply imposes a few sentences over the backdrop of the dramatic stones to let us know she has paid for her sins.

No matter how many times we revisit this book, with each new reading Tess Durbeyfield's tragic story is as fresh and painful as the first time we experienced it. She is a victim of economy, the patriarchy, and the bad luck of meeting a bad man and another bad man posing as a good man. All the forces, including the parents who should have protected instead of exploited her, her husband who should have banished his double standard instead of his wife, and society who should have first punished the abuser and not the abused, are all complicit in the tragedy that was Tess's life and her death.

Bibliography

Tess of the D'Urbervilles: A Pure Woman (1891)

Works Cited

Hardy, Thomas. Introduction by James Wood. *Tess of the D'Urbervilles*. New York: Modern Library Classics, 2001.
———. *Tess of the D'Urbervilles: A Pure Woman*. Introduction by Marcelle Clements. Signet Classics, 2006.

—GS

TYLER DURDEN

First Appearance: *Fight Club*
Date of First Appearance: 1996
Author: Chuck Palahniuk (1962–)

Remember this. The people you're trying to step on, we're everyone you depend on. We're the people who do your laundry and cook your food and serve your dinner. . . . We are cooks and taxi drivers and we know everything about you. . . . We control every part of your life.

Even before a shirtless, abdominally ripped, and bloody Brad Pitt made him iconic in the 1999 movie, Tyler Durden was unforgettable. The swaggering antihero of Chuck Palahniuk's debut novel, *Fight Club*, he strutted into literature as a model of anarchic masculinity, an antidote to the emasculation of men in the white-collar wage-earning world, a force of pure aggression unavailable to a post–baby boomer generation raised on sensitive feelings and support groups. As the founder of a club where his followers reconnect with their innate brutality by taking turns beating each other senseless, Tyler insists that only through pain can a man know he's truly alive. He's the id unleashed, a terrorist rebelling against consumerism's false wants, and a cult leader preaching a bare-knuckled philosophy of primitivism that's fascistic in all but name.

He also doesn't exist—a fact many readers tempted to buy into his revolutionary agenda tend to forget.

Fight Club is narrated by Tyler's foil, an unnamed young professional who feels defeated by the numbness of his job and the antiseptic conditions of modern life. The narrator spends much of his time catching flights to endless business meetings, causing him perpetual insomnia. During a vacation to a nude beach he meets Tyler, who asks for his address. Sometime later, when he returns home, the narrator discovers his hermetically sealed, climate-controlled apartment has been blown to smithereens. As the police investigate the explosion, he receives a mysterious summons from Tyler. The stranger offers the narrator a place to stay, but on one condition: "I want you to hit me as hard as you can," he insists.

Throughout the novel, Palahniuk cuts back and forth in time, creating a dislocating sense of disorder that nicely conveys the chaos Tyler wants to ignite. Initially, the saboteur is content to perform quiet acts of subversion. At the theater where he works as a part-time film projectionist he splices single frames of genitalia into the movie reels so penises and vaginas flash before customers' eyes for one-sixtieth of a second. At his other job as a waiter he urinates in soup tureens and farts on serving carts of Boccone Dolce served to Junior Leaguers who never know better because the meringue absorbs the odor. He steals fat from liposuction treatments and renders it into soap. More ominously, he dabbles in explosives.

Tyler's real coup comes when he and the narrator establish their fight club and discover how many disillusioned men long to get their limp masculinity hard. The narrator himself is electrified: before, his only outlet for his anger was to clean his apartment, but now he can wiggle loose teeth in his jaw. The clubs quickly evolve into the next stage of Tyler's plan, a quasi-terrorist group called Project Mayhem. Foot soldiers dubbed "space monkeys" revel in destruction, paintballing statues and defacing corporate towers. The narrator is so enthralled he dreams of wiping his ass with the *Mona Lisa*.

At the core of Durden's anger is his insistence that modern men have been abandoned by their fathers. If we can't win the love of God, the ultimate father figure, he insists, at least we can get his attention and earn his hate. His ultimate aim is to bring about a cultural ice age, taking humanity back to survivalist mode so men can stalk elks outside of department stores and rappel up the kudzu that will grow over the Sears Tower. The space monkeys are mostly happy to worship him and spread his cult of personality.

Project Mayhem taps into such a deep reservoir of pent-up anger that no matter where the narrator goes young men ask him if he knows the name Tyler Durden. The twist of *Fight Club*, of course, is that the narrator *is* Tyler—or rather Tyler is the narrator's alter ego. When he discovers his split personality, the narrator decides he must stop Project Mayhem, leading to an epic confrontation on the roof of a skyscraper Tyler is set to detonate. The movie version departs significantly from Palahniuk's original plot: On film the narrator (played by Edward Norton) shoots himself to kill off Tyler, but he's too late, and Project Mayhem's bombs destroy the financial district the narrator peers down upon—a tableau that even two years before 9/11 many reviewers found objectionably immoral. In the novel, the suicide attempt fails miserably, and the narrator wakes up in a hospital, his face permanently disfigured. To his horror he discovers that the anarchy he's loosed upon the world still roils. Orderlies with bruised and stitched faces address him as "Mr. Durden" in subversive whispers, promising they're still hard at work on Project Mayhem. "We look forward to getting you back," one says in the book's final line.

Fight Club isn't a subtle novel. To make his point about feminized men, Palahniuk includes a tragic character named Big Bob, a former bodybuilder whose testicular cancer has cost him his balls (any other word seems to violate the spirit of the book) and who grows male breasts, or "bitch tits." Tyler's philosophy itself is a fairly paint-by-numbers mixture of Marx's critique of capitalism and Nietzschean nihilism. And symbolism doesn't get much more basic when the space monkeys don black shirts à la Mussolini's goons as their uniform.

Yet there's no denying that in the mid-1990s *Fight Club* tapped into Generation X disgruntlement, both its resentment of its absentee fathers and the service economy it seemed doomed to toil in. The novel and movie's cult cred has kept Tyler Durden politically relevant throughout the decades since. Allusions to *Fight Club* have popped up in an unsettlingly diverse range of political movements: in the 1999 Seattle riots protesting globalization during the World Trade Organization Ministerial Conference, at protests against both the Democrat and Republican Conventions in 2000, and at the 2011 Occupy Wall Street movement, to name a few.

Its most enduring influence, however—much to Palahniuk's chagrin—has been in the alt-right movement, the loose coalition of predominantly male far-right fringe groups railing against identity politics and gender equality, usually in unapologetically racist and sexist language. Google "*Fight Club* and politics" and one discovers an array of websites that adapt Tyler's most memorable lines to legitimate their belligerent grievances. The alt-right even found its favorite insult to politically correct sensibilities in Tyler's message to his followers: "You are not special. You're not a beautiful and unique snowflake."

Not surprisingly, few Tyler Durden fans acknowledge that Palahniuk's narrator wants to kill off his alter ego, or that *Fight Club* satirizes brute masculinity as much as it celebrates it. Pointing out those inconvenient facts would probably get us labeled snowflakes, though—or maybe a punch in the face.

Bibliography

Fight Club (1996)

—KC

E

KATNISS EVERDEEN

First Appearance: *The Hunger Games*
Date of First Appearance: 2008
Author: Suzanne Collins (1962–)

Katniss. It's the plant I was named for. And I heard my father's voice joking, "As long as you can find yourself, you'll never starve."

In young adult fiction, boys traditionally hog the action. Whether Twain's Tom Sawyer and Huckleberry Finn, Jim Hawkins in Robert Louis Stevenson's *Treasure Island* (1883), Mowgli in Rudyard Kipling's *The Jungle Book* (1894), or Ender Wiggin in Orson Scott Card's *Ender's Game* (1985), young heroes test their moral mettle by lighting out either for the territories, the high seas, or universes far, far away. Girls, when present at all, are usually love interests, or they're confined to home, as in Louisa May Alcott's *Little Women* (1868). This was still true as recently as the new millennium: Hermione Granger may not get the Becky Thatcher treatment in J. K. Rowling's phenomenally successful Harry Potter series (1997–2007), but she still plays second fiddle to Harry himself.

The gender divide in YA fiction didn't begin to collapse until the late 2000s. And it did so thanks to a single dynamic young woman: Katniss Everdeen, the narrator of Suzanne Collins's megaselling *The Hunger Games* (2008), and its two equally successful sequels, *Catching Fire* (2009) and *Mockingjay* (2010).

Katniss is a female Theseus, the mythological Roman warrior who battles the evil King Minos by entering the labyrinth to kill the Minotaur. In Collins's case, Minos is the dictatorial President Coriolanus Snow, the head of the repressive government of a postapocalyptic America called Panem. Ruling from a metropolis known as the Capitol, the Big Brother–like Snow and his ministers exploit the country's twelve districts to feed its decadent lifestyle. Each year the Capitol demands that the districts send two competitors to its Hunger Games as a tribute, just as Minos demanded human sacrifices from the Athenians he conquered.

When her younger sister, Prim, is selected for the games, the sixteen-year-old Katniss volunteers to take her place in the duel-to-the-death competitions. Evoking the legend of Artemis the hunter as well as Theseus, Katniss is well trained as an archer and woodsman, having grown up foraging in the forests around District 12 to feed her mother and siblings, her father having died in a coal-mining explosion when she was a child. The Hunger Games themselves are a version of the Roman bread and circuses that pitted gladiators in fatal exhibitions cheered on by crowds drunk on bloodlust and gore. In Panem, the games are broadcast for the lurid entertainment of the Capitol's similarly degenerate population.

Not unlike Joseph Campbell's hero with a thousand faces, Katniss must uphold her instinctive moral code as she fights to survive; throughout Collins's first installment, she embodies the virtues of self-sacrifice, loyalty to allies, and honor in battle. In *Catching Fire* and *Mockingjay*, she goes on to become a freedom fighter, first inspiring the oppressed districts to rebel against the Capitol and then leading a guerilla assassination squad to rid Panem of Snow. In the end, Katniss must confront the fact that the rebel forces she fights alongside are just as capable of atrocity as the tyrants they seek to overthrow. After learning that resistance leaders bombed their own troops and then framed Snow for the casualties (including Prim) to win a propaganda campaign, she executes not the dictator she has helped unseat but the revolution's own amoral leader, Alma Coin. In a world where power inevitably corrupts those who hold it, the hero must maintain her moral autonomy and stand for good. The series ends with an epilogue that flashes forward to show an adult Katniss still emotionally struggling twenty years after her acquittal for Coin's murder on grounds of insanity. She soothes her post-traumatic stress from her ordeal by reminding herself of humane acts she has witnessed throughout her life. "There are much worse games to play," the final line reads.

At first glance, Collins's trilogy seems to empower its heroine simply by casting her in the traditional role of the strong-but-silent male warrior. As a female protagonist, Katniss is unusual for how emotionally remote she is. Beneath her taciturn front, though, is a complex and often ambiguous revision of gender roles. As Collins admitted, *The Hunger Games* was inspired by reality television in addition to classical mythology, particularly in the way that story lines that supposedly emerge spontaneously in unscripted series are contrived behind the scenes to appeal to viewer desires. And after violence, no desire in the Capitol sells like romance. From the moment Katniss enters the games, a team of advisers and stylists packages her to maximize her appeal and win gifts from sponsors. Mentoring her is an alcoholic former champion, Haymitch Abernathy; a stylist, Cinna; and a gaudy chaperone, Effie Trinket. The key to Katniss's success, according to them, is to play the role of a "star-crossed lover" with a childhood acquaintance, Peeta Mellark, her district's other competitor.

Katniss resists this romance plot because she has a more natural connection to Gale Hawthorne, a fellow hunter. Their bond is platonic, though, and more often than not she's content to be alone than with either boy. Yet to survive the games she must act the part of a conventional girl in love, allowing herself to be dressed and presented as Peeta's happy fiancée in interviews with the games' master of ceremonies, Caesar Flickerman. The contrived romance becomes a national obsession, turning Katniss and Peeta into celebrities. Her choice of a wedding gown even makes ratings history—at least until the gown bursts into flames and reveals itself as the defiant costume of the mockingjay, the symbol of rebel resistance against the Capitol.

Throughout the trilogy, Peeta, not Katniss, inhabits the conventional female role, professing his true love for Katniss live on television and requiring her to rescue him from several damsel-in-distress scenarios. Yet Peeta's sensitivity and creativity also teach Katniss to fuse her anger and resolve with characteristics that their dystopia deems vulnerabilities, including empathy, nurturing, and intuition. As the couple build a mutually rewarding interdependency, their melding of traits makes it difficult to ascribe attributes to a specific gender: Katniss and Peeta come to embody together the best of each sex. The melding also leads Katniss to recognize the limitations of her other suitor's rage for revolution. In his fury to topple the Snow government, Gale inadvertently provides Coin the weapons that kill Prim and her fellow rebels. The greatest sign of Katniss's growth comes in the epilogue, where, having made Panem safe for children by ending the games, she can overcome her antipathy toward motherhood, which she associates with passivity and victimization. Yet even in adulthood Katniss remains unconventional: Collins makes it clear that Peeta was the one desperate for a family, and that he needed several years of convincing his wife before she agreed to bear children.

In pop-culture commentaries, Katniss's nontraditional femininity often sets her in opposition to another contemporary heroine of a massively popular YA franchise, Bella Swan in Stephenie Meyer's *Twilight* series (2005–2008), who by contrast seems far more passive and dependent on male approval. Yet Katniss's arc of development also sets her apart from "kick-ass" female action heroes like Lisbeth Salander, the punk computer hacker of Stieg Larsson's *The Girl with the Dragon Tattoo* novels. Lisbeth is a fantastic creation in her own right, avenging misogyny and abuse as if she were Dirty Harry in a goth hoodie, but she changes little from novel to novel, and is sometimes so sexualized as to seem a male fantasy. Katniss, meanwhile, is that rare round character whose growth doesn't resolve predictably.

She proves that girls who're incendiary don't have to burn out but can remain gender rebels long after the war is won.

Bibliography

The Hunger Games (2008)
Catching Fire (2009)
Mockingjay (2010)

—KC

JANE EYRE

First Appearance: *Jane Eyre*
Date of First Appearance: 1847
Author: Charlotte Brontë (1816–1855)

I am no bird; and no net ensnares me; I am a free human being, with an independent will; I am not an angel, and I will not be one till I die; I will be myself.

Jane Eyre is one of many literary orphans—including British cousins Harry Potter, Oliver Twist, and a variety of other Dickens kin—who populate the pages of novels and garner sympathy for their plight. Undeterred by a geography of misery and with determination to claim herself, Jane boldly announces, "I must dislike those who, whatever I do to please them, persist in disliking me. I must resist those who punish me unjustly." The strength of her self-defense, combined with the "poor girl marries the prince" scenario, and topped off with a dollop of empathy for a gutsy young woman buffeted by the cruel winds of fate, Jane's story solidifies our conviction that she is worthy of the attention we continue to give her.

Charlotte Brontë establishes in Jane a forbearance that only breaks on rare occasions to discharge the arrows of indignation when she is pushed to the brink. Her dignity flows from an unexplained fount of self-worth in spite of being poor, diminutive, and constantly referred to as unattractive. Whether she is the original "plain Jane" from whom we get the term or just an unwitting precursor to the now-familiar phrase, no one seems to know, but with such a verdict on her head and no dowry to entice marriageable prospects, Jane's future looks grim. As readers, we expect the journey to be fraught with misery—this is the typical scenario we find endearing—but we also have confidence in her pluck as she faces the tribulations a good plotline will inevitably throw in her path. We need not worry, however, because these tales nearly always end with a large surprise inheritance kicking in at the last minute to tie everything up in a satisfying bow.

What is perhaps more relevant to a modern audience, especially a feminist one, is the shift from the novel's orphan-centric theme to the second section's focus on the future of an unmarried woman. Because Jane is not a well-situated female with family prominence and/or a pretty face, she is not easily tracked for matrimony. No handsome prince is waiting for her to claim the wayward glass slipper. Lacking the proper accoutrements for marriage, she looks to one of the few alternative prospects allotted to her while some ill-fated fictional girls in other novels succumb to the world's oldest profession and the fatalistic end such tragedies often produce. Jane remains socially appropriate, takes up her new position as a governess, and begins a journey encompassing plot-twisting turns and the slow burn of an unlikely romance.

Jane's new employer, Mr. Rochester, turns out to be an intellectual soul mate, and like her, he is no looker. Unlike her, he's a male who has inherited money, and his pocketbook significantly outweighs his not-so-handsome mug, so he's all set. Or so we would think. In details long enough to fill the Victorian novel this is, Jane and Rochester move through an awkward courtship and to the brink of marriage Brontë's readership wildly cheers on as just rewards for a plain girl with a big brain and a sassy disposition. Wouldn't you know (well, not really—who would have guessed?), there is a madwoman locked up in the attic who's hell-bent on destroying the wedding veil of her husband's betrothed. The tough cookie that Jane is, she refuses to marry a man who already has a wife, a guy who begs her to proceed with the nuptials and simply ignore the crazy woman upstairs who occasionally gets loose to wreak havoc around the manor. Waving the symbolic flag of self-respect, Jane dismisses her would-be groom by saying, "I care for myself. The more solitary, the more friendless, the more unsustained I am, the more I will respect myself." The readers silently cheer her on with a "You go, girl!" and at this point, Jane does just that.

Plot details proliferate, many of them requiring some willing suspension of disbelief after Jane runs away, but cutting to the chase, she eventually follows a premonition leading her back to Thornfield where she finds the estate in ruins after poor Mrs. Rochester sets it on fire, jumps to her death, and leaves behind her widower who is blinded and severely maimed trying to save her. In a gender-reversing turn of events, Jane comes to his rescue, their love is immediately restored, and she proclaims with a bold assertion, "Reader, I married him." Rochester later miraculously gains sight in one eye, enough to see his newborn son, and they live happily ever after on Jane's newfound wealth. (Did we forget to mention that Ms. Eyre is now an heiress? Fun play on words, Brontë!)

The continued popularity of *Jane Eyre*, even with its scrappy heroine and the slanted but ultimate endgame of fairy-tale coupling, is still quite remarkable considering the gap between publication in 1847 and a current, seemingly more liberated audience who apparently still hasn't had enough of that age-old story. Virginia Woolf had earlier pondered this enigma when writing, "As we open *Jane Eyre* once more we cannot stifle the suspicion that we shall find her world of imagination as antiquated, mid-Victorian, and out of date as the parsonage on the moor. . . . So we open *Jane Eyre*; and in two pages every doubt is swept clean from our minds." For a significant number of feminists from Woolf forward, the work becomes an important manifesto (womanifesto?), with Jane representing strong females who overcome, and Bertha, the madwoman in the attic, signifying patriarchal oppression and its resultant feminist rage.

In print constantly since its publication, *Jane Eyre* has been retold and reworked a remarkable number of times, especially in new mediums between the 1950s and the present. These include a prequel, at least seven sequels, sci-fi and erotic "mash-ups," comic book versions, and adaptations in film, television, theater, ballet, opera, musicals, and symphonies. An ever-growing list of productions have hailed marquee actors and directors whose names continue to draw new audiences beyond those who have firsthand familiarity with Brontë's work. Famous leading men over the years such as George C. Scott, Orson Welles, Charlton Heston, William Hurt, Timothy Dalton, and Michael Fassbender have played the Byronic, broodingly passionate Mr. Rochester. With the exception of Joan Fontaine in 1943, less famous actresses played Jane, perhaps because she is characterized as unattractive, so smoldering sexpots took other roles. Smaller parts featured a young Elizabeth Taylor (sexpot in the making) as Helen Byrnes, Judy Dench as Mrs. Fairfax, and Anna Paquin as the childhood Jane, and the movie remakes continue.

In the end, *Jane Eyre* is a compelling tale of a quiet girl who rises to victory even in the cold, windswept landscape where men hold all the money, make all the rules, and keep women in their place, except when they can't. And aren't women even more interesting and attractive in the ways that should count when their brains, wit, and integrity are the jewels in their crown? "Yes," so say we all.

Bibliography

Jane Eyre (1847)

Work Cited

Woolf, Virginia. *The Common Reader*. New York: Harcourt, Brace, 1925.

—GS

F

ATTICUS FINCH

First Appearance: *To Kill a Mockingbird*
Date of First Appearance: 1960
Author: Harper Lee (1926–2016)

There are some men in this world who are born to do our unpleasant jobs for us.

There may be no more noble father figure anywhere in literature than Harper Lee's widower Atticus Finch, the central hero of her 1960 southern tale *To Kill a Mockingbird*. And for those of a certain age, that version is indelibly bound up with Gregory Peck's 1962 film incarnation. The novel won the Pulitzer Prize for Fiction in 1961, and Peck won the Academy Award for Best Actor in 1963, each honor marking the strength of this story and one of its central characters. In both renderings, Atticus is the epitome of a southern gentleman complete with a three-piece linen suit and slow-paced cadence the heat of the South seems to imbue. But more importantly, he is the embodiment of the moral playbook needed then, during the civil rights era when the novel was published, and now, to set the example we might wish all our fathers and community, national, and world leaders would take to heart.

Most of what we know of Atticus, the name by which his children also call him, we learn from his adult daughter Jean Louise as she reminiscences about her childhood through the lens of the rearview mirror. Appropriately nicknamed "Scout," perhaps because of her overobservant nature, she constantly questions Atticus for what he does and why he does it. He is unlike other dads who are young enough to play football with their sons, enjoy hunting, occasionally get drunk and engage in a fistfight or otherwise exhibit the more demonstrably "manly" qualities he seems to lack. Scout's surprise in discovering when he shoots a rabid dog that Atticus has a dead-accurate aim raises her level of admiration disproportionally to the often lukewarm responses she manages for the sage advice offered with annoying frequency to an impetuous daughter prone to reaction rather than tempered response. Notwithstanding Scout's moderated adoration, we who are eavesdropping on the Finch family are drawn to rally support for the "Atticus for Sainthood" fan club.

At the heart of what makes Atticus Finch one of the most loved fictional characters of all time is the insistence that his children, and we by association, call out their better angels as they walk among the downtrodden who are often abused by "proper" society. One aspect of Harper Lee's genius in the telling of this story is that she provides multiple chances to learn compassionate behavior through Atticus's exchanges with the two victims central to parallel yet ultimately intertwining plots—the poor, black, wrongfully accused Tom Robinson and the debilitatingly shy and misunderstood recluse Boo Radley, and incidentally, other poor white families and their disadvantaged children as well. *To Kill a Mockingbird* becomes more than just a referendum on racism as it is often touted; it is a call to practice human kindness, tolerance, and Good Samaritan values in a broader swath. Atticus does not fail to model these virtues in his children's presence, in his community, and in our hearts.

Respect for Atticus is at its height when he not only accepts the assignment of defending a black man accused of raping a white woman; he actually leans into it with the full conviction of his purpose. In answer to Scout's question about why he does so, he replies that his conscience demands him to, even though he's "licked a hundred years before [he] started." He faces down an angry mob ready to exact their own justice in an attempt to lynch Robinson before he has the right to fair and impartial judgment. And at the close of that trial, Atticus's remarkably eloquent arguments about dignity and compassion are among the most reasoned and humane that literature has to offer. We hold our collective breaths with the hope that what is no doubt doomed before Atticus utters an opening statement will miraculously turn in the direction of true justice. We already know the verdict, though, if we're honest with ourselves, but Atticus's valiant attempt only serves to heighten our respect for him. The quiet but profound admiration the balcony's African American onlookers demonstrate as he passes further solidifies Atticus as a hero for the black community, for those in the white community who are able to transcend racial division, and for generations of readers who have clung to the figure who is just the stuff we want our heroes to be made of.

The 2018 opening in Montgomery, Alabama, of a memorial to the collective South's thousands of lynching victims attests to the history Atticus's arguments could not override in the 1930s pre–civil rights South, and the July 2015 publication of Harper Lee's second published novel *Go Set a Watchman* has dramatic implications for our view of him as the perfect champion of decency and civility. In the novel said to be a rejected first draft of *To Kill a Mockingbird* and set chronologically twenty years later, Jean Louise returns to Macon and discovers her father actually opposes desegregation and the NAACP and has even attended a KKK meeting. From this new angle of observation, some critics have pointed out signs that this perspective exists even through a few statements in *Mockingbird*. This notion shattered nearly everyone who read the novel and idolized Atticus Finch, but *Washington Post* columnist Peggy Noonan calms our fears by reminding us that he is a fictional character drawn and shaped to fit the writer's purpose. Were he real, he would have human fallibility and no doubt disappoint us at some point in some way. And as Noonan says, "Atticus never lived and can never die, and if you want to visit him you can pick up a book."

Noonan makes a couple of good points about our propensity to create heroes who are beyond the borders of reality, and about the beauty of literature—that we can freeze these characters in time so they won't fail us. Forgetting the Atticus of *Watchman,* a novel many readers wish had remained unknown and unpublished, we can celebrate the Atticus of *To Kill a Mockingbird* whose biggest flaw is really an endearing quality. He operates on the naïve belief that most people are kind at heart if we just understand them well enough on a deeper level. In the novel's closing lines even after Tom Robinson's wrongful conviction and murder, Bob Ewell's attack on the Finch children, and the necessity of Boo Radley's becoming a killer to save them, we celebrate one of Atticus's most famous phrases, one that President Barack Obama chose to cite in his 2017 presidential Farewell Address: "You never really understand a person until you consider things from his point of view . . . until you climb into his skin and walk around in it."

For those who love symbols, the novel is full of them, and the mockingbird of the title's fame, the one Atticus tells his children it is a sin to kill, exemplifies all the defenseless victims society would seek to destroy. Because at least in this book he tries to save them, and through his children he instills in the next generation that moral code as well, we hail thee, Atticus Finch!

Bibliography

To Kill a Mockingbird (1960)

Works Cited

Noonan, Peggy. "Don't Mourn Atticus Finch." *Wall Street Journal,* July 24, 2015.
Obama, Barack. "Farewell Address." Transcript. *Los Angeles Times,* January 10, 2017.

—GS

HUCKLEBERRY FINN

First Appearance: *The Adventures of Tom Sawyer*
Date of First Appearance: 1876
Author: Mark Twain (1835–1910)

I felt good and all washed clean of sin for the first time I had ever felt so in my life, and I knowed I could pray now. But I didn't do it straight off, but laid the paper down and set there thinking—thinking how good it was all this happened so, and how near I come to being lost and going to hell. And went on thinking. And got to thinking over our trip down the river; and I see Jim before me all the time: in the day and in the night-time, sometimes moonlight, sometimes storms, and we a-floating along, talking and singing and laughing. But somehow I couldn't seem to strike no places to harden me against him, but only the other kind.

"All modern American literature," Ernest Hemingway once wrote, "comes from one book by Mark Twain called *Huckleberry Finn.*"

If that's the case, then Huck Finn is the representative American. He's not the first "American Adam" whose innate individualism sends him lighting out for the territory to escape a society that wants to "sivilize" him, but he is the one whose vernacular voice and vagabond roving most enduringly embody the innocence, impish freedom, and intuitive sense of right and wrong that America likes to believe animates its national spirit. First introduced in Mark Twain's *The Adventures of Tom Sawyer* (1876), Huck did not come into his own until nine years later when he starred in his own picaresque, where his journeys transcend the larks and escapades of children's literature to become a profound moral satire of American failings, including its myths of childhood, its educational system, and, most controversially, its racism. *Adventures of Huckleberry Finn* was neither an easy book to write, nor its message easy to sell. It no sooner hit bookshelves in 1885 than stuffy institutions like the Concord Public Library banned it for its coarse language. Nearly 140 years later, school systems strike it from their curricula for fear of the controversy its more than 200 uses of "nigger" will spark. If the puckish Huck never seems to wear out his welcome—he has been adapted into more than 100 movies, TV series, Broadway musicals, and even, recently, manga comics, and has inspired countless other imitators—he never seems to stop upsetting people either.

According to Twain's autobiography (which, remarkably, before 2010 was only published piecemeal), Huck was inspired by a childhood friend in Hannibal, Missouri, named Tom Blakenship. At once irredeemably indolent and yet kindhearted, Blakenship was in all but name an orphan. As the former Samuel Clemens recalled, because Tom had total freedom he seemed entirely happy. When first conceived from Blakenship's mold, Huck was little more than a sidekick. Twain describes him in *Tom Sawyer* as "conscience free" and as smoking and swearing constantly. Yet he gives Huck precious little to do but tag along as Tom plays pirate, unearths buried treasure, and tries to inform the clueless town of St. Petersburg without getting himself murdered that the malevolent Injun Joe killed Doc Robinson, not the wrongly tried Muff Potter. Mostly Huck is a foil to Becky Thatcher, Tom's love interest. If courting Becky will pull Tom into a world of politesse and etiquette, Huck represents a life of footloose exploits, free of responsibility.

Eager for an income stream in the lucrative world of children's literature, Twain began planning for a *Tom Sawyer* sequel almost immediately after the book's publication. Indeed, *Adventures of Huckleberry Finn* evolved from deleted portions of its predecessor that described Huck's adoption by Widow Douglas, which Twain had been advised, wrongfully he concluded, to cut. His most important departure was to allow Huck to speak in the first person, something he had denied Tom, much to his regret. He completed 400 quick pages, then grew frustrated and set the manuscript aside for three years. After attempting a revision again in 1879–1880, he set Huck aside again for *another* three years. It took a trip to Mississippi and New Orleans where he witnessed how little Emancipation had improved the lives of blacks in the South to inspire a return to the story. Twain realized that the fate of a runaway slave named Jim he'd introduced into the plot as a companion to Huck provided an opportunity for an adult indictment of America's woeful treatment of its nonwhite population, and not just a diverting children's book.

In effect, Twain was able to finish the novel by transforming the plot from a series of episodic adventures into the story of his hero's moral development. In the novel's early portions, Huck is acted upon more than he is an actor. Not only are

Widow Douglas and Miss Watson trying to teach him religion, but his drunken father, Pap, kidnaps him to steal the reward money he and Tom earn for recovering treasure in *Tom Sawyer*. Huck fakes his death and escapes to Jackson Island, where he discovers Jim making his way across the Mississippi River to freedom in Illinois. In an improbable digression, Huck dresses as a girl to perform reconnaissance in town, where he learns Jim is wanted for Huck's supposed demise. Huck and Jim set off on a raft but are momentarily split up when a steamship smashes into them. What follows are some of the funniest extended set pieces in American literature.

First, Huck gets swept up in a Hatfields-and-McCoys-style feud between two families, the Grangerfords and the Shepherdsons. He is forced to listen to the mawkish poetry of the late Emmeline Grangerford, who fancied herself an elegiac artist. When two young members of the clans elope together, a bloody shootout wipes out the Grangerfords, including Huck's friend and Emmeline's brother, Buck. Subsequently, Huck, reunited with Jim, encounters a pair of grifters who pass themselves off as a lost English duke and the Dauphin, the rightful heir to the French throne. The duo perpetuate several scams Huck and Jim are forced to partake in, until Huck's conscience forces him to derail one of their plots. The duke and the Dauphin turn around and sell Jim down the river.

In the novel's most serious passage—contained in chapter 31—Huck weighs his responsibility to Jim, who has put himself in danger for the boy, against society's laws. Realizing helping a man escape from slavery will make him a criminal, Huck declares, "All right then, I'll go hell," and he sets off to save his friend.

But it's at this point that critics traditionally accuse Twain of fumbling his story line. "If you read [the novel]," Hemingway added as a caveat to his praise, "you must stop where the Nigger Jim is stolen from the boys. That is the real end. The rest is just cheating." In another improbable twist, Tom Sawyer turns out to be the nephew of the Phelps family that buys Jim. Rather than simply break Jim free, Twain forces Huck to help instigate a series of prankish intrigues at Jim's expense that end with Tom shot in the leg. The diversions are all for naught: As Tom has known all along, Jim has been legally free since he and Huck disappeared, emancipated by his dead owner's will.

Despite Tom's injection into the story, Huck's voice dominates in the novel—and nowhere more powerfully than in the final paragraph, where he insists he must "light out" of society because civilization corrupts. If only for this statement alone he is the voice of American individualism. In the context of a razor-sharp satire about America's moral failings, though, the line resonates with the core appeal of the American mythos: freedom as unlimited as the frontier itself.

Bibliography

The Adventures of Tom Sawyer (1876)
Adventures of Huckleberry Finn (1885)

Works Cited

Hemingway, Ernest. *Green Hills of Africa*. New York: Scribner's, 1935.
Twain, Mark. *Autobiography of Mark Twain*. 3 vols. Berkeley: University of California Press, 2010–2015.

—KC

HENRY FLEMING

First Appearance: "Private Fleming / His Various Battles"
in Bacheller-Johnson Newspaper Syndicate papers
Date of First Appearance: December 3–9, 1894
Author: Stephen Crane (1871–1900)

It was not well to drive men into final corners; at those moments they could all develop teeth and claws.

"The cold passed reluctantly from the earth, and the retiring fogs revealed an army stretched out on the hills, resting. As the landscape changed from brown to green, the army awakened, and began to tremble with eagerness at the noise of rumors." These lines begin Stephen Crane's Civil War novel *The Red Badge of Courage* and set the stage for what his young soldier is about to experience as he impatiently awaits initiation into battle. Crane describes Henry Fleming simply as "the youth" who becomes a sort of "everyman" and a psychological trove for discussion of existential questions about the nature of fear, death, and humanity's place in the universe. War serves as the catalyst for this contemplation, and in the course of a few days through this accelerated bildungsroman—a fancy word describing the journey to adulthood—young Henry will convince himself that he has grown from youthful naïveté to manhood through his traumatic journey. In examining the emotional complexity of such a voyage, Crane sets a standard for writers to follow who will tell their own stories of youth engaged in the theater of war.

Many critiques of the novel suggest the work had such a strong sense of verisimilitude that Crane must have experienced the cataclysm firsthand to have written so truly about it through Henry's eyes. Yet Crane, born nearly a decade after the war's end, used his journalist's training to interview war veterans and create a narrative that seemed the product of keen observation. He conjured a soldier who collectively represents a military unit purposely not identified as Northern or Southern. Fleming is simply one man among many in blue uniforms fighting against many others outfitted in gray. The major battle in which Henry participates goes unnamed as well, and his experience becomes universal. Henry Fleming can be any soldier in any war at any time.

Whether consciously or not, Crane taps into the rising interest in psychology Freud and Jung were generating around the time of *The Red Badge of Courage*'s 1895 publication. He shifts narrative focus so that Fleming's inner thoughts occupy at least as much literary real estate as the description of his external actions. Crane uses a narrative voice-over to reveal what makes Henry tick, rather than relying on his immature braggadocio as the novel opens or his grandiose proclamation at the end when he says, "He had been to touch the great death, and found that, after all, it was but the great death. He was a man." Henry's journey is fraught with seismic shifts in who he sees himself to be—bold and courageous or scared and uncertain—and we simultaneously assess him critically or sympathetically in return.

By its very nature, war works against the human instinct for survival, and Henry's emotional vacillations demonstrate his own interior battles. Will he be a man and risk death, or will he run and save himself? The epic poetry from ancient Greece and Rome boasts of warriors' bravery, and Roman poet Horace made famous the phrase "*Dolce et decorum est, pro patria mori*," an idea later grandly rejected by World War I poet Wilfred Owen, who calls it "the old lie." His emotionally charged poetic imagery urges potential soldiers and their countries of origin to embrace the reality that it is not sweet and honorable to die for one's fatherland. It is slaughter on a grand scale. Crane, Tolstoy, and other nineteenth-century writers began questioning the frenzied rhetoric of propaganda used to dupe young men like Henry. Ernest Hemingway in his own war/antiwar novel *A Farewell to Arms* builds upon Crane's critique of propagandistic power when his soldier, Frederic Henry, reflects: "Abstract words such as glory, honor, courage, or hallow were obscene," because they hold manipulative power with potentially deadly consequences. Frederick (Henry) Fleming, names too similar to be accidental, meld into one symbolic soldier representing all the young men who will fall headlong into this trap and volunteer to fight.

Henry feigns frustration that his troop isn't immediately engaged in bloody conflict, and he questions comrades about how they will respond to action. In doing so he reveals to the reader, if to no one else, his fear of being seen as a coward. When he does run as the first skirmish gets tough, he rationalizes his response as appropriate by noticing that hurling a pinecone at a squirrel causes the animal to flee—an action followed by an expected reaction. In this way he justifies his sense of nature's plan for self-preservation. On the other hand, when circumstances push him toward an act viewed as brave, even foolhardy, as he pries the flag from the dead flag bearer's hands and charges forward, he is propelled by innate response more than choice. Both actions demonstrate that Henry is hostage to circumstances. One isn't any truer than the other, and his supposed cowardice and bravery are mere results of the pressures bubbling up at the moment, not conscious acts.

Henry's experience will also deconstruct romanticized views about being killed or wounded. He longs for a red badge, an injury that would signify his heroism, but the posture of a dead soldier he comes upon in the woods undermines such glory. It isn't blood or a gaping wound that Henry notices; it's the dehumanizing ants that scurry across the dead man's face. When he does incur a wound, it has false merit because he acquires it by being hit with a rifle butt of another fleeing soldier, and Henry is simply in his path. There is no honor or glory in this marker, just simple shame. But again, Henry can excuse himself because "he had performed his mistakes in the dark, so he was still a man." In a later published short story, "The Veteran," Fleming is back as an old man who admits to his grandson about the war, "You bet I was afraid," which disappoints the boy. Later the barn catches fire and the old soldier dies trying to rescue the horses. Crane continues to underscore the opposition between self-preservation and bravery.

In a simple poem from his collection *War Is Kind*, Crane sums up what Henry struggles to learn: "A man said to the universe: 'Sir, I exist!' 'However,' replied the universe, 'the fact has not created in me a sense of obligation.'" Henry is important to himself, not to a grand and impersonal nature and certainly not to the construct of war. This legacy of reconsidering lofty ideals abruptly butted against war's threat to individual sanctity ties itself to many of the compelling war novels to follow. In addition to Hemingway's noted work, *All Quiet on the Western Front*, *Catch -22*, *Slaughterhouse-Five*, *The Naked and the Dead*, and *If I Should Die in a Combat Zone*, to name some of the most noted ones, all add their own poignancy about what it means to be like Henry Fleming, wanting to be a man in society's eyes yet wanting to preserve himself against war's bad odds.

Bibliography

The Red Badge of Courage: An Episode of the American War (1895)

Works Cited

Crane, Stephen. *The Red Badge of Courage & "The Veteran."* Modern Library Classics, 2000.
———. *War Is Kind and Other Lines.* New York: Frederick A. Stokes, 1899.
Hemingway, Ernest. *A Farewell to Arms.* Scribner, 1929.
Owen, Wilfred. *The Collected Poems of Wilfred Owen.* New York: New Directions, 1965.

—GS

FRANKENSTEIN'S CREATURE

First Appearance: *Frankenstein, or The Modern Prometheus*
Date of First Appearance: 1818
Author: Mary Shelley (1797–1851)

I am malicious because I am miserable. Am I not shunned and hated by all mankind? You, my creator, would tear me to pieces and triumph; remember that, and tell me why I should pity man more than he pities me? You would not call it murder if you could precipitate me into one of those ice-rifts and destroy my frame, the work of your own hands. Shall I respect man when he condemns me? Let him live with me in the interchange of kindness, and instead of injury I would bestow every benefit upon him with tears of gratitude at his acceptance. But that cannot be; the human senses are insurmountable barriers to our union. Yet mine shall not be the submission of abject slavery.

His face—at least the one Hollywood gave him in 1931 in his most enduring incarnation—is so instantly recognizable that we often forget he doesn't have a name. Out of convenience audiences refer to him by his maker's distinctly German surname, which was borrowed from a real-life castle overlooking the city of Darmstadt in the Odenwald Mountains. Throughout the novel that spawned him, however, he is simply known as "the fiend," "the ogre," "the daemon," "the devil," and even "the vile insect." Those scared by him are apt to call him Frankenstein's Monster; those who feel sorry for him, viewing him as a cautionary tale of science run amuck, refer to him as Frankenstein's Creature.

Whatever he's dubbed, he's always spoken of as less than human, as bestial, even though he is stitched together from body parts reanimated through the supernatural art of alchemy. Described as hideous and deformed, he is a figure of profound sorrow, suffering from isolation and loneliness. As much terror as he inspires in anyone unlucky enough to gaze upon him, he symbolizes the anguish of being vilified and ostracized—an anguish that hardens into rage and a vow of revenge against the man who invented and then abandoned him. "I ought to be thy Adam," he tells his creator. "But I am rather the fallen angel, whom thou drivest from joy for no misdeed."

The story of how Mary Shelley was inspired to write *Frankenstein, or The Modern Prometheus*, her debut novel, published when she was all of twenty years old, is almost as famous as the story of Dr. Victor Frankenstein and his much-maligned monster. In June 1816, the then Mary Godwin and her lover and future husband, the Romantic poet Percy Shelley, were summering outside of Geneva, Switzerland, when their mercurial celebrity companion, Lord Byron, suggested a competition to test who could produce the best ghost story. While others abandoned the contest, Shelley claimed a dream came to her in which a "pale student" of the "unhallowed arts" tried to flee a horrific creature he invented. The novel, published anonymously in early 1818, combined elements of the gothic, with its emphasis on irrational, supernatural events, with tales of Romantic rebels who, like the mythological Prometheus or Faust, flaunted the limitations of human knowledge pursuing divine power.

What made Shelley's tale especially contemporary was Dr. Frankenstein's use of laboratory science to create a new life form. In particular, her hero employs chemically generated electricity, or what was known as "galvanism" (a peculiar fascination of Percy Shelley's that led some critics to assume he and not Mary wrote the novel). Unusually graphic in its violence, the novel drew the attention of dramatists who quickly staged adaptations, intrigued by the melodramatic spectacle of depicting the occult. The popularity in London of Richard Brinsley Peake's *Presumption, or The Fate of Frankenstein* in 1823—the first version to feature the famous line "It lives!"—led to Shelley publishing a second edition of the book under her name. She revised the novel in 1831, cutting much of the philosophizing and making Victor Frankenstein more of a villain than a tragic hero to appeal to a wider audience disturbed by the radical morbidity. Critics have debated ever since which version is superior.

In Peake's dramatization, the actor portraying "————" (as the unnamed creature was credited) painted his face green, his body blue, and donned a toga, associating the "beast" with Third World "primitives." By the end of the nineteenth century, Frankenstein's monster was specifically costumed as an African. In America, both before and after the Civil War, political cartoons often rendered him as a menacing black man. In other instances, he was portrayed as an immigrant, whether as Irish or "Mongolian" (because of Shelley's description of his "yellow skin"). As such associations reveal, the creature has always been a metaphor. At various points the violence he unleashes in Dr. Frankenstein's world has been interpreted as a symbol of the French Revolution, of slave and labor uprisings, and even of socialism. His ability to function as an allegory of historical change did not end in 1931 when makeup artist Jack Pierce collaborated with Boris Karloff to fix the creature's features into its most famous form for James Whale's movie adaptation; the movie Frankenstein's flat head, green skin, and neck bolts have all been interpreted as eugenicists' view of the feebleminded, devolved lower classes.

Two things usually surprise readers who discover Shelley's novel only after watching Karloff's three portrayals of the creature, or subsequent ones by Lon Chaney Jr. and Bela Lugosi—or even any of the innumerable parodies that riff on Pierce's makeup, such as *The Munsters* TV show (1964–1966) or Mel Brooks's *Young Frankenstein* (1974), where, of course, the name is pronounced "Fronk-en-steen." The first striking aspect is that the original *Frankenstein* is a frame narrative cast in the form of an epistolary novel. In letters home to his sister, explorer Captain Robert Walton describes rescuing a nearly frozen Victor Frankenstein from an ice floe on an expedition to the North Pole. Dr. Frankenstein narrates his family background and academic studies in detail; not until chapter 5 do we actually glimpse the creature's translucent yellow skin, which barely covers the muscles and arteries of its eight-foot frame, or its straight black lips.

Rather than watch the creature rise and terrorize the countryside, though, we listen to the doctor recount how he fled in terror, only to return later to discover the daemon has fled. We also learn of the murder of Victor's brother, William, and the execution of his nanny, Justine, who Frankenstein is convinced the creature has framed to punish him. Not until chapter 10 do we actually encounter the monster, at which point the drama feels so flat we may not appreciate the real shock:

It not only lives—it speaks!

In the King's English, the creature describes how it learned language by eavesdropping on a poor family. It also notes the influential books it read. But the real pathos begins when the "wretch" sees his reflection in a pool and is shocked by his own hideousness. Knowing society will never accept him, the creature demands Dr. Frankenstein create him a mate so he won't spend his existence in solitude. When his maker initially refuses, the monster swears vengeance: "If I cannot inspire love, I will cause fear, and chiefly towards you my archenemy, because my creator, do I swear inextinguishable hatred."

Giving the creature a voice, Shelley made him a version of Lucifer from Milton's *Paradise Lost*, a child cast into the wilderness without love or protection, cursing the creator who abandoned him. The subsequent plot, in which the doctor briefly attempts to create a companion to protect his loved ones, only to change his mind for fear of destroying the human race, is suspenseful enough. True to his promise, the creature ruins Frankenstein's life by killing his best friend, Clerval, and his fiancée, Elizabeth. In many ways, though, its greatest tragedy is outliving the creator who dies trying to destroy his own invention. In our last glimpse of the creature, it floats away from Walton's ship, a figure of infinite solitude who can no longer bide its time until death for resenting ever being born.

"Even that enemy of God and man"—Lucifer—"had friends and associates in his desolation," the creature mourns. "I am alone."

Bibliography

Frankenstein, or The Modern Prometheus (1818)

—KC

G

DOROTHY GALE

First Appearance: *The Wonderful Wizard of Oz*
Date of First Appearance: 1900
Author: L. Frank Baum (1856–1919)

"Where is Kansas?" asked the man, in surprise.

"I don't know," replied Dorothy, sorrowfully; "but it is my home, and I'm sure it's somewhere."

Books sometimes become eclipsed by the popularity of the films they inspire, but that isn't how it started for L. Frank Baum's *The Wonderful Wizard of Oz*, the first in a prolific series of novels that continued with thirteen sequels written by the author, nineteen more created by a writer hired after his death, and even more by other authors beyond that. Harry Potter apparently has nothing on Dorothy for popularity in her day. While most of these *Oz* editions have been relegated to the dusty shelves of neglect, the original story of Dorothy Gale's journey lives on, even if best known by the current citizenry through the still widely popular 1939 film version featuring Judy Garland's star-making performance. The film owes much of its success to the imaginative story line and cast of characters Baum created, and in spite of the title that seems to indicate a wizard as the protagonist, it is really Dorothy, a teenage orphan from Kansas, who takes center stage. She and her little dog, Toto, join an oddball collection of friends—a lion, a scarecrow, and a tin woodman—for a fanciful journey away from an uneventful life on the farm to an alternate universe where Dorothy finds obstacles she must conquer and a great white male at the end of the road to help her find the way home. Wouldn't you know, though, it's really a good female witch, some magic slippers (what's with the shoes in children's stories?), and Dorothy's own powers that do the trick.

Both the novel and the film use a tornado as the vehicle that propels Dorothy away from the drab, windswept plains of her Kansas home to a Technicolor landscape with a yellow brick road running through it. While at times she feels lost and frightened, and who wouldn't with all those weird creatures and a bad witch on the loose, Dorothy is a spunky girl who isn't afraid to speak up for herself when she feels threatened or needs to protect her friends. In fact, though the original book doesn't offer a last name, Baum created one for the 1902 spin-off Broadway play and uses it as a pun when she introduces herself by saying, "I am Dorothy, and I am one of the Kansas Gales," to which the Scarecrow replies, "That accounts for your breezy manner." It is Dorothy's manner and determination that carries the menagerie of characters through the dangers of their journey to find what they are missing—courage, a heart, and a brain—the traits Dorothy has in full measure.

Baum noted that *The Adventures of Alice in Wonderland* served as inspiration for his own children's book, and comparisons are easy to draw. Beyond title similarity and the perhaps coincidental wardrobe choice of a blue-and-white dress, Alice and Dorothy both have strong personalities, and they both enter a magical land with talking animals and other oddities. Each novel was clearly designed for a children's audience, was immediately and enormously popular, and spawned countless retellings of the story through related books and remakes in cartoon animation, live action, television, and film over the more than a century since each appeared in print.

Sadly, each also suffers from a critical need to take the joy out of simple childhood amusement by digging for hidden adult-world themes that relegate the discussion to intellectual tedium rather than amusement: Oz as a metaphor for rising populism of the time, the yellow brick road as a symbol of the monetary gold standard, Dorothy's silver shoes—the color they were in the novel—as a representation of free silver monetization, the forest as the quagmire depicting deep-seated emotional trauma, and the journey in its totality as an epic battle between good and evil. Can't a yellow brick road sometimes just be an attempt to add a pop of color to boring blacktop? Never mind morals to the story; sometimes we want a road just to be a road so we can read our bedtime story and go to sleep. (Not so much with the movie. The part with the witch in the castle is still scary.)

Having denigrated the idea that children's stories must have a higher pedagogical purpose, the novel does have something important to teach. Dorothy is a strong role model in an age when girls were trained to defer to men to solve their problems, to save the day, and then to make them princesses—really, by that we mean wives, mothers, and chief cooks and bottle washers. Instead, Dorothy is in charge of three males of various species or nonspecies, four if you count Toto, who seems to be male too. She leads them through the forest, the sleep-inducing poppy field, and a host of other roadblocks in their episodic travels. And it is Dorothy who heads the charge against the Wicked Witch of the West and her minions of winged monkeys and succeeds in melting her into oblivion with a pail of water. In doing so, Dorothy fulfills the Wizard's demand before he will fulfill (fail to fulfill) their request to help them get home.

Dorothy is yet another in the line of literary orphans who rise to the challenge of a world filled with danger, uncertainty, and disappointment, and Ralph Waldo Emerson's call for self-reliance isn't lost on her. The magic shoes the Good Witch of the North encourages Dorothy to take from off the feet of the dead witch Dorothy's house has landed on become a sort of talisman used to access her own power. But it is the ensemble experience that becomes the heart and soul of the journey with Dorothy leading the search on both the literal path and the figurative one. She realizes the need for a symbolic home found through community with others, and it is the comradery she shares with the Lion, the Tin Woodman, and the Scarecrow as they overcome obstacles along the way that is the true gift Dorothy finds—the value of home the heart seeks.

Dorothy Gale's story is as popular and as ingrained in the culture today as it was in 1900. A contemporary revisionist makeover, Broadway's *Wicked*, has expanded the arms of community to include the evil witch in the circle of empathy, and *The Wiz: The Super Soul Musical* had earlier shown that the story isn't just about white people from Kansas anymore. But from whatever angle the story is told, *The Wonderful Wizard of Oz* has become a lasting part of the culture, and the film has added its own cult iconography. Dorothy's sequined ruby-red shoes, called "the holy grail of Hollywood memorabilia," were recently recovered after being missing for more than a decade, and their value is now estimated at potential millions. Now those are some magical shoes!

Though L. Frank Baum was said to have created so many sequels to Dorothy's story in order to keep financially afloat, *The Wonderful Wizard of Oz* was a gold mine in the ways that really count. Dorothy's adventure remains a lasting icon of childhood fantasy tales and a wonderfully entertaining read.

Bibliography

The Wonderful Wizard of Oz (1900)
The Marvelous Land of Oz (1904)
Ozma of Oz (1907)
Dorothy and the Wizard of Oz (1908)
The Road to Oz (1909)
The Emerald City of Oz (1910)
The Patchwork Girl of Oz (1913)
Tik-Tok of Oz (1914)
The Scarecrow of Oz (1915)
Rinkitink in Oz (1916)
The Lost Princess of Oz (1917)
The Tin Woodman of Oz (1918)
The Magic of Oz (1919)
Glinda of Oz (1920)

Works Cited

Brown, William F., playwright. *The Wiz: The Super Soul Musical*. Music and lyrics by Charlie Smalls. First performance, Morris A. Mechanic Theatre, Baltimore, October 21, 1977.

Holzman, Winnie, playwright. *Wicked*. Music and lyrics by Stephen Schwartz. First performance, Curran Theatre, San Francisco, May 28, 2003.

Karnowski, Steven. "Sting Operation Recovered Dorothy's Stolen Ruby Slippers." Associated Press, September 4, 2018.

—GS

T. S. GARP

First Appearance: *The World according to Garp*
Date of First Appearance: 1978
Author: John Irving (1942–)

You only grow by coming to the end of something and by beginning something else.

The World according to Garp was the novel that brought John Irving fame, a cult hit that put him on the covers of national magazines and sparked a "Believe in Garp" movement. With the novel, Irving bucked a cultural trend. As a writer for *Rolling Stone* noted, "Most Seventies fiction has been about disengagement; *Garp* is about engagement, with ordinary life, family life, public life, over the long haul, even if its characters are the sort of folk who would, were life to allow it, prefer to keep to themselves." The episodic novel is a pre-cradle-to-grave story that tracks Garp from his school days through postgrad travel in Europe to his less-than-perfect marriage and years trying to make it as a writer.

"T. S." stands for "Technical Sergeant," and Garp is the last name of the incapacitated ball turret gunner that nurse Jenny Fields, who wanted a child but "as little to do with a peter as possible," mounted without his consent. Ironically, the woman who would go on to become a famous feminist icon essentially raped a dying man in order to conceive. But Garp's story really begins when his mother takes a live-in nursing job at an all-boys prep school so her son can get a good education. That's when we begin to see his struggle to navigate the considerable wake she leaves. Garp is the story of a fatherless male trying to find his identity, a celebrity's child trying to push out from under the shadow of a parent, and a man trying to balance career and domestic life. But Irving is pretty clear about what's admirable in his protagonist: "Garp was a kind of heroic survivor."

As a youngster, Garp is as naïve as he is eager to embrace life. When he goes after a pigeon on the school roof with a lacrosse stick and gets trapped in a gutter in the pouring rain, his mother climbs right out there after him. "Mom?" he says. "Don't let go." And she doesn't—for more than a decade. When Garp decides to become a writer and pens a short story every month while at Steering School, where he is a champion wrestler, Mom decides she's also going to write. When graduation gets closer and Garp says he's thinking of going to Europe, Mom announces she's going with him. The day he graduates and is looking forward to celebrating, before he can ask to go out with friends she buys him beer and says, "Go ahead and get drunk if you want to." Garp responds, "Jesus, Mom," yet drinks with her anyway in their infirmary wing apartment, wondering if *everything* will be this anticlimactic. Even in Europe, his mother, writing a feminist account of her life without men, "cramps" her son's style. They go to a red-light district in Vienna, where Jenny wants to talk with a hooker about lust. Garp, who speaks German, interprets while they haggle over price. After an hour of translating, Garp is startled when his mother asks if he wants the hooker. Well, yes, he says, and she gives him the money. Yet she gets angry with him when he seems to know that she got a good price. That pretty much sums up the tension that Garp feels as well, some of it inherently inherited contradictions and some of it the result of a clash between his sympathetic feminism and a male libido strong enough to drive him to seduce girls and women . . . then wonder, guiltily, about the thin line that separates rape and seduction.

Garp is an interesting character precisely because he's a walking set of contradictions, with the novel's main conflict the one Garp has with himself. His impatience, quick temper, and simmering resentment often get in the way of empathy, yet he can be warmly human too. When that Viennese hooker becomes ill and is dying, Garp goes to visit her and holds her hand. Stateside, when he's jogging in the park and comes upon a naked ten-year-old girl who's obviously been attacked, he helps the police track down the molester and becomes outraged when the legal system lets the man go. Likewise, while Garp makes fun of the women who have come to live with his mother after her book makes her a feminist icon— Ellen James Society members who have removed their tongues in sympathy for an eleven-year-old who was raped and had her tongue cut out so she could not speak of it—later in life Garp will sit next to the real James on an airplane and become deeply moved and committed to her.

At one point in the novel Garp says that rape has been too much a part of his life, but so have mangled body parts. When he was only five years old he had a chunk of his ear bitten off by the dog of the Percys, a family his mother detested but who made him feel his own uniqueness more than she did. It was why he liked to hang around there. On the night of his graduation, after his mother falls asleep, he goes to the Percy house drunk and looking to have sex with Cushie Percy again. Instead, after seeing the dog, he impulsively executes a wrestling takedown and bites off a huge chunk of the animal's ear. Later, married to his coach's daughter and with two young sons that he's taking care of, Garp returns home with the boys and turns off the headlights before cruising into the driveway "blind," a trick he's often done. But the student his English professor wife is having an affair with has parked in the driveway, and Garp smashes into the car. His youngest son is killed, his oldest son loses an eye, and Garp breaks his jaw and mangles his tongue, ironically aligning him with the James Society women. But the student doesn't get off scot-free. His penis is mostly bitten off during the violent collision that will take years for Garp and his wife, Helen, to put in their past. That night and the dog-ear incident will shape Garp as much as his encounters with feminism and feminists.

Garp wrestles with his attitudes toward "lust" throughout years of sex with girls his own age, his marriage, a strange wife-swapping episode, his adultery with two babysitters, and Helen's affair with a student. But nothing seems to have affected him as much as the encounter with that ten-year-old assault victim he once helped. Because men are naturally lustful, Garp concludes, rape "made men feel guilt by association," so much so that when he next goes to make love to his wife he can't help but think of the "three-pack of condoms nestled patiently in his pocket, coiled like snakes." And he realizes he doesn't want a daughter, "because of *bad* men, certainly; but even, he thought, because of men like *me*." He may be a man, but Garp is also clearly his mother's son. Just as Garp observes that his mom remained a nurse all her life, he's always the wrestler, grappling with his own contradictions.

Bibliography

The World according to Garp (1978)

Work Cited

Marcus, Greil. "The World of 'The World according to Garp' (the *Rolling Stone* Interview with John Irving—12/13/79)." GreilMarcus.net. February 26, 2018. https://greilmarcus .net/2018/02/26/the-world-of-the-world-according-to-garp-interview-with-john -irving-12-13-79/.

—JP

JAY GATSBY

First Appearance: *The Great Gatsby*
Date of First Appearance: 1925
Author: F. Scott Fitzgerald (1896–1940)

Can't repeat the past? Why of course you can!

Countless characters enter the popular consciousness but not many become brand names. The hero of F. Scott Fitzgerald's *The Great Gatsby* radiates such style that his memorable cognomen has been borrowed—often without regard for copyright—for boutiques, bars, clothing lines, hair wax, bedsheets, and even sugar packets. Maybe it's inevitable that a man who wears pink suits and shows off his latest imported-from-England shirts would become a fashion icon. Yet for all the product tie-ins, and for all the Gatsby galas thrown so people who spend their lives trapped in business casual can doll up for an evening as a flapper or slicker, the mysterious millionaire of West Egg, New York, doesn't endure because he embodies elegance. He is, rather, a poignant figure who symbolizes deeply ingrained American contradictions.

To some, Gatsby's tragedy is his innocence and optimism; to others it's his delusions of grandeur and crass fixation with money and possessions. Like most self-made men, he is an inveterate liar who falls victim to his own baloney; others defend him as a victim of class boundaries that aren't supposed to exist in America. At heart he is all of these things, but he'd be none of them if not for what the novel's narrator, Nick Carraway, calls his "limitless capacity for wonder," his insistence that life should be commensurate (a favorite Fitzgerald word) with the imagination's ability to picture it. That makes Gatsby literature's greatest beautiful dreamer, embodying the delicacy but the obduracy of aspiration too.

F. Scott Fitzgerald was born into a fading middle-class family, the son of an unprosperous salesman and an eccentric mother whose money floated the household. As an adolescent in St. Paul, Minnesota, he was acutely aware that his peers were more affluent. Later as a Princeton undergraduate he overheard a family member of his debutante girlfriend Ginevra King say, "Poor boys shouldn't think of marrying rich girls." He never truly recovered from the snub, even reexperiencing that rejection a few years later when Zelda Sayre insisted she couldn't marry a penniless writer. As Fitzgerald's career took off (quickly changing Zelda's mind), his fiction focused on ambitious young men trying to prove themselves worthy of wealthier "golden girls" whose affection granted entry into a world of privilege. Early attempts to tell this tale, like the 1922 story "Winter Dreams," were overly sentimental. At the ripe old age of twenty-seven, eager to produce an enduringly beautiful work, Fitzgerald elevated the scenario with greater nuance and more deliberate craft. The result lent his prototypical hero two arresting qualities his predecessors lacked—mystery and mystique.

So beguiling is Jay Gatsby's charisma that guests swarming the lavish parties he hosts, but only hovers on the periphery of, can't help but gossip about him. Rumors say he was a German spy during the Great War, that his uncle was Baron von Hindenburg, that he is a bootlegger, or that he killed a man. To Nick, Gatsby's every gesture feels rehearsed, right down to his smile. His favorite endearment—"old sport"—is a laughable affectation. The stories he tells about growing up a young rajah come straight out of adventure novels.

Yet no matter how flagrant Gatsby's fibs or how stagy his mannerisms, Nick is fascinated instead of offended. That's because Fitzgerald was writing at a time when American culture was fixated more by personality than character, more by magnetism than by honesty or integrity. Self-help books promoted the idea that anyone could be as interesting as Valentino if they just mastered a few fundamentals of charm or elocution. The difference is, those manuals insisted their advice brought out a real self that was inhibited by society. The curiosity Gatsby generates suggests that audacity bedazzles observers more than authenticity. Everyone partaking of his elaborate pageantry suspects he's pulling a con, but nobody objects—they admire the thoroughness with which he sells his grand illusion. In the end, the only one Gatsby fools is himself, and it brings about his downfall.

The novel's core poignancy is that Gatsby believes in the American dream. That's a thesis hammered into cliché by roughly 1,837,766 student term papers over the decades. Yet no amount of hackneyed interpretation can render Gatsby's unshakable faith in his dream trite while rereading Fitzgerald's elegiac prose. Most famously, *The Great Gatsby* ends with an arresting passage in which Nick recognizes in his friend's romanticism the very essence of the shining city on a hill the American ideal is founded on. The dream is a cat-and-mouse game: The more we fail it, the more we chase it, which is why, as Fitzgerald writes, like Gatsby, America is doomed to paddle headlong into a current that carries it forever back to an origin story that it never once lived up to. A more sardonic writer would have debunked the dream, costing his hero his innocence. Yet one marvel of *Gatsby* is Fitzgerald's generosity in not disillusioning his main character. Right up to the moment he dies, Gatsby believes in that symbolic green light, convinced that the woman whose approval confirms his ability to create himself out of nothing more than the "ineffable gaudiness" of his ambition, Daisy Fay Buchanan, will come back to him.

Instead, he ends up at the bottom of his pool, shot to death by a lowly garage owner after Daisy's vile husband, Tom, convinces the grieving man that Gatsby, not himself, has been having an affair with his wife, and that Gatsby, not Daisy, mowed the poor mistress down when she rushed into the road to run away with her lover amid the ash heaps separating New York City and Long Island. As Nick insists, the rich survive by carelessness and indifference, while dreamers like

Gatsby and Myrtle Wilson, the woman, pay for the ultimate price for believing in limitless possibility.

When *The Great Gatsby* was published, Charles Scribner's Sons marketed it as a satire. Gatsby was a modern-day Trimalchio, his gauche ostentation equating the Roaring Twenties with "the crude, flaming days of the later Roman Empire." Not until after Fitzgerald's premature death in 1940 did the novel become a national touchstone. Fitzgerald wants us, like Nick, to half disapprove, half approve of his hero and of America, too, seeing both as innocently garish and garishly innocent. Adaptations, unfortunately, tend to veer to one extreme or the other. In the two most famous Hollywood versions, Robert Redford (1974) plays Gatsby as a passive blank slate, handsome but postured, while Leonardo DiCaprio (2013) emphasizes his feverish impatience to be accepted. Both also sold *The Great Gatsby* as a love story, which is only true if one tacks "self-" to the front of that description.

Dressed in Fitzgerald's lyrical style, though, Gatsby's self-deception makes him seem as vulnerable as fraudulent, too guileless to even be a patsy of his patron Meyer Wolfsheim's scams. Even if Jay Gatsby is phony to the bone, he's still America's truest believer.

Bibliography

The Great Gatsby (1925)

Work Cited

Fitzgerald, F. Scott. "Winter Dreams." *Metropolitan*, December 1922.

—KC

HOLLY GOLIGHTLY

First Appearance: *Breakfast at Tiffany's* in *Esquire*
Date of First Appearance: November 1958
Author: Truman Capote (1924–1984)

Be anything but a coward, a pretender, an emotional crook, a whore: I'd rather have cancer than a dishonest heart. That's not being pious. Just practical.

Say the name "Holly Golightly" and most audiences picture the perky, waifish Audrey Hepburn in a sleeveless black dress, hair in a high-piled bun adorned with a diamanté, a cigarette holder pinched in the fingers of an elbow-length satin glove. Fictional characters don't often become fashion icons, but thanks to Blake Edwards's classic 1961 romantic comedy, the heroine of *Breakfast at Tiffany's* routinely inspires clothing, jewelry, and makeup lines.

Truman Capote's original 1958 novella is often described as darker than its cinematic counterpart, but that's not the right word: it's coarser. Holly refers to "dykes" and calls a rival a "twat." One of her suitors complains she serves men "horseshit on a platter." In a scene that PETA would likely protest, she abandons a pet cat she refuses to name so she won't get attached to it with an unsentimental farewell: "I said fuck off!"

F-bombs like Holly's were still rare in fiction in the late 1950s. Capote insisted on the profanity even though it meant publishing the story in *Esquire* rather than the far more lucrative *Harper's Bazaar*. Yet he objected when critics called his heroine a call girl, preferring the more euphemistic "geisha," meaning young women unapologetically okay with men paying them "powder-room money" for the pleasure of their company. In this regard, Holly is a descendant of Lorelei Lee in Anita Loos's *Gentlemen Prefer Blondes* (1925), which had recently been a blockbuster Broadway musical and film, the latter starring Capote's friend Marilyn Monroe (whom Capote wanted to play Holly instead of Hepburn). Holly is far more self-aware than Loos's stereotypical dumb blonde, though, even if her suitors, burdened with silly names like Salvatore "Sally" Tomato and Rutherford "Rusty" Trawler, are only slightly more believable than the cartoonish old coots who lust after Lorelei. *Gentlemen Prefer Blondes* is a slapstick farce, but *Breakfast at Tiffany's* made its splash claiming to treat realistically the lifestyle of an emerging class of independent, metropolitan women. As their spokeswoman, Holly Golightly enjoys affairs, travels the world, and even smokes pot at her windowsill singing Kurt Weill, without ever being punished for being a "bad girl." The worst she may suffer, Capote writes, is a restless heart.

As with most iconic American characters, Holly's story is about identity. She's a version of Jay Gatsby, a nobody who capitalizes upon her good looks and social ambition. Capote's unnamed narrator even serves as her Nick Carraway, framing her in an aura of mystery she wouldn't possess if she spoke in the first person. (Unlike the movie's "Paul Varjak," played by George Peppard, Capote's narrator, whom Holly dubs "Fred" after her beloved brother, isn't a romantic suitor—most critics assume he is gay.) As also with Gatsby, Holly's past catches up with her. Midnovella, an old man named Doc Golightly appears, revealing her real name, Lulamae Barnes, and that she's the runaway child bride he married when she was fourteen. If the lesson of *The Great Gatsby* is that we can't transcend our social origins to become whoever we wish we were, *Breakfast at Tiffany's* says just the opposite. Every scrape and setback Holly gets into flows right off her back. She's implicated in a drug ring, gets dumped by a Brazilian fiancé after suffering a miscarriage, and loses her brother to World War II. Yet these plot twists don't derail her American dream. That's because Holly Golightly is what in a later era would be called a "free spirit." The Daisy Buchanan she pursues isn't even a person—she's after fun and adventure. The calling card above her mailbox claims her full name is "Holiday Golightly," her occupation "traveling."

During a party, one of Holly's male patrons, the overcologned Hollywood agent O. J. Berman, dismisses her as "a phony" before quickly correcting himself, insisting she's a "real phony" because she "believes all this crap she believes." The paradox of the "real phony" suggests the possibilities of identity in the mid-twentieth century that made Holly such an appealing character: As self-help literature of the period insisted, we're free to invent ourselves externally as long as we're true to our inner self. *Breakfast at Tiffany's* is chock-full of proclamations making this point, as if Capote were writing a book of proverbs for audacious nonconformists. Holly would rather be "natural" than "normal," insisting society forces us to falsify ourselves in return for safety and security. It's the message of other great literary rebels of the 1950s who aren't quite as fashion conscious, like Jack Kerouac's Dean Moriarty. If Capote hadn't caustically dismissed *On the Road* ("That's not writing, that's typing"), Holly Golightly might've been a member of the Beat generation instead of a "society gal."

But while Capote's great accomplishment is treating Holly with a lightness of both theme and style, that doesn't mean his heroine doesn't pay a price for remaining "unto-thyself" honest. Holly suffers bouts of the "red means," or angst. Her only cure is a trip to Tiffany's, not because diamonds are a girl's best friend but because the luxury store, with its rich smell of silver and alligator-skin wallets, feels like a place where nothing bad could ever happen. If there's a hint of sadness to *Breakfast at Tiffany's*, it's that free spirits may never find that safe space. The story ends on a wistful note as the narrator remembers spotting Holly's cat in a New York City apartment window after Holly abandoned it, looking happy and at home. Not having heard from Holly for more than fifteen years, the narrator can only hope she is too—though his tone implies he doubts it. Settling down would be a self-betrayal.

Unfortunately, Hepburn's iconic portrayal of Holly has overshadowed her more complicated literary inspiration, despite the movie aging badly. (Mickey Rooney's racist caricature of Holly's Japanese neighbor, Mr. Yunioshi, renders it unwatchable at points.) Attempts to update the character usually fare poorly. Neither a 1966 Broadway musical, a 1969 TV pilot, nor two early twenty-first-century stage adaptations proved successful. That's because Holly Golightly belongs to her era as much as she does Hepburn's or even Capote's. She's a creature of that late fifties/early sixties dawn of the sexual revolution when the Pill and Helen Gurley Brown said a single girl was classy if she regarded sex pragmatically instead of romantically. A few decades earlier and she would've been Daisy Miller or Brett Ashley, punished for roaming free. A decade later, she'd be a cautionary tale of late 1960s excesses—like Maria Wyeth in Joan Didion's *Play It as It Lays* (1970), or, even worse, a Manson girl. Such a fate would disappoint what we most love about her.

Her admirers, whether her suitors or her readers, want to believe that no matter where Holly goes, she lands lightly.

Bibliography

Breakfast at Tiffany's (1958)

—KC

H

MISS HAVISHAM

First Appearance: *Great Expectations*
Date of First Appearance: Serialized 1860–1861, published 1861
Author: Charles Dickens (1812–1870)

Ask no questions, and you'll be told no lies.

Charles Dickens created many remarkable males in his repertoire of great characters, though very few females, and *Great Expectations*'s Miss Havisham is a lady readers will never forget. Like the old English nursery rhyme whose famed Diddle, Diddle Dumpling went to bed with one shoe off and one shoe on, Miss Havisham remains for her adult lifetime half-shod and wearing the decayed wedding dress she hasn't undonned since she stopped the clock at the precise moment of her jilting—twenty minutes to nine—on the morning of her pending nuptials. Leaving aside thinking too deeply about the impractical aspects of that choice, the psychological nether regions this calls into play become as fascinating a second thread of the novel as the central one surrounding Pip, the young boy whose expectations we watch unfold through the expanse of this twisting plot. In true Dickensian style, each branch of the interwoven story lines bears interesting fruit, and Miss Havisham is certainly a peach ripe for plucking as a case study in pathological grief and the art of revenge.

The fact that Miss Havisham (Have-a-shame) is essentially bereft of a given first name and is identified only by the nonwedded signifier "Miss" accentuates both the weight society places on females of marriageable age who have failed to become "Mrs. Somebody," and the long-lasting affair with shame and vengeance she will perpetuate in lieu of moving on in a healthy way with the rest of her life. She is indeed frozen in time, an object of complete emotional paralysis who becomes physically bound to the place of her trauma and transfixed in time. When young Pip is summoned to meet Miss Havisham years after the moment of her disgrace, the yellowed and slowly disintegrating bridal gown has more resemblance to a burial shroud than to the apparel that was meant to usher her into wedded bliss. She remains entombed in her equally decaying mausoleum of a family estate appropriately named Satis House. Though the Latin translation of "satis" is "enough" and has its own significant relevance, "stasis" also comes to mind with its hard-to-miss implications.

If Miss Havisham had chosen removing herself from society to wallow privately in grief she would have been a character interesting enough to merit our attention on that quality alone. And we might have even encouraged her to use any energy her ultradepressed state allowed to target the object of her jilting, the man who had wronged her not only through that action but by also absconding with much of her significantly large inheritance. In that act she is doubly duped because her half brother had participated in the swindle with the would-be husband. We might offer sympathy for her plight and say, "You get 'em, Missy!" Instead, we come to find her a truly grotesque figure rather than simply a tragic one because of the diabolic plot she crafts to seek revenge not on the objects of her humiliation but on a blameless next generation. She adopts a young girl named Estella, and as she grows to be a beauty Miss Havisham instructs her to "break their hearts, my pride and hope, break their hearts and have no mercy." In this way, Miss Havisham pays the revenge forward to undeserving innocents and moves from victim to victimizer, from shamed to shameful.

This transformation and the mental anguish causing such untethering from human kindness has made Miss Havisham the enduring figure of curiosity she continues to be. She represents just the type of emotionally stunted, darkly brooding, and gothically twisted figure William Faulkner, a great admirer of Dickens, finds so alluring. At least two of his own fictional females have a clear sisterhood with Dickens's bitter spinster. Like Miss Havisham, Rosa Coldfield in *Absalom, Absalom!* and Miss Emily Grierson in the short story "A Rose for Emily" have both been jilted and suffer their own forms of emotional inertia. But Faulkner takes Miss Havisham's molded wedding cake set out for the reception that was never to be held a step further with Miss Emily. Readers are shocked at the story's end to discover not only the body of the lover she likely murdered to keep from leaving her, but that the bed shows signs of her having lain there with the corpse. Dickens and his Miss Havisham would be impressed!

Carol Ann Duffy, the first female British poet laureate, is also enamored with the concept of Miss Havisham's grief and "love's hate behind a white veil." Her jilted lover in a poem simply titled "Havisham" has "dark green pebbles for eyes," calling up the color often associated with envy or jealous rage and has "ropes on the back of my hands I could strangle with." The persona petitions at the end to "give me a male corpse for a long slow honeymoon," and she reminds the listener, "Don't think it's only the heart that b-b-b-breaks." Duffy captures female rage and resulting insanity so clearly evocative of Dickens's Havisham and other nineteenth-century fictional women and moves the voice to a powerful interior monologue capable of eliciting a deeper, more personal tone to the wrath. The effect is bone-chilling and speaks with a freedom Dickens would certainly have relished.

Dickens must have felt *Great Expectations* was too dark, even for a Victorian novel, so he offered a bit of reprieve for Miss Havisham near the story's sad end. The eternal old maid finally sees the misery her actions have wrought not just for herself, but upon Pip and Estella as the progeny of her revenge. Purged by this awareness, Miss Havisham cries out for Pip to forgive her, which he does, and then, consumed literally by fire and figuratively by guilt, she dies shortly thereafter. In the original ending, however, Dickens pulls the reader back to darkness by momentarily reuniting the couple only to wrench them apart forever. After a friend's protestation, he recants with a second possibility that they meet again, and Pip sees "no shadow of another parting from her." This vague hope remains ambiguous, so Dickens gets his toast and his tea too by satisfying two opposing camps.

Dickens's Miss Havisham has gained what one critic calls the "afterlife of a memorable character." She is indeed unforgettable, and we half want to know and are equally half-horrified by the possibility of a real Miss Havisham molding away out there somewhere. But whether she is based on a real story or not isn't the point. Her case takes on literary transcendence. She may represent our own fears about failure to be loved, a rejection that has lifetime effects no matter if we willfully allow them free play as Miss Havisham did or whether they become powerful subterranean forces. She haunts us for the possibility of what a human soul in conflict with itself might be capable or incapable of bearing. Perhaps Dickens's hope through this dark tale is a cry for the warmth of humanity, not the icy heart Miss Havisham has replaced in her own chest and in Estella's, but for the warm one that is meant to beat there.

Bibliography

Great Expectations (1861)

Works Cited

Duffy, Carol Ann. *Mean Time.* London: Anvil, 1993.
Letissier, Georges. "The Havisham Affair or the Afterlife of a Memorable Fixture." *Études anglaises* 65, no. 1 (2012): 30–42.

—GS

EUGENE HENDERSON

First Appearance: *Henderson the Rain King*
Date of First Appearance: 1959
Author: Saul Bellow (1915–2005)

Society is what beats me. Alone I can be pretty good, but let me go among people and there's the devil to pay.

"Gene" Henderson would seem to have it all. An Ivy Leaguer and millionaire (thanks to inherited money), he's been married to his second wife for twenty years, and she's devoted enough to bail him out when he drinks too much (which is always) and gets into brawls at the country saloons near his hobby farm. A bit of a lazy bum by his own admission, he putters around his pig farm, peruses the books his father left him, waxes philosophical, or, "a little deaf," scratches away at a violin to relieve stress. But now that Henderson is fifty-five he's having one heck of a delayed midlife crisis.

The problem is that Henderson is restless and uneasy, still looking for meaning and hoping to find a cure for his existential angst. He worries that his next coming-of-age will be one where "as the years go by, you're just like other people you have seen, with all those peculiar human ailments." Henderson thinks, "Who wants it? Who needs it? These things occupy the place where a man's soul should be." Plus, he's feeling a bit guilty and needing to get away because during the last fight he had with his wife, the housekeeper suffered a heart attack and died. Henderson pinned a "do not disturb" note on her and impulsively took off for Africa with an old friend—and his bride—on their honeymoon. Later, when Mrs. Newlywed holds a grudge against him for not kissing her at the wedding, he decides to go his own way. He hires a guide named Romilayu and leaves in a jeep they soon abandon in favor of walking.

Henderson tells his own story, and as James Parker writes in a *New York Times* article, what stands out with every reading and rereading is "the ugly-beautiful, slangy, blustery, 'Dream Songs'-jazzy bravado-and-bellyache voice of Henderson"—whose inner voice continues to say, "I want, I want." On the one hand, Henderson is an obvious symbol of affluent ennui and arrogance, but there's also a universal vulnerability as he desperately tries to do something meaningful, only to create a series of mishaps with disastrous results. Henderson may play at life with the same bored restlessness as he tackles other hobbies, but his efforts never seem token because he is so earnest and, when his attempts go comically awry, apologetic.

Even before he leaves for Africa, there's something striking about the image of Henderson standing on a ladder in his library, looking for a quote about self-forgiveness that he remembered seeing in one of his father's books. As he stands on the ladder and pulls book after book off the shelf, shaking them to see if the paper with the quote will fall out, he instead only produces a cascade of dollar bills of various denominations that his father had a habit of using for bookmarks.

At six feet four inches tall and 230 pounds, Henderson is a strong fellow with "an enormous head, rugged, with hair like Persian lambs' fur. Suspicious eyes, usually narrowed. Blustery ways. A great nose." His face, we're told, can seem like "the clang of a bell" because he's hard of hearing on the right side and he has a "way of swinging the left into position." The only survivor of three siblings, he can be moody, rough, cynical, and probably a bit mad. We hear about his second marriage to Lily in some depth, but his narrative is so self-deprecating that it's mostly anecdotes about his misbehavior—as when he fell off a tractor, drunk, and boorishly entered the house as Lily was entertaining. He wiped his nose and mustache with his fingers before saying, "How do you do?" and shaking hands with everyone—including, as a gag, his wife. He could be cruel, too, as when he would threaten to shoot himself, knowing full well how traumatized Lily was that her father took his life using a gun. But the thing of it is, Henderson *knows* he's a louse, and a part of him needs to go to Africa because he's convinced that there he can do something to somehow atone for all the rotten things he's done or make up for his lost dream of becoming a doctor. At the very least, he hopes the Africa trip will help him keep death at bay.

"Africa reached my feelings right away even in the air, from which it looked like the ancient bed of mankind," says Henderson, who soon after embarking on his epic walkabout has two tribal encounters. When he meets the fictional cattle-raising Arnewi they are in the midst of a serious drought. Henderson's first impulse is to give the children a treat, as he did in Italy during World War II. Lacking that, with a First World audacity he pulls out his lighter and sets a bush on fire. Rather than gasping in wonder, the people, led by a girl, all cry . . . which he interprets as a cry for help. "I feel it. Maybe a lion has eaten her family? Are there man-eaters around here? Ask her, Romilayu. Say that I've come to help."

It was another display of white arrogance, but again Henderson can't help himself. That's one of the things that make him so interesting. He says and does completely inappropriate things, yet he continues to be aware that he's behaving badly. After the burning bush incident, he acts godlike as Conrad's Lord Jim until he meets King Itelo and thinks, "Here was someone who obviously had been around, as he spoke English, and I had been boasting . . . and setting bushes on fire . . . and making like a regular clown." Henderson, who says he's so fierce that even his pigs are afraid of him, ends up wrestling Itelo and gains the tribe's respect. But then he persuades Itelo to let him try to solve their water problem. They can't use the water from the village cistern because it's been taken over by frogs. Henderson's solution? Gunpowder, which unfortunately blows up the entire cistern, releasing the reservoir despite Henderson's comic efforts to serve as a human dam. An equally comic melodrama follows as Henderson tells Itelo, "Stab me . . . and don't forgive me. I couldn't stand it. I'd rather be dead." When he offers to repair the cistern he's told, "Bettah you not, sir" and asked to leave the village.

Henderson has better luck with the Wariri, whom he first scoffs at because they are smaller and shorter than the Arnewi. But here, in another drought-plagued land, he acquires his name—Sungo, the Rain King—after he asks King Dahfu to allow him to relocate a heavy wooden statue of the cloud goddess, and shortly thereafter it actually rains. Thanks to Dahfu, he finally appears to grow and approach that elusive something he's been looking for—which is symbolically proven after he's elevated to king following Dahfu's death, and, knowing it was sabotage and not trusting the Wariri, he heads home with a lion cub that the Wariri believe contains the soul of his friend. And he tells Romilayu, "Where I go he goes." It was his only baggage, now.

Bibliography

Henderson the Rain King (1959)

Work Cited

Parker, James, and Francine Prose. "Bookends: What's It Like Reading Saul Bellow's 'Henderson the Rain King' Today?" *New York Times*, April 28, 2015. https://www.nytimes.com/2015/05/03/books/review/whats-it-like-reading-saul-bellows-henderson-the-rain-king-today.html.

—JP

SHERLOCK HOLMES

First Appearance: *A Study in Scarlet* in *Beeton's Christmas Annual*
Date of First Appearance: December 1887
Author: Arthur Conan Doyle (1859–1930)

My life is spent in one long effort to escape from the commonplaces of existence—these little problems help me to do so.

"Elementary, my dear Watson."

People who know nothing else about Sherlock Holmes seem to know that catchphrase and the way the famous detective, who routinely outdeduced Scotland Yard, would begin to explain his thought process to companion Dr. John Watson. But the phrase never appeared in any of the four novels or fifty-six short stories featuring Holmes. Basil Rathbone uttered that catchphrase in *The Adventures of Sherlock Holmes* (1939), and it became a part of the detective's lingo and legend.

Edgar Allan Poe may have established the genre with Detective Dupin in "The Murders in the Rue Morgue" (1841), but it was Arthur Conan Doyle who created the world's most celebrated sleuth—a brainy logician who, Chloe Fox says, according to *Guinness World Records*, is the "most portrayed movie character" of all time. Some seventy actors have played him in more than 200 films, with the most enduring performances coming from Rathbone between 1939 and 1946 and Robert Downey Jr. playing the character more recently in tongue-in-cheek action films. Disney even got into the act with *The Great Mouse Detective*, in which an animated rodent version matches wits with archenemy Professor Ratigan, who is clearly a variation of Holmes's nemesis, Professor Moriarty.

In the fiction, Holmes famously resides at 221B Baker Street, and in an early version he was called Sherrinford Holmes, while his sidekick was Ormond Sacker. That early draft laid the groundwork for the sophisticated and scientific-minded Holmes, whom many suspect was named for one of Doyle's favorite writers, Oliver Wendell Holmes. Holmes was described as a philosopher and collector of rare violins who had access to his own chemical laboratory. Biographer Russell Miller traces the character's roots to the University of Edinburgh Medical School, where Doyle as a student encountered a celebrated professor known as "a master of observation, logic and deduction, possessing almost clairvoyant powers of diagnoses." And Dr. Joseph Bell's physical characteristics match the description Doyle offers for Holmes in the debut novel, *A Study in Scarlet* (1887). Like Bell, Holmes is tall and lean with piercing eyes, a hawk nose, square chin, and hands "blotted with ink and stained with chemicals." In this first mystery, Holmes is further described as "a little queer in his ideas—an enthusiast in some branches of science" who had invented a microscopic test to distinguish new blood from old. That interest in better crime solving through chemistry would lead to his becoming the only fictional character to receive a fellowship from the Royal Society of Chemistry. It also made him hugely popular. As Miller explains, "The superhero of the Victorian era, a knight errant with Watson as his Sancho Panza, Holmes appeared on the scene" when science "was the new obsession and Holmes was the embodiment of scientific investigations." His eccentricities also endear him to readers, who must smile every time he affixes a letter to his mantelpiece with a pocketknife or pulls tobacco from the Turkish slipper in which it was stored.

Readers learn about Holmes through Watson, who is introduced by a mutual friend as a possible roommate, and the two hit it off. Holmes is, according to Watson, "not a difficult man to live with . . . quiet in his ways, and his habits were regular." Usually in bed by 10:00 p.m. and already working at the lab before Watson awakes each morning, Holmes mostly interacts with Watson when he's working on a case. Watson is "stimulated" by his curiosity for the extraordinary Holmes, and the more he tags along and engages with Holmes, the more his "respect for his powers of analysis increased wondrously."

Holmes demonstrates a parlor-trick level of observation and deduction upon first meeting Watson, remarking, "You have been in Afghanistan, I perceive." Astonished, Watson counters, "How on earth did you know?" It was the way he held his arm, the result of a wound gotten while serving in the army medical corps. That near-sideshow level of observation and deduction has entertained generations throughout the years.

"You remind me of Edgar Allan Poe's Dupin," remarks Watson, who becomes not only Holmes's friend but his biographer as well. "I had no idea that such individuals did exist outside of stories." From the beginning, the Holmes stories were presented to readers as the "reminiscences of John H. Watson, late of the army medical department"—no doubt one reason why so many readers think of him as a real person. Of the 400 Sherlock Holmes societies that exist worldwide, some are dedicated to playing the Holmes game, of trying to verify biographical details to confirm he's real. "Now in my opinion," Holmes replies, "Dupin was a very inferior fellow. That trick of his breaking in on his friends' thoughts with an apropos remark after a quarter of an hour's silence is really very showy and superficial. He had some analytic genius, no doubt; but he was by no means such a phenomenon as Poe appeared to imagine." That dismissal may seem like a criticism, but it's Doyle's way of acknowledging a debt while also trying to set Holmes apart from "regular" police detectives. In fact, some fans and scholars believe that's why Doyle has his hero using cocaine, which was legal in Victorian England.

Many readers have gotten their impressions of Victorian and Edwardian England through Holmes, vicariously navigating the misty streets of London with him as he solves cases for clients ranging from monarchs and governments to lowly tradesmen and governesses. Holmes's last adventure was published twelve years before the British government created its "Keep Calm and Carry On" campaign, but if he were yet alive he could have been the poster child. The epitome of steadiness, after both men bring down a dangerous murderer by simultaneously shooting at him, Holmes notices a poisonous dart that had barely missed them. Watson tells readers, "Holmes smiled at it and shrugged his shoulders in his easy fashion, but I confess that it turned me sick to think of the horrible death which had passed so close to us that night."

Holmes and Watson often carried service pistols, and Holmes, a master of disguises with above-average strength, is an expert bare-knuckle boxer who knows enough jujitsu to combine the forms into a version he calls "baritsu." A proper gentleman, Holmes also carries a cane, which he uses when necessary, since he is an expert fencer. But it's his brain that people most remember and celebrate.

Holmes has "an extraordinary genius for minutiae," Watson observes, and readers find his breadth of knowledge entertaining, even though, as biographers point out, there are many inaccuracies. "It is very customary for pawnbrokers in England, when they take a watch, to scratch the numbers of the ticket with a pin-point upon the inside of a case," Holmes declares, his mind already racing forward. Watson, representing the reader's point of view, will be the first to admit he finds it hard to keep up, after which Holmes will say something like, "I hardly expected that you would. Let me see if I can make it clearer." Though a visit to the Sherlock Holmes Museum on Baker Street would be fun, for most fans, just trying to keep up with Holmes in print is pleasure enough.

Bibliography

A Study in Scarlet (1887)
The Sign of the Four (1890)
The Adventures of Sherlock Holmes (1892)
The Memoirs of Sherlock Holmes (1894)
The Hound of the Baskervilles (1901–1902)
The Return of Sherlock Holmes (1905)
His Last Bow: Some Reminiscences of Sherlock Holmes (1917)
The Case-Book of Sherlock Holmes (1927)
The Complete Sherlock Holmes (1930)

Works Cited

Fox, Chloe. "Sherlock Holmes: Pipe Dreams." *Telegraph*, December 15, 2009. https://www.telegraph.co.uk/culture/film/6789921/Sherlock-Holmes-pipe-dreams.html.

Lycett, Andrew. *The Man Who Created Sherlock Holmes: The Life and Times of Sir Arthur Conan Doyle*. New York: Free Press, 2007.

Miller, Russell. *The Adventures of Arthur Conan Doyle: A Biography*. New York: Thomas Dunne Books, 2008.

—JP

HUMBERT HUMBERT

First Appearance: *Lolita*
Date of First Appearance: 1955
Author: Vladimir Nabokov (1899–1977)

I touched her hot, opening lips with the utmost piety, tiny sips, nothing salacious; but she, with an impatient wriggle, pressed her mouth to mine so hard that I felt her big front teeth and shared in the peppermint taste of her saliva.

He's the most memorable character we wish we could forget: an eloquent, funny narrator whose words must be resisted rather than enjoyed, lest we find ourselves seduced by his wit and the pathos of his self-contempt and fail to realize that behind his tribute to the "aurochs and angels" of art's transcendent beauty lurk the evasions of the most odious sort of criminal: the pedophile. He's Humbert Humbert, the voice of Vladimir Nabokov's *Lolita*, a novel that tests our ability not to fall for the two most knee-jerk reactions a character can provoke in a reader: to be repulsed and to feel empathy.

Of course, *Lolita* exploits other desires audiences may seek in literature. On one level, this "confession of a white widowed male"—a subtitle meant to evoke 1950s pulp exploitation paperbacks—appeals to the "low" urge for pornography. This was a desire, admittedly, much harder to gratify in Nabokov's era when explicit rutting wasn't a computer click away. But enticing tawdry appetites is part of the joke of *Lolita*. Humbert takes nearly 130 pages to reach the moment he has his way with his twelve-year-old stepdaughter Dolores Haze in room 342 of the Enchanted Hunters hotel: "By six she was wide awake," he anticlimactically reports, "and by six fifteen we were technically lovers." At the same time, the novel is equally contemptuous of dressing up these illicit desires in literary language. Humbert Humbert may drop big words such as "callypygean" or "olisbos"—fancy terms for shapely buttocks and dildo, respectively—but he never explains his degeneracy more clearly than when describing Lolita's reaction to the assault: "She started complaining of pains, said she could not sit, said I had torn something inside of her."

Lolita is at heart about coercion and resistance—and, despite its subject matter, the struggle over consent is more rhetorical than sexual. (Legally, after all, there is no such thing as consent with a twelve-year-old.) Humbert's inability to accept responsibility for his actions begins with writing under a pseudonym, even though he's in jail, charged with murdering another of the girl's abusers, his real name presumably a matter of public record. He describes being hospitalized for madness, hoping readers will view his predilection as mental illness. At other times "H. H." wants us to believe he's a naïve romantic who fell prey to an emotionally obtuse preteenager who couldn't appreciate the danger her blossoming sexuality put them both in. He refuses to use the word "pedophilia" to describe his condition, preferring "nympholepsy," and calls upon poetic precedent to justify his pathology, citing Dante, Petrarch, and Edgar Allan Poe as artists who, like him, were sophisticated enough to appreciate the mix of innocence and vulgarity that nymphets radiate. He even turns to Freud for an answer, explaining that at fourteen he was on the verge of losing his virginity with his first love (whom he dubs, after Poe, Annabel) when they were interrupted, leaving him attempting to consummate that relationship deep into adulthood.

But perhaps Humbert Humbert's most subtle weapon of coercion is his self-loathing. Throughout the story, this European émigré deprecates his pretensions as much as he turns down his nose at American crassness, even portraying himself as a comic dupe. He claims to hate himself for despoiling Lolita, insisting if he were his own judge he would sentence himself to thirty-six years in prison for statutory rape (though none for murder). Yet his humor and self-hatred are really a front for the point he most wants to persuade us of: Even if he hurt Lolita, he can make amends by immortalizing her in art.

Think of *Lolita* as the greatest tragicomedy ever about molestation, and the challenge of getting a bead on Nabokov's notoriously misunderstood novel becomes apparent. The subject matter was so offensive that initially no American publisher would touch the book; it first appeared under the aegis of Paris's Olympia Press, an imprint known for erotica and avant-garde nose thumbing. Three years later, when Putnam's released the first American edition, it sold 100,000 copies in three weeks on the strength of its "indecent" reputation. The name "Lolita" quickly became an unfortunate synonym for jailbait precocity and ingénue allure, with decades of paperbacks featuring cover images of young women suggestively licking lollipops or applying lipstick to their parted lips. (Most of these tableaux were inspired by the poster for Stanley Kubrick's 1962 relatively chaste movie adaptation rather than the novel itself.)

Humbert Humbert, meanwhile, became a byword for any middle-aged man's attraction to forbidden virginal fruit. Readers have had a hard time separating the narrator from his creator—not because Humbert's longings were in any way autobiographical (far from it) but because his language is so Nabokovian, tessellated with allusions, puns, and leitmotifs. The great challenge of reading *Lolita* is admiring and enjoying its aesthetic brilliance while recognizing that Humbert's use of those very same tools is pure evasion.

Humbert enters Lolita's life in May 1947 when he rents a room from the child's widowed mother, Charlotte, in the staid eastern town of Ramsdale. The early chapters parody the novel of manners. Nabokov exposes the lewd goings-on behind small-town America's polite facade, culminating in an icky scene in which Humbert discovers how to masturbate with Lolita, legs stretched across his lap, none the wiser. When Charlotte is fatally (and conveniently) run over after discovering Humbert's depravity in his diary, he absconds with his stepdaughter on a yearlong cross-country picaresque that parodies the American road trip. Here Nabokov's sardonic humor obscures just how controlling of his charge Humbert grows after he has intercourse with Lolita, threatening her with reform school if she disobeys, bribing her for sex with spare change that he steals back, denigrating her as both symbol and symptom of American popular culture.

Eventually he tries to provide her some semblance of a normal life, settling down in another homey burg, Beardsley. At thirteen, Lolita grows rebellious, and over the school year Humbert suspects she's planning to run away. Paranoid, he takes to the road again, only to discover an ominous figure, a doppelgänger, shadows his every move. Two months into this second flight, Lolita escape his clutches.

Only later does he discover how. At seventeen, Dolores, now married and pregnant, contacts Humbert, asking for her mother's inheritance. During their final conversation—unbeknownst to her stepfather, a preface informs us, Lolita subsequently dies in childbirth—she reveals her rescuer was Clare Quilty, a playwright and family friend. Quilty relished taunting Humbert but tossed Dolly (Lolita) aside when she refused to participate in his orgies and pornography. Shocked at how worn Lolita is, Humbert suddenly understands the damage he's caused and attempts to expiate himself by killing Quilty. While waiting trial, he writes the confession we read, his own attempt at self-exoneration—though an artistic one, not a moral one. The story, Humbert insists, will repay Lolita for the innocence he stole by carrying her into "the refuge of art" where sonnets are prophetic and paintings endure thanks to the mysteries of their "durable pigments."

Once again we must separate the author from his character. In the voice of Nabokov, the final passage counts as among the most beautiful descriptions ever of the immortality we want to believe great art achieves.

Coming from Humbert Humbert, though, we can't buy a word of it.

Bibliography

Lolita (1955)

—KC

I

INVISIBLE MAN

First Appearance: *Invisible Man*
Date of First Appearance: 1952
Author: Ralph Ellison (1913–1994)

He was shot because he was black and because he resisted. Mainly because he was black.

Not to be confused with H. G. Wells's mad scientist who actually *becomes* invisible, the nameless narrator of Ralph Ellison's 1952 novel is figuratively invisible—a metaphor for the African American experience. "Except for its upper levels, where it tends to merge with the American whole," Ellison writes in his working notes for the novel, "negro life is a world psychologically apart." Ellison's narrator is a man "born into a tragic irrational situation, who attempts to respond to it as though it were completely logical. He has accepted the definition of himself handed down by the white South and the paternalism of northern philanthropy." *Invisible Man* may be the story of one man's experience, but that experience carries tremendous symbolic weight. Ellison's character is constantly asking questions of a philosophical, social, or ethical nature.

The idea for the novel came to Ellison in the forties when he was typing away in a Vermont barn, and one afternoon his "fingers took over and typed what was to become the very first sentence . . . 'I am an invisible man'"—a line so outrageous that his first impulse was to throw it away. Then he asked himself, *Who would make such a statement?* That intrigued him. Suddenly he remembered a "blackface comedian bragging on the stage of Harlem's Apollo Theatre to the effect that each generation of his family was becoming so progressively black that no one, not even its own mother, had ever been able to see the two-year-old baby" and the audience "roared with laughter." It occurred to Ellison that whites seldom look past "the abstraction 'Negro' to the specific 'man.' Thus a Negro is rendered invisible—and to an extent invincible when he, as our hero comes to do, attempts to take advantage of the white man's psychological blind spot." In the novel, that's echoed by a black doctor who only found employment as a veterinarian: "Behold! a walking zombie! Already he's learned to repress not only his emotions but his humanity. He's invisible."

The idea of humanity diminished to the point of invisibility is driven home in the novel's most chilling yet memorable sequence. After the narrator, Invisible Man, delivers a well-received valedictorian address at his southern high school, he's invited to give the same speech at a gathering of the "town's big shots." When he arrives they're wearing tuxedos, drinking whiskey, and smoking cigars, and he's surprised to learn that before he's allowed to give his speech, he must box with black classmates in a "battle royal" for the men's amusement. The ten boys are stripped to the waist, given boxing shorts and gloves, and expected to slug it out in a makeshift ring, all at the same time, blindfolded, in front of these tipsy white pillars of society: bankers, lawyers, judges, doctors, fire chiefs, teachers, merchants, and pastors.

Before the fight, the men bring out a completely naked blonde. "Some of the boys stood with lowered heads, trembling," the narrator recalls. "I felt a wave of irrational guilt and fear. My teeth chattered, my skin turned to goose flesh, my knees knocked." She dances for the men and the boys, and later, when the battle royal begins, the now-blindfolded narrator says, "I could no longer control my emotions. I had no dignity. I stumbled about like a baby or a drunken man." He feels blows landing and goes down, head hitting the floor. "I lay prone, pretending that I was knocked out, but felt myself seized by hands and yanked to my feet. 'Get going, black boy! Mix it up!'" The harder they fight, the more frenzied the crowd becomes. After it's over, the emcee calls them to get their money, winner first. On a rug there are coins, bills, and gold pieces. "Boys, it's all yours," one man says. "That's right, Sambo," says another. But when they try to get their payment, they discover the rug has been electrified. "My hair bristled up on my head as I shook myself free," the narrator says. "My muscles jumped, my nerves jangled, writhed." He hears the men's laughter. "Pick it up, goddamnit, pick it up!"

White privilege follows him to a black college, where the black president asks him to drive one of their richest white benefactors around town. But when the man wants to go off the beaten path to see the real "Negro" experience and the narrator takes him to an area where they end up in a bar/brothel, the man is injured. Afterward the president is annoyed that a smart fellow like the narrator either doesn't know how or refuses to play the game. "You're nobody, son. You don't exist—can't you see that? The white folk tell everybody what to think." He kicks the narrator out of school but sends him to New York to find summer employment with what turns out to be a letter of damnation rather than recommendation. Stranded in a strange city with all doors closed to him, the narrator takes a job in the engine room of a paint factory. There, as a new hire entering shortly before a strike, he's treated like a scab by the workers but also attacked by his antiunion foreman. Landing in the hospital, he awakens to find white doctors taking the opportunity to use him for experimentation—an interesting allusion to Wells's sci-fi hero.

Invisible Man is a political novel in which a flesh-and-blood narrator finds himself wrestling with issues of personal, racial, and social identity. When he witnesses a white marshal evicting a feeble, elderly black couple, he gives an impromptu impassioned speech to bystanders and draws the attention of the local organization of socialists. They offer him work, and after training he becomes the party's chief spokesperson in Harlem. He believes he's speaking out for the downtrodden until he encounters a backlash from black nationalists who accuse him of playing the white game instead of working to better the lives of black people—which, of course, is the exact opposite of what the black college president had accused him of doing.

The most vocal (and agitated) among the nationalists calls himself Ras the Exhorter (a.k.a. Ras the Destroyer), and things escalate so much that the narrator must run for his life. Eventually he goes off the grid. One night, he says, in the dark he accidentally bumped into a man who called him vile names. The narrator shouted at the man, insisting he apologize, ready to slit his throat until he realized the man truly did not see him as another man, another human. "Now, aware of my invisibility, I live rent-free in a building rented strictly to whites, in a section of the basement that was shut off and forgotten during the nineteenth century, which I discovered when I was trying to escape in the night from Ras the Destroyer." But he's not destined to "hibernate" for long. Readers realized this earlier when the narrator spoke at the funeral of a former "Brotherhood" acquaintance. The man had been reduced to selling paper Sambo marionettes, and when the cop pushed him and used the N-word, something in him snapped. And the narrator's eulogy resonates as much as today's headlines.

Bibliography

Invisible Man (1952)

Work Cited

Callahan, John F. *Ralph Ellison's Invisible Man: A Casebook*. New York: Oxford University Press, 2004.

—JP

J

HENRY JEKYLL / EDWARD HYDE

First Appearance: *The Strange Case of Dr. Jekyll and Mr. Hyde*
Date of First Appearance: 1886
Author: Robert Louis Stevenson (1850–1894)

*At that time my virtue slumbered; my evil, kept awake by ambition, was alert and swift
to seize the occasion; and the thing that was projected was Edward Hyde.*

The duality of man is one of those overarching philosophical concepts popularly discussed in psychology classes, used as the context for many a sermon from the high pulpit, and as the theme for scores of horror novels, especially gothic ones, penned by mostly English writers. Mary Shelley's *Frankenstein* (1818) set the nineteenth century's gold standard for contemplation of the subject, and society churned with fear that the civilization priding itself on its achievements and level of human superiority was only a facade hiding the baseness that lurked below the surface and might at some inopportune moment come snarling to the forefront. The British seemed particularly pent up and susceptible to that fear, and this is precisely the situation put forward in Robert Louis Stevenson's classic novella *The Strange Case of Dr. Jekyll and Mr. Hyde*, a short work with a big impact. As society's upper crust partook of proper high tea every afternoon with their pinkies raised at an appropriate angle away from their fine bone china teacups, they secretly worried that a gentleman by day might become an evil boogeyman by night. And indeed, he does.

Dr. Henry Jekyll appears on the scene in Victorian English society with its strict moral expectations imposed like a symbolic iron girdle or chastity belt designed to keep pent-up inner passions imprisoned. On the surface Dr. Jekyll is what he needs to be: a well-educated London doctor, a person of highly refined morals, and a respected member of the community who throws dinner parties, gives to charity, and behaves like a perfect English gentleman minding his p's and q's. But in the darker recesses of his intellect he is fascinated with the conflict between good and evil, and as a scientist he hopes to find this distinction through experimentation using himself as the petri dish. And what a germ culture he discovers! By swallowing a potion he concocts, Dr. Jekyll's physical and emotional being becomes hideously contorted as Mr. Edward Hyde enters the arena of human depravity, and a star monster is born.

Dr. Jekyll is fully conscious that his inner demon, who bears another name and grotesquely distorted physical appearance, is an extension of himself. He and Edward are personalities in polar opposition, to be sure, but they are offspring of the same mind. Jekyll confesses to himself, "I stood already committed to a profound duplicity of me," and he realizes that "of the two natures that contended in the field of my consciousness, even if I could rightly be said to be either, it was only because I was radically both." The critical element here is that in realizing this, he not only fails to destroy the darker side of himself, he gives in to it. His having struggled to keep Hyde repressed, in fact, had only strengthened his dark persuasions, and in finally giving in to Hyde's urging to be freed, Jekyll admits that because "my devil had been long caged, he came out roaring."

The fact that there were real circumstances paralleling the Jekyll and Hyde dual personality certainly compounded interest in the novella's subject. Stevenson had written an earlier play for the London stage called *Deacon Brody, or The Double Life* about a real case of a well-respected Scottish church deacon convicted of surprising crimes and eventually hanged. And two years after *Jekyll and Hyde*, the story was also linked to the White Castle murders, better known as Jack the Ripper murders, occurring between August 31 and November 8, 1888, in a seedy section of London. The actor playing Hyde in the theater's version at the time was so convincing as the monster that at one point he was even suspected of being the murderer, and because the victims had organs missing there was suspicion that the killer might, like Dr. Jekyll, have been a physician. Fear ran so rampant about Jekyll and Hyde scenarios that anyone could be suspect now that human depravity had been so clearly linked to previously unquestioned members of proper society.

Interest in human nature's potential for depravity may have had a specific earlier influence as well. Charles Darwin's work cannot be denied at least tangentially as a force gaining notoriety in popular consumption and may have prompted Stevenson's turn from his previous fiction's lighter tone to this much more sinister timbre. Darwin's theory in *On the Origin of Species* (1859) and *The Descent of Man* (1871)—the evolution of man from the lowest life forms, through apes, and finally to humans—shook the Christian world and Wordsworthian Romantic sensibilities espousing the idea that "trailing clouds of glory do we come / From God, who is our home." If our origins are bestial instead of celestial, then what are we to think about humanity's animal instincts and potential for evil? What are the stops that may be put on these urges to keep them submerged, or in Dr. Jekyll's case, what forces might cause them to be released?

The Strange Case of Dr. Jekyll and Mr. Hyde and other fictional and real forays into the human psyche became the basis for a number of psychological premises. Sigmund Freud invested much of his life's work on his theory of the psyche and its division not solely cleaved into good and evil halves but into the three stages of ego. Edward Hyde is a perfect representation of Freud's pure "id," the part of the mind that controls base instincts. Fitting Henry Jekyll into Freud's "superego" controlling moral conscience and the "ego" balancing these is a bit more difficult, since he is aware of Hyde but does not control him. Current pop psychology has coined the "Jekyll and Hyde" effect or split personality, and clinical psychology uses the academic label "dissociative identity disorder" for more than one distinct personality found within the same body. Though not originating the concept, Stevenson's novel certainly popularized it.

Putting clinical psychology aside, *Jekyll and Hyde* made a lasting fictional splash and no doubt inspired many works to follow, including H. G. Wells's *The Island of Doctor Moreau* (1896) and Bram Stoker's *Dracula* (1897). These and a slew of so-called shilling shockers—what we today label as pulp fiction or mass-market thrillers—fed on sensationalism and fascination with the fear that our socially acceptable veneer could so easily be shattered. To relieve the dramatically dark side of the story, many versions to follow also played with humorous derivatives of Stevenson's morose tale with stories such as *Dr. Pyckle and Mr. Pryde, Dr. Jerkyl's Hide, Hyde and Go Tweet, Jekyll and Heidi,* and so forth, thus creating a spoof on something too dark to dwell on without some comic relief. Even Warner Bros. released cartoons spoofing the Jekyll/Hyde phenomenon.

Whether a story of individual human depravity or a moral cautionary tale about society as a whole, we continue to be fascinated by this macabre and mesmerizing tale, and we can only agree with Dr. Jekyll's pronouncement that the internal battle between our better angels and our basest demons is "as old and commonplace as man."

Bibliography

The Strange Case of Dr. Jekyll and Mr. Hyde (1886)

Work Cited

Wikipedia. S.v. "Adaptations of *Strange Case of Dr. Jekyll and Mr. Hyde.*" Accessed October 10, 2018. https://en.wikipedia.org/wiki/Adaptations_of_Strange_Case_of_Dr._Jekyll _and_Mr._Hyde.

—GS

MA JOAD

First Appearance: *The Grapes of Wrath*
Date of First Appearance: 1939
Author: John Steinbeck (1902–1968)

Her hazel eyes seemed to have experienced all possible tragedy and to have mounted pain and suffering like steps into a high calm and a superhuman understanding.

The Dust Bowl of the 1930s added insult to injury during the decade of the Great Depression, and no group seemed more displaced by these two economic disasters than the Oklahoma tenant farmers derogatorily nicknamed "Okies." As the blight on the American agricultural belt worsened, these farmers and their families took to the road with the few belongings they could strap to their beat-up jalopies, and in a sad version of *The Beverly Hillbillies* they headed to California in search of a new life. John Steinbeck poignantly captures this historical drama in his 1939 novel *The Grapes of Wrath*, which cast a glaring spotlight on the "have-nots" that the American dream of prosperity had abandoned. Steinbeck focused the novel's social commentary on one family, the Joads, who become emblematic of the great human migration and the struggle to retain pride in self and family while their means of subsistence crumbles beneath them. Ma Joad rises out of this saga as one of the most memorable mothers in fiction.

The matriarch of the Joad family is a simple, uneducated farmer's wife living quietly in the shadow of her menfolk. She keenly understands and respects the burden put on males as head of the family, and she has faith that as long as the men don't break under the pressure, the family will be all right too. Ma senses, though, cracks forming and recognizes that such strife can cause even good people to lash out, so she and the other wives facing similar calamity leave "the men alone to figure and to wonder in the dust." These husbands and fathers scratch in dirt that no longer yields crops, will give no answers, and acquiesces to the winds buffeting both the people and the soil from which they have come. Ma and her community of women obediently support their men and quietly dismantle their homes and the life they have known.

As one event followed by another erodes Pa Joad's control over the family's destiny and causes him to falter where he needs to be strong, Ma steps in with a swiftness that forever alters the family dynamics. When needed, she wields authority with a cast iron skillet, a car jack handle, or a sharp tongue to safeguard her family, and she just as passionately displays her gentle, humanitarian spirit by feeding other family's hungry children, nursing the sick, and assisting the downtrodden. Ma's selflessness as she eases Granma's death in the back of the moving truck while shielding the family from this trauma is only one among many illustrations of her sheer determination, deep love, and true grit.

Ma Joad doesn't have a first name in the novel; she is simply Ma, the "citadel of the family, the strong place that could not be taken." Like forged steel, the fires of tribulation she faces seem to burnish her character rather than destroy it through the cascade of calamity she suffers: the initial loss of the homestead; the gypsy-like existence on the road; the deaths stacked nearly back to back—the family dog the first day out, swiftly followed by the deaths of Grampa, Granma, the Reverend Jim Casy, and finally daughter Rose of Sharon's stillborn baby; and added to this horrific compilation, the desertions of son Noah and son-in-law Connie, her son Tom's forced flight after he commits murder while fighting for the migrants' cause, and Pa's collapsed authority under the weight of these losses. Through it all, Ma Joad stands as the family's pillar and toward the end of the novel delivers her life-affirming proclamation: "Woman got all her life in her arms . . . it's all one flow, like a stream, little eddies, little waterfalls, but the river, it goes right on. Woman looks at it like that. We ain't gonna die out."

Ma's travails do more than just engage readers on an emotional level. Her strength draws sympathy for the litany of misfortune engulfing the Joad family and other fellow migrants along the famous Route 66 or in the camps known as Hoovervilles that served as temporary pit stops for a moving army of the disenfranchised. Steinbeck's poignant rendering in real time of a national crisis brought down to the personal level gained much attention and garnered important political support in high places. While reading *The Grapes of Wrath*, Eleanor Roosevelt was particularly drawn to Ma's character and heralded her in the First Lady's popular *My Day* column by saying, "Somehow I cannot imagine thinking of 'Ma' without, at the same time, thinking of the love 'that passeth all understanding.'" Nor did Mrs. Roosevelt stop there. She championed the marginalized masses throughout the nation, supported her husband's platforms for relief, testified in Congress about the plight of migrant workers, and helped encourage the passing of labor law reform. On the surface, Ma Joad and Eleanor Roosevelt have almost nothing in common, but in a remarkable way Ma dominates her circle of influence with the same vigor the nation's First Lady did, and with much less to draw on for the task. Noted Steinbeck biographer Susan Shillinglaw goes so far as to say what national politics really needs in the twenty-first century is Ma Joad in the White House and that "President Ma would be a beacon for all women and all men." Now that would be some sort of populism!

Early in the novel Ma suggests to her son Tom, whose inability to tolerate injustice is both his cross and his crown, that if everyone got mad in unison the power of the people might be enough to topple the powerful. Steinbeck underscores this socialism in making the Joads' experience a synecdoche of a more sweeping nature, even a righteous cause. The opening lines of the Civil War song "The Battle Hymn of the Republic," from which the novel takes its title, suggest conflict no less epic than "the coming of the Lord" who in his anger at the world's state "hath trampled out the vineyards where the grapes of wrath are stored." That California's vineyards are one source of the conflict creates a doubly delicious symbolism.

Steinbeck's tour de force hit such a collective nerve that it went from a first printing and several reprints to a major motion picture release in less than a year. John Ford's adaptation starring Henry Fonda is considered one of the great movies of all time, and Fonda's star power no doubt helped the film's popularity as a worthy tribute to the Pulitzer Prize–winning novel consistently listed on virtually every Top 100 reading list. But Ma is the true star, in both book and film, and her "We're the people that live. . . . We're the people" speech near the end is the emotional epiphany that solidifies her as the heart and soul of a fractured community. She is the fictional embodiment of the crisis, and while the novel leaves Tom Joad stealthily fighting for the people and likely becoming a martyr for the cause, Ma Joad is holding the family together and marching them quietly onward.

Bibliography

The Grapes of Wrath (1939)

Works Cited

Roosevelt, Eleanor. *My Day*. June 28, 1939.
Shillinglaw, Susan. "75 Years after *The Grapes of Wrath*, We Need Ma Joad in the White House." *Washington Post*, April 18, 2014.

—GS

K

ANNA KARENINA

First Appearance: *Anna Karenina* in *The Russian Messenger*
Date of First Appearance: 1875–1877
Author: Leo Tolstoy (1828–1910)

Respect was invented to cover the empty place where love should be. And if you don't love me anymore, it would be better and more honest to say so.

When Leo Tolstoy's *Anna Karenina* was serialized in *The Russian Messenger* from 1875 to 1877 and published in book form in 1878, it appealed to audiences as much as today's reality television series on lifestyles of the rich and famous. Since the October Revolution of 1917 ended the age of royalty in Russia, readers have been even more fascinated with that bygone era. Though the egalitarian in us may prefer a society where everyone exists on the same economic plane, it's also part of human nature to fantasize about living a life of opulence and entitlement—or to be reassured that royalty and the upper class have problems too.

"More than any other book, it persuades me that there is such a thing as human nature, and that some part of that nature remains fundamentally unaffected by history and culture," author Francine Prose told Jilly Cooper and the *Guardian*, adding that *Anna Karenina* reminds her to pay closer attention to the world. "I've always loved the scene in which Anna, having met the charming Vronsky, returns home to her husband and is struck by how unattractive his ears are. How could something like that not stand up to, and transcend, the so-called test of time?" Prose isn't alone in her praise. *The Top Ten: Writers Pick Their Favorite Books* (2007) asked 125 writers to list their top ten greatest works of fiction. After the final tally, *Anna Karenina* emerged as Number 1.

With Countess Anna Arkadyevna Karenina, Tolstoy gives readers a realistically flawed heroine who is as passionate as she is intelligent, and as strong as she is independent. More importantly, he gives us a character so believably complicated and contradictory that even Anna struggles at times to comprehend why she behaves as she does. By novel's end, other characters are deeply affected by her fate, yet they have remarkably different takeaways. One writes her off as a "bad woman," while another ponders her tragedy and has a revelation that we all have the power to inject positivity into our lives. Her story makes readers question what it means to live a life of fulfillment, and to what extent morality and society's approval should shape individual needs and desires. Is our existence a sacrifice to be made in the service of idealism, family, or community, or does pursuing one's own destiny and happiness matter just as much, if not more? In the end, the most romantic question implied by Anna's plight is this: Is love more important than everything else?

Anna thinks so, and because she risks everything for love and defies societal conventions in the process, she has become an inspiration to generations. The novel has spawned a radio dramatization, two touring stage productions, two multiseason television series, and more than twenty films—the earliest coming in 1911, and the most recent being Joe Wright's theatrical-style 2012 adaptation starring Keira Knightley as Anna. As a reviewer for *Rolling Stone* observed, Wright "shakes things up by setting his film in a 19th-century theater to emphasize Anna's artificial life in Russian society"—which is consistent with one of the novel's themes of behavior as performance in upper-class Russian society. "There wasn't anything I couldn't relate to, and that was the most shocking thing in itself," Knightley told *Elle* magazine. "Certainly being a woman now is much easier. Nonetheless, we live in societies with rules, and if you break them, the pack [can] turn against you." Wright's production, with a screenplay by Tom Stoppard, emphasizes the double standard of an elitist Russian society that forgives and accepts Anna's brother after his adulterous dalliance, but ostracizes Anna for her own genuinely loving affair with a dashing military man. The film suggests that Anna ultimately plunges into depression because of society's rejection of her, but in the novel it's more complicated.

"Let me tell you candidly my opinion," Anna's brother says. "You married a man twenty years older than yourself. You married him without love and not knowing what love was. It was a mistake, let's admit." It was a mistake made, too, because of a rumor spread by the cold and unfeeling Karenin's aunt, which suggested he had "already compromised the girl and that he was honor bound to make her an offer." Accepting a marriage forced upon them by a gossiping and rigid society wasn't the only mistake Anna would make—another thing that reinforces her humanness. The novel's main narrative follows Anna on an emotional and psychological journey of passion, disillusionment, confusion, and resentment. Love makes people crazy, and it certainly does Anna, who wrestles with the same sorts of problems and questions that readers do. Anna has a marriage of "prudence," but when she charms Count Vronsky at a Moscow ball with a smile that "set him on fire," they begin the passionate affair that continues even after she informs her husband, and he refuses to grant a divorce. Karenin, who has a government job and plans on seeking elected office, wants to keep up appearances—to play the "game" society requires of its transgressors. But as Anna continues to see Vronsky away from home (and eventually *in* the Karenin home), "the position was one of misery for all three."

The novel begins, "Happy families are all alike; every unhappy family is unhappy in its own way." Unlike some literary heroines who seem unsuited for or traumatized by motherhood, Anna is a good mother who treasures her eight-year-old son and has a vibrancy that draws others to her. When she spends the day with her sister-in-law and her children, the little ones cling to her throughout the visit, and when they race to hug her goodbye she runs laughing to meet them, calling, "All together" and embracing the "throng of swarming children, shrieking with delight." Anna is full of life, and that attracts adults to her as well. "Besides wit, grace, and beauty, she had truth," one young man says of her. "She had no wish to hide from him the bitterness of her position," he thinks. "What a marvelous, sweet and unhappy woman!"

Anna Karenina ends sadly, of course, because it is, after all, a Russian novel—which is also why the book runs close to 900 pages in translation and there are so many main characters that you need a chart to keep them all straight. Like Jay Gatsby, Anna doesn't make an appearance until well into the novel—chapter 18. Later, after she meets her tragic end, the novel continues for nineteen more chapters. But it's her story that propels the novel. All the other characters are foils and counterpoints.

In 2018, the famed Bolshoi Ballet debuted *Anna Karenina* with Olga Smirnova dancing the lead role in an adaptation that sets the story in the present day. "The tragedy of Anna and Vronsky in the book is the impossibility of divorce at the time," Smirnova says. "But today, because everyone can file for a divorce, it is not such a tragedy." As a result, the ballet focuses on the forces that influence Anna's decisions throughout the novel and the emotional and psychological states that she experiences—which, of course, are the elements that make the novel itself timeless, and Anna a wonderfully complicated character.

Bibliography

Anna Karenina: A Novel in Eight Parts (1878)

Works Cited

Banka, Mike. "Keira Knightley on Her Starring Role in 'Anna Karenina." *Elle*, November 15, 2012. https://www.elle.com/culture/movies-tv/news/a16239/keira-knightley-interview/.

Cooper, Jilly. "Why Leo Tolstoy's Anna Karenina Transcends the Ages." *Guardian*, September 1, 2012. https://www.theguardian.com/film/2012/sep/02/anna-karenina-tolstoy-five-writers.

Shpakova, Anna. "An 'Anna Karenina' for Our Times at Moscow's Bolshoi Theatre." NPR. March 23, 2018. https://www.npr.org/2018/03/23/595199671/an-anna-karenina-for-our-times-at-moscow-s-bolshoi-theatre.

Travers, Peter. "Anna Karenina." *Rolling Stone*, November 15, 2012. https://www.rollingstone.com/movies/movie-reviews/anna-karenina-128192/.

Zane, J. Peder. *The Top Ten: Writers Pick Their Favorite Books*. W. W. Norton, 2007.

—JP

MICK KELLY

First Appearance: *The Heart Is a Lonely Hunter*
Date of First Appearance: 1940
Author: Carson McCullers (1917–1967)

But there's one thing I would give anything for. And that's a piano. If we had a piano I'd practice every single night and learn every piece in the world.

As the filmmaking Farrelly brothers might say, *There's Something about Mick*—the main female character in Carson McCullers's 1940 novel *The Heart Is a Lonely Hunter*. Maybe it's the restless energy that comes from being on the cusp of adolescence. Maybe it's the incongruence of a rough tomboy from a poor family hearing music in her head all the time and wanting to become a famous composer-conductor. Or maybe it's that Mick is always thinking, and there's so much for her to process as life tries to spin her in circles.

Biff Brannan notices. He owns a café two blocks from the house Mick's parents' opened to boarders after her father couldn't find work. The youngest girl of six Kelly children, Mick stops in his café several nights a week for a hot chocolate and Biff always gives her a discount. He's fascinated by this "gangling, towheaded youngster, a girl of about twelve" who wears "khaki shorts, a blue shirt, and tennis shoes—so that at first glance she was like a very young boy." One night she asks to buy a pack of cigarettes and he asks if her parents know she's out after midnight. After she leaves, Biff has second thoughts about selling her tobacco, not knowing she's taken up smoking because at 5'6" Mick is *hoping* cigarettes will stunt her growth. Biff "thought of the way Mick narrowed her eyes and pushed back the bangs of her hair with the palm of her hand. He thought of her hoarse, boyish voice and of her habit of hitching up her khaki shorts and swaggering like a cowboy in the picture show. A feeling of tenderness came in him." That feeling makes him uneasy. Later in the novel, after Biff's wife dies, he feels especially drawn to Mick again, wanting to "reach out his hand and touch her sunburned, tousled hair—but not as he had ever touched a woman." That, too, makes him uneasy, for if it isn't sexual, what is it?

When Mick's own father needs to tell someone how isolated he feels being a provider who's not providing, he turns to Mick, not his wife or her siblings. People at the vocational high school she attends also respond to her differently, because she received "special permission and took mechanical shop like a boy." And at the house where Mick would sneak into a dark yard every night and hide in a bush next to a window to listen to Mozart and Beethoven playing on the radio, if the rich people who lived there knew about Mick they would also sense she's far from typical. Then there's Portia, the daughter of a black doctor in town who, despite the Kelly family's poverty, works for them as their cook. Mick reminds Portia of her own father: neither goes to church, and neither seems sure about God. Although Mick and Portia argue, Portia loves her and can't help but notice Mick is always lost in thought. Portia is convinced that "one of these days she going to really surprise somebody. But whether that going to be a good surprise or a bad surprise I just don't know."

Harry, the boy next door, has always been drawn to her. Though he's Jewish and lately can only talk about Hitler and the threat of Fascism, at a party that functions as Mick's coming-out—with peanut butter and jelly sandwiches and punch and her father writing out the "prom" cards—he presents a card so he can walk with her, though she can see there's nothing written on it. Later, in winter, they will ride their bikes sixteen miles to go swimming. As the narrator tells it from Mick's point of view, while waiting around she is full of restless energy. "Music was in her mind. Just to be doing something she picked up a ten-penny nail and drove it into the steps with a few good wallops." On their swimming excursion Harry tells her, "It used to be I had some big ambition for myself all the time," but not anymore. Seeing the look on Harry's face makes her feel sad, and before you know it she's daring him to go skinny-dipping.

Mick is a mixture of restless energy, confusing emotions, and raw potential. Ironically, the one person who doesn't seem to see something special in her is John Singer, a mute who, after losing his best friend and fellow mute roommate of ten years to "the state insane asylum" 200 miles away, had taken a room at the Kellys' boardinghouse. Mick practiced piano every day at the local gym, then deliberately walked past the store where Singer worked. "Then every night she waited on the front porch for him to come home. Sometimes she followed him upstairs. She sat on the bed and watched him put away his hat and undo the button on his collar and brush his hair. For some reason it was like they had a secret together. Or like they waited to tell each other things that had never been said before." Their imagined connection is symbolized by his name and her habit of singing everywhere she goes.

Though the song came later, readers can almost hear her vocalizing "Up on the Roof" as she climbs to the top peak of a new two-story house being built in the neighborhood, something most kids were afraid to do. "Nerve, Mick, you've got to keep nerve," she says as she almost slips on the way down. She goes inside the construction and adds to the graffiti: "EDISON, DICK TRACY, MUSSOLINI, M.K. [her initials]," and on the opposite wall, she writes a "very bad word" with chalk she brought with her—"PUSSY"—and her initials underneath. Mick is complicated and so richly drawn that Sondra Locke received an Oscar nomination for portraying her in the 1968 film adaptation.

McCullers was only twenty-two when she wrote her first novel, and there's something about the way she describes Mick and her complex feelings and thought processes that really make Mick stand out among fictional characters. Mick paints pictures with titles like "Sea Gull with Back Broken in Storm" and writes music in notebooks she keeps in an old hatbox alongside pieces of instruments she's using to build her own violin. When older, she has a beer and ice cream sundae, together. Unlike other girls "scared a man would come out from somewhere and put his teapot in them like they was married," she walks and sings late at night, unconcerned, convinced she can run from the biggest attackers and beat the smaller ones. She grapples with or tries to understand pubescence and the loss of virginity her thirteenth summer, as well as her sister's serious illness, her family's extreme poverty, the incarceration and mistreatment of Portia's brother, the death of a close friend, and ultimately the mixture of feelings and dreams that makes her who she is. When her younger brother asks, after overhearing a slur, "Are we common, Mick?" she responds, "*I'm* not." And it's the truest thing she says.

Bibliography

The Heart Is a Lonely Hunter (1940)

—JP

KURTZ

First Appearance: "The Heart of Darkness" in *Blackwood's Magazine*
Date of First Appearance: February–April 1899
Author: Joseph Conrad (1857–1924)

The horror! The horror!

Joseph Conrad's mysterious Mr. Kurtz from *Heart of Darkness* isn't exactly an enlightened or politically correct figure. He's an ivory trader, which justifiably angers animal rights activists, and he's a commercial arm of colonialism, which ought to infuriate anyone sensitive to the many ways in which Western powers used their might to oppress peoples and loot precious resources and national treasures. Anyone who's antiracism and who values humility and fair treatment of others can't be thrilled, either, that Kurtz set himself up as a "god" among the tribal people of the Congo River basin, or that he used cannibals to attack other tribes in order to acquire more ivory. But Kurtz also happens to be literature's most memorable "shadow character," whose haunting offstage presence is felt throughout the novella—even though he doesn't appear until twenty pages or so from the end. While we see him only briefly when he's sick and dying, Kurtz remains at the center of the narrative, an elusive key to interpreting the book's symbolic title and an ongoing obsession for the narrator.

On a trading company pleasure boat anchored in the Thames, Charles Marlow tells the story of how he traveled to Africa to captain a river steamboat transporting ivory collected by the most successful agent in company history—a "phantom" named Kurtz, who comes up constantly in conversation and seems to reside somewhere in the back of his mind almost every minute of his journey. Even seemingly unrelated details often have to do with our understanding of Kurtz. In one such instance, when Marlow goes to Brussels and undergoes a routine physical exam, the doctor brings up the issue of madness and remarks that once men are in Africa, "changes take place inside."

After a thirty-day ship's voyage to the company's coastal station in Africa, Marlow hears from the chief accountant about "a very remarkable person" in charge of an important trading post. But there's also hesitancy. "When you see Mr. Kurtz, tell him from me that everything here . . . is very satisfactory. I don't like to write to him—with those messengers of ours you never know who may get hold of your letter—at that Central Station." After an outburst over "those savages," the accountant predicts Kurtz will "go far, very far. He will be a somebody in the Administration before long. They, above—the Council in Europe, you know—mean him to be." Kurtz eventually looms so large in Marlow's mind that when he keeps hearing the man might be dead, he's first angry and then disappointed, having "traveled all this way for the sole purpose of talking to Mr. Kurtz. . . . Hadn't I been told in all the tones of jealousy and admiration that he had collected, bartered, swindled, or stolen more ivory than all the other agents put together?"

Part of what makes Kurtz a compelling character is the shroud of mystery that surrounds him. He is legendary, but controversial. Marlow overhears one agent complaining about Kurtz's methods and how he's ruining the trade for everyone else. Meanwhile, the Central Station manager thought it a happy "accident" Marlow's boat was wrecked so he couldn't disembark immediately on the two-month journey to reach Kurtz. Does he mean to sabotage Kurtz or replace him without his superiors' knowledge? Kurtz "got the tribe to follow him" and they "adored him," but when Marlow and the manager steam upriver and their boat is attacked, it's unclear whether the cannibals attack because they don't want their beloved Kurtz leaving, whether they think it is someone hostile, or whether they attack at Kurtz's command. Such a swirl of confusion!

When Kurtz finally appears he makes a grand entrance, emerging from the jungle on a stretcher borne by a large group of men "waist-deep in the grass" who appear suddenly "as though they had come up from the ground," while "a cry arose." Then, "as if by enchantment, streams of human beings—of naked human beings . . . were poured into the clearing. . . . The bushes shook, the grass swayed for a time, and then everything stood still in attentive immobility." When Kurtz sits up, Marlow sees that he is "lank and with an uplifted arm" that extends "commandingly." He looks to be "at least seven feet long," though the narrator muses that "Kurtz" in German means "short." When the covering slips off, Marlow can see the man's rib cage. "It was as though an animated image of death carved out of old ivory had been shaking its hand with menaces at a motionless crowd of men made of dark and glittering bronze." Then, as Kurtz opens his mouth wide, the narrator imagines that "he had wanted to swallow all the air, all the earth, all the men before him." The narrator hears a deep voice and realizes Kurtz "must have been shouting," though this "shadow looked satiated and calm." When he finally speaks to Marlow, who had trekked 200 miles from the coast, he says, "I am glad"—nothing nearly as profound as Marlow might have hoped.

Readers, like Marlow, must piece together their impressions in order to make sense of Kurtz and understand why he looms so large. At Central Station, Marlow overhears the barely competent manager and a relative conspire against Kurtz, whose methods disgust and frighten them. In the interior, Marlow finds the devotion of two Kurtz's aides almost disciple-like. Yet, he says of one, "I did not envy him his devotion to Kurtz," further clouding the waters for readers hoping for the mystery of Kurtz to finally be explained.

Heart of Darkness was first published as a three-part serial in *Blackwood's Magazine* in 1899, with book publication following in 1902. It has been frequently taught in high schools and colleges, but those who haven't encountered Kurtz in their English classes likely learned about him through watching Francis Ford Coppola's inventive 1979 screen adaptation, *Apocalypse Now*. Coppola updated the story by setting it in the Vietnam War, with Marlon Brando playing Col. Walter E. Kurtz—sent to Vietnam to compile a report on the failings of current military policies, just as Conrad's Kurtz was asked to compile a report on best practices to control the "natives." Colonel Kurtz took a group of Green Berets and their families deep into the jungle, where from a base camp they launched attacks on the Vietcong—just as Conrad's Kurtz had an indigenous lover and used her tribe to attack surrounding peoples. His methods—which included staking the heads of tribal enemies in a circle around his hut—struck fear in the hearts of men.

In the end, Kurtz is best known for his last words: "The horror! The horror!" Does he mean darkest Africa? Human nature? What isolation does to a man? What *greed* does to a man? Since Kurtz's report to the Society for the Suppression of Savage Customs ends with his recommendation to "exterminate all the brutes!" readers can only hope that his last spoken words indicate that he was aware he had become more savage than any of the "natives" he encountered or wrote about. And yet, he remains hauntingly mysterious.

Bibliography

Youth: A Narrative and Two Other Stories (1902)

—JP

M

JOSEPHINE "JO" MARCH

First Appearance: *Little Women*
Date of First Appearance: 1868
Author: Louisa May Alcott (1832–1888)

I've got the key to my castle in the air, but whether I can unlock the door remains to be seen.

Little Women found itself on nearly every young girl's reading list from the time of its publication in 1868 through the twentieth century, and Louisa May Alcott's novel is now being discovered by a new audience of millennials. In a 2017 adaptation, Maya Hawke, the daughter of Hollywood's Uma Thurman and Ethan Hawke, took on the role of central character Josephine (Jo) March, who is by far the most colorful of the March family's four daughters. In some ways Jo is a bookish Northern Scarlett O'Hara verging on womanhood in the middle of the Civil War and chafing at the constrictions that define who she should be, rather than who she wants to be. Virtually all *Little Women* fans love Jo because of that struggle, and perhaps at least subconsciously they see her independent nature as mirroring their own sensibilities. They want Jo to be the trailblazer for their secret rebellions and heart's passions, and incidentally, they want her to marry the boy next door—but more about that later.

Some really remarkable, self-possessed women pay homage to Jo March as the specific source of their *Little Women* adoration and their own inspiration. It comes as no surprise that female writers relate to Jo as a young nineteenth-century wannabe author thwarted from following her passion. Gertrude Stein, Cynthia Ozick, Barbara Kingsolver, Joyce Carol Oates, Nora Ephron, Ursula K. Le Guin, Ann Petry, and Anna Quindlen, representing a wide range of genres, have picked up the pen to express their love for Jo. They are joined by J. K. Rowling, arguably the most popular writer on the planet, who said, "It is hard to overstate what she meant to a small, plain girl called Jo, who had a hot temper and a burning ambition to be a writer." But the range of women from other disciplines who also have a strong bond with Jo is equally remarkable. Feminist Simone de Beauvoir, punk rocker and artist Patti Smith, and politician Hillary Clinton all profess their connection to Jo's intelligence and unconventional desires. She represents for these diverse women a bridge into the new century and the freedom to burst open opportunities to pursue their desires in earnest. Jo March becomes both the poster girl and flag carrier for this cause.

The paradigm for women in the mid-1800s had been clear. They were expected to be submissive wives whose duty was to follow the ideal of the era's famous poem "The Angel in the House," which espoused that "man must be pleased" and doing so "is woman's pleasure." (Note to reader: Perfect restraint being practiced here by not supplying a snarky retort! Okay, returning to authorial tone.) Young girls were merely women in training, and Alcott's coming-of-age story plies the cult of family and domesticity that the century's readers consumed in large doses. Jo can be crammed into that mold as she accepts familial expectations, and her devotion to the March family is undisputable. She makes sacrifices to boost waning finances by selling her hair—a weird nineteenth-century way to make money—as well as contributing her earnings from outside the home, nursing her dying sister Beth, and respecting and honoring her parents. Jo as dutiful daughter? Check.

Alcott performs an amazing tightrope act appealing to Victorian mores while also nuancing Jo's story in ways that connect the aforementioned high-profile women and other modern readers who could only have been imagined a century and a half earlier. Instead of painting her into the domestic corner, Alcott presents Jo as a tomboy with a boy's name who is referred to by Mr. March as his "son Jo," and the somewhat effeminate next-door neighbor Laurie with a typically female name calls her "dear fellow." Jo does not want to be a wife, and she underscores this by saying, "I'm happy as I am, and love my liberty too well to be in a hurry to give it up for any mortal man." You get the picture. Alcott is stirring up gender stereotypes more than a century before others found the courage to do so.

The backstories to novels are often compelling, but Jo's is especially so. Everyone agrees she is Alcott's alter ego as a rebellious pseudoboy with no desire for the expected endgame of marriage and motherhood. Nothing shocking there, as Alcott remained unwed. But what few know is that the original publication's long title, *Little Women: Meg, Jo, Beth, and Amy. The Story of Their Lives. A Girl's Book*, highlights "girls" and therefore drops the plot off before marriage becomes an issue. The version everyone now knows includes in one collective binding the follow-up, *Good Wives*, practically forced on Alcott by her publisher because so many readers wanted to know what happened to the March girls and who they married. More importantly, they wanted to know if Jo married Laurie. The rebellious streak that created Jo also caused Alcott's frustration that readers believed marriage "was the only aim and end of a woman's life." (Perhaps a double meaning on the second half of that phrase.) She stubbornly proclaimed, "I *won't* marry Jo to Laurie to please anyone." She also told a friend that "out of perversity" she created a marriage that didn't satisfy the romantics. Touché, Louisa May!

Alcott's solution was to twist the knife a bit while seeming to acquiesce. In the *Good Wives* portion of *Little Women*, Jo is twenty-five when she marries, practically an official Victorian spinster by then, and she chooses a nontraditional husband, a much older, well-educated though unattractive and somewhat uncouth German professor, and it is Jo's inherited money, not his earnings, that provides the home in which they will raise their two boys. Like Brontë's Jane Eyre who only marries when she is financially independent and can choose not to, Jo acts rather than reacts to life. She will not be some man's "little woman," but a partner holding at least some of the reins to her own future's carriage.

Both Alcott and the readers have expressed some disappointment in the ending, however. We all love Jo bucking the system, and we want her to be the rebel who defies the drag of domesticity, but we would also like the happily-ever-after life with the boy we've decided is perfect for her. Essay after essay written by smart, accomplished, feminist-leaning women all bemoan Alcott's subversion. The eNotes website even put out a call for unhappy readers to submit alternate endings, and some interesting ones have come forward—and a multiracial family with Jo's LGBTQ persuasion was no doubt inevitable.

The conflicted feelings readers have about Jo March's future only seems to strengthen their devotion and interest, though. The nineteenth-century youth novel with a bit of a disappointing conclusion still rates high with audiences. The BBC's Big Read ranked it No. 18 on their "Nation's Best Loved Novel" list, and it is consistently included on many Top 100 ratings of literary texts. Alcott may not have delivered the readers' perfect ending in *Little Women*, but she certainly got her message across.

Bibliography

Little Women (1868)
Good Wives (1869) (published in England as separate volumes, usually as one volume in America)
Little Men, or Life at Plumfield with Jo's Boys (1871)
Jo's Boys, and How They Turned Out: A Sequel to Little Men (1886)

Works Cited

BBC's The Big Read Top 100. 2003. https://www.bbc.co.uk/arts/bigread/top100.shtml.
Lanzendorfer, Joy. "10 Things You Might Not Know about *Little Women*." *Mental Floss*, May 21, 2018.
Patmore, Coventry. *The Angel in the House*. London: John W. Parker and Son, 1858.
Rowling, J. K. "J. K. Rowling: By the Book." *New York Times Sunday Book Review*, October 11, 2012.

—GS

PHILIP MARLOWE

First Appearance: *The Big Sleep*
Date of First Appearance: 1939
Author: Raymond Chandler (1888–1959)

I needed a drink, I needed a lot of life insurance, I needed a vacation, I needed a home in the country. What I had was a coat, a hat and a gun. I put them on and went out of the room.—Farewell, My Lovely

He wasn't the first private dick to confront corruption in the mean streets, but he was the first to do it with a sense of chivalric resolve. Readers today have forgotten most of the first-generation Prohibition-era gumshoes who took detective fiction out of the quaint parlors of C. Auguste Dupin and Sherlock Holmes and relocated it to the dens of iniquity where killer kingpins and femmes fatales wreak their mayhem. Carroll John Daly's Three Gun Terry Mack and Race Williams, Raoul Whitfield's Jo Garr, and George Harmon Coxe's Flashgun Casey are names familiar mainly to scholars of *Black Mask*, the pulp rag credited with popularizing hardboiled crime fiction. Dashiell Hammett's the Continental Op and Sam Spade remain iconic, foundational figures in the genre, but audiences influenced by their countless descendants are often shocked by how nihilistic they seem, as if they were infected by the same "blood simple" impulses of the forces they fight.

The moral sensibility of the private investigator—the idea of the PI as a knight-errant who stares down wrongdoing with bruised but unbendable idealism—comes instead from Raymond Chandler's contribution to the art form, Philip Marlowe. Wisecracking and world weary, Marlowe brought a poetic melancholy to the voice of the crime fighter that elevated the stakes from lurid, escapist entertainment to literary poignancy. Hardly a fictional flatfoot in novels, films, or television since he debuted in *The Big Sleep* (1939) isn't a variation on his prototype.

Chandler was forty-four and fired from his job as an oil-industry accounting executive for alcoholism when he broke into *Black Mask* with "Blackmailers Don't Shoot." For the moment, the detective's name was Mallory, an allusion to Sir Thomas Malory, author of *Le Morte d'Arthur* (1485) and an indication of the writer's attachment to medieval literature's chivalric tradition. Over the next six years Chandler eked out nearly two dozen pulp stories with names like "Trouble Is My Business" whose heroes were known as Carmady, Ted Malvern, or John Dalmas, but who all shared the same basic characteristics: They were loners who viewed their home base of Los Angeles as a microcosm of civic greed and hedonism, and they were as philosophical as they were quick to draw their gat. Eventually, Chandler settled on the name Philip Marlowe, evoking the Renaissance playwright Christopher Marlowe, suggesting the author's interest in richly intricate Elizabethan language, which became a trademark of his novels' narrative style.

One reason Marlowe stands out as a character is that Chandler's plots are often so byzantine that readers tend to remember his sarcastic asides more than the dizzying twists and turns. As the author joked, whenever he found he'd written himself into a corner he simply had two men enter the scene with guns drawn and followed that plot strand wherever it might lead him. *The Big Sleep* involves blackmail, pornography, a dead chauffeur, a missing husband, and two spoiled sister-heirs to an oil fortune whose ailing father will go to any length necessary to protect. *Farewell, My Lovely* (1941) starts in a black nightclub with a grotesquely muscular, hot-tempered ex-con named Moose Malloy on the prowl for his missing girlfriend, Velma Valento, leading Marlowe into a vortex of stolen jewelry, marijuana, phony psychics, dope-peddling doctors, and a bribe-dealing gambler who controls LA's dirty nearby neighbor, Bay City (Santa Monica). *The Long Goodbye* (1953) features a dead wife and her supposedly suicided husband/murderer, a $5,000 bill, an aging Hemingway-styled writer hampered by alcoholism, his untrustworthy spouse, the trauma of World War II, and a case of bad cosmetic surgery. Through all the treachery and deception, Marlowe maintains a hard-bitten idealism, even though the novels usually end with the characters he most tried to assist backstabbing or disappointing him in ways large or small.

Chandler completed seven Marlowe novels in just under twenty years. Compared to the detective novelists who followed in his wake, such as the indefatigable John D. MacDonald (Travis McGee) or Ross Macdonald (Lew Archer), he was far from prolific. Both his drinking and his financial dependency on Hollywood scriptwriting stymied his output. The three aforementioned Marlowe entries are uncontested classics; the other four are wildly inconsistent, although all have their flashes of brilliance. Despite the varying quality, Marlowe remains remarkably consistent throughout them (except for his age). Readers learn only bits and pieces of his backstory. His parents are dead and he has no siblings; he attended some college; he cut his legal teeth working for the district attorney but was fired for insubordination. He has no home life, living in a small apartment and later a rented house, but spending most of his time in his office in the Cahuenga Building on Hollywood Boulevard. Only in *The Long Goodbye* and *Playback* (1958), Chandler's final novel, is he given any romantic life, taking up with Linda Loring. The pair would have married in *The Poodle Springs Story* if the author hadn't died only four chapters into it. (In 1988, one of Chandler's most successful heirs, Robert B. Parker, finished the novel to mixed reviews.) Otherwise, the most we know of Marlowe is his preferences in booze (whiskey), the cars he drives and the cigarettes he smokes (Camels), and the fact that he's a self-described "romantic": "I hear voices crying in the night and I go see what's the matter," he says in *Goodbye*.

The abstraction serves him well: As many critics have noted, Marlowe is best thought of as less a person than as an attitude, a voice of stoic but unshakable idealism. After his fourth novel, *The Lady in the Lake* (1943), Chandler published the quintessential credo of the hardboiled detective, "The Simple Art of Murder," in which he spelled out Marlowe's stance. "If there were enough like him," the piece concludes, "the world would be a very safe place to live in, without becoming too dull to live in."

Marlowe made an immediate and enduring splash not only in crime fiction but on the radio and in film as well. Three different actors portrayed him on the silver screen before Humphrey Bogart's definitive turn in Howard Hawks's *The Big Sleep* in 1946 (featuring a script coauthored by William Faulkner). In the 1940s and 1950s at least seven different radio series featured either adaptations of Chandler novels or new adventures by spin-off writers. There have also been periodic efforts to update Marlowe to post-1960s sensibilities. James Garner's charming interpretation of the character in the 1969 movie *Marlowe* led directly to his popular turn in the 1974–1980 TV series *The Rockford Files*. Elliott Gould's more bumbling version in Robert Altman's 1973 adaptation of *The Long Goodbye*, however, remains divisive. The most successful update is probably Thomas Pynchon's shambolic Doc Sportello in *Inherent Vice* (2009), a pot-smoking, hippie version of the character untangling conspiracies in the Manson era (and one that owes a debt to Roger L. Simon's Moses Wine, the first baby boomer Marlowe who debuted in 1973's *The Big Fix*).

Although acclaimed novelists such as John Banville (writing as Benjamin Black) and Lawrence Osborne have kept Marlowe alive with their authorized novels *The Black-Eyed Blonde* (2014) and *Only to Sleep* (2018), respectively, the PI's voice remains most stinging in the original novels. "I see him always in a lonely street, in lonely rooms," his creator wrote shortly before his death, "puzzled but never quite defeated."

Bibliography

The Big Sleep (1939)
Farewell, My Lovely (1941)
The High Window (1942)
The Lady in the Lake (1943)
The Little Sister (1949)
The Long Goodbye (1953)
Playback (1958)

—KC

JANE MARPLE

First Appearance: "The Tuesday Night Club" in *The Royal Magazine*
Date of First Appearance: December 1927
Author: Agatha Christie (1890–1976)

It has just happened that I have found myself in the vicinity of murder rather more often than would seem normal.

Following on the heels of Agatha Christie's hugely successful first sleuth, Hercule Poirot, one might not expect any room left for Miss Jane Marple to carve out her own fame. One would be wrong. The white-haired, seemingly unremarkable, bird-watching, gardening-loving, brocade- and lace-donning spinster in her late sixties or early seventies who passively knits in the background is as far as she could get from the vision we might conjure for a steel-trap mind, "nothing escapes my keen observation" detective type. In her first novel appearance in *The Murder at the Vicarage* (1930), her nondescript demeanor is contrasted against another old maid described as "a mixture of vinegar and gush," and we are told, "of the two Miss Marple is much more dangerous." She is fully aware of the advantage and slyly acknowledges, "Sitting here with one's knitting one just sees the facts." So, with Miss Marple's arrival on the scene, add to the list of literary English old maids another remarkable but on the surface seemingly very ordinary lady who holds her own against all the great male figures penned by great male writers. Christie's Miss Marple takes her place alongside the indomitable Brontë and Austen single ladies who have made their own way in a man's world.

Contrary to bursting on the crime-detective scene in a flashy, grandstanding way, Miss Marple gets a slow start by being briefly introduced and then going almost unnoticed—precisely the point—and therefore becoming privy to the goings-on without being suspected of the danger she poses to others' secrets. She only appears infrequently, quietly observing and gathering clues without anyone's awareness she is even on the trail until near the end of the book when she puts together the pieces of the mystery and solves the crime that professionals have failed to unravel. She adopts as her distinct style a modus operandi similar to that employed by the famous tortoise, whose slow but meticulous progress toward the finish line eventually surpasses all the hares racing past the best clues and failing to accomplish the task.

Miss Marple has the advantage of holding two firm beliefs that aid in her crime-solving success. The first is that rather than seeing small villages as sanctuaries of human kindness, her opinion is quite the opposite: "There is a great deal of wickedness in village life." Secondly, she does not support the idea of humanity's innate goodness. Staring from the pessimistic point of view that all people are capable of anything and that expecting the worst is the best practice, she frees herself to assess upstanding pillars of the community on an equal plane of evil possibility with those who are more likely to be most suspected. In a later story, she will corroborate the consistency of her belief by noting, "It really is very dangerous to believe people. I never have for years." Christie borrows this quality from her own grandmother, of whom she says, "Although a completely cheerful person, she always expected the worst of anyone and everything. And with almost frightening accuracy (she was) usually proved right." Her literary doppelgänger is as well.

Christie brings Miss Marple to life later in her writing career and offers an explanation for creating a second more private PI. After years of writing about Poirot, Christie confesses that she grew tired of him, his fussy ways, and his arrogant attitude. Pairing the two was not a choice, she says, because although they are of similar age and could have bumped into each other on a particularly complicated case needing a double amount of "small gray cells," as Poirot calls them, she writes that he as "a complete egoist, would not like being taught his business or having suggestions made to him by an elderly spinster lady." Such a collaboration would have been an interesting meeting of the minds or maybe a showdown of the sleuths, though, and not having the opportunity to peek in on that history-making case seems a real loss.

In sharp contrast to Poirot, Marple didn't travel the world, didn't seem concerned about fine food or wine, and wasn't meticulous in her wardrobe choice. She preferred to blend into the background rather than stick out like a well-dressed, attention-getting center of the crowd. But like Poirot, she was unencumbered by a spouse or children and had the advantage of being able to pour her full attention into solving a crime. Also like Poirot, she was adroit at observing behavior, gathering clues, deducing what was relevant and what was extraneous, and arriving at a conclusion that had seemed obvious to no one else, in her case even to the trained professionals whose job she was usurping without pay or help, and often with little praise.

Christie seemed to enjoy coming at crime-solving fiction from a female perspective, but she also regretted that "Miss Marple was born at the age of sixty-five to seventy—which as with Poirot, proved unfortunate, because she was going to have to last a long time in my life. If I had had any second sight I would have provided myself with a precocious schoolboy as my first detective; then he could have grown old with me." Somehow, this seems to be less than truthful, though, and it's more believable that spending as much time as Christie did with these two main characters—more than seventy books featuring one or the other and countless short stories—she had to love for them as they were; they were, after all, children of her own creation. Marple is less of an amusing character than Poirot, but Christie didn't kill her off as she did him, if that counts for anything.

The detective genre translates perfectly to television and film, and Miss Marple has starred many times in both mediums. Her character lures the audience in with that harmless grandmotherly demeanor and then enthralls them with her nimble skill at cracking even the most seemingly unsolvable cases. Being a creation of British origin, she has come to be considered a national treasure, and the BBC's *Agatha Christie's Miss Marple* series played by Joan Hickson was a television staple from 1984 until 1992, spanning all twelve of the original novels in which she appeared. Crossing the pond, the series also played on *PBS Mysteries!* some years later. Film icons Helen Hayes, Angela Lansbury, and Margaret Rutherford brought Miss Marple to life on the screen, and Lansbury went on to star from 1984 to 1996 in an American television knockoff series, *Murder She Wrote*, in which her character combined Christie's talent as a mystery writer and Marple's skill as a detective.

Highbrow literary critics often scoff at the mystery/detective fiction genre. The books are popular with the masses, after all—a fast-food equivalent to a highly nourishing meal—but millions of readers would beg to differ. Some satisfying fast food is good for the soul every now and then, isn't it?

Bibliography

Novels

The Murder at the Vicarage (1930)
The Thirteen Problems (1932) short-story collection also published as *The Tuesday Night Club*
The Body in the Library (1942)
The Moving Finger (1942)
A Murder Is Announced (1950)
They Do It with Mirrors (1952) also published as *Murder with Mirrors*
A Pocket Full of Rye (1953)
4:50 from Paddington (1957) also published as *What Mrs. McGillicuddy Saw!*
The Adventure of the Christmas Pudding (1960)
The Mirror Crack'd from Side to Side (1962) also published as *The Mirror Crack'd*
A Caribbean Mystery (1964)
At Bertram's Hotel (1965)
Nemesis (1971)
Sleeping Murder (1976)

Short Stories

From *The Thirteen Problems* (1932) short-story collection also published as *The Tuesday Night Club*: "The Tuesday Night Club," "The Idol House of Astart," "Ingots of Gold," "The Bloodstained Pavement," "Motive v. Opportunity," "The Thumbmark of St. Peter," "The Blue Geranium," "The Companion," "The Four Suspects," "A Christmas Tragedy," "The Herb of Death," "The Affair at the Bungalow," "Death by Drowning"
From *The Regatta Mystery and Other Stories* (1939): "Miss Marple Tells a Story"
From *Three Blind Mice and Other Stories* (1950) also published as *The Mousetrap*: "Strange Jest," "The Case of the Perfect Maid," "The Case of the Caretaker," "Tape-Measure Murder"
From *Double Sin and Other Stories* (1961): "Greenshaw's Folly," "Sanctuary"

Works Cited

Adams, Stephen. "Agatha Christie Used Her Grandmother as a Model for Miss Marple, New Tapes Reveal." *Telegraph*, September 15, 2008.

Bolin, Alice. "Miss Marple vs. the Mansplainers: Agatha Christie's Feminist Detective Hero." *Electric Lit*, May 15, 2015.

—GS

OSKAR MATZERATH

First Appearance: *The Tin Drum*
Date of First Appearance: 1959
Author: Günter Grass (1927–2015)

I shall try to dictate a quieter chapter to my drum, even though the subject of my next chapter calls for an orchestra of ravenous wild men.

Oskar Matzerath is one of the most original characters in literature, and to tell his story Günter Grass uses a mash-up of genres—a blend of realism, fantasy, magic realism, social commentary, and comic satire. In *The Tin Drum* (*Die Blechtrommel*), Oskar asks, "What novel—or what else in the world—can have the epic scope of a photographic album?" Oskar tries to reconstruct his life from memories of a 120-page photo album that was among his most cherished childhood possessions, with an engaging voice that's somehow wise, funny, poetic, and poignant, often at the same time. But there *is* an X factor: Oskar is telling his photograph-inspired story with the assistance of a toy drum he needs to bang on . . . from the confines of his room in a Polish mental hospital in the early 1950s. Over the course of his thirty-year life, he has always needed to bang on a toy drum, and when he breaks it he finds a replacement.

Is he crazy? You be the judge. Born in 1924 with the mind of an adult, Oskar becomes immediately disenchanted with life after hearing his mother's husband, a grocer named Matzerath, say with frightening certainty that young Oskar will also become a grocer in adulthood. Never mind that Matzerath may or may not be his biological father (a very young Oskar discerns that his mother is continuing an affair with Cousin Jan that began before he was born). He's made his decision, so when, on his third birthday, he finally receives the toy tin drum and drumsticks he had been awaiting—in infancy he had heard his mother say, "When little Oskar is three, he will have a toy drum"—he executes his exit strategy.

"It was then that I declared, resolved, and determined that I would never under any circumstances be a politician, much less a grocer, that I would stop right there, remain as I was—and so I did; for many years I not only stayed the same size but clung to the same attire." He accomplishes this by taking advantage of Matzerath leaving the cellar trapdoor open on his third birthday. With no one watching, having just received his tin drum, little Oskar toddles down the sixteen worn steps and hides his drum among the flour sacks for safekeeping. Then he climbs back up to the ninth step and launches himself, landing on his head on the concrete floor. Recalling the four weeks he spent in the hospital, Oskar gloats, "On my very first day as a drummer I had succeeded in giving the world a sign; my case was explained even before the grownups so much as suspected the true nature of the condition I myself had induced. Forever after the story was: on his third birthday our little Oskar fell down the cellar stairs, no bones were broken, but he just wouldn't grow any more." A scientific enigma, Oskar adds, "And I began to drum." When someone tried to take his drum he would scream so piercingly that glass would break. The same was true with his singing, and he had a talent for shattering glass. "Today as I lie here in my mental hospital, I often regret the power I had in those days to project my voice through the wintry night to thaw frost flowers on glass, cut holes in shopwindows, and show thieves the way."

Bruno, his "keeper" at the asylum, watches Oskar through a peephole and allows him to drum three to four hours daily. Oskar needs his drum "which, when handled adroitly and patiently, remembers all the incidentals that I need to get the essential down on paper." With Oskar, Grass blurs the line between normalcy and mental illness. Case in point: He ends up here because he found the severed finger of a nun he liked and he confessed to her murder, just because he needed solitude and quiet to think about his life and write his memoirs. Then again, Oskar's whole life seems to skate along the thin line that separates sanity from insanity. How else to describe a character who has his first sexual experience with his father/stepfather's second wife, and at three feet tall joins a troupe of little people who perform for the German troops at the front line, then becomes the Fagin-like leader of a gang of child criminals who call him "Jesus," works as a nude model, and in an ironic moment of accidental success that would resurface in such later novels as *Forrest Gump* forms a jazz trio with two friends and becomes rich and famous?

In telling his story, Oskar drifts back and forth between the narrative first person ("I") and third person ("Oskar"), tantalizing readers to look for a pattern that might help understand what makes Oskar tick. "Mama would throw me out with the bath water," he writes, "and yet she would share my bath. When I sang windowpanes to pieces, Mama was on hand with putty. . . . When Mama died, the red flames on my drum casing paled a little; but the white lacquer became whiter than ever and so dazzling that Oskar was sometimes obliged to close his eyes."

Ultimately, though, it's Oskar's attention to detail and his wry, subtly self-deprecating way of telling a story that makes him so much fun to read. Comic descriptions abound. When he has his first sexual encounter with Matzerath's second wife, for example, he writes, "It was quite beyond me why Maria, with oddly pursed lips, should whistle while removing her shoes, two high notes, two low notes, and while stripping off her socks. Whistling like the driver of a brewery truck, she took off the flowery dress . . . dropped her brassiere, and still without finding a tune, whistled frantically" while pulling off her panties. Later, "shaking her head, she picked her hairs from between my lips and said, in a tone of surprise, 'What a little rascal you are! You start up and you don't know what's what, and then you cry.'" The 1979 film adaptation won the Palme d'Or at Cannes and the Academy Award for Best Foreign Language Film, but the scene above proved highly controversial, and the novel remains so.

Grass said he was a supporter of the Social Democratic Party of Germany, and in his "frolicsome black fables," as the committee phrased it when awarding him the Nobel Prize, he created a novel that paints the political landscape with the same brush of sanity/insanity he uses for his main character. *The Tin Drum* pushed German readers to come to terms with their recent Nazi past. Decades later, though, Grass's standing as "moralist-in-chief of German letters" would come into question with his late-life admission that he was a soldier in the Waffen SS. He, as much as anyone, would have had the need to come to terms with Nazism. Yet, because many have interpreted Oskar's beating of the drum as a subconscious protest against middle-class complacency in the face of political upheaval, the phrase "to beat a tin drum"—to draw attention to a cause by creating a ruckus—has become a part of our cultural idiom.

Bibliography

The Tin Drum (1959)

Work Cited

"The Hypocrite's Halo." Editorial. *Washington Times*, August 20, 2006. https://www.washingtontimes.com/news/2006/aug/20/20060820-104132-7171r/.

—JP

MERLIN

First Appearance: *History of the Kings of Britain*
Date of First Appearance: circa 1135
Author: Geoffrey of Monmouth (1095–1155)

Learn why the world wags and what wags it. That is the only thing the mind can never exhaust, never alienate, never be tortured by, never fear or distrust, and never dream of regretting.—The Once and Future King

Sorcerer, wizard, wise old sage, counselor to kings, protector of kingdoms, foreseer of the future. These qualities identify Merlin, a character whose history spans nearly 1,000 years and who has held kings in his hands and kingdoms in his grasp. Every wizard, warlock, or magician gracing the pages of fiction since the early Middle Ages or appearing larger than life in film from its advent at the turn of the twentieth century owes homage to this mythic man as their progenitor. Doctor Who in a BBC television show about a traveler through time says, "He has many many names. But in my reckoning he is Merlin." His legendary figure, often dressed in flowing robes, wearing a pointed hat or a hood, and sporting a long gray or white beard, has been re-created in such figures as *The Hobbit* and *The Lord of the Rings'* Gandalf, *Star Wars'* Obi-Wan Kenobi, and *Harry Potter*'s Albus Dumbledore. Through these widely popular figures and many more, Merlin's identity and influence continue to resonate, and he shows no sign of disappearing anytime soon.

The mysterious figure, fictionalized from Anglo-Saxon legend, would later come to be associated with King Arthur, Camelot, the Knights of the Round Table, and the search for the Holy Grail. He first appears in print around 1135 in Geof-frey of Monmouth's composite *History of the Kings of Britain* and later singularly in *Life of Merlin* and *Merlin's Prophecies*, but his history goes back several centuries to British folklore somewhere between the sixth and eighth centuries. He seems to be an amalgamation of two men, a figure referred to as "Wildman of the Woods," and a fatherless boy called Ambrosius born of a noblewoman—some stories say a nun of noble birth—and a demon or incubus, thus the likely origin of his su-pernatural powers. The idea of a person unbounded by society either by birth or by choice holds such fascination in any age and culture that the telling and retell-ing of Merlin's story proliferates from there: French poet Robert de Boron a few decades after Monmouth's history, a mid-fifteenth-century *Prose Merlin* version composed by multiple authors from Boron's poem, Sir Thomas Malory's 1485 *Le Morte d'Arthur*, Tennyson's *Idylls of the King* (1859–1885), T. H. White's *Once and Future King* (1958), and on and on with new stories about Merlin or tales beyond these with characters whose authors have clearly been inspired by him.

Though in the realm of present Merlinesque characters his renown is somewhat eclipsed by Frodo's tutor, Luke Skywalker's mentor, or Harry Potter's teacher, who are all derivatives of Merlin, imitation clearly is the truest form of flattery. He is the first literary figure to have embodied magical powers to promote a story's action. He can shape-change to become another figure or use his powers to alter someone else's appearance, teleport himself in time and space, move boulders to create Stonehenge, or cause a sword to be encased in stone only to be removed by a worthy successor to the crown. He is the force behind the scenes more than in front of them, but Merlin's powers make him invaluable to king and kingdom, and his ability to transcend time ultimately gives him authority beyond the earthy climes kings occupy.

Merlin has been described as an archetype, a figure bearing important traits re-current in human history, and he fits a couple of significant categories that famed psychologist Carl Jung notes. First, he is the "helper figure" whose keen grasp of circumstances, prophetic insight, intelligence, and a willingness to minister and to mentor serve him well, and he not only assists one king, he is counselor to three British rulers: King Vertigern, the first and least well known; his successor Uther Pendragon, who is Arthur's father; and finally, Arthur himself. Merlin also might be interpreted through *The Hero with a Thousand Faces* and what Joseph Campbell calls the monomyth. In this structure an assistant/helper fills an important role of seeing the hero safely through a treacherous journey often in a land filled with magical elements and back home to receive the rewards bestowed upon him for his success. In comedic or satiric versions, this figure might be called a sidekick as Merlin appears in some versions of the Arthurian tale, or he can equally be portrayed as a necromancer with darker intent.

Whether Merlin is considered a prophet of good purpose or a wizard whose powers derive from evil depends on the time frame of the tale, who is telling the story, and the ideology, pagan or Christian, most prominent in the version being tapped into at the time. Merlin the wizard, descendant from demonic lineage, becomes more dominant in renderings where magic is central for control and can sometimes be misused for evil purposes. In these stories he is able to alter circumstances, shape-shift for deceptive purposes, and wield power over others to do his bidding or the bidding of the king against their will. Merlin the prophet functions more as wise counsel guiding the king and ensuring the safe succession and wise rule of the next heir.

But even the young Merlin grows old in spite of his magical abilities, and he becomes another archetype, the wise old man. This is the role, accompanied with the visual of the robe and white beard, so well associated with Merlin unless you're a Generation Xer or a millennial, in which case the various progeny suitable to the era's top magical sage take precedence. The wise old man is tasked first through his powers of prophetic vision to identify the young would-be hero capable of being a grand leader of men. Merlin, in at least Malory's later version of the Arthurian legend, goes a step further in fulfilling this role first by creating the spell that alters Uther Pendragon's appearance so he can sleep with the Duke of Cornwall's wife and conceive Arthur. He then takes the child away to be groomed for his future. Once the wise old man has fulfilled his role and his ward has been safely secured as an effective leader, he then serves as spiritual and sometime tactical counsel until such time when he is either killed off, or in Merlin's case is magically locked away to allow the hero full reign.

Merlin is a fascinating character in his own right, and equally important, he keeps good company. King Arthur, Queen Guinevere, Sir Lancelot, Galahad, Gawain and the Knights of the Round Table, Morgan le Fay, the Lady of the Lake. There is not a dull one in the bunch, and collectively their tale is as engaging as human drama gets. The litmus test of any good story is how many times it can be told, enhanced, altered, and adapted and still be a best seller or box office hit. For Merlin and his bevy of friends, the ticker is still counting.

Bibliography

History of the Kings of Britain (circa 1135)
Life of Merlin (circa 1150)
Merlin's Prophecies (circa 1155)
Prose Merlin (circa 1450–1460)
Le Morte d'Arthur (1485)
Idylls of the King (1859)
The Once and Future King (1958)

Works Cited

Campbell, Joseph. *The Hero with a Thousand Faces*. New York: Pantheon Books, 1949.

Jung, Carl. *Archetypes and the Collective Unconscious*. Trans. R. F. C. Hull. Volume 9, Part 1. Princeton University Press, 1969.

Richardson, Rob. "Travels through Time and Space: Part Seven: Sylvester McCoy." *Expert Comics News and Reviews*, April 11, 2013.

—GS

MEURSAULT

First Appearance: *L'Étranger* (*The Stranger*)
Date of First Appearance: 1942
Author: Albert Camus (1913–1960)

I had been right, I was still right, I was always right. I had lived my life one way and I could just as well have lived it another. I had done this and I hadn't done that. I hadn't done this thing but I had done another. And so?

Rarely has a philosophy found as perfect a voice for expressing its view of the universe as existentialism does in Albert Camus's story of a French Algerian man who, for inexplicable reasons, kills an Arab and is condemned to death. Camus may have rejected the assumption that he was an existentialist, insisting instead he was an absurdist, but the bleakness of both schools' insistence that moral absolutes neither explain nor guide human behavior is nowhere in literature better dramatized than in the anomie of his narrator, a young clerk named only Meursault. Speaking in clipped, Hemingwayesque sentences, Camus's antihero is a puzzling study in detachment whose inexpressive demeanor is presented as the only authentic response to death.

From the short novel's opening paragraph, in which Meursault states that his Maman (mother) has passed away but that it doesn't mean anything to him, to its conclusion, in which he imagines a crowd greeting his execution with cries of hatred, Camus's speaker is an emotional blank slate. He doesn't grapple with conscience as fellow murderer Raskolnikov does in Dostoevsky's *Crime and Punishment* (1866), nor is he a martyr for a social crisis like racism as does another convicted killer, Bigger Thomas in Richard Wright's *Native Son* (1940). Only in the closing pages does Meursault show any emotion, exploding at a priest who talks to him about God. Otherwise, he remains detached, which is why he inspires conflicting interpretations. He's a character who can't be made to care. When death is the ultimate fact of life, he says, what's the point?

Camus once summed up his novel by saying, "In our society, any man who doesn't cry at his mother's funeral is liable to be condemned to death." What he meant was that Meursault chooses not to behave as other people expect—he doesn't "play the game." When he attends his mother's funeral, he fails to demonstrate the grief other people expect. He doesn't want to see his mother in her casket one final time, and he doesn't cry as her friends do during her memorial. The next day, Marie, a former acquaintance he invites to a movie after an afternoon at the beach, is startled to discover among his clothes a black tie worn as a sign of mourning—nothing in Meursault's behavior hints that he's suffered such a recent loss. Later, when Marie asks if he loves her, his blunt reply is "probably not." As the original UK translation of Camus's title states, Meursault is *The Outsider*—his actions don't make sense to others because he speaks as he feels at any given moment, without trying to conform to anyone's idea of what's normal.

Meursault's most inexplicable action is his unmotivated murder of an unnamed Arab on an Algerian beach. He might have claimed self-defense, for he first encountered his victim in a scuffle over the man's sister, prompted after Meursault's friend Raymond beat the woman. Yet the killing happens after this fight; Meursault returns to the scene of the confrontation with a borrowed gun, and not for revenge either. Going or not going, he says, is all the same to him. And while the Arab pulls a knife on him that catches the glare of the sun and blinds Meursault, suggesting he might fire mistakenly, or by unconscious impulse, he doesn't just pull the trigger once—he shoots the man four more times. Four short knocks on the door of unhappiness, he calls the shots.

The second half of *The Stranger* depicts society's effort to make sense of the crime, something Meursault, not surprisingly by now, sees little purpose in attempting. His court-appointed lawyer wants him to claim his grief over Maman's death means he wasn't in his right mind; the examining magistrate gives up on persuading him to beg God's mercy and calls him "Monsieur Antichrist." Because his friend Raymond is reportedly a pimp, the prosecuting attorney says the killing happens because he consorts with known criminals. The court sentences Meursault to death—by guillotine, no less—mostly because of his apparent callousness.

Despite his inexpressiveness, Meursault does find contentment at the novel's end by accepting the inevitability of death. Whether this year or two decades in the future doesn't matter: the finality is the same. To the priest whose duty is to comfort the condemned, this seems like utter hopelessness, and he promises to pray for the murderer—a condescending offer that prompts Meursault's final, cathartic outburst. In his view, the priest is just as condemned as he is, because they will both die, and any hope of spiritual transcendence is self-deception. Meursault's sudden rage shatters the priest, but Meursault himself doesn't really understand how it cleanses him of the worst disease humanity can perpetuate—hope—until ship sirens awaken him in the middle of the night, and he suddenly feels at one with "the gentle indifference of the world." Accepting death, he claims he's happy—and that he was happy, too, before he murdered the Arab.

Meursault's claim takes us back to the beginning of the novel, where we realize that for all his apathy, he really does enjoy satisfying moments of pleasure. He loves to sleep, and he enjoys sex with Marie. He likes food and coffee, swimming at the beach, and the intense sun and ocean smell of Algiers . . . at least when they're not blinding him as he points a gun at somebody. These sensations from our physical environment, Camus insists, are our only source of meaning—not abstractions like values or social mores, but the intensity of feeling our physical environment gives us. Higher meanings are just self-delusions; all we have is the here and now.

Understanding why Meursault became so iconic in literature has a lot to do with the context in which he first appeared. *L'Étranger* was written shortly before France fell to the Nazis at the outset of World War II; when it was published under the Vichy regime in 1942, Hitler's censors had to okay it. The novel slipped by because (a) it didn't overtly criticize the Nazis and (b) it wasn't by or about a Jew. Yet Meursault's story, along with Camus's accompanying essay on the absurd, *The Myth of Sisyphus*, made an immediate splash among resistance forces who found in it (thanks to a positive review by Jean-Paul Sartre)—confirmation that neither faith, patriotism, nor honor would help them survive the occupation, much less regain their country. Survival would mean engaging the moment without dogma or sentimentality and recognizing that no rational explanation for the horrors of Hitler existed. After the war, Camus would soften *The Stranger*'s severity in his occupation allegory *The Plague* (1947), but no character in that novel can compete with Meursault—mostly thanks to his uncompromisingly oblique voice.

In recent decades, readers have explored Meursault's Algerian identity and his relationship to the Arabic population during France's colonial rule (which didn't end until 1962, two years after Camus's death). Postcolonial readings of *The Stranger* abound, many questioning whether reductively referring to the murder victim as "the Arab" reflects a colonialist mind-set on the part of Meursault (and Camus), with others arguing that Meursault's prosecution victimizes him comparably to Algeria's oppressed peoples. The difficulty of answering this question has recently been tackled by Algerian novelist Kamel Daoud, whose marvelous *The Meursault Investigation* (2013) gives the victim a name (Musa) while recasting the story of *The Stranger* from the point of view of his surviving family members.

Bibliography

L'Étranger (1942)

Work Cited

Kamel, Daoud. *Meursault, contre-enquête*. Hydra, Algeria: Barzakh Editions, 2013. English version: *The Meursault Investigation*. Trans. John Cullen. New York: Other Press, 2015.

—KC

THE MISFIT

First Appearance: "A Good Man Is Hard to Find" in *The Avon Book of Modern Writing*
Date of First Appearance: 1953
Author: Flannery O'Connor (1925–1964)

Jesus was the only One that ever raised the dead and He shouldn't have done it. He thrown everything off balance. If He did what He said, then it's nothing for you to do but throw away everything and follow Him, and if He didn't, then it's nothing for you to do but enjoy the few minutes you got left the best way you can—by killing somebody or burning down his house or doing some other meanness to him.

The author would've preferred the victim of the crime be cited as the most memorable character from her most famous story. For Flannery O'Connor, the unnamed grandmother of "A Good Man Is Hard to Find," a woman viciously murdered for assuring a stone-cold killer nicknamed the Misfit that he's deep down a moral man, is an agent of grace—albeit a deeply fallible one. In a 1963 essay called "A Reasonable Use of the Unreasonable," O'Connor claimed that the grandmother plants the mustard seed of God's irresistible redemption in the soul of the escaped convict a mere second before he blows her head off. The old woman's words will haunt her killer, the writer insisted, until at some future date he stops rebelling against divine authority and transforms into the proselytizer O'Connor believed all mortals were born to be. Don't get distracted by the dead bodies, she said. The underlying religious message was more important than the story's slick hard-boiled surface, even if the Misfit does get the story's coolest line: "She would have been a good woman . . . if it had been somebody there to shoot her every minute of her life."

With a deep sigh, O'Connor admitted her words likely fell on deaf ears; give readers a choice between an upstanding citizen and a bad man with a loaded shotgun, and they'll go for the latter. Although she didn't say it, one imagines her thinking her audience would only accept the theological message if they, like the grandmother, were staring down the end of two loaded barrels.

Yet with all due respect to the grandmother, the Misfit is indeed the character who makes "A Good Man Is Hard to Find" such a wickedly acerbic satire of hollow faith in a secular age. Although he doesn't appear until the final scene, his presence is felt throughout—first as a parody of the breathless media sensationalism that turns crime sprees into a form of cultural entertainment, and then as an unremittingly bleak embodiment of amoral violence, one who rationalizes his evil as the only sane response to life. In effect, the Misfit bridges two traditions of modern crime writing. Before he enters the story, the danger he presents to society seems so distant that his evil feels unreal, not unlike that of the bad guys in first-generation pulp fiction with similarly cartoonish nicknames like "Whisper" or "The Beast." When the killer and his henchmen appear calmly wielding guns, though, he offers an emotionally detached but intellectually reasoned rejection of theological good. His calm embrace of the fallen world boils down to his credo: "No pleasure but meanness." His ability to rationalize evil makes him a bone-chilling cousin to such nihilistic antiheroes as Meursault in Albert Camus's *The Stranger* (1942), Lou Ford in Jim Thompson's noir classic *The Killer inside Me* (1952), or Robert Mitchum's preacher-turned-serial killer in Charles Laughton's 1955 film *The Night of the Hunter*. As more than one critic has argued, the Misfit is a godfather to the serial killers who populate today's fiction and TV crime shows, making him a harbinger of our queasy desire to peek into the dark underbelly of the soul.

Part of what makes "A Good Man Is Hard to Find" such an effective short story is the startling tonal shift it takes when the Misfit enters the plot as a kind of anticowboy, shirtless and in stolen jeans. The first half of the text is a rollicking satire of the midcentury South's changing landscape, perhaps second only to Vladimir Nabokov's *Lolita* (1955) in using a road trip to parody the gaucheries of American popular culture. Packed into a car with her son, Bailey, his wife, and his obnoxious children for a Florida vacation, the grandmother witnesses a culture far more transitory and disconnected than the Tennessee of her relatives. In a world of garish roadside distractions, from comic books and jukeboxes to billboards screaming in all caps and exclamation points to greasy BBQ stands run by men like Red Sammy Butts whose punning names reduce them to stereotypical goobers, newspaper accounts of the Misfit's crimes just seem like one more disposable amusement. The grandmother revels in gossiping about the on-the-lam felon, masking her enjoyment of the suspense he brings to her dull life with the cheap nostalgia of lamenting that the world has gone to pot.

Not that the grandmother is the good person she laments there aren't more of. She doesn't much care for her grandchildren, John Wesley and June Star (who are admittedly obnoxious). The malicious pleasure she gets from telling the story of a "nigger boy" who once ate a watermelon intended for her because her "gentleman" suitor, Edgar Atkins Teagarden, carved his initials in it ("E.A.T.") is hardly Christian in spirit. It's when the grandmother's cat, Pitty Sing, causes Bailey to wreck the car on an isolated dirt road and the Misfit descends on the stranded family that the woman's true hypocrisy is revealed. She not only blurts out the spree killer's name when she recognizes his face, dooming the family to be shot in the woods, pleading for their lives, but she also insists the Misfit wouldn't possibly shoot a lady because he doesn't have "common blood." Her equivalence between goodness and simplistic Christian piety is as transparent as it is desperate; by the time she's muttering "Jesus, Jesus," she sounds as if she's swearing, not praying.

In contrast to her superficial pleas, the Misfit's beliefs are fascinatingly complex. As the former gospel singer and undertaker reveals, he can't remember the crime that first sent him to the penitentiary. It doesn't really matter because original sin already condemns humanity to guilt before it can ever choose evil on its own. Committing crimes is his way of owning or "signing for" the bad deeds for which God has prejudged his children. The Misfit also rejects the idea of believing without proof that Christ redeemed humanity, because that would require a leap of faith that further robs individuals of choice. If Jesus did rise from the dead, then people should have no excuse for not following him, but if he didn't, then humanity has no reason not to indulge in evil because life is unfair suffering. The Misfit wants theological certainty; in its absence, he thinks he can only enjoy the brutality of rebelling.

In the end, though, not even evil relieves doubt. When the grandmother touches his shoulder attempting some gesture of motherly comfort, the Misfit shoots her dead. One of his henchmen laughs, but the story ends with the killer's sharp rebuke of his own philosophy that meanness is enjoyable: "It ain't no pleasure in life," he grunts. No killer in literature seems to enjoy his job less, which somehow makes the Misfit even cooler.

Bibliography

The Avon Book of Modern Writing (1953)
A Good Man Is Hard to Find (1955)

Work Cited

O'Connor, Flannery. "On Her Own Work: A Reasonable Use of the Unreasonable." In *Mystery and Manners: Occasional Prose*, edited by Sally and Robert Fitzgerald, 107–14. New York: Farrar, Straus and Giroux, 1970.

—KC

GUY MONTAG

First Appearance: "The Fireman" in *Galaxy Science Fiction*
Date of First Appearance: February 1951
Author: Ray Bradbury (1920–2012)

There must be something in books, something we can't imagine, to make a woman stay in a burning house.

Aldous Huxley helped forge discussion of a dystopian "brave new world" with his 1932 novel of the same name, George Orwell followed with *Animal Farm* (1945) and *Nineteen Eighty-Four* (1949), and Ray Bradbury soon joined in with his publication *Fahrenheit 451* (1953), voted "one of the best dystopian novels of all time" by *Paste* magazine. Bibliophiles were horrified by a society that deemed books so dangerous they not only had to be banned, but also burned along with the houses in which they were found, and the book-loving perpetrators immediately arrested. The idea was shocking. It still is. The novel's opening sentence was "It is a pleasure to burn," and its protagonist Guy Montag serves as a fireman whose job is not to put out fires, but to start them—chiefly for the purpose of destroying books. He readily does so until his thinking is jogged, and he begins to question the process, which is precisely the danger meant to be stifled. Like all dystopian novels, interrogating a futuristic society leads to an interrogation of the path that got them there and what that connection is to the current status quo. Guy Montag becomes the book's social conscience, the instrument through which questioning occurs, and as such, he is as relevant now as he was more than half a century ago and will be a half century from now, and no doubt beyond.

Guy's first name and generalized characterization portray him as a nondescript cog in a large wheel controlled by an indistinct entity, and this is the position he and the masses have intentionally been lulled into accepting. His teenage neighbor Clarisse has been less susceptible to the mind-dulling, hypnotic condition under which everyone has fallen because she and her family don't watch the giant screen on their wall, and her relatively innocent questions cause Guy to probe his own thoughts about why things are the way they are. She asks if firemen's original job was to put out fires rather than start them, and he laughs uncomfortably but can't put his finger on why. When she asks if he's happy, Guy confesses that he feels "his body divide itself . . . the two halves grinding one upon the other." This scrutiny of his own thoughts seems too subversive at first, so he justifies it as Clarisse projecting her thoughts onto him. He also rejects the idea that he is in control of his hands' actions, but rather that they have a volition of their own. Eventually, Guy confronts his mindless following of edicts, and he begins secretly challenging ideas, even though he is one of the enforcers meant to keep thoughts at bay by destroying the books. Guy slowly begins to rebel by hiding and reading books, and eventually he exchanges using actual fire for participating in an intellectual firestorm when he joins the few resisters left at the end of the novel's cathartic mass destruction.

Bradbury's purpose behind creating Guy Montag and *Fahrenheit 451* seems obvious. Aren't all dystopian novels a rebellion against government, and this one certainly has that flavor as well. Early on when asked where the idea came from, Bradbury said, "Well, Hitler, of course. When I was 15, he burned the books in the streets of Berlin. Then along the way I learned about the libraries in Alexandria burning 5000 years ago. That grieved my soul. Since I'm self-educated, that means my educators—the libraries—are in danger. And if it could happen in Alexandria, if it could happen in Berlin, maybe it could happen somewhere up ahead, and my heroes would be killed." This connection to Hitler's actions led many to believe that Guy Montag and his world were products of Bradbury's rebellion against politics, though he denies the book was meant as an antigovernment invective. It is certainly easy to see why it might be read that way, though.

Autocratic regimes ruling with unchecked power had proved highly dangerous and were targeted and defeated in the previous decade's world war. Nazis in Germany had not just burned in the streets books they saw as subversive; they began incinerating en masse people who didn't agree with them or those they deemed inferior. But even post–World War II, it wasn't long before the 1950s House Un-American Activities Committee under Senator Joe McCarthy made people starkly aware that government was watching them, and blacklisting, censorship, and other punishments were doled out to those who didn't fit the accepted mold. Again, this seems like an easy assumption for what inspired Bradbury's novel and Guy Montag as his mouthpiece fighting such crimes against individual freedom.

The real motivator, Bradbury revealed in an interview much later, was radio and television. He said, "I wasn't worried about freedom. I was worried about people turned into morons by T.V." He saw listening and viewing as antithetical to reading, and "this sort of hopscotching existence makes it almost impossible for people, myself included, to sit down and get into a novel again." With television relatively new at the time he was writing the book, he anticipated its hypnotic qualities as the opioid of the masses, and Guy Montag's wife becomes the zombie reflecting what is happening in all the houses. Interestingly, this concept has reared its head again, this time with discussion about the danger of social media as the new opioid with its large-scale ability to be abused. HBO released its version of *Fahrenheit 451* in May 2018, and it is widely seen as ticking "all the right dystopian-horror boxes"—but it doesn't have the power of Bradbury's text.

In the novel, aside from the obvious danger of being found out as a rebel, the dilemma Montag faces is that he must think for himself and understand the value of books if he is going to risk so much to read them, and, like other resisters, to preserve them through memory. Books contradict each other, even themselves, and they require analysis, hypothesis, synthesis, and decisions about philosophical beliefs. Reading and digesting a book is serious business and can develop heretics against whatever regime is currently dominant. They are powerful tools, and Montag comes to understand that and to protect the privilege.

The novel ends as a large flash appears on the horizon, and it's clear that the city has been destroyed—not completely apocalyptic, however, because Montag and the others who become the keepers of the books they have memorized will carry the seeds to rebuild. The stories will be told over and over, an idea later copied in the 1985 film *Mad Max: Beyond Thunderdome*, as part of the past's heritage that will become the tales informing the future. Montag has memorized the biblical passage "To everything there is a season. A time to break down, and a time to build up," and the destruction and rebirth described in that passage come full circle as he and his friends usher in a new dawn.

Bibliography

Fahrenheit 451 (1953)

Works Cited

Bradbury, Ray. Interview by Dana Gioia. "Creating *Fahrenheit 451*." *National Endowment for the Arts Magazine*, 3, 2006.
"Bradbury on Censorship/Television." Video clip. RayBradbury.com. Accessed October 16, 2018. http://www.raybradbury.com/at_home_clips.html.
Gilbert, Sarah. "*Fahrenheit 451* Tackles the Evils of Social Media." *Atlantic*, May 19, 2018.
Jackson, Frannie and *Paste* staff. "The 30 Best Dystopian Novels of All Time." *Paste* magazine, May 29, 2018.

—GS

DEAN MORIARTY

First Appearance: *On the Road*
Date of First Appearance: 1957
Author: Jack Kerouac (1922–1969)

A kind of holy lightning I saw flashing from his excitement and his visions, which he described so torrentially that people in buses looked around to see the "overexcited nut." In the West he'd spent a third of his time in the poolhall, a third in jail, and a third in the public library. They'd seen him rushing eagerly down the winter streets, bareheaded, carrying books to the poolhall, or climbing trees to get into the attics of buddies where he spent days reading or hiding from the law.

Some characters become famous because they're based on famous people. Others become literary idols and end up making the people they're based on famous. That's the case with Dean Moriarty, the "holy goof" who embodies America's restless energy and reckless velocity in Jack Kerouac's beatnik classic *On the Road*. Both in biographical background and personality, Dean is inseparable from the man who inspired him, Neal Cassady (1926–1968). Kerouac spent his career mythologizing the charisma Cassady exuded, seeing in him a spontaneity and vibrancy akin to the improvisational riffing of jazz musicians. While the author was convinced he captured those qualities better in his novel *Visions of Cody* (an excerpted version was published in 1960, but the complete text appeared only posthumously in 1972). *On the Road* is the book that turned both men into cult heroes and made the Beat generation's boundary-breaking spirit of exploration and adventure an antidote to the 1950s' staid conservatism. Over the decade that followed, Kerouac's novel inspired beatniks, hipsters, and hippies to seek enlightenment in the unconventional. Cassady soon discovered that fans of *On the Road* expected the real-life Dean to live up to the legend. The notoriety cost him jail time and likely contributed to his premature death at forty-one.

From the opening sentence, Dean Moriarty dominates *On the Road*. Kerouac's alter ego narrator, Sal Paradise, hears stories of him, then reads philosophical letters he mails, even before the two meet. When Dean shows up in New York City along with his teenage bride, Marylou, Sal inadvertently interrupts them having sex. From this auspicious introduction, Sal learns his new friend's three main impulses are carnal, criminal, and literary. Dean wants to be a writer but needs Sal to teach him how. He is also relatively fresh from reform school, having done time for heisting cars to joyride, but his "criminality" isn't pathological or psychotic. It's a "wild yea-saying outburst of American joy," a quest for two things usually depicted as antitheses: knowledge and kicks.

Structurally, *On the Road* is divided between four cross-country trips Sal takes between 1947 and 1950. The first, set a year after the friends' initial meeting, leads Sal alone to Denver, where he learns that Dean grew up the son of an alcoholic hobo who left him to fend for himself in downtown pool halls. Dean appears in this journey only long enough to introduce his new wife, Camille, before Sal heads for San Francisco for adventures of his own. In the following year's odyssey, Dean summons the narrator for a trip to New Orleans, accompanied now again by Marylou; as Sal realizes, his friend's gusto renders him incapable of settling down with one woman for long. Sal is even shocked when Dean invites him to sleep with his girl. In a scene highlighted in the 2012 movie starring Kristen Stewart, Marylou sits naked between the two men and strokes their penises with cold cream. (At least one radical aspect of Cassady *On the Road* suppresses, though, is his bisexuality; Kerouac doesn't allow Dean to bed Carlo Marx as Cassady did that character's inspiration, poet Allen Ginsberg.) The most significant event occurs when Dean accompanies Sal to a bebop jazz performance where the musicians' effortless virtuosity leads Dean to introduce his idea of "IT," the epiphany one achieves by diving into the adrenaline of experience without concern for rational thought.

Dean doesn't fully articulate his theory until Sal's third journey, set in 1949, by which point their intellectual circle is fed up with Dean's selfish hedonism. When their mutual friend Galatea Dunkel takes Dean to task for his constant philandering, Sal realizes the criticism is pointless: Dean is "the Idiot, the Imbecile, the Saint of the lot . . . the HOLY GOOF." This latter term places him in the tradition of the holy fool, of sages who speak wisdom in bouts of madness—though in Dean's case "madness" is passionate intensity, not insanity. To him "IT" is a transcendent moment in which time stops and one experiences pure beatitude or bliss, something the duo feels when they arrive in Chicago and watch their jazz hero, pianist George Shearing, perform.

By the fourth journey, though, the mood darkens, and Sal wonders if Dean's energies can be put to a productive purpose. By now Dean is the father of four children, two with Camille, an illegitimate one out west, and a new one with his latest girlfriend, Inez, whom he marries without bothering to divorce Camille. Sal's growing impatience comes to a head in Mexico when he comes down with dysentery and Dean abandons him to rush back to Inez. Sal considers him a "rat." The novel ends with two final encounters, the first showing that Dean hasn't changed (he is back with Camille, though he wants Inez to live across town from them), the second admitting that he has. For reasons Kerouac doesn't explain, Dean rolls briefly through New York but "he couldn't talk anymore and said nothing." Saddened, Sal decides the old Dean is gone but the new one will go on, though he can't shake Dean's influence on his sensibility. In a melancholy final paragraph, he pictures the immensity of America and its endless circling roadways, as circuitous as his thoughts, and all he can say is, "I think of Dean Moriarty."

Kerouac followed *On the Road* with a dozen Beat generation novels, some featuring another version of Dean Moriarty with a different name, Cody Pomeray. By the mid-1960s, their creator grew to resent bitterly his fame as the king of the Beats and denounced the burgeoning hippie movement—often truculently, as when he appeared slurring and bloated, nearly unrecognizable, on William F. Buckley's syndicated TV show *Firing Line* a year before his 1969 death. Cassady's fame had an equally tragic effect. Largely because of *On the Road*'s notoriety, police in 1958 entrapped the real-life Dean in a pot bust that cost him two years in San Quentin. Emerging as a countercultural hero, Cassady fell into the trap of trying to live up to his wild and reckless reputation, traveling frenetically but aimlessly, ingesting dangerous amounts of LSD, and serving as a guru to Ken Kesey's Merry Pranksters in 1964. In early 1968, reportedly under the influence of Seconal, he passed out on a Mexican railroad track and died of exposure. "Thank God," his ex-wife Carolyn—Camille in *On the Road*—said. "Released at last."

Despite the enduring fascination with Neal Cassady, Dean Moriarty is more than a simple transcription of the man who inspired him. As Kerouac mythologizes him, Dean incarnates the paradoxes of America. Restless even as he exhausts his natural resources, he represents an ideal that remains on the go even as it's running on empty.

Bibliography

On the Road (1957)

Works Cited

Kerouac, Jack. *Excerpts from Visions of Cody*. New York: New Directions, 1960.
———. *Visions of Cody*. New York: McGraw-Hill, 1972.

—KC

O

OFFRED

First Appearance: *The Handmaid's Tale*
Date of First Appearance: 1985
Author: Margaret Atwood (1939–)

My name isn't Offred, I have another name, which nobody uses now because it's forbidden. I tell myself it doesn't matter, your name is like your telephone number, useful only to others; but what I tell myself is wrong, it does matter.

Political novels rarely age well. Few readers today revisit Philip Roth's *Our Gang* (1971), a venomous Nixon satire that appeared *before* Watergate, and fewer still read Henry Adams's *Democracy* (1880), about a populist president abusing executive power. For every well-remembered *Phineas Finn* (1869) or *All the King's Men* (1946) by Anthony Trollope and Robert Penn Warren, respectively, only specialists recall George Meredith's *Beauchamp's Career* (1875) or Howard Spring's *Fame Is the Spur* (1940).

Even when a political novel does endure, the plot usually overshadows its characters. George Orwell's *Animal Farm* (1945) is eternally topical, but neither Snowball, Napoleon, nor Squealor are memorable as personalities—they're allegories, rather, of specific political positions. Not everybody in a political novel gets to be as iconic as Tom Joad or Atticus Finch.

Margaret Atwood's *The Handmaid's Tale* is the rare example of a novel that roars back into relevance after decades in print. Initially, this dystopian warning against totalitarian repression of women was viewed as protesting 1980s religious fundamentalism, whether the Iranian Revolution's ayatollahs or America's own Reaganite Christian right. Set in a near future in which a theocracy called Gilead has overthrown the United States, the novel details how women are enslaved as breeders during an infertility crisis. Atwood's most disturbing prediction is a ritual called "the Ceremony," in which the master impregnates an ovulating handmaid as she lies in his wife's lap, a proxy vagina.

The Handmaid's Tale was cited in abortion-rights debates up through the 1992 election of the pro-choice Bill Clinton, but perceptions of its parallels to specific era events tapered throughout the late 1980s. A 1990 film adaptation with a Harold

Pinter screenplay didn't allude to period incursions against women's freedoms, such as the rise of the charismatic fundamentalist Randall Terry and his Operation Rescue movement, which blockaded abortion clinics and heckled patients seeking reproductive health services. One left-leaning reviewer dismissed the movie's grim vision of women's future as "paranoid poppycock" before adding "just like the book." Throughout the quarter century that followed, the novel was consistently taught and studied, its radical bona fides certified whenever a library or school board banned it as antireligious or obscene. Yet its vision no longer seemed foreboding.

All that changed, however, in 2016 with the election of Donald J. Trump. The first president in American history whose popularity swelled, especially among Christian evangelicals, whenever he insulted a woman, Trump normalized misogyny while promising a return to right-wing patriarchal authority. Not even getting caught on tape bragging of sexually assaulting women by "grab[bing] 'em by the pussy" derailed his path to the White House. Six months after Trump's surprise victory—won through the electoral college, not the popular vote—the streaming platform Hulu premiered a television adaptation of *The Handmaid's Tale*, and suddenly Atwood's novel was more topical than it was during its original vogue. Images from the narrative became key symbols of the anti-Trump, pro-women "resistance" at marches and demonstrations. Protestors donned the signature red cloaks and white wimples (head coverings) that mark the handmaids' chattel status in Gilead. The costume, reminiscent of the Puritan era, has proved an effectively theatrical statement of defiance not only in America; women have worn it as well at protests in Argentina, Ireland, and numerous other countries. Literature doesn't get much more relevant.

What's curious about *The Handmaid's Tale* as protest literature, though, is how remarkably unrevolutionary its central character is. Known as Offred—or "Of Fred," referring to Fred Waterford, "The Commander" whose household she serves—Atwood's narrator isn't, on the surface, a rebel. She doesn't overthrow Gilead's reigning regime as does Theo Faron in P. D. James's comparable parable of infertility and oppression, *The Children of Men* (1992). Nor is she Katniss Everdeen, the female insurrectionist in Suzanne Collins's young adult fantasy *The Hunger Games* (2008–2010). Offred instead is relatively passive. Her closest analogue may be Winston Smith in Orwell's *Nineteen Eighty-Four* (1949), but even he joins a resistance movement and is tortured by Big Brother's chief enforcer. Offred only hears whispers of revolution, and the novel's ambiguous ending doesn't say whether the fomenting uprising determines her fate. Comparing herself to her friend Moira, who battles to escape Gilead, Offred admits to feeling like a "wimp." Atwood eschews her audience's desire to see female freedom fighters warring against male domination. Offred's perspective allows her instead to explore how cultures coerce people into accepting oppression as natural, and how silent acts of resistance undermine that ingrained order. *The Handmaid's Tale* suggests that street-fighting women won't topple the patriarchy. Rather, freedom's first step is to subvert instilled beliefs privately.

The first thing Gilead expects handmaids to forget, for example, is their past. Yet Offred meticulously curates memories of her previous life. She remembers her mother, an antipornography feminist who once led Take Back the Night marches; her husband, Luke, whose fate she's not sure of; and her daughter, who Gilead deemed illegitimate because Luke was divorced and who was handed to a prominent family to raise. Offred also recounts her indoctrination at the Red (Re-education) Center, where under the brutal discipline of Aunt Lydia she was trained into servility.

As she services the Commander and his unhappy wife, Serena Joy (a former televangelist), Offred witnesses the hypocrisies of Gilead's elites. The Commander initiates a taboo relationship with her, inviting her to play Scrabble in his "forbidden" room. The game is indicative of how crucial language is to Offred's quiet rebellion: because handmaids are prohibited from reading, she ponders words incessantly, enjoying their sensuality and developing personal meanings. Later, the Commander escorts her to a government-operated brothel called Jezebel's, where the Republic's leaders indulge their sexual fantasies with sterilized women who dress up as cheerleaders and baby dolls. (Offred discovers Moira working here.)

Serena Joy likewise breaks Gilead's rigid cultural rules, encouraging Offred to begin a sexual relationship with the Commander's chauffeur, Nick. Suspecting that her husband is sterile, the wife hopes the pair will conceive a child she can raise as her own. What Serena Joy never expects is that Offred will enjoy sex with Nick, finding rebellion in intimacy. She also never suspects Nick of belonging to the Mayday Underground and plotting Offred's escape. In the final scene, armed officers who may be the Eyes of God, the secret police, or Mayday revolutionaries forcibly take Offred from the Commander's house; whether she is headed for darkness or light is unclear.

The novel's final section flashes forward nearly 200 years to an academic analysis of Offred's narrative, which, we learn, she recorded onto cassettes discovered long after Gilead's fall. A scholar, Professor Pieixoto, laments that her story can't be substantiated because few records from "the Gileadean regime" survive. Atwood's point is twofold. She parodies how women's stories are always framed within male commentary that judges female voices. She also emphasizes how women are excluded from history because their stories only survive in fragments and ephemera like Offred's tapes.

The only way women's history will survive, *The Handmaid's Tale* insists, is for women to speak up now, which Atwood will no doubt do in the impending sequel she announced she was writing in late 2018, *The Testaments*.

Bibliography

The Handmaid's Tale (1985)

—KC

KATHERINE SCARLETT O'HARA

First Appearance: *Gone with the Wind*
Date of First Appearance: 1939
Author: Margaret Mitchell (1900–1949)

I'm afraid I'll die and go to hell.

Gone with the Wind was the perfect summer read during those teen years when the practice of baking one's oiled skin to a golden brown was in vogue, however ironically oppositional that act was to Scarlett O'Hara's equal efforts to keep her sixteen-year-old skin pristinely pale. The deep whiteness of Margaret Mitchell's Southern lady-in-training bespeaks a privileged rank built on the scarred backs of slaves who made her world possible, but that fact made little or no difference to a young and completely self-indulgent Scarlett. Talk of the pending Civil War was only a rude interruption at barbecues where she expected to be the object of all the young men's attention, including those promised to other girls. While the novel's title suggests the destruction of a whole class and its way of life, such serious social, racial, and economic issues were not the driving factors compelling Mitchell's heroine, or the novel's typical young readers for that matter. *Gone with the Wind*'s more-than-800-page epic tale owes its lasting popularity to one source—Miss Scarlett O'Hara.

No matter what side of the Mason-Dixon Line one calls home, or which emblematic flag is sacred, Scarlett represents a stereotyped vision of the Southern belle and her antebellum lifestyle we have come to perceive as historical reality. We can close our eyes and see her billowing whale-boned gown and hear the deep Southern drawl as she calls to yet another would-be suitor strolling up the expansive plantation lawn past live oaks dripping Spanish moss. We imagine ourselves standing on the wide porch of Scarlett's beloved Tara while gazing out at the sunset over the red Georgia clay and tobacco and cotton plants in rows as far as the horizon's reach. This is the romanticized South we like to conjure, the one to which Scarlett was born and expected to gain ascendency. But Mitchell brilliantly sets her novel as the Civil War begins and extends it over the course of the Reconstruction era that follows so she can unfold one of the fictional South's most stubbornly resilient women against such a backdrop. Like the region that has shaped her, and with God and us as her witnesses, we watch Scarlett pledge to rise again and again because no matter what setbacks come along, "tomorrow is another day."

The 1989 film *Steel Magnolias* popularized the new image of the Southern woman forged in metal cloaked under the facade of a delicate blossom. Scarlett O'Hara is trained to be a proper young woman of plantation aristocracy, but she is more akin to the region's new generation of ladies. Her name gives the first clue to that nature as a tough cookie rather than a shrinking violet, to mix metaphors. Mitchell originally called Scarlett "Pansy" but was convinced at the last minute to change the name because, like a magnolia, the pansy implies a weakness Scarlett does not possess. She begrudgingly, though expertly, deploys the helpless "I need a man to protect me" aura to cover her headstrong, independent nature considered unbecoming for a well-bred daughter of the plantation. But Scarlett more appropriately calls to mind a fiery personality that will erupt when she fails to hide her steel under the petal's velvety cover, and O'Hara to add the combustible disposition often linked to her Irish heritage.

Scarlett is the bad girl we should hate but can't stop ourselves from loving. As NPR contributor Karen Grigsby Bates writes, "She is the founding mother of the Me generation" whose "unabashed self-interest" is "delicious" and "kind of like flipping off the Mean Girls' table in the school lunchroom," though Scarlett is one of the mean girls too. She acts to fulfill her narcissistic nature at a cost to others' happiness, she throws childish tantrums even as she grows into womanhood, and she masterfully plies phony coquettishness to steal other women's beaus for her own purposes. But we've also seen her chafe at counterfeit female helplessness, single-handedly build a successful business, and drive a horse and wagon with her sister-in-law and newborn nephew through burning Atlanta while fighting off marauding troops as she hurries home to protect Tara. Scarlett is Technicolor against the genteel milquetoast who surround her. She holds her nose and dives into whatever is necessary, first to achieve her own spoiled and self-indulgent desires, and then, because she refuses to lose the real battle, the fight for her home. The fact that the most devastating war on American soil is smack-dab in the middle of her personal and emotional landscape is significant only because it is the wall in her way. All men, all battles, all problems are only objects to hurdle or to employ in her plan to save what she loves, including herself.

Scarlett will marry her first husband to get back at Ashley Wilkes, a man we come to be sick of long before Scarlett does. She will wed her second husband, her sister's fiancé, and usurp his money to make ends meet as the war takes its toll on the plantation economy, and she will accept her third husband, Rhett Butler, because he is happy to allow his money to flaunt ascendency over those who look down on her breaches of Southern etiquette. Scarlett employs what one critic calls "sex work"—more politely referred to as feminine wiles—because she will get what she needs. But she also keeps her family and freed slaves from starving, murders a Yankee who threatens their safety, and stops Southern whites from forcing her off the beloved homestead by raising taxes she can't pay.

Scarlett's transcendence to film and popular culture also underscores the power of her personality. In Metro-Goldwyn-Mayer's three-hour-and-forty-five-minute blockbuster, she appears in virtually every scene, and this larger-than-life Scarlett forever embeds its British-born star Vivien Leigh in our mind's eye as the visual prototype. Leigh's drawled "Rheeett, eif yewh goowh whaaire shahl Eeye goowh? Whaaht shahll Eeye dewh?" rings true, at least to Yankee-born ears, and Clark Gable's "Frankly, my dear, I don't give a damn" ranks as the number one quote on the American Film Institute's list of top movie lines. Carol Burnett's spin-off "Went with the Wind" is one of television's classic spoofs with Scarlett descending Tara's grand staircase wearing a dress fashioned from her mother's velvet curtains, as she does in the book, but Burnett's brilliant version includes the curtain rod poking out from the shoulders of the dress with Scarlett explaining that she "saw it in the window and just had to have it." And Alice Randall's 2001 novel *The Wind Done Gone* provides us with a revisionist story from the view of one of Tara's slaves.

Despite her selfish nature, even to the end, Scarlett O'Hara continues to reverberate with a contemporary audience because she is a realist and a survivor. When she first meets Rhett, who has just caught her in an embarrassing moment that he impolitely notices, she responds, "Sir, you are no gentleman," to which he replies, "And you, miss, are no lady. . . . Don't think I hold that against you."

Neither do we.

Bibliography

Gone with the Wind (1939)

Work Cited

Bates, Karen Grigsby. "Shrew, Selfish Scarlett: A Complicated Heroine." NPR, *All Things Considered*, January 28, 2008.

—GS

ORLANDO

First Appearance: *Orlando: A Biography*
Date of First Appearance: 1928
Author: Virginia Woolf (1882–1941)

Now, the obscurity, which divides the sexes and lets linger innumerable impurities in its gloom, was removed, and if there is anything in what the poet says about truth and beauty, this affection gained in beauty what it lost in falsity.

If you're unlucky in literature, you wake up one morning like Kafka's Gregor Samsa and discover you've turned into a cockroach. If the gods are on your side, though, you hop out of bed as the titular hero of Virginia Woolf's 1928 romp through history does at the age of thirty and find you're suddenly a woman. You also find nobody makes a particularly big deal of it. You live on for some 300 years, barely aging, and you crank out innumerable works of poetry and drama, hobnobbing along the way with some of the greats of British literature, including John Dryden and Alexander Pope. You get to experience the great biological honor that separates women from men—bearing children—but you aren't hampered by the limitations men have traditionally imposed upon women. You get to love whom you want to love, dress however you wish, and travel anywhere you like.

Most of all, you get to be whomever you want to be, which means you're not confined to being one thing. It sounds like a great life, and Virginia Woolf has great fun writing it in *Orlando: A Biography*. The novel gives us a main protagonist who enjoys something denied most other characters in literature: absolute freedom of identity.

Orlando is at once a satire of biography (replete with pompous footnotes), a takeoff on literary criticism and the dubious mechanics of reputation building, a treatise on how the interior experience of time is more fulfilling that the outwardly measured world of clocks and schedules, and a biting commentary on how women's contributions to literary history are minimized—a theme shared by Woolf's highly influential essay *A Room of One's Own*, which she wrote at the same time as this book.

But perhaps the best description of *Orlando* comes from Nigel Nicolson, whose mother inspired the titular character: The novel is "the longest and most charming love letter in literature." Woolf and Vita Sackville-West were intimately involved at the height of their careers, and their relationship helped the former overcome the trauma of the childhood sexual abuse she suffered at the hands of her older stepbrothers. Having completed several dark explorations of the postwar world, including the classics *Mrs. Dalloway* (1925) and *To the Lighthouse* (1927), Woolf felt in need of an "escapade"; *Orlando* was her opportunity "to kick up my heels & be off." Although rightly celebrated as a comic masterpiece, the book is also recognized as a landmark in LGBTQ literature, revered as one of the earliest works to dismiss gender as a social construct with little fixed relevance to biological sex. Because they were published the same year, the exuberant *Orlando* is often contrasted to Radclyffe Hall's gloomy *The Well of Loneliness*, which portrays same-sex attraction as a shameful and crippling invitation to dissatisfaction. Woolf's novel, by contrast, unabashedly celebrates androgyny as emotionally freeing and fulfilling.

Orlando's tale begins during the reign of Queen Elizabeth, when the teenager meets the royal family and his father is gifted a large estate where the boy will spend much of the next three centuries. The estate is based on the Kent country house known as Knole that had been in Sackville-West's family since the sixteenth century; Woolf relished her visits there. Queen Elizabeth soon makes young Orlando her treasurer and takes him as her lover until his affections roam elsewhere, and he is exiled. When he returns to royal favor under James I he meets a Russian princess named Sasha, but their affair is short-lived. Orlando turns to writing, eschewing company to produce nearly fifty works by the age of twenty-five. Eventually, he befriends a famous author named Nick Green who pens a satire of Orlando's privileged existence, embarrassing him. Later, the young man travels to Constantinople to serve as ambassador on behalf of the empire. After earning the title duke, he falls into a seven-day stupor and wakes up to discover he's a woman. The transformation proves just one more adventure, though. Soon Orlando is off, living with gypsies and taking up with a sea captain.

Eventually, she returns home to discover her property at risk. Because Orlando is no longer a man, she can't claim ownership of her estate, and heirs from a woman in Constantinople who duped her into marriage before her sex change claim the house is theirs. Soon another man intrudes upon her world when all Orlando wants to do is write. A former lover, Harriet, reveals that she's actually a man named Harry and pressures her into eloping to Turkey. After several comic misadventures, Orlando declines and moves instead into high society, attending balls where she's exposed to the blather of leading literary men. She soon begins dressing in men's clothes from her old life, finding them more congenial to moving through the social world.

As the eighteenth century gives way to the nineteenth and the stuffier Victorian age settles in, Orlando realizes she must have a husband to keep her freedom. She meets Marmaduke Bonthrop Shelmerdine, or "Shel," who agrees to wed her, finding in her the strength to accept his feminine qualities. They marry and have a child, but as a sailor Shel must return to the sea. Orlando waits patiently at her estate, whose ownership has been kindly decided in her favor. One night, upon hearing an airplane, she exposes her breasts to the moon, whereupon Shel conveniently leaps from an aircraft to her side. The novel ends with the clock striking midnight, welcoming a new day: October 11, 1928—which just happens to be the same date Virginia Woolf published *Orlando*.

What makes Orlando him-/herself unique as a character is the utter lack of gender confusion. To be a man and a woman at the same time is natural to him/her, and the life choices made regarding clothing and marriage to Shel are a matter of practical experience. Orlando marries in the Victorian age because it is what she has to do to continue to pursue her true passion, which is writing. That's not to say those demands don't spark frustration and require intellectual pondering. Yet they are depicted as difficulties of existing as one or the other sex because of constraints imposed by social institutions.

Orlando proved to be Woolf's greatest commercial success, selling some 8,000 copies in its first year—not exactly a blockbuster, but more than double what any previous novel had sold, and enough to gain her a level of financial security throughout the next thirteen years before her 1941 suicide. The book has been a perpetual favorite for adaptation precisely because Orlando enjoys the best of both worlds. Most popularly, Sally Potter's 1992 film introduced actress Tilda Swinton to audiences, though the script departs from Woolf's original by making Orlando's sex change the result of an identity crisis. In 2010, writer-director Sarah Rule staged a more faithful adaptation in New York and later Australia that was praised for the very thing that makes the novel a rewarding read: its frivolity. As a gender rebel, Orlando promises us that both time and identity can be fluid and fun.

Bibliography

Orlando: A Biography (1928)

—KC

P

PAPA (THE MAN)

First Appearance: *The Road*
Date of First Appearance: 2006
Author: Cormac McCarthy (1933–)

You have to carry the fire . . . inside you. It was always there. I can see it.

Few postapocalyptic novels are as grim and unrelenting as Cormac McCarthy's 2006 Pulitzer Prize–winning story of a father and son wandering south to find the sea after an unnamed catastrophe destroys civilization. Written in a minimalist yet poetic style that gives the story the gravity of a parable, the book captures better than any other in its genre the sheer tediousness of surviving in a world where nothing matters but the barest essentials of existence: food, shelter, and avoiding predators. Even names are a luxury in this ash-blanketed landscape. The two main characters are known only as "the man" and "the boy." The latter refers to his father as "Papa," but his love and admiration are an innocence that will become a vulnerability if he doesn't learn to guard himself against evil. The man is sick and knows he's likely to die before his son reaches adulthood. The best he can do for the child is bequeath him the knowledge to continue on. Yet despite the grueling struggle to persist, the father also understands that staying alive isn't enough. The boy and the world alike need a value system to live for. As he insists to his son, even in a posthuman environment there must be goodness.

McCarthy sets us up to read *The Road* as a story of heroism, of a father going to extraordinary ends to protect his child. On the surface, the man is the last knight, susceptible to temptation and despair yet never abandoning his quest, a Fisher King redeeming the land that won't be renewed. The medieval references aren't inappropriate considering that in draft the book was originally titled *The Grail*. In this regard, the novel appeals to our desire to believe that parents won't abandon us—at least, that our father figures won't abandon us, given that the man's wife and the boy's mother commits suicide very soon after the unnamed cataclysmic event—perhaps a nuclear bomb, perhaps a meteorite—transforms the world at precisely 1:17 one morning years earlier into an "ashen scabland."

The novel's most dramatic moments certainly demonstrate the father's resilient commitment to the boy. In one action sequence a menacing forager happens upon them in the woods and draws a knife before the man shoots him in the head, spending one of the only two bullets they have for protection. The stranger belongs to a marauding group of cannibals traveling by truck and plundering any stragglers they come across; from the father's tense exchange with the scavenger it's clear the gang will kill them, probably after raping the child. When the father later returns to where the dead man's body should lie, he discovers nothing but bones and a pool of guts—the truck people eat their own corpses. The father's struggle is to reassure the boy that the two of them aren't the only good guys left in the world.

Despite the man's heroism, he can't protect the child from discovering the depths of depravity to which humanity has sunk. In one horrific episode, the travelers come across a plantation house where they discover humans chained in a cellar, stored as livestock. *The Road*'s most gruesome moment occurs when they discover the remains of a fire with a headless, gutted infant skewered on a spit. "I'm sorry" is all the father can say.

Yet as much as McCarthy dramatizes the father's struggle to protect the boy, the novel makes it clear very quickly that the man is dependent on the child. His desperate love for his son reflects *his* need to believe that the child is a vessel of hope. He describes the boy as his "warrant," his purpose. If the child isn't God's word, he tells himself, God never existed. Elsewhere he refers to his son as his "golden chalice." As he later confesses to himself, the boy is all that stands between him and death. His belief stands in contrast even to the survivors they encounter who haven't succumbed to cannibalism. When the man and the boy meet an old man in the road who calls himself Ely—a version of the biblical prophet Eli—the Buddha-like figure declares, "There is no God and we are his prophets." The man needs his son so he doesn't fall into a similar state of despair and long for death.

In several scenes, the grueling journey—its pace hobbled by cold, hunger, and diarrhea—pushes the man beyond his limits, and the child must remind him of the need to maintain hope. In one scene, the father refuses to help a man burned by lightning in the road, much to the boy's confusion and tears. Later, the boy breaks down crying when the man refuses to allow him to write a note for people who might follow in their tracks. The father worries the note might lead the bad guys to them, then realizes the child thinks all people have gone bad and that they'll always be alone and isolated. Elsewhere, the father and son overtake a thief who has stolen their cart of foodstuffs and clothing and the man angrily strips the pilferer of everything he possesses, abandoning him naked in the road. His anger upsets the boy, who begs his father to show the stranger one bit of charity. The father refuses, insisting the thief didn't show them any mercy. Exhausted, he chides the child for questioning his decisions, insisting the boy isn't the one who has to worry about them. "Yes, I am," the boy replies. "I am the one."

In such moments, McCarthy makes it clear that the child is a Christ figure. In a world where the "last host of Christendom" can expire as easily as a snowflake, the man must save the child to save himself. Despite his failings, he does so until hit in the leg by an arrow from a stranger in a window the pair innocently passes. The wound depletes the man's energy, and in his final words he tells the child he must "carry the light"—a responsibility the boy seems likely to uphold after a surrogate family adopts him, and he speaks to his father's memory as if he's speaking to God.

Bibliography

The Road (2006)

—KC

PETER PAN

First Appearance: *The Little White Bird*
Date of First Appearance: 1902
Author: J. M. Barrie (1860–1937)

Never is an awfully long time.

"I'll never grow up, never grow up, never grow up. Not me!" Perhaps the most memorable line from Disney's 1953 *Peter Pan* animated musical takes its cue from author J. M. Barrie's 1904 play with its alternate title *The Boy Who Wouldn't Grow Up*. This sentiment taps into two important psychological touchpoints—a wish to retain a childlike state of innocence and the realization that this idealized Shangri-La is impossible to sustain. Unless, of course, you're Peter Pan. Add to Peter's perpetual youth, his magical ability to fly, the pixie dust–trailing fairy Tinkerbell, the Darling family children headed by pseudo–mother figure Wendy and guarded by a nanny-substituting Saint Bernard, a band of Lost Boys, a sundry cast of runaways and otherwise caricatured outcasts, an evil pirate captain and swashbuckling shipmates, and a man-eating crocodile, and you've got the makings of a classic children's tale.

The popularity Barrie experienced with multiple play and novel versions of *Peter Pan* from 1902 to 1911 made clear the public's appetite for the whimsical fairy tale and its eternal boy. Generations since then have first heard, then read, and then shared with their children the story of Peter, and the proliferation of retellings from every possible angle and medium has solidified his rise to iconic status. Starting with Disney's mid-twentieth-century version, *Peter Pan* has been animated in print and film and brought to life onstage and on television in a *Pan* renaissance accelerating since 2000 with many well-known Hollywood stars and producers tying their names to the story's variant plots and emphasis. Peter has, in fact, transcended from simply being a novel protagonist to expanded roles as a Broadway and box office hit and a pop-media star with all the glittery fame that ensues.

Disney's cheerful but formulaic version set the standard for many renditions to follow that showcased Peter as a bossy, confident, self-involved teenage boy who wears a simple tunic, tights, and pointy shoes and hat—a nod to the earlier Robin Hood image propelling young males to wear medieval-style clothing and engage in mock sword fights in their backyards. The pretend Nottingham Forest shifts to

Neverland, or Never Never Land in some versions, and Robin's band of merry men become updated as Peter's Lost Boys. This look is so iconic, in fact, that it became the prototype for an often-donned Halloween costume gender-neutralized perhaps to follow the popular practice of using a small female adult as the lead role in plays and live-action television versions. Children festooned as Peter can even stoke up on the pseudo-healthy Peter Pan peanut butter with twenty-first-century crunchy and reduced-fat versions before brandishing their swords to raid neighborhood candy stashes, a.k.a. pirates' booty.

What has been all but lost to contemporary audiences, however, is the evolution of Peter Pan's character, and the circumstances of his origin may shed some light on why he continues to be so endearing more than a century after his creation. In the earliest rendition, *The Little White Bird*, Peter is a seven-day-old baby described as half-bird—perhaps the initial source of his ability to fly—who escapes out an open window and wanders into Kensington Park where he first meets fairies. Upon his homecoming he finds the window closed, but he can see his mother has replaced him with a new baby, so he flees to the park again, never to return. In most subsequent versions, Peter flies back to an open London window, this time at the home of the Darlings, but he always retreats to Neverland and his orphaned status despite the family's offer to adopt him as well as the tribe of Lost Boys, who also decline to embrace a permanent family.

On its surface, *Peter Pan* presents its namesake with the escapist adventure of a boy's imagination and a joyful respite from the restrictions of childhood and parental rules. Peter gleefully exclaims, "I'm youth, I'm joy, I'm a little bird that has broken out of the egg." What young boy or girl hasn't dreamed of becoming a temporary fugitive from bothersome adults, bedtime imprisonments, and a dutiful life? As such, Peter's tale of escape will likely remain standard repertoire long into the future as we engage in the willful suspension of disbelief required to fully engulf ourselves in Neverland's promise of freedom. Even if only for a fleeting moment, we eagerly accept Peter's edict to "think of all the joy you'll find when you leave the world behind and bid your cares goodbye."

As with most enduring children's tales, however, adult themes lurk just below the threshold of their ebullient surface, and the story of Peter Pan is no exception. He is not just the leader of the Lost Boys, he is the original Lost Boy, and in spite of his eternal freedom from the fetters of accountability, he is also essentially stuck in time. In a sort of repeated *Groundhog Day*, he will have to endure watching generations come and go as he remains unendingly youthful. Wendy will grow into womanhood and have children of her own, and they will in turn have children, and "all children, except one, [will] grow up," if we exempt the Peter of Steven Spielberg's 1991 revisionist *Hook*, where Robin Williams plays the grown-up boy who has himself become a father.

Relative to Barrie's earliest embodiment of Peter, the origins of his last name might readily be traced to the Greek Pan, a mythical god of rustic creatures said to be half-animal. Like the fictional Greeks Oedipus and Electra, whose names have been appropriated as psychoanalytical terms by Freud and Jung, respectively, contemporary clinical practitioners have unofficially linked Peter's behavior and his name to men who fail to accept the yoke of male maturation. The Peter Pan syndrome's badge of dishonor highlights the shadowy side of his legacy and the consequences of failing to embrace life's natural progression.

Barrie's story is, in fact, darker than contemporary interpretations. Captain Hook is bedeviled by his nemesis the crocodile with its ticking alarm clock—an easy symbol of death to which he inevitably succumbs. At one point Peter also proclaims, "To die will be an awfully big adventure," signaling that Peter might welcome death as a release. Cultural adaptations and the need for contemporary pleasantness in children's tales shifted to a much "happily-ever-after" aura with Peter exclaiming in several later versions, "To live would be an awfully big adventure," and thus a lane opens for ever-expanding approaches to what Peter might do or whom he might be in the infinite time allowed him as an immortal soul.

Peter Pan's legacy provides much more than the popular tale of youthful impetuousness and invincibility. He has become a deeply embedded cultural icon speaking perhaps as much to adulthood's fears and losses as to childhood's dreams. But whether Peter represents a heroic figure or a rebel with an ambiguous or absent cause, he is a mainstay in the collective memory of generations growing up with post–Industrial Revolution's fear of lost worlds and lost innocence.

Bibliography

The Little White Bird (1902)
Peter Pan, or The Boy Who Wouldn't Grow Up (play) (1904)
Peter in Kensington Gardens (1906)
When Wendy Grew Up—An Afterthought (1908)
Peter and Wendy (1911)

—GS

PIGGY

First Appearance: *Lord of the Flies*
Date of First Appearance: 1954
Author: William Golding (1911–1993)

It's them that haven't no common sense that make trouble on this island.

In 1954, when an atomic-fallout monster named Godzilla was stomping movie-set skyscrapers, William Golding published a dystopian novel about British school-boys trying to survive on a deserted island following the crash of their evacuation plane not long after an A-bomb had been dropped. The obvious antiwar message aside, what shocked readers of *Lord of the Flies* was Golding's bleak view of human nature—that with no adults on the island the boys instinctively would form their own society but quickly devolve into primitive savagery.

"*Kill the beast. Cut her throat. Spill her blood*," the choirboys turned hunters chant, and each time they have the chance to kill one of the island's wild pigs they do so with increasing brutality, ecstasy, and fierce tribalism. They go from timidly poking at a vine-ensnared piglet with their handmade spears and knives to working together as a group to butcher them, then celebrate with bloodthirsty chants and gleeful reenactments. "I cut the pig's throat," brags Jack, the leader of the hunters, while after another kill they laugh at how one spear penetrated: "Right up her ass!" By novel's end they will put a pig's head on a sharpened stick—a symbol of their savagery they dub *Lord of the Flies* (a translation of "Beelzebub," the Philistine god).

Ironically, the most hauntingly memorable character in the book is named Piggy, a "very fat" boy with a "button nose" and glasses who, as his nickname suggests, provides a parallel target for the boys' aggressiveness and cruelty. As with the island pigs, it begins gradually, but steadily escalates. When we first meet him, Piggy has a hard time keeping up with his fit companion Ralph as they walk through the jungle—especially since, as he tells Ralph with "a tone of pride," he was the only boy in his school who had asthma ("Ass-mar?" Ralph ridicules; "Sucks to your ass-mar!"). "And I've been wearing specs since I was three." Even twelve-year-old Ralph, who will become the closest thing to a friend that Piggy will find on the island, treats him poorly from the start, thinking of him in piglike terms ("in a few seconds the fat boy's grunts were behind him"). And he laughs and shouts, "Piggy! Piggy!" when the boy whispers the nickname kids called him back at his school. Orphaned, he tells Ralph, "I used to live with my auntie. She kept a candy store. I used to get ever so many candies. As many as I liked." Later Ralph will violate the boy's confidence by telling everyone his name is "Piggy," though Piggy had begged him not to tell any other survivors they might encounter. Evoking reader sympathy from the very beginning, Piggy strikes a chord in anyone who's ever been or has known a child who was picked on.

In a novel that's full of symbols, Piggy is also connected to each of them on some level. When Ralph sees something in the lagoon, it's Piggy who identifies the object and its use: "I seen one like that before. On someone's back wall. A conch he called it. He used to blow it and then his mum would come. It's ever so valuable." Piggy is the one to suggest blowing it to call others to a meeting and coaches Ralph until he gets more than a "low farting noise" out of it. The conch becomes the boys' symbol of power. Whoever holds it gets to speak—though Piggy ironically will be denied that right ("Shut up, Fatty!") because he's the fat kid, the kid with glasses, the kid with asthma, the smart kid that everyone picks on, the one with all the ideas but not the bearing to be chief.

Throughout the novel, Piggy is the voice of reason, the voice of logic, as his glasses symbolize. When Ralph says his military dad will rescue them because somebody at the airport will tell him about the crash, Piggy says, "Not them. Didn't you hear what the pilot said? About the atom bomb? They're all dead. . . . This is an island. Nobody don't know we're here. . . . We may stay here till we die," he says, prophetically. Piggy's glasses reflect the sun and are associated with light. Later, when the boys try to build a signal fire to attract the attention of any passing ships or planes, they realize that they can use Piggy's glasses to start the fire, and those glasses become synonymous with that flame and take on importance beyond the intellectualism they typically suggest. But the boys take and use his glasses without his permission, and that becomes another act of bullying, another violation. As the others grow wilder and paint their faces, Piggy remains "the only boy on the island whose hair never seemed to grow"—long hair being a symbol for wildness.

But Piggy isn't just a passive victim who shrinks from his tormentors. He states his opinions despite the consequences. When Jack abandons the rescue fire to go hunting, Piggy chastises him for blowing a chance to signal a passing ship—"You didn't ought to have let that fire out. You said you'd keep the smoke going"—but absorbs a vicious punch to the gut that follows, and a blow to the face that breaks one lens of his glasses. On another occasion, when the assembly refuses to give a small boy a chance to speak and they laugh after making him cry, Piggy stands up for the boy, shouting, "Let him have the conch! Let him have it!" In another instance, when the boys grow fearful talking about a "beast" one of the children claims to have seen, Piggy scoffs, "Nuts!" and indignantly says, "I don't believe in no ghosts—ever!" That prompts another abusive response from Jack, who wrestles the conch shell away from him: "Who cares what you believe—Fatty!"

Twice *Lord of the Flies* was adapted for film, and twice it fell short of capturing the power of the novel's descriptions and horrific implications. A good but not great black-and-white version was made just nine years after the book was published, and even an R-rated color version made in 1990 was no match for readers' imaginations, with the addition of F-bombs doing little to add impact. Elsewhere in pop culture, Iron Maiden released a rock song titled "Lord of the Flies" and goth-rock band Nosferatu cut an album with the same title, but mostly it's the novel and the characters themselves that have resonated for all these years.

Though not intended as young adult fiction, *Lord of the Flies* has been read primarily by students of all ages and has had an undeniable influence on the young adult fiction genre. As Golding acknowledged in an interview with *Young Entertainment*, "*The Hunger Games* trilogy does an excellent job of reframing a lot of the same issues I wrote about in *Lord of the Flies*." The novel remains chilling because, as Golding suggests, bullying remains an inhuman part of human nature.

Bibliography

Lord of the Flies (1954)

Work Cited

Laub, Mordechai. "William-Golding-Lord-of-the-Flies-Interview." *Young Entertainment*, September 17, 2014. https://youngentertainmentmag.com/william-golding-lord-of-the -flies-interview/.

—JP

BILLY PILGRIM

First Appearance: *Slaughterhouse-Five, or
The Children's Crusade: A Duty-Dance with Death*
Date of First Appearance: 1969
Author: Kurt Vonnegut (1922–2007)

Among the things Billy Pilgrim could not change were the past, the present, and the future.

"I'm just a poor, wayfaring stranger. A traveler through this world of woe. And there's no sickness toil or danger, in that bright world to which I go." These opening lines to a popular American gospel/folk lyric could be the theme song of Billy

Pilgrim, Kurt Vonnegut's most iconic character, who lives up to his surname as a wanderer through the landscape of war and its aftermath while shifting in and out of time between this earth and a world beyond. Vonnegut's extended title, *Slaughterhouse-Five, or The Children's Crusade: A Duty-Dance with Death*, is expansive enough to allow speculation about what makes Billy tick. Is he a Christ or Antichrist figure, a war or antiwar hero, a lunatic or a person maintaining sanity in a creative way, a prophet holding secrets to life or a person who has gone off the rails? These questions suggest the complexity Vonnegut creates in this strange, hard-to-classify novel, and they perhaps offer clues to why Billy Pilgrim becomes a counterculture hero for the turbulent age into which he emerges at the book's 1969 publication date. His absurdist experience provides a grand metaphor, a glimpse into the existential quandary about the meaning of life and man's inhumanity toward man. And if all that is too heavy, Vonnegut serves up Billy's angst in typical sardonic humor, so the reading goes down easier.

Slaughterhouse-Five can be both deeply probing and elusive, but one thing seems clear. Billy Pilgrim is neither a war hero in the traditional sense, nor an antiwar hero. He is simply a survivor, an optometrist whose vision about life is hypersensitive though he fails to act upon his insights, and he becomes a nonhero floating through life passively acted upon rather than being actively engaged. He doesn't save women and children during the bombing of Dresden. After the cataclysm, Billy simply emerges from the underground meat slaughterhouse where he is working as a prisoner of war. He doesn't rescue victims from the rubble; he collects corpses as part of his prisoner duties.

At the end of the war Vonnegut's soldier finds himself, or loses himself, by becoming "unstuck" in time and perhaps untethered to reality, but whether he is sane or not isn't the central point. The crux of the matter rests on Billy's ability to exist in the midst of modernist angst and chaos in a postwar generation. And the beauty of Billy's delayed debut—the novel's publication nearly a quarter century after the end of World War II—is that for his reading audience Billy's relevance isn't postwar at all; it lies at the heart of a cultural crisis immediately consequential to a new generation. If we allow the life on a written page to have a vital existence through those who embrace it, Billy provides a living example of what the counterculture of the turbulent 1960s and 1970s Vietnam War protests could glom onto for their own antiwar revolution. As one writer so aptly put it, Vonnegut uses Billy, as Michael Crichton notes, "to lift the lid of the garbage can, and dispassionately examine the contents." He leaves the reader to fill in the passion that the aftermath of incendiary bombs has sucked out of Billy.

Whether Billy's experiences are real with actual time travel and alien abduction to the planet Tralfamadore or a symptom of what we now call post-traumatic stress syndrome, either way what happens to Billy is symptomatic of his trauma. From the outset, Vonnegut uses the novel's title to clue us in to Billy's postwar struggle and his efforts to learn how to exist in a world that had enlisted children to wage a crusade over religious ideals, where a new group of war wagers had blown up complete innocents for no vital strategic value. Billy gets that human existence is an unavoidable duty-dance with death, except in the Tralfamadorian sense where death can be undone by simply moving to another spot in time because it is only one point on a fluid continuum. Such a plot mitigates the horror of war or death, which need not be an inevitable end to existence. When Billy's daughter asks what his military experience had been like, he thinks to himself, "Everything was beautiful, and nothing hurt." The statement dramatically counters his real experience and highlights one of Billy's coping mechanisms—to simply replace reality with fantasy when verisimilitude is too overwhelming. He believes it would make a perfect epitaph for a tombstone—a marker that the body now lying beneath the stone had nothing but good to say about life; that is, if he weren't dead.

Billy echoes an earlier Vonnegut character from *Mother Night* who says, "It's all I've seen, all I've been through that makes it damn nearly impossible to say anything. I've lost the knack of making sense. I speak gibberish to the civilized world, and it replies in kind." In Vonnegut's view, transferred from that novel to *Slaughterhouse-Five* and to Billy, actively generating mass death through engagement in war is a human debacle of mind-boggling proportion. And even though Billy is an assistant chaplain in his official military capacity, religion offers no solace. It merely functions as an institution that seems not only resigned to human suffering, it instead teaches that pain is all part of a vast eternal plan to whip humans into shape in order to earn a better life elsewhere in some distant heaven.

The only way to live in the absurdity of such a universe is to be either creative or passive. Billy seems to be both, and he coins the phrase "So it goes," which appears more than 100 times in the novel as his antidote to the inexplicable. One hundred and thirty-five thousand residents of a beautiful historic city are annihilated, a man is shot dead for stealing a teapot, a nation glamorizes war by making movies with handsome male leads like John Wayne and Frank Sinatra as heroes, mothers worry that their sleeping babies will grow up to be soldiers, aliens capture humans and put them on exhibit in a distant planet's zoo, an optometrist is assassinated for no apparent reason. And "so it goes" in Billy Pilgrim's world.

At one point, Billy watches a movie of the war played in reverse in his head. The brilliance of this— the idea that a stupid, ugly, and deadly set of actions could be rewound to be undone—is perhaps the point where Tralfamadorian circular time or bopping back and forth in chronology has its origins. But even if such reversal were possible, the world's population is still human. In a POW scene early in the book, an American soldier called out of line and punished for an insignificant action asks, "Why me?" The response he gets from the German guard is "Vy you? Vy anybody?" As the novel closes, Vonnegut skips back to the end of the war and the release of prisoners. Billy hears the birds singing to each other, and one says to him, "Poo-tee-weet." It is about as useful an explanation for the human condition as anything offered in this century, and Billy Pilgrim knows it.

Bibliography

Slaughterhouse-Five (1969)

Works Cited

Crichton, Michael. "Slaughterhouse-Five." In *The Critic as Artist: Essays on Books 1920–1972*, edited by Gilbert A. Harrison, 100–107. New York: Liveright, 1972.
Vonnegut, Kurt. *Mother Night*. Greenwich, CT: Fawcett, 1962.

—GS

FLEUR PILLAGER

First Appearance: "Fleur" in *Esquire*
Date of First Appearance: August 1986
Author: Louise Erdrich (1954–)

I'm going to slice you open and take out your guts and hang them on the walls. Then I'm going back home to live on the land you took.

Fleur Pillager isn't as well known as others in this book. Although mentioned or described in seven novels, she's mostly featured in *Tracks* (1988) and *Four Souls* (2004). We first meet her in an excerpt from *Tracks* that was published in the August 1986 *Esquire* and reprinted in *O. Henry Prize Stories, 1987*. Drawing upon her Chippewa heritage, Louise Erdrich created a character that's rich even for the wonderfully varied cast she revisits in her loosely connected novels. And Fleur is easily one of the most mystical and fiercest females in literature.

How mystical and fierce?

Kirkus Reviews called Fleur "a water-witch, whose ease in love and revenge and self-confidence makes her a frighteningly awesome presence to most men and women."

In *The Beet Queen*, published a month after the *Esquire* story, Fleur is an old woman—someone her own great-granddaughter considers "spooky." She comes from a Chippewa family rumored to know the secret ways to "cure or kill." Raised on the shores of Matchimanito Lake, Fleur drowned twice before adulthood—first as a child, and again as a teenager, each time coming back to life. It was rumored that Misshepeshu, the spirit of the lake, grabbed her both times and had his way with her the second time. Two men who first saved her disappeared soon afterward. When she fell in the lake as a fifteen-year-old, she washed ashore, "her skin a dull dead gray," and the man attending to her heard her hiss, "You take my place." He became so afraid that afterward he wouldn't leave his house . . . and drowned when he slipped and fell in a new bathtub his sons had brought him. "Men stayed clear of Fleur Pillager after the second drowning," reports Pauline Puyat, one of two narrators in *Tracks*. "Even though she was good-looking, nobody dared to court her because it was clear that Misshepeshu, the water man, the monster, wanted her for himself."

Fleur is a consummate survivor. When the other *Tracks* narrator, tribal elder Nanapush, goes to the Pillager cabin to check on the family following a tuberculosis epidemic, he finds all Pillagers dead except for seventeen-year-old Fleur, who is feverish and "wild as a filthy wolf, a big bony girl whose sudden bursts of strength and snarling" terrifies the tribal policeman who accompanies him.

Fleur transforms into a bear in several of the novels, and Pauline recounts how after Fleur went out one night, she followed the girl's tracks in the morning and saw where her bare feet had changed into the claws and pads of a bear. Animal transformations are part of the Chippewa world, and such episodes further establish Fleur as a force to be reckoned with. Her fury is fully unleashed in the nearby town of Argus, where she had gone to earn money to pay her family's government land allotment fees. There she works at a butcher shop with white men who see something in her that "made their brains hum." Fleur stuns them one day by pulling up a chair to join their poker game—something women just didn't do. When they see she can "stack and riffle, divide the cards, spill them to each player in a blur, rake and shuffle again," it further agitates the men. One night after she stuffs her winnings inside her dress, the men beat and rape her—though she fights the whole time and makes eye contact with Pauline, whom she spies hiding in the shadows, silently watching. The next day, a mysterious tornado tears through the town, destroying the butcher shop and killing her three assailants.

One suspects that in Fleur's mind that squared things, because when she returns home and Nanapush asks about a story Pauline has been telling, she smiles and says, "Uncle, the Puyat lies." As Erdrich told one interviewer, Pauline is "afraid of Fleur, as many women who allow themselves to be controlled are threatened by women who do as they please." Fleur isn't just strong—she's headstrong, and not afraid to live by herself at the cabin, chopping wood, shooting game, and catching fish. Even when she takes a lover named Eli who begins living with her at the cabin, it's on her terms—though one suspects it amuses her, too, to give gossips more to talk about and create a certain uncertainty about the father of the baby she's carrying after Argus. Though a jealous Pauline uses "love medicine" to bewitch Eli so he has an affair with a younger Chippewa woman, Fleur's response is classic: She lets him back in the cabin but refuses to cook, clean, or touch or talk to him. It drives him crazy. Eventually she will fully accept him, but on her own terms. When Eli's mother, Margaret, moves in with them, Fleur shows a different kind of stubborn strength. After her "mother-in-law" is attacked and shamed by men who shave her head, Fleur curses the men, and one of them does, in fact, die. To further show her support, Fleur shaves her own head to match Margaret's—an act of proud solidarity and defiance. But Fleur also has what Nanapush recognizes as "the mysterious self-contempt of the survivor."

Readers see Fleur in times of weakness, too, as when she nearly dies in childbirth and copes with depression after a second baby is stillborn. Then, upon learning that the money she gave Margaret and her son, Nector, to pay her land fees was instead used to pay their own, Fleur clutches a boulder to her chest and walks into the lake, drowning a third time—though Eli revives her and she hisses, "Nector will take my place!" The drowning gives her renewed strength for revenge. The day before the white men take possession of the land, Fleur quietly, secretly takes an ax to every tree on the property. Then, in *Four Souls* (2004), after sending her daughter Lulu off to government school, she plots an elaborate revenge on the man most responsible, hiring on as his family's laundress in order to get close. When she realizes the man is unwell, she first nurses him back to health because "she wanted the man healthy so she could destroy him fresh."

Fleur's flaw—aside from being a vigilante-style scourge—is an arrogance that "held her back" sometimes. When she finally does put a knife to the man's throat and says, "I am the woman whose land you stole," she realizes he's stolen so many family parcels from young women that he truly can't remember her. But when he promises to divorce his wife and marry her and do anything she wants, the opportunistic Fleur spares his life, lives with him in Minneapolis society, raises a "surprise" child by him, and when his empire crumbles, returns to the reservation in search of healing. That is, she does to him what he has been doing to women all along. Fleur's lives—for she has many—are fascinating and her character so sensitive to justice that Father Damien, assigned to minister Christianity to the Chippewa, thinks fondly of her and even goes to Pillager island when it's time for him to die . . . hoping to see Fleur once more.

Bibliography

Love Medicine (1984)
The Beet Queen (1986)
Tracks (1988)
The Bingo Palace (1994)
The Last Report on the Miracles at Little No Horse (2001)
Four Souls (2004)
The Painted Drum (2005)

Works Cited

Beidler, Peter G., and Gay Barton. *A Reader's Guide to the Novels of Louise Erdrich*. Columbia: University of Missouri Press, 2006.

Chavkin, Allan, and Nancy Feyl Chavkin. "An Interview with Louise Erdrich." In *Conversations with Louise Erdrich and Michael Dorris*, edited by Allan Chavkin and Nancy Feyl Chavkin, 220–53. Jackson: University Press of Mississippi, 1994.

"*Tracks*, by Louise Erdrich." *Kirkus Reviews*, August 15, 1988. Posted online September 22, 2011. https://www.kirkusreviews.com/book-reviews/louise-erdrich/tracks-6/.

—JP

HERCULE POIROT

First Appearance: *The Mysterious Affair at Styles*
Date of First Appearance: 1920
Author: Agatha Christie (1890–1976)

I do not approve of murder.

Hercule Poirot in his short five-feet-four-inch, perfectly coiffed and mustachioed, impeccably dressed self, stands toe to toe with Sherlock Holmes and alongside Miss Jane Marple in the triumvirate of famous British sleuths, though he would be the first to say he is Belgian—being English would have put him too directly in competition with Sir Arthur Conan Doyle's famous investigator. Poirot resides primarily in England after the first Great War, however, and is the precursor to his elderly fictional relative, Miss Jane Marple, also Christie's brainchild. In the popular detective genre, one could not possess a better pedigree. Between 1920 and 1975, this Belgian PI was the star of thirty-three novels, one play, and more than sixty short stories, and his escapades make up a good portion of the more than 2 billion (yes, *billion*) copies of Christie's crime-solving mysteries worldwide sales, ranking third only to the Bible and Shakespeare.

Throughout his career, Poirot distinguishes himself with his flamboyant persona, complete with an idiosyncratic accent, an old-fashioned and overstyled but immaculate wardrobe, and a curled and waxed handlebar mustache, yet it is his preferred investigative style that ultimately solidifies his place as one of the greats in nineteenth-century detective fiction. Though keen forensic work and meticulous crime scene investigation are important, and he isn't above occasionally snooping in drawers, he prefers a more cerebral approach for his professional methodology, and he prides himself on using "the little gray cells" of brain matter he sees as his most effective tool and his superpower. When criticized for a seeming lack of engagement, he retorts, "You have the mistaken idea implanted in your head that a detective is necessarily a man who puts on a false beard and hides behind a pillar! The false beard, it is *vieux jeu*, and shadowing is only done by the lowest branch of my profession. The Hercule Poirots, my friend, need only to sit back in a chair and think."

His investigation starts with the key question of why a crime has been committed, and he favors a psychological approach in getting to the bottom of the quandary about the "who" in the "whodunit" equation. Poirot doesn't regard assumptions, often sees oppositional evidence as telling—love hiding hate, hate concealing passionate connection, indifference shrouding supreme interest—and his keen sense of how humans think and act propels him to supersleuth status. He notes that "there is always a danger of accepting facts as proved, which are really nothing of the kind," and he bows to no one's inspection of these but his own. His arrogance is off-putting but also backed up by his success, which is not to be disputed.

Sometimes Poirot takes his show on the road, notably in two of the most popular stories from Christie's series—*Murder on the Orient Express* (1934) and *Death on the Nile* (1937). Murder committed in the claustrophobic/no-escape-hatch setting of a train and a ship, coupled with the movement through an exotic foreign backdrop, heightens the dramatic tension that makes for great escapist fiction. During much of his career Poirot is on the move solving murders on land, air, and sea; on trains, planes, and boats; and in any number of places one can be murdered—Egypt, Eastern Europe, Mesopotamia, Jordan, to name a few.

As we would expect, the tales of Hercule Poirot are not limited to the page, and they make for equally satisfying thrillers for filmgoers, television audiences, and theatergoers. He debuted on-screen in the 1931 film *Alibi*, which had been adapted from an earlier play, and he appeared in various flicks for the next few decades. Poirot made his biggest media splashes starting in the sixties with Tony Randall's portrayal of him in *The ABC Murders* (1966), followed by British actor Albert Finney appearing as Poirot in *Orient Express* (1974) with a star-studded cast that guaranteed attention paid if the Christie/Poirot combination were not already enough draw. Sean Connery, John Gielgud, Vanessa Redgrave, Michael York, Anthony Perkins, Lauren Bacall, and Ingrid Bergman with an Oscar-winning performance cinched the movie's box office draw. This success was followed by British actor of Russian descent Peter Ustinov playing the lead in 1978's *Death on the Nile*, once again with an all-star cast, this time featuring Bette Davis, David

Niven, Mia Farrow, Angela Lansbury, and Jack Ward. In total, more than twenty actors have played the famous investigator, including David Suchet who filled those patent leather shoes in the television series *Agatha Christie: Poirot*, which had a remarkable twenty-five-year run from 1989 until 2013.

Hercule Poirot made his swan song appearance in terms of Agatha Christie's contributions in the appropriately named 1975 novel *Curtain*, closing with the famed detective's death. Christie confessed that Poirot had gotten a little cocky and allowed himself to become "an egocentric creep," so his exit was a literary murder of sorts, though he was old so she had at least softened the approaching blow, and we know who did it. The *New York Times* treated his demise as if he were a real person and placed the announcement on the front page under the headline "Hercule Poirot Is Dead; Famed Belgian Detective." In a perfectly dead-panned tone of solemnity and respect, the article honored his memory by saying: "Mr. Poirot achieved fame as a private investigator after he retired as a member of the Belgian police force in 1904. His career, as chronicled in the novels of Dame Agatha Christie, his creator, was one of the most illustrious in fiction." The tribute went on to say that though he had suffered declining health in the recent years, he could be seen at a local nursing home "wearing a wig and false mustaches to mask the signs of age that offended his vanity. In his active days, he was always impeccably dressed." This last statement would have made the always fastidious detective proud. As *Gentleman's Gazette* noted, "It seems likely that a little dust would cause the quaint, dandified Belgian gentleman more pain than a bullet wound," and circumstantial evidence would seem to bear this out.

Popular fictional characters often refuse to stay dead, and Poirot is no exception. Author Sophie Hannah has published *The Mystery of Three Quarters: The New Hercule Poirot Mystery* (2018) authorized by the Agatha Christie estate because apparently there are more murders to be solved and money to be made. Poirot had at one point confessed, "It is my weakness, it has always been my weakness, to desire to show off," so one has to believe he wouldn't mind having more chances to do so. Perhaps as amazingly prolific as Christie was, but because she had grown tired of writing about him herself, it's not beyond the realm of possibility that she would be happy to have the help.

Bibliography

Short-story collections have the abbreviation "ss."

The Mysterious Affair at Styles (1920)
The Murder on the Links (1923)
Poirot Investigates (1924, ss)
The Murder of Roger Ackroyd (1926)
The Big Four (1927)
The Mystery of the Blue Train (1928)
Black Coffee (1930 play; novel adapted from play, 1998)
Peril at End House (1932)
Lord Edgware Dies (1933) also published as *Thirteen at Dinner*
Murder on the Orient Express (1934) also published as *Murder in the Calais Coach*
Three Act Tragedy (1935) also published as *Murder in Three Acts*

Death in the Clouds (1935) also published as *Death in the Air*
The A. B. C. Murders (1936) also published as *The Alphabet Murders*
Murder in Mesopotamia (1936)
Cards on the Table (1936)
Dumb Witness (1937) also published as *Poirot Loses a Client*
Death on the Nile (1937) also published as *Murder on the Nile* and as *Hidden Horizon*
Murder in the Mews (1937, ss) also published as *Dead Man's Mirror*
Appointment with Death (1938)
Hercule Poirot's Christmas (1938) also published as *Murder for Christmas* and as *A Holiday for Murder*
The Regatta Mystery and Other Stories (1939, ss)
Sad Cypress (1940)
One, Two, Buckle My Shoe (1940) also published as *Overdose of Death* and as *The Patriotic Murders*
Evil under the Sun (1941)
Five Little Pigs (1942) also published as *Murder in Retrospect*
The Hollow (1946) also published as *Murder after Hours*
The Labours of Hercules (1947, ss)
Taken at the Flood (1948) also published as *There Is a Tide*
The Under Dog and Other Stories (1951, ss)
Mrs. McGinty's Dead (1952) also published as *Blood Will Tell*
After the Funeral (1952) also published as *Funerals Are Fatal*
Hickory Dickory Dock (1955) also published as *Hickory Dickory Death*
Dead Man's Folly (1956)
Cat among the Pigeons (1959)
The Adventure of the Christmas Pudding (1960, ss)
Double Sin and Other Stories (1961, ss)
The Clocks (1963)
Third Girl (1966)
Hallowe'en Party (1969)
Elephants Can Remember (1972)
Poirot's Early Cases (1974, ss)
Curtain (written about 1940, published 1975)
Problem at Pollensa Bay and Other Stories (1991, ss)

Works Cited

Bolin, Alice. "Miss Marple vs. the Mansplainers: Agatha Christie's Feminist Detective Hero." *Electric Lit*, May 15, 2015.
Christie, Agatha. *Dumb Witness*. New York: Dodd, Mead, 1937.
———. *Five Little Pigs*. New York: Dodd, Mead, 1942.
Laskaug, Thomas. "Hercule Poirot Is Dead; Famed Belgian Detective." *New York Times*. August 6, 1975.
Schneider, Sven Raphael. "Hercule Poirot and His Suits, Overcoats and Dressing Gowns." *Gentleman's Gazette*, December 30, 2011.

—GS

EDNA PONTELLIER

First Appearance: *The Awakening*
Date of First Appearance: 1899
Author: Kate Chopin (1850–1904)

I would give up the unessential; I would give my money, I would give my life for my children; but I wouldn't give myself.

"She grew daring and reckless, overestimating her strength. She wanted to swim far out, where no woman had swum before." These two lines from Kate Chopin's 1899 publication of *The Awakening*, originally titled *A Solitary Soul*, say so much in such few words about her central character Edna Pontellier and the unexpected path she will choose. Mrs. Pontellier steps onto the fictional stage after three prominent novels by nineteenth-century male authors had centered on the suicide of a female protagonist: Gustave Flaubert's *Madame Bovary* (1857), Leo Tolstoy's *Anna Karenina* (1878), and Stephen Crane's *Maggie: A Girl of the Streets* (1893). Public captivation with the subject seemed clear if the three earlier books' popularity were any gauge, but it wasn't until Chopin's novel that a female author tackled such a delicate and uncomfortable topic in full. This is not surprising, as the few women writers who were publishing in the century tended to focus on a more domesticated theme. In the male-authored books on the subject, two of the females had committed suicide after failed adulterous affairs, and one after having resorted to prostitution when her family rejected her. Even though these works projected a sympathetic view of women's traumas, death was the inevitable end for their sins against the social order. Proper ladies would not write about such a topic, but Chopin wasn't a proper lady by the standards of her day. She was a cigar-smoking, non-sidesaddle-horseback-riding divorcée who preferred the company of men. She also chose for her protagonist Edna Pontellier to reject the role of wife and mother. Like her male counterparts' treatment of female suicides, Chopin's lady would have to pay the price to appease the general readership, but in that action, Edna claims herself in a way that will many decades later make her a feminist emblem, a symbolic country in which to plant their flag.

One might ask why a wife and mother who chooses to commit suicide rather than continue in these roles is a memorable character for anything other than making a horrible choice. Criticism both at the time of the novel's publication, and lingering still, sees Edna as a prime example of self-centeredness. It's hard not to agree in some respects. Chopin makes it clear that her husband Leonce is *not* a wife beater, but a kind and considerate husband, if a somewhat less-than-passionate one. Her two sons are not uncontrollable monsters, and she has help taking care of them and her household. She and the children vacation through the summer at a lush Grand Isle resort away from the heat of New Orleans while Leonce remains in the city to work, only escaping on weekends to join them. Even so, let's face it, not everyone is cut out to be a mother, or a housewife no less, and for females in particular, marriage naturally followed by motherhood was really the only acceptable woman's vocation, like it or not. The alternative was spinsterhood, which was always projected as a sad and often sordid existence. Edna made the choice any respectable woman of her generation would make.

Chopin places Edna in the middle of two extreme female role models. The first is Mademoiselle Reisz, who is an independent woman and musician living a somewhat shabby life but a free one, existing on her own earnings. As Edna shows signs of wanting to explore her creative side, Mlle Reisz wisely advises that "to succeed, the artist must possess the courageous soul . . . the soul that dares and defies." Her words are a warning as much as they are advice because she understands the personal strength necessary to live outside the confines of expectation. Madame Adele Ratignolle represents the second and more conventional model for what Edna should aspire to be. She is the supreme example of motherhood and its self-abnegation. In the midst of an agonizing birth scene Edna has been called to attend, and as she inwardly rebels against the "ways of nature" and its "scene of torture," Adele, without being conscious of the effect her words will have, reminds Edna to "think of the children. . . . Remember the children!" For Edna, little middle ground seems possible between these two extremes.

As Edna contemplates her growing discontent, "she wanted something to happen—something, anything: she did not know what." She finds two escapes from her life, one socially acceptable to a point, and the other, completely unacceptable. She comes to realize she would like to paint, and in fact she takes it up in earnest. There is one problem: How does she sustain herself financially in this way? It is not a lucrative profession for most men, and certainly not for women. Edna refuses to use her husband's money to escape from him, but she will no longer be one of his possessions either. Her second independent activity is to engage in extramarital relationships, the first one through heavy flirting that evolves into infatuation and then love but no physical relationship, and the second, a strictly sexual liaison with a known rake who opens Edna's eyes to passion but fails to pair it with romance. She slowly realizes that neither husband nor her lovers provide the "taste of life's delirium" she seeks.

Edna also realizes that her children are not a source of happiness, and the joy of motherhood all women are by nature supposed to embrace eludes her. In fact, "the children appeared before her like antagonists who had overcome her, who had overpowered and sought to drag her into the soul's slavery for the rest of her days." This emotion goes way past postpartum depression, describing a heavy maternal angst to which she is only just becoming fully awakened. As Edna in the last few pages of the novel moves toward her final act veiled as a potential accidental drowning, though all signs point toward conscious choice, in her last thoughts of them she says, "But they need not have thought that they could possess her, body and soul." With that, Edna swims past the point of no return. Lest we think of her as heartless and completely void of love, she had earlier confessed to Adele that she would "give her life for her children," but she would never give herself. The sadness is that she sees no compromise here either.

Edna had earlier in the summer learned to swim and reveled in the freedom of that activity. The sea becomes the symbolic warm and salty amniotic fluid of the womb that gives birth to her initial sense of freedom and provides the soft and gentle "close embrace" of death as she realizes she is not strong enough to seize such a luxurious possession as herself. Edna's suicide, and that she saw no way to find herself except to lose herself, was shocking at the time and remains jolting more than a century later, but her experience also serves as a stark reminder of the struggle to maintain a sovereignty when female identity has for so long been tied to something other than selfhood.

Bibliography

The Awakening (1899)

—GS

ALEXANDER PORTNOY

First Appearance: "A Jewish Patient Begins His Analysis" in *Esquire*
Date of First Appearance: April 1967
Author: Philip Roth (1933–2018)

I am marked like a road map from head to toe with my repressions. You can travel the length and breadth of my body over superhighways of shame and inhibition and fear.

"I'd love to meet him, but I wouldn't want to shake his hand."

Jacqueline Susann cracked that joke to Johnny Carson on *The Tonight Show* in 1969, irked that reviewers compared her sexy blockbuster *The Love Machine* to her surprise competition for the top of the best seller lists, Philip Roth's *Portnoy's Complaint*. Susann aimed the quip at her rival writer, but it applies equally to the book's thirty-three-year-old narrator, Alexander Portnoy. Because *Portnoy's Complaint* sparked a tornado of both titters and condemnation over its graphic descriptions of onanism, its protagonist holds the dubious distinction of being literature's most famous masturbator.

Yet Portnoy is memorable for more than taking a—err—hands-on approach to his identity crisis. He remains among the most obsessive self-loathers in fiction, his neuroses indicative of both the repressive conformity of middle-class Jewish American culture and the confusing freedoms of the 1960s' sexual revolution. Bawdy and self-lacerating, *Portnoy's Complaint*—first excerpted in *Esquire*, *Partisan Review*, and *New American Review* in 1967—holds the unlikely honor of being American literature's most complex analysis of shame and guilt this side of Hawthorne's *The Scarlet Letter* (1850), a novel with which it has absolutely nothing else in common. Despite its demeaning treatment of women, it remains a landmark in American humor, bridging the gap between the literary monologue and stand-up comedy.

Portnoy's Complaint unfolds in the form of a therapy session, its hero directly addressing his psychologist, Dr. Spielvogel, from the analyst's couch. Outwardly, the patient is an accomplished civil servant as New York City's assistant commissioner for human opportunity; behind closed doors, he compulsively indulges his sexual appetites, convinced that the pressure to be publicly successful denies him inner pleasures he feels excruciating guilt for even desiring. As befits Roth's satirical disdain for Freud ("Let's put the Id back in Yid!" Portnoy declares at several points), the chief culprit of the character's angst is his mother, Sophie. Often misjudged as a stereotypically suffocating Jewish mother, Mrs. Portnoy is both overweening and overprotective, making her son dependent on approval he yearns to rebel against. Well into Alex's adolescence she bangs on the bathroom door, asking about the condition of his "poopie" while reprimanding him (wrongly) for eating diarrhea-inducing french fries at his after-school hangout. Portnoy's father, Jack, is more remote, suffering from constipation and serving as a symbol of the Jewish assimilation into the American mainstream Portnoy wants to flout.

Between his mother's omnipresence and his father's cowed humility, Portnoy finds his only avenue for self-expression in (to quote a chapter title) "whacking off." And lo, the amount of semen one must wade through in this novel! Portnoy describes "firing [his] wad" into all manner of receptacles, from toilets to cored apples to his sister's brassiere. Most notoriously, he confesses to violating a slice of liver intended for the family dinner table. At another point Portnoy shoots himself in the eye with his own emission.

The comedy turns darker—more chauvinistic—after Alex loses his virginity and becomes addicted to seducing women. His first sexual contact is with Bubbles Girardi, an eighteen-year-old high school dropout who bequeaths manual stimulation on inexperienced teenagers—but only if they ejaculate within fifty strokes. In college he dates Kay Campbell, who inaugurates the novel's unsettling habit of dubbing women with derogatory nicknames. Kay is "The Pumpkin," an Iowa coed who takes Portnoy home for Thanksgiving, where he realizes that despite their shared intellectual interests she will never convert to Judaism. All of Alex's conquests are shikses, or gentile women. In bedding them, Portnoy enacts a double form of rebellion, rejecting his parents' prohibitions against "consorting with Christian girls"—another chapter title—and asserting through his virility his prowess at penetrating, literally and figuratively, anti-Semitic goyim culture. After the Pumpkin comes "The Pilgrim," Sarah Abbott Maulsby, whose uptight New England refinement Portnoy wants to sully to assuage his bitter feelings of Jewish exclusion. Their relationship roars to a stop over Portnoy's insistence she perform fellatio.

The woman bearing the brunt of his animus, though, is Mary Jane Reed, a.k.a. "The Monkey," so named because of some unspecified sex act she admits to performing before meeting Alex. Mary Jane's rural West Virginia background allows Portnoy to feel intellectually superior while embarrassing him deeply; in her willingness to cede to his sexual wants the Monkey appears to crave his denigration, though she claims she gives in because she loves him, which repulses Alex. As Portnoy comes to realize, he cannot reconcile the idea of love and sex because the former connotes responsibility and attachment, while the latter is simply a form of power. His ultimate act of humiliating the Monkey happens during a tour of Italy when he hires a prostitute for a threesome. He subsequently abandons Mary Jane when she threatens to leap off a balcony unless he marries her.

Only when Portnoy visits Israel does he begin to understand his condition. First he seduces a female lieutenant in the Jewish army, discovering to his horror that he's impotent. He next picks up Naomi, whom he calls "The Jewish Pumpkin" before dubbing her "The Heroine" because she's the one who finally forces him to confront his callowness. Naomi insists that Portnoy hides behind self-deprecation to avoid accepting his Jewish heritage and becoming a real man. Her rejection—which leaves Portnoy curled on the floor, clinging to her leg and begging to perform cunnilingus to prove himself—doesn't cure his inner conflict, but it does send him to Dr. Spielvogel for treatment. The story ends with a long rant in which Portnoy tries to exorcise his anger at society's arbitrary prohibitions (such as tearing off mattress tags) without succumbing to self-indulgent, destructive rebellion (like screaming "Up society's ass, Copper!" at authorities, which he longs to do). The monologue climaxes in a primal scream that leads to the literal "punch line," in which Dr. Spielvogel signals, despite Portnoy's voluble confession, that the healing journey has only just begun: "So . . . now vee may perhaps to begin. Yes?"

In later years, Roth would describe *Portnoy* as a creative breakthrough that allowed him to abandon literary décor and "let it rip" with profanity and explicit sex, elevating obscenity to art. The book's notoriety drove sales up to 400,000 hardbacks in its first year alone and nearly 4 million paperbacks by the mid-1970s, turning Roth into a celebrity outside of literary circles. Yet the novel also inspired bruising, hyperbolic condemnation, especially from Jewish intellectuals. Gershom Scholem claimed *Portnoy's Complaint* did more damage to Jews than the "Protocols of the Learned Elders of Zion," the spurious bible of anti-Semitism. Irving Howe said the greatest insult one could give it was to read it twice. Despite their objections, the novel became a touchstone of the era's obsession with sex.

What is remarkable is how little Portnoy's voice has aged. Reading the novel on its fiftieth anniversary is like listening to an expertly delivered comedy routine that could be delivered today. Profane in his self-deprecation, Alexander Portnoy is a case study in self-flagellation, even when he's not whacking off.

Bibliography

Portnoy's Complaint (1969)

Works Cited

Howe, Irving. "Philip Roth Reconsidered." *Commentary* December 1972: 69–77.
Scholem, Gershom. "*Portnoy's Complaint.*" Trans. E. E. Siskin. *CCARJ* (Central Conference of American Rabbis Journal), June 1970: 56–58.

—KC

HARRY POTTER

First Appearance: *Harry Potter and the Philosopher's Stone*
Date of First Appearance: 1997
Author: J. K. Rowling (1965–)

Well, we've never had a great Defense Against the Dark Arts teacher, have we?

Only one character in this book has his own theme park world, and that's J. K. Rowling's boy hero, Harry Potter. *The Wizarding World of Harry Potter* at Universal Orlando Resort, Universal Studios Hollywood, and Universal Studios Japan features a facsimile of the Hogwarts School of Witchcraft and Wizardry, where

young Harry and his witch/wizard friends studied magic. Visitors can ride a rep-
lica Hogwarts Express train that transported gifted youngsters from the Muggle
(nonmagical) world to Hogwarts, and they can wave interactive wands as they
explore sections of Diagon Alley and other re-creations from the books and popular film series. The immersive "worlds" were an instant success, with attendance
at the Hollywood park increasing 60 percent when the Potter attraction opened.

If that doesn't make Harry Potter seem like a pop-culture phenomenon, consider this: According to fan site Pottermore, more than 500 million Harry Potter
books have been sold worldwide in eighty languages, with the last volume, *Harry
Potter and the Deathly Hallows*, setting a Guinness World Record for the most novels sold on the day of release. In the U.S. alone, that final volume had a first printing of 12 million copies, with midnight book-release parties prompting long lines.
And the Warner Bros. film series is the third highest grossing, behind only Marvel
Universe and *Star Wars*. Though it may seem like a footnote by comparison, some
universities are now offering courses on the Harry Potter books, and at least three
volumes of academic criticism have been published in addition to the dozens of
fan books and guides.

Though written for young readers, the Potter fantasies are also popular with
adults, perhaps because the main character is as surprisingly complex as any in
literature. Rowling said that Harry was in her head for seventeen years and "feels
like this ghostly son in my life . . . a prism through which I view death, in its many
forms." Harry is an appealing combination of ordinary young man and reluctant
savior, and because of the latter he must deal with more deaths than most characters or readers. He loses his parents, his godfather, two beloved mentors, several
classmates, cherished friends, and even his wizard's owl, Hedwig—all because
they were close to Harry, the archetypal "chosen one." From the age of one, when
the evil wizard Voldemort killed Harry's magical parents and tried to kill him as
well, Harry becomes known throughout the wizarding world as "The Boy Who
Lived"—the only one to survive the Killing Curse, with a scar on his forehead the
shape of a lightning bolt to prove it. That fateful night, wizards secretly took him
to his Muggle aunt Petunia to be raised beyond the Dark Lord's penetrating vision.

In the Potter books, Voldemort, like Hitler, is obsessed with racial purity. He and
his followers wish to exterminate all Mudbloods (witches and wizards with Muggle
blood). In other parallels to Nazi Germany, Voldemort's followers remove a diver-
sity fountain and install a might-makes-right statue in its place, they replace liberal
Hogwarts faculty with their own teachers and fascist rules, and they replace knowledge with propaganda. The books, which begin when Harry gets an invitation to attend Hogwarts at age eleven, start out light but grow increasingly darker and more
violent. Harry is a quiet and generally shy lad who soon realizes if he doesn't act, if
he doesn't follow his destiny, many more people will die. Gradually he develops his
magical powers and, because of recurring visions that connect him to Voldemort,
begins to understand his special status. In addition to having the same coming-of-
age character arc as many young heroes—he is seventeen in the last installment—a
second arc tracks his growth as prime wizard, and a third has him gradually understanding and accepting that he must die in order to kill Voldemort.

All of this makes Harry an interesting character, but he's also a likable one who
comes across like the boy next door. As late as the fifth book he's described as "a

skinny, black-haired, bespectacled boy who had the pinched, slightly unhealthy look of someone who has grown a lot in a short space of time. His jeans were torn and dirty, his T-shirt baggy and faded, and the soles of his trainers were peeling away from the uppers." Harry doesn't just look average, he's also ordinary in other respects. He's not the best student, and he's not good at everything he attempts. He has a hot temper, and there are many times when he'd rather hang out with friends or play Quidditch than be "the chosen one." When he comes late to a potions class and is told to grab a textbook from the shelves, he finds one in which a student calling himself the "Half-Blood Prince" made corrections that turn out to be, well, *correct*. Does Harry show the teacher? No. In what could be construed as a form of cheating, he pilfers the book and continues to use it in order to excel in the class. Things like that make him interestingly *human*.

Teachers generally try not to favor him, but the other students have grown up hearing about the legendary Harry Potter, and frankly some of them are sick of it. So he also has resentment and rivalries to contend with, and as his hormones kick in he has crushes and relationship confusion, along with friends to confide in—chief among them the brainy Hermione Granger and the easily embarrassed Ron Weasley. Rowling said that while Hogwarts headmaster Albus Dumbledore is the character she'd most love to have dinner with and Hermione is the one most like her, her favorite character is still Harry. And he's certainly the novel's richest character, because he grows and matures throughout the books in far more depth than the others, and readers have full access to his psychological and emotional struggles.

As Harry bonds with Dumbledore, readers will recognize the Arthur-Merlin archetype at work, but later another archetype surfaces when Harry becomes instrumental in leading an underground student rebellion called Dumbledore's Army; he becomes a revolutionary figure, and the fascist establishment Ministry of Magic prints posters labeling Potter as "Undesirable #1." Rowling said that, for her, "absolute heroism is rebuilding after that kind of trauma, and I can think of nothing more noble than he's actually living what Dumbledore preached."

Harry, of course, defeats Voldemort, but Daniel Radcliffe, who played Potter in the eight films (the seventh book was split in half), said he thought the young wizard's biggest achievement was that he "created an appetite for literature." Even nonreaders became readers because of Harry. Though Christian parents worried unnecessarily that the Potter books would become a gateway into the world of the occult, as one Christian writer explained, the books deal with values that are solid models of citizenship, such as "friendship, family, self-sacrifice, temptations and the dangers of giving in, courage, the power of love, facing fears, the deepest desires of our hearts, growing up, bullying, protecting the innocent, dealing with injustice, helping those who are enslaved, racial bigotry, class snobbery, international cooperation, life and death, hatred, torture, tyranny, and terrorism—all relevant issues in today's world."

Bibliography

Harry Potter and the Philosopher's Stone (1997)
Harry Potter and the Chamber of Secrets (1998)
Harry Potter and the Prisoner of Azkaban (1999)
Harry Potter and the Goblet of Fire (2000)

Harry Potter and the Order of the Phoenix (2003)
Harry Potter and the Half-Blood Prince (2005)
Harry Potter and the Deathly Hallows (2007)

Works Cited

Associated Press. "Harry Potter Is a Modern Phenomenon." *Today*, July 2, 2007. http://
    www.today.com/id/19491516/ns/today-today_entertainment/t/harry-potter-modern
    -phenomenon/#.W4C68H5Om-o.
Burkhart, Gina. *A Parent's Guide to Harry Potter.* Downers Grove, IL: InterVarsity, 2005.
"A Conversation between JK Rowling and Daniel Radcliffe." YouTube video, 53:03.
    Posted September 22, 2013, by HarryPotterAdmirer. https://www.youtube.com/watch
    ?v=7BdVHWz1DPU.
Flood, Alison. "JK Rowling Reveals Her Favourite Harry Potter Character." *Guardian*,
    May 16, 2011. https://www.theguardian.com/childrens-books-site/2011/may/16/jk
    -rowling-favourite-harry-potter-character.
Niles, Robert. "The Power of Magic: USH Attendance up 60% after Potter." *Theme Park
    Insider*. April 27, 2017. https://www.themeparkinsider.com/flume/201704/5551/.
Pottermore News Team. "500 Million Harry Potter Books Have Now Been Sold World-
    wide." Pottermore.com. February 1, 2018. https://www.pottermore.com/news/500
    -million-harry-potter-books-have-now-been-sold-worldwide.
Wood, Jennifer M. "10 Highest-Grossing Movie Franchises of All Time." *Mental Floss*, April
    30, 2018. http://mentalfloss.com/article/70920/10-highest-grossing-movie-franchises
    -all-time.

—JP

HESTER PRYNNE

First Appearance: *The Scarlet Letter*
Date of First Appearance: 1850
Author: Nathaniel Hawthorne (1804–1864)

Why are we taught to be ashamed—of love?

Old classics never die; they just keep haunting high school English classes as students might testify of Nathaniel Hawthorne's *The Scarlet Letter*, published in 1850. Contemporary readers often find the language only a tad less antiquated than Shakespeare's, and on its surface the novel seems to have little in common with twenty-first-century teenagers, except perhaps the topic of unwanted pregnancy and the havoc it wreaks on one's social life. So why make them read the book? Because Hester Prynne is one of the rock stars of fiction, and she needs no qualifiers of literary period, gender, or nationality to hold her own against any protagonist on a ranked list. As one website recently put it, "Hester is our homegirl." This phrase may not translate well a century from now, but the qualities that make Hester an enduring figure will.

  As Hester emerges from a seventeenth-century Boston prison at the novel's opening carrying a three-month-old child, she exudes dignity and grace in the face of all that would rob her of both. Much to the surprise of the dour towns-people who expect to see a broken woman, her statuesque figure and stunning beauty make "a halo of the misfortune and ignominy in which she was envel-oped." Hawthorne sure knows how to embellish a phrase! Hester's beauty has not only withstood the months of dismal incarceration, she has transcended her punishment, and the narrator goes so far as to say that if a stray Papist were to be wandering in this Puritan burg, he might be reminded of the Madonna herself holding the holy child. Not bad for an adulterous woman clutching the object of her sin to her breast.

Emblazoned upon the chest of her simple Puritan frock Hester Prynne has at-tached a fantastically embroidered scarlet "A" sure to draw attention. That letter forever linked to her has become arguably one of the three most identifiable sym-bols in all of literature, in company with Gatsby's green light and the white whale Moby-Dick. We are never told in the novel, nor do we need to be, that Hester has committed adultery; the proof is evident for all to see because she has lived unaccompanied by her husband for the past two years. What is equally clear is that Hester takes the nearly intolerable walk of shame, head held high and with a muted but almost haughty look of self-possession. Her body language validates acceptance of the punishment without apology for the crime.

So why in the mid-nineteenth century does Hawthorne create this seventeenth-century narrative of female woe? As a matter of possible historical inspiration, in 1845 his friend and fellow transcendentalist Margaret Fuller published her feminist work *Woman in the Nineteenth Century*, and in 1848 Susan B. Anthony and Elizabeth Cady Stanton held the first women's rights conference. If we are to believe the novel's preface, "The Custom House," we know that Hawthorne's literary persona discovers a package bearing the red "A" along with a narrative relaying the curious circumstances of a woman's life. This seems a contrived authentication for a tale he is about to weave, but we do know that Hawthorne's great-great-grandfather John Hathorne had been a judge at the Salem witch tri-als, one of America's darkest hours of disgrace and wrongful accusation, and the younger Hawthorne was presumably ashamed enough to change the spelling of his name to diminish the connection.

If we believe Hawthorne's personal shame, we understand more fully his deep-seated need to make Hester a sympathetic figure. Her years of penance become steadily more self-induced than forced upon her. She silently points to the letter to remind passersby not to sully themselves through association with her. She shuns all social interaction but administers mercy to those in need. Hester tolerates cruel censure for an act she did not commit alone, and she protects the identity of the two men who continue to wrong her—the husband who mysteriously appears the day of her public shaming and demands silence so he can secretly exact slow torture upon the man who cuckolded him, and the Reverend Arthur Dimmesdale who wallows in his own guilt at not acknowledging his paternity and complic-ity. Because of Hester's honorable response to her punishment, fellow Bostonians come to believe the scarlet letter "A" means "able" or "angel," and in the end we might only find fault with her not for the act of adultery but for her failure to denounce both her husband for his cruel and silent revenge, and her lover for his cowardice and self-absorption.

The history of public humiliation no doubt goes back as far as the chronicling of human nature, but from Hawthorne's novel forward, Hester and the scarlet letter have become synonymous with using such sentencing not to punctuate a crime so much as to humiliate the perpetrator. With all-too-frequent regularity, newspaper headlines echo Hester's scarlet letter with judges ordering convicted defendants to stand in public holding a sign describing their transgressions. Florida even had on its books until 2002 a so-called *Scarlet Letter* law requiring unwed pregnant women to publish names of their sexual partners so potential fathers might be identified before babies could be put up for adoption.

But through all this discussion of sin, we neglect an important element in Hester. She is a young and beautiful woman, capable of deep physical and emotional passion. However ill advised, her love for Arthur Dimmesdale extends presumably beyond the grave, though with his dying breath he robs her of even this hope by declaring the vanity of such ignominious thoughts. Remaining true to him, and to her own nature, Hester gets the last word, and returns to the scene of the crime to be buried next to the man whom she would not let disavow her, even in death.

John Updike, at first glance, might be an unlikely source for discussion about Hester Prynne, but he found her so inescapable to a contemporary discussion of sex that he wrote a twentieth-century revisionist trilogy—one book for each of *The Scarlet Letter*'s three central characters—where in Hester's updated tale the title's single letter *S.* evokes the connection. Updike reminds us that Hester is a sexual being, irrepressible and "a mythic version of every woman's attempt to integrate her sexuality with societal demands." Such a tribute speaks to the engagement Hawthorne's Mistress Prynne continues to create as a symbol in our cultural psyche.

More than four centuries dead in historic context and more than a century and a half since her fictional debut, Hester still haunts us. Her unjust punishment resonates. Her desire to be understood and accepted for who she is and not identified only for what she has done tugs at our own personal episodes of mistreatment, no doubt far less severe, but wounding nonetheless. And above all else, the dignity with which Hester bears this incongruity is the true example Hawthorne sets. In *The Scarlet Letter* Hester claims, "This badge hath taught me—it daily teaches me," and the beauty is that it can daily teach us as well the lessons of tolerance and forgiveness not always easily found or practiced.

Bibliography

The Scarlet Letter (1850)

Works Cited

Fuller, Margaret. *Woman in the Nineteenth Century*. New York: Greeley and McElrath, 1845.
Updike, John. Interview by Andrea Seabrook. "Hester Prynne: Sinner, Victim, Object, Winner." NPR, *All Things Considered*, March 2, 2008.

—GS

Q

QUASIMODO

First Appearance: *The Hunchback of Notre-Dame*
Date of First Appearance: 1831
Author: Victor Hugo (1802–1885)

My misfortune is that I'm still too much like a man; I wish I were a beast outright, like that goat.

When we first meet Quasimodo in the year 1482, the bell ringer at Notre-Dame Cathedral is called a "baboon," a "devil of a man"—someone who looks like "a giant that had been broken and awkwardly mended." He's a "Cyclops" who is almost as broad as he is tall, with one eye completely obscured by an enormous wart and one tooth protruding like "the tusk of an elephant." And, of course, there's that infamous fleshy hunchback.

During the Festival of Fools, costumed Parisians celebrate in the plaza near the cathedral. Quasimodo, who had been watching from the shadows, is proclaimed the pope of fools because of his "masquerade." Hoisted on a platform, he's cheered . . . until neighbors recognize him and everyone realizes his ugliness is no mask. Instantly the women hide their faces. Someone who lives in the shadow of Notre-Dame grumbles that at night she hears him "scrambling in the gutter. With the cats." Another has caught him peering in her window and is convinced Quasimodo consorts with witches. "He's constantly upon our roofs" and "casts spells at us down the chimneys." He's "mischievous as he's ugly," another complains. But however deformed, Quasimodo is still a twenty-year-old man. Later in the novel, when he spies a beautiful gypsy girl who often dances in the plaza, he can't help but fall in love with her—though he can't fully process his feelings because his brain is "a peculiar medium."

With *The Hunchback of Notre-Dame*, Victor Hugo offered readers a unique and more interesting twist on the "Beauty and the Beast" fairy tale. Rather than a handsome prince who's merely transformed by a magic spell, Quasimodo is a freak of nature, a human so physically deformed that others see him as monstrous. His condition is alarmingly real and frighteningly permanent, and the way people respond to him is hurtful, even to someone who doesn't have the same intellect or range of human experience. A sculptor's recently found memoirs suggest that Hugo may have gotten the idea from seeing a hunchback stone carver working on the restoration of Notre-Dame. But Quasimodo is much more than a mutant. Despite his deformities, he has "a certain gait denoting vigour, agility, and courage—a strange exception to the everlasting rule which prescribes that strength, like beauty, shall result from harmony."

Quasimodo is fit and agile enough to climb all over the cathedral's facade, with "no other help than the projections of its architecture and sculpture." Having lived inside Notre-Dame since he was adopted by the stern cleric Claude Frollo, who would become archdeacon, Quasimodo took to the cathedral "like a tortoise to its shell." He explored every inch, from the deepest recesses to the tallest spires. As he clambered up and down the front of the cathedral, he must have seemed like a medieval Spider-Man to the people of Paris—and a wonder to nineteenth-century readers as well.

Quasimodo is most in his element when he's among the fifteen bells in the cathedral towers. Frollo taught him to speak, read, and write, but in giving Quasimodo the bells to ring, it was like "giving Juliet to Romeo." Quasimodo rings them for any occasion and what seems to neighbors like no occasion at all. The bells have names and Quasimodo talks to them, encouraging them to ring their loudest as he looks down at the swarm of people 200 feet below. At times he throws himself on the largest bell—Marie, his favorite—riding her and hugging her as she rings, becoming "a strange centaur, half man half bell." Ringing those bells all these years has made Quasimodo deaf, but he is most alive when he's with them. That's because while he loves Frollo, his master seems incapable of loving in return. In fact, one of the novel's most interesting contrasts comes from the lust that drives Frollo as he watches Esmeralda dance, compared to the pure, innocent love that Quasimodo feels for her.

Frollo's lust drives him to send Quasimodo to kidnap Esmeralda and bring her to him, and Quasimodo tries to do what he's told, tossing aside a man who tries to help her and behaving like a wild animal when apprehended—even foaming at the mouth. Quasimodo is more beast than human when we first encounter him, which is reinforced as we watch him riding Marie and uttering a single ejaculation: "Vah!" But the tipping point occurs when a magistrate sentences Quasimodo to the public pillory. Stripped to his waist and bound to a platform, Quasimodo breathes "heavily, like a calf when its head hangs tossing about over the side of the butchers cart." He's whipped until he bleeds, while the crowd shouts insults and throws stones at him. But after Esmeralda emerges from the crowd to give him a drink, we see a change in him—proof of the transformative power of love.

Readers begin to witness Quasimodo's human side after Frollo tries to assuage his lust by having Esmeralda arrested and sentenced to hang. Given the chance to say a final penance on the steps of Notre-Dame, she's swept off by Quasimodo who, like King Kong would later do with Fay Wray, scampers to the top of the building with her. There he famously shouts, "Sanctuary!" while a crowd that had assembled below approves. Later, when we see him stop by her "cell" in the upper part of the cathedral, we realize how articulate he can be, how sensitive. Yet, though his "beauty" recognizes how basically good and kind he is, she still cannot think of him as anything but a "poor devil"—even when she awakens to find him looking at her and he responds, "Don't be afraid. I'm your friend. I was come to look at you sleeping. That doesn't hurt you, does it, that I should come and see you asleep?"

It's Quasimodo who has the revelation: "Never did I see my ugliness as I do now," he says. "When I compare myself to you, I do indeed pity myself, poor unhappy monster that I am." As Quasimodo looks at one of the cathedral's famed stone gargoyles and thinks, "Oh, why am I not made of stone like thee?" it's a moment worthy of Hamlet and his skull.

Not surprisingly, *The Hunchback of Notre-Dame* has been embraced by popular culture, though the story is often changed to be happier than the one Hugo wrote, which ends with Frollo tossed from the heights of Notre-Dame, Esmeralda hanged in the plaza, and a disconsolate Quasimodo disappearing forever . . . only to be found years later in a site where bodies had been dumped, his misshapen skeleton entwined with that of a woman's. Played by such Hollywood icons as Lon Chaney, Charles Laughton, and Anthony Quinn, Quasimodo has appeared in dozens of film and television adaptations, including several TV miniseries and a famous Disney animated film. But he's also appeared in dozens of operas, ballets, and theatrical performances—including an 1836 opera with libretto by Hugo himself. And there have been video games, comics, and even radio serials based on the character and his story . . . which have turned out to be timeless.

Bibliography

The Hunchback of Notre-Dame (1831)

Work Cited

Nikkhah, Roya. "Real-Life Quasimodo Uncovered in Tate Archives." *Daily Telegraph*, August 15, 2010. https://www.telegraph.co.uk/culture/books/artsandentertainment booksreview/7945634/Real-life-Quasimodo-uncovered-in-Tate-archives.html.

—JP

DON QUIXOTE

First Appearance: *El Ingenioso Hidalgo Don Quixote de la Mancha*
Date of First Appearance: 1605
Author: Miguel de Cervantes (1547–1616)

The desire of achieving fame is a powerful incentive.

In an 1868 letter to his niece, Fyodor Dostoevsky wrote, "Of all the beautiful individuals in Christian literature, one stands out as the most perfect, Don Quixote. But he is beautiful only because he is ridiculous."

Anyone who knows the adjective "quixotic"—meaning "extravagantly chivalrous or romantic; visionary, impractical, or impracticable"—knows that it refers to Don Quixote, Miguel de Cervantes's seventeenth-century comic hero. *The Ingenious*

Gentleman Don Quixote of La Mancha was published as a parody of romances in 1605 and became so popular that spurious versions popped up, which Cervantes referenced in a second installment published in 1615. Like Cervantes, who was a frail fifty-eight-year-old when the first volume appeared, Quixote has seen better days. Unlike Cervantes, a failed writer who worked as a tax collector and served time in prison when his numbers didn't add up, Quixote is a man of some means. Wealthy enough to have a housekeeper and curate to take care of him and his house, he immerses himself in books day and night, reading romantic tales of knights-errant, maidens in distress, and honors won in single combat at home and abroad. "At last, when his wits were gone beyond repair," readers are told, he decides "to win a greater amount of honor for himself and serve his country at the same time, to become a knight-errant and roam the world on horseback." Shining up old pieces of armor left him by his great-grandfather, this early do-it-yourselfer makes "a kind of half-helmet" out of thin board reinforced with a few strips of iron, grabs an old lance, and sets off on a "steed" dubbed Rocinante that's really a broken-down nag. He dreams of the "sweet lady" he will rescue and even gives this imaginary beauty a name: Dulcinea del Toboso.

Though early readers found the earnest but crazy nobleman appealingly funny, centuries later Don Quixote is often thought of as the unofficial patron saint of impossible dreamers. As much as the novel, people today will have heard of him because of "The Impossible Dream," the principal song from the 1965 Broadway musical *Man of La Mancha* that's sung by Quixote as a way of explaining why he does what he does. Yes, he's old and crazy enough to mistake a windmill for a four-armed monster, source of the expression "tilting at windmills" (fighting an imaginary enemy). Yes, he's paranoid enough to think that he has a mortal enemy—an evil wizard named the Enchanter—who is changing all of his romantic projections into shabby reality, and yes he fancies himself a knight accompanied by his "squire," a portly farmer that he recruits. But Don Quixote somehow speaks to the yearnings of unfulfilled human experience.

The old man who refuses to let chivalry and adventure die, or to go gently (and unimaginatively) into his own good night, has inspired more than thirty films, four ballets, four operas, and dozens of orchestral suites and symphonies. Contemporary musicians from folk to rap have released "Don Quixote" songs, and Quixote has inspired such visual artists as Pablo Picasso, Salvador Dali, and Honoré Daumier. Because he is associated with travel and pilgrimages, Quixote also turns up in the names of bars, restaurants, karaoke clubs, and B&Bs all over the world. So universally beloved is he that statues of him occupy prominent spaces in numerous countries, including Spain, Belgium, Mexico, Cuba, China, and the U.S.— where he can be seen in San Francisco's Golden Gate Park and on the grounds of the John F. Kennedy Center for the Performing Arts in Washington, D.C.

Because of the depth of characterization, *Don Quixote* is widely considered to be the first modern European novel, and at more than 500,000 words, it's also one of the longest. The episodic or "picaresque" novel follows the exploits of Don Quixote and his sidekick, Sancho Panza, whom he promises there's "no telling what adventure might occur which would win them an island, and then he would be left to be the governor of it." But from the moment Quixote charges a windmill with his lance and gets knocked off his horse by the blades, Sancho realizes that his main duty as squire will be to protect his master from himself, and that includes humoring him by going along with his cockeyed perception of the world. But Quixote is not merely mad or totally comic. He recognizes his madness at times and even defends his romantic perceptions.

"I wish the pain in this rib would subside somewhat so that I might be able, Sancho, to show you how wrong you are," Quixote says after that first battle turned battering fails to knock some sense into him. He *prefers* to see the world in romantic terms, and, for reasons the reader must discern, needs to see himself as a knighterrant, compelled to pursue grand adventures. Although an innkeeper, not royalty, knights him using a book instead of a sword, it doesn't matter to Quixote, whose misadventures are often based on his misperceptions or misunderstandings. In one such episode, Quixote takes off his armor but places it right next to a community water trough; whenever people approach to drink, he thinks they are trying to steal his armor and uses his lance to knock them down. He charges a caravan because they won't acknowledge that the imagined Dulcinea is the most beautiful in the world, and they beat him with his own lance. He fights a group angered that his horse tried to mate with their mares and gets knocked unconscious, and he attacks a religious group carrying a large image of the Virgin Mary because he thinks they're transporting a fair maiden against her will. He charges a funeral because he thinks the coffin contains a great knight who must be avenged, and when he and his squire attack a chain gang (to free the oppressed), the prisoners fight to help win their release but then turn on the knight-extremely-errant when he insists they go to Toboso and tell Dulcinea how bravely he fought. And Don Quixote gets so caught up in a puppet show where Moors chase after a knight and fair damsel that he suddenly rushes the stage to attack the puppets, thinking it all real.

Throughout the book, such comic misadventures are balanced by stories both men tell to pass the time, like Chaucer's pilgrims, and the contemplative and philosophical Quixote also engages his squire and others in discussions of such weighty topics as knighthood, books, wealth, fame, honor, duty, love, intelligence, parenting, and beauty—all the while seeming quite sane, thereby complicating readers' opinion of him.

In the end, after friends try to get "the madness out of Don Quixote's noodle" and stage a joust that results in his bitter defeat, he is so crushed that on his deathbed he recants his romantic notions. But like the readers who have grown to love Don Quixote and admire his persistent idealism, friends miss the old Quixote, and Sancho delivers the final word on his madness: "The grade A madness that a man can be guilty of in this life is to die without good reason, without anyone killing him, slain only by the hands of melancholy."

Bibliography

El Ingenioso Hidalgo Don Quixote de la Mancha (1605, 1615)

Works Cited

Loseff, Lev. "Dostoevsky & 'Don Quixote.'" *New York Review of Books*, November 19, 1998. https://www.nybooks.com/articles/1998/11/19/dostoevsky-don-quixote/.
Putnam, Samuel, translator and editor. Introduction to *The Portable Cervantes*. New York: Penguin, 1978.

—JP

R

RODION ROMANOVICH RASKOLNIKOV

First Appearance: *Crime and Punishment*
Date of First Appearance: 1866
Author: Fyodor Dostoevsky (1821–1881)

And how could such an atrocious thing come into my head? What filthy things my heart is capable of.

At the corner of Stolyarny and Grazhdansky Streets in St. Petersburg, Russia, there's a house with the words "Home of Raskolnikov" carved in relief. More than 150 years after Fyodor Dostoevsky created him, Rodion Raskolnikov remains one of the most infamous characters in fiction—so much so that sites associated with him continue to be popular with tourists. With Raskolnikov, Dostoevsky stretched the accepted notion of a novel's "protagonist" to include a man with a split personality whose criminal acts and psychological profile would spur countless other stories of criminal minds and the causal relationships between poverty, mental instability, and crime.

Literature's most famous law student turned criminal turned rehabilitated citizen may not have even come into being if it wasn't for the inequalities of society that Dostoevsky experienced firsthand. Like his character, Dostoevsky was educated but poor, and though their crimes were different (protesting censorship versus murder), both men served out a sentence in Siberia. After dropping out of school because of finances, twenty-three-year-old Raskolnikov is down to pawning his last two sentimental keepsakes. He dresses in rags and lives in a garret that's more "cupboard" than room—what his mother calls "wretched lodging . . . like a tomb." Forced to sleep on an old torn sofa, he becomes increasingly agitated each time he must deal with Alyona, the pawnbroker, growing ever more resentful of her and her wealth. As Raskolnikov boldly tells an officer of the law while passionately arguing hypotheticals (as current and even former students are apt to do), "On one side we have a stupid, senseless, worthless, spiteful, ailing horrid old woman, not simply useless but doing actual mischief, who has not an idea what she is living for herself," and "on the other side, fresh young lives thrown away for want of help. . . . Kill her, take her money and with the help of it devote oneself to the service of humanity and the good of all. . . . One death, and a hundred lives in exchange—it's simple arithmetic!" But it's probably not the smartest conversation to have if, like Raskolnikov, you've spent the last month first entertaining the thought, then imagining the act, and finally planning the details of the murder.

Then again, Raskolnikov isn't your typical murderer. When he was at school he helped care for a tubercular fellow student and even, after the student died, took on the responsibility of caring for the student's aged and infirmed father. If that's not enough to balance his moral ledger, he once rescued two small children from a house fire and frequently gives what little money he has to people in need. But as even his mother concedes, Raskolnikov is a walking contradiction: both generous and "haughty," and morosely withdrawn yet also hot tempered. He's a loner who hides from everyone "like a tortoise in its shell," but emerges from time to time to help others. Part of the problem is that this young man, described as being even more attractive than his sister, has "overwrought nerves" and an "irritable condition, verging on hypochondria." So is it his condition, the extreme poverty, or a combination of the two that makes him "unhinged"? What drives Raskolnikov to behave in ways that puzzle and shock even him?

Raskolnikov has given this much thought, and "it was his conviction that this eclipse of reason and failure of will-power attacked a man like a disease developed gradually and reached its highest point just before the perpetration of the crime, continued with equal violence at the moment of the crime . . . then passed off like any other disease." If it were so, he reasons, it would explain why so many crimes are "so badly concealed and so easily detected." Significantly, right before he commits the murder, "a sudden giddiness came over him," whereas afterward he was beset by "a sort of blankness, even dreaminess." Later, when police question him, he faints, as if weakened by disease. But elsewhere in the novel Raskolnikov offers a different explanation for his criminal behavior. In confessing to the crime he says, "I want to prove one thing only, that the devil led me on then and he has shown me since that I had not the right to take that path, because I am just such a louse as all the rest." He insists, "It was the devil that killed that old woman, not I."

As a character, Raskolnikov invites study and speculation, especially when he himself is prone to philosophizing. "He doesn't jeer at things, not because he hasn't the wit, but as though he hadn't time to waste on such trifles." He tends to focus—and obsess—on one or two things at a time, like the inequity between the wealthy pawnbroker and all of the poor people who have to deal with her nastiness and threats if they're just one day late with an interest payment. He's also especially sensitive about women and morality. When he sees a very young teenage girl drunk in the streets and crossing her legs "indecorously," he fends off a rich man who he perceives meant to take advantage of the girl, and even goes so far as to summon a policeman and share his suspicions. In another instance, when he impulsively goes into a basement tavern for the first time in his life, he meets an unemployed alcoholic who shares his sad story of poverty so extreme that his wife had forced his daughter from a previous marriage to sell herself for money. It has a profound effect on Raskolnikov.

Most famously, though, there's Raskolnikov's theory of criminals that reads like a corruption of liberal thought. He believes that there are two kinds of men: those who are temperamentally conservative and law abiding and "live under control and love to be controlled," and those who "transgress the law," people who are "disposed to destruction according to their capacities." The latter, he argues, "seek in varied ways the destruction of the present for the sake of the better." Throughout *Crime and Punishment*, readers are invited to consider whether that's revolutionary or criminal thought. To Raskolnikov, the crime almost seems like a purification, after which "it will be over and everything will begin afresh"—though even this thought astounds him. When Raskolnikov tells his mother he gifted the money she had given him to the wife of the drunk he had met in the tavern and begs her forgiveness, she assures him, "I am sure that everything you do is very good." His reply is chilling: "'Don't be too sure,' he answered, twisting his mouth into a smile."

As David Mikics writes in the *New Statesman*, when Dostoevsky briefly shifts the point of view to the pawnbroker's sister at the moment she's going to be killed, "We've spent so much time with the murderer, in our slow, captivated reading of the book, that we can't just reject him now. But we also know that, when he scorns the sacredness of human life, he has done the unforgivable." Raskolnikov will have his happy ending, but as we consider his outcome we also naturally reflect on the victims, whose endings were quite the opposite.

Bibliography

Crime and Punishment (1866)

Works Cited

Mikics, David. "What *Crime and Punishment* Can Teach You That the Internet Can't." *New Statesman*, November 25, 2013. https://www.newstatesman.com/cultural-capital/2013/11/what-crime-and-punishment-can-teach-you-internet-cant.
Zakharova, Alisa. "St. Petersburg in the Footsteps of Raskolnikov." *Russia Beyond*, July 14, 2013. https://www.rbth.com/literature/2013/07/14/st_petersburg_in_the_footsteps_of_raskolnikov_28057.html.

—JP

IGNATIUS J. REILLY

First Appearance: *A Confederacy of Dunces*
Date of First Appearance: 1980
Author: John Kennedy Toole (1937–1969)

I had a rather apocalyptic battle with a starving prostitute. Had it not been for my superior brawn, she would have sacked my wagon.

And the title of Best Hot Dog Vendor in Literature goes to . . . Ignatius J. Reilly, who also happens to be Best Mama's Boy—though he's certain he's not, even if he does spend as much time finding ways to stay at home as he does trying to get out from under her thumb.

A Confederacy of Dunces was published eleven years after the suicide of its author, John Kennedy Toole, largely due to the persistence of Toole's overbearing mother and the advocacy of southern writer Walker Percy. In his foreword to the Pulitzer Prize–winning novel, Percy wrote that protagonist Ignatius J. Reilly is a "slob extraordinary, a mad Oliver Hardy, a fat Don Quixote, a perverse Thomas Aquinas rolled into one." At age thirty, Reilly is a year younger than Toole was when he killed himself, suffering from mental illness and dejected after his manuscript was repeatedly rejected. Some characters are just along for the ride, but the corpulent Reilly, so big his hands are described as "paws," is absurdly unique. Without him, the novel would never have been become a cult classic with a fan base as devoted as *The Rocky Horror Picture Show* crowds. Reilly is so big in New Orleans, where the novel is set, that a life-size bronze statue of him was erected in the 800 block of Canal Street in a pose that mimics the novel's opening, with Reilly waiting for his mother:

> A green hunting cap squeezed the top of the fleshy balloon of a head. The green earflaps, full of large ears and uncut hair and the fine bristles that grew in the ears themselves, stuck out on either side like turn signals indicating two directions at once. Full, pursed lips protruded beneath the bushy black moustache and, at their corners, sank into little folds filled with disapproval and potato chip crumbs. In the shadow under the green visor of the cap Ignatius J. Reilly's supercilious blue and yellow eyes looked down upon the other people waiting under the clock at the D.H. Holmes department store, studying the crowd of people for signs of bad taste in dress.

Throughout this comic novel the educated but slovenly and lazy Reilly rails against modern society, reluctantly yields to his mother's nagging, and navigates a series of job attempts. Along the way he corresponds with a hippie ex-girlfriend and interacts with colorful New Orleans characters, while Mrs. Reilly serves as his enabler, would-be mentor, or tormentor (it's hard to tell which). That Reilly has been embraced as a pop-culture icon, albeit an underground one, is crazy ironic, since the character *despises* pop culture. He attends showings of popular films only to loudly complain, and working as a hot dog vendor he berates a Pirate's Alley painter for "the offenses which you have committed to canvas." Convinced that everything went downhill after the Middle Ages, Reilly writes in one of his Big Chief tablets, "With the breakdown of the Medieval system, the gods of Chaos, Lunacy, and Bad Taste gained ascendancy." As a trained medievalist he wrote a monograph about it and sent it to the rare book room at Tulane University, but he's fairly certain they never accepted his "gift"—as certain as he is that he's a misunderstood genius.

Reilly knows New Orleans well because he's only left the city once and was so traumatized by a failed bus trip to Baton Rouge to interview for a university medievalist position that he never left town again. But he's like no professor or medievalist anyone would recognize, preferring to hobnob with far less erudite folks. Reilly and his mother pass the time with a stripper at a club called Night of Joy, but when he sees her performing a lady pirate striptease as Harlett O'Hara he rushes the stage, only to have her cockatoo attack him, disorienting him so much that he's almost hit by a bus after he staggers outside.

Percy was right. Reilly *is* a little like a fat Don Quixote or an angry/crazy version of the fat half of the Laurel and Hardy comedy duo, and that's what makes him the kind of train wreck of a fictional character that's impossible to ignore. Unable to keep a job and plagued by a bloated stomach and chronic belching, Reilly often lies in bed "contemplating the unfortunate turn that events had taken since the Reformation" and masturbating, during which he pictures an ex-girlfriend who suspects he's a homosexual. He may wear a Mickey Mouse watch and may want to register sodomites, but just as you're ready to write him off as an absurd comic invention, he says or does something that reminds you that he's certainly not the only socially awkward person to fancy himself smarter than anyone else and retreat to his bedroom sanctuary when things upset him too much. Although the typical basement/bedroom dweller who lives with his mother as an adult *usually* doesn't contemplate Boethius and cry, "Oh, Fortuna, blind heedless goddess, I am strapped to your wheel. Do not crush me beneath your spokes"—you could certainly picture hipsters doing so if it became trendy. While he's not the first dependent underachieving adult to hear his mother insist that he *has* to get a job to help pay the bills, he's probably the only medievalist who thinks he's too good for this century to find employment—especially when past history suggests it's futile to even try. After all, a job at a public library lasted less than a day, and he was fired from his last teaching job for throwing students' papers out the window (they were *not* too good for this century).

"Ken" Toole's academic friend Pat Rickels said in the *Independent Weekly* that Toole "made fun about everything and everybody," but that Ignatius J. Reilly seemed to be a composite character. When the first chapter was published in *New Orleans* magazine, she said that it was "so obviously Ken and so obviously Bob Byrne," Toole's office mate and fellow English instructor at the University of Louisiana, Lafayette. "Everything in Bobby is in Ignatius," Rickels said. "His size, his indigestion, his greed, his love of Boethius. All of his little verbal tags are in Ignatius, being under the wing of his mama, all of his strange medieval obsessions."

Reilly wanders the streets "like a Mardi Gras" though it's not even February, wearing a long scarf and carrying a plastic pirate sword. When a young man scoffs that he looks "like Charles Laughton in drag as Queen of the Gypsies," Reilly "began to strike the young man's calves" with his sword and throws one of his "elephantine desert boots" at him, proclaiming, "I am the avenging sword of taste and decency." When he finally does leave home for good, he tells his ex-girlfriend he wants to bring *all* his notes. "We must never let them fall into the hands of my mother. She may make a fortune from them. It would be too ironic."

Bibliography

A Confederacy of Dunces (1980)

Work Cited

Tutwiler, Mary. "The Lafayette Confederacy." *Independent Weekly*, July 20, 2005. http://theind.com/article-160-The-Lafayette-Confederacy.html.

—JP

RENO

First Appearance: *The Flamethrowers*
Date of First Appearance: 2013
Author: Rachel Kushner (1968–)

I had to watch out for potholes, and cabs that came to sudden stops, but crossing Broadway, zooming up Spring Street, passing trucks, hanging a left onto the Bowery, the broadness of the street, the tall buildings in the north distance, the sense of being in, but not of, the city, moving through it with real velocity, wind in my face, were magical.

When published in 2013, Rachel Kushner's *The Flamethrowers* dazzled critics like few novels in recent history. For one thing, its subject matter and geography were astonishingly broad and varied. Although unified by its 1970s time frame, the plot leaps from land speed racing in the salt flats of Utah to New York City's avant-garde art world, exploring photography and models known as "China girls" (the face models on film leaders whose skin tone allowed lab techs to calibrate their color processing) to the rise of Italian Fascism (with flashbacks to World War I and the emergence of Mussolini), revolutionary politics, Brazilian rubber plantations, and the industrial history of tires. Across this vast backdrop, Kushner proves herself a master stylist with idiosyncratic imagery and lush description whose thick viscosity avoids stalling the brisk pace.

The most divisive element of the novel, though, proved to be Kushner's narrator, a young woman known only as Reno after her Nevada hometown. *The Flamethrowers* is her coming-of-age story, but while like a typical picaresque hero, her role is more to observe the world than to shape it; she is never wide-eyed or endangered by her naïveté, no matter the risks she takes. She's a reflecting presence, but not a wallflower—more than one reviewer was baffled by how "macho" she behaves. Yet other readers say she's too unemotional. Some find her aloof, comparing her voice to the hip detachment of vintage Joan Didion, a not-inappropriate comparison given the era the book depicts. In a novel obsessed with fire and burning, Reno never allows herself to get overheated. She's the essence of cool.

At heart, *The Flamethrowers* is about theatricality and artifice in art, and whether they have any real-world influence on political protest and socioeconomic change. The answer seems obvious when one looks to the backstory of T. P. Valera, whose association with F. T. Marinetti's futurism movement and military experience during World War I in the Arditi, the Italian Army's special forces, lead him to join Mussolini's Fascists in the 1920s. From there Valera rises in Italian society as the founder of a motorcycle company, surviving World War II to become a major influence on state politics into the 1970s. As Kushner demonstrates, the futurists' anarchic aesthetic of velocity, violence, and technology directly influenced the Fascists and after World War II was reified into a strain of capitalism that allowed Valera to build tire plants in the forests of Brazil and ruthlessly exploit his workers.

The aesthetically pleasing design and exhilarating rush of the motorcycle as a symbol of cultural rebellion, however, obscures the more nefarious aspects of these connections. By the 1970s, as Reno arrives in New York City and becomes the girlfriend of Valera's son, Sandro, a well-known minimalist in the art world, the relationship between aesthetics and culture is not so much concealed by commerce as it is tenuous from the threat of irrelevance. Contemporary artists are just as avant-garde as Marinetti's followers, but the force of historical motion no longer speeds toward either the disaster of world wars or the "progress" of industrialization and development. Instead, art and time both seem to spin their wheels.

In our first glimpse of Reno, she wrecks a Moto Valera cycle during a race in the Bonneville Salt Flats of Utah. She is only nominally a racer; her main goal is to photograph her tracks for an art project. But the crash leads a crew for a hybrid motorcycle/automobile to appreciate Reno's thirst for risk, and they soon help her set the land speed record for a woman (a feat modeled on the 1960s' career of racer Lee Breedlove). In a traditional novel, the crash and subsequent land speed record would form the climactic trajectory of Reno's story, dramatizing the heroic resolve and drive to conquer limitations. But for Kushner, events in Utah are merely a vehicle for transporting Reno abroad to Italy, where at the invitation of the Valera family she's to participate in promotional events for the company. Events both personal and political intervene. At Lake Como outside Milan, Reno discovers that Sandro is romantically involved with his cousin, and she abandons him for the groundskeeper Gianni, who just happens to be a leader of a leftist movement called the Autonomists.

Sweeping her off to Rome, Gianni introduces Reno to the labor protests against the Valera Company's treatment of its workers, which Kushner sets against the historical unrest in Italy known as the Movement of '77. She witnesses street riots and, it's implied, becomes the unknowing conduit by which terrorists kidnap and later kill Sandro's brother Roberto, who heads the company and is infamous for his exploitation of his workforce. We never know for certain, because the final section recounts how after Reno helped smuggle Gianni into France he failed to show up for their rendezvous. "Leave with no answer," reads the final line. "Move on to the next question." The chronological ending actually appears some ninety pages earlier, when in Roberto's absence Sandro is called home to take over the family company. As Sandro sits on the runway, a blackout hits New York City (based on the famous July 13–14, 1977, NYC blackout), stranding him. But Reno rides through the darkened city on her Moto Valera, a "performance" that feels "pure" to her: "It was only a motorcycle," she says, "but it felt like a mode of being."

The question that lingers at the end of *The Flamethrowers* is exactly what Reno learns from this period of her life. The two conclusions are intentionally indeterminate, a fact that polarized readers. Yet in press for the novel Kushner made it clear she wasn't interested in the traditional "novel of development" that depicts personal growth. Some reviewers complained that for all the novel's heat, Reno herself lacked warmth—a criterion that other commentators interpreted as sexist for demanding that a female character display heart. As defenders argued, one reason Reno seems so emotionally removed is that in art and politics women are frequently sidelined, their ambitions and ideas unnoticed amid the endless bluster of aggressive men. Who are the real flamethrowers? Kushner asks of these men. The capitalists who sell us the vehicles to indulge our desire for motion and velocity, or the incendiary artists who sell us the rebellious ideas we perform riding them?

In the end, *The Flamethrowers* isn't interested in answering that question, because it's irrelevant to Reno. As they used to say in the 1970s, she just keeps on truckin'. That's what makes her an enigmatic character. Through her, Kushner allows readers to enjoy a virtuoso voice that is unheard if not ignored in every group she affiliates with—the voice of a woman who, in the end, would rather ride off to new experiences rather than either mow down or burn down any world where she's taken for granted.

Bibliography

The Flamethrowers (2013)

—KC

S

LISBETH SALANDER

First Appearance: *Män som hatar kvinnor* (*The Girl with the Dragon Tattoo*)
Date of First Appearance: 2005
Author: Stieg Larsson (1954–2004)

I'm going to speak plainly. . . . This video shows you raping a mentally handicapped twenty-four-year-old girl for whom you were appointed guardian. And you have no idea how mentally handicapped I can be if push comes to shove.

She's one of the unlikeliest action-adventure heroines in popular fiction: a Swedish punk-goth loner in Doc Marten boots, not even five feet tall and slight but formidably pierced and tattooed, a brilliant computer hacker and internet sleuth, possibly suffering from Asperger's syndrome but definitely antisocial, bisexual, and unapologetically promiscuous, a fearless motorcyclist with a photographic memory, and a victim of child abuse and sexual assault bent on punishing misogyny with her own brand of vigilante justice, which often borders on ritualistic torture.

As conceived by Stieg Larsson—a Stockholm-based left-leaning muckraker journalist who died of a heart attack at fifty in 2004 before the first installment of his *Millennium* trilogy crime series was published—Lisbeth Salander is the rare female antihero who is allowed to remain remote, unlikable, and fraught with enough glaring contradictions to make her divisive. She is at once a feminist icon and a male superhero fantasy. Larsson subjects her to an almost unbearable amount of violence to symbolize the threats suffered by everyday women, but not unlike James Bond there's never any doubt that she will escape and wreak revenge. Throughout the three novels Larsson drafted before his premature death, including those known by the English titles *The Girl with the Dragon Tattoo*, *The Girl Who Played with Fire*, and *The Girl Who Kicked the Hornet's Nest*, Lisbeth exposes Scandinavia's fascist past and still festering neo-Nazi/skinhead subcultures, loots the offshore accounts of an evil capitalist baron, outs her estranged crime-boss father as an ex–Russian spy, and destroys a secret government cabal intent on covering up crimes committed in the name of national security.

Somewhere amid these adventures she also finds time to get a very controversial set of breast implants.

Larsson told close friends that a shameful memory inspired Lisbeth. At the age of fifteen, he witnessed a trio of friends gang-rape a teenage girl near his hometown of Umea. After he failed to intervene, he tried to apologize to the victim, but she refused to forgive him, and the memory haunted him over the decades, inspiring him to become an advocate for women's rights. At the height of Lisbeth's popularity in 2010 another acquaintance of Larsson's threw doubt on the story, claiming the writer admitted to hearing about the rape secondhand and passing it off as his own. In the only interview he gave about the *Millennium* trilogy, he claimed the character came from a completely different source: Lisbeth was an adult version of Pippi Longstocking, the unruly, rebellious children's book hero created by fellow Swede Astrid Lindgren.

Whatever her origins, Lisbeth was intended as a vehicle for Larsson's leftist politics. Throughout the series, she teams up with journalist Mikael Blomkvist, the editor of a struggling political magazine called *Millennium*, which Larsson closely modeled on the antiracism publication *Expo* that he cofounded in 1995 and ran on a shoestring budget until his death.

In the first entry in the series—its original Swedish title translates into *Men Who Hate Women*—Lisbeth meets Blomkvist when a retired industrialist named Henrik Vanger hires her to conduct a background check on the reporter. After he discovers she's hacked into his computer, the pair team up to solve the 1966 disappearance of Vanger's grandniece Harriet, who the old man believes has been murdered by a member of his wealthy family. Improbably, Lisbeth and Blomkvist become lovers, but the hacker is volatile and aloof, and the duo ends up chasing leads independently. Eventually they discover Harriet's brother Martin is a serial killer. In a reversal of the usual gender dynamic in thrillers, Lisbeth rescues Blomkvist from the murderer's clutches and chases the culprit to his death on her motorcycle. She also breaks into the bank accounts of Mikael's nemesis, the robber baron Hans-Erik Wennerström, helping herself to some $260 million of his illicit fortune and planting an anonymous tip that leads to his murder.

The two sequels in the original series delve deep in Lisbeth's backstory. In *The Girl Who Played with Fire* she discovers the father she thought she burned to death as a child for beating her mother is alive and running a sex-trafficking ring. With Blomkvist's assistance, she further learns that Alexander Zalachenko was once a Russian spy whom the Swedish government has long protected to cover up its own Cold War crimes. "Zala," as the kingpin is known, frames Lisbeth for several murders, leading to her and her new lover Miriam Wu's vilification in the tabloid press as lesbians. Eventually, Lisbeth confronts her violent father, only to discover that the menacing giant who has been trailing her throughout much of the plot is her half brother, Ronald Niedermann, who serves as Zala's henchman. Suffice it to say, the family reunion is not a happy one. *Hornet's Nest*, meanwhile, finds Lisbeth fighting the shadowy governmental organization that protected Zalachenko. Known as the Section, the group attempts to manipulate the justice system to institutionalize her, a sham Blomkvist helps her expose before they reconcile.

Larsson's plots are bafflingly complex and implausible, but they are even more notorious for the sexual sadism Lisbeth avenges. In *Dragon Tattoo*'s most infamous scene, her legal guardian, Nils Bjurman, brutally rapes her. Lisbeth secretly videotapes the assault, then later returns to Bjurman's apartment to torture him, violating him anally with a sex toy and tattooing "I AM A SADISTIC PIG, PERVERT, AND RAPIST" on his belly before blackmailing him into giving her control over her finances. The graphic depiction of violence against women here and in other scenes—such as when in *Fire* Zala shoots his daughter in the head and leaves her for dead, forcing Lisbeth to dig her way out of her own grave—has raised concerns that the novels are exploitative. Larsson's defenders deny the charge, insisting that the heroine's "physical feminism" symbolizes women's refusal to redress abuse only in traditionally feminine or unaggressive ways, such as relying on the justice system.

Both Lisbeth's and Larsson's feminist bona fides have been challenged on other grounds, though. Next to the Bjurman episode, the most commented upon moment is the breast augmentation the punk purchases with stolen funds at the start of *Fire*. So head scratching is this plot detail that Larsson's official website devotes a whole section to it, inviting readers to debate whether the enhancement is consistent with Lisbeth's character or an inevitable example of how the male gaze undermines even the best progressive intentions of an author.

At its peak, Larsson's massively popular trilogy inspired a highly praised three-part Swedish film adaptation starring Noomi Rapace, a Swedish miniseries called *Millennium*, a sequence of English-language graphic novels, and a popular American movie directed by David Fincher (who also directed *Fight Club*). Although its popularity peaked circa 2010, the franchise has been continued in recent years with novelist David Lagercrantz hatching further Lisbeth Salander adventures in *The Girl in the Spider's Web* (2011)—itself adapted into a 2018 American film—and *The Girl Who Takes an Eye for an Eye* (2017). Only time will tell if Lisbeth becomes an institution like James Bond, but her impact is already apparent in the profusion of "ass-kicking" feminist action heroines who have emerged in her wake.

She is truly the Girl Who Kicked Open the Door.

Bibliography

The Girl with the Dragon Tattoo (2008 in English)
The Girl Who Played with Fire (2009 in English)
The Girl Who Kicked the Hornet's Nest (2009 in English)

—KC

SANTIAGO

First Appearance: *The Old Man and the Sea* in *Life*
Date of First Appearance: September 1, 1952
Author: Ernest Hemingway (1899–1961)

Have faith in the Yankees my son.

It's hard to believe that readers could be captivated by an old man alone with his thoughts in a skiff, but there's something remarkable about Ernest Hemingway's simple Cuban fisherman. After eighty-four fishless days, Santiago sails farther from shore than any other fisherman. He battles and boats a record-size Atlantic blue marlin, but loses the eighteen-foot fish to sharks, leaving him to return to his village with the remains lashed to the side of his sixteen-foot boat. In winning for losing, or vice versa, Santiago is typical of the Hemingway hero, but also Hemingway's most sympathetic character—maybe even one of the great sympathetic characters in literature.

Hemingway's earlier heroes were often self-centered, jaded, impulsive, self-destructive, and testosterone driven—but not Santiago. Though other fishermen make fun of him for his bad luck and his patched-up shirt and sail, Santiago does not get angry. He carries himself with a quiet dignity and remains close to the boy who fished with him from the time he was five until the now-teenage boy's parents made him switch to a luckier boat after the old man's fortieth day without a fish. The battle with the marlin and sharks may constitute the main narrative, but as Hemingway biographer Carlos Baker notes, it's the relationship between Santiago and the boy Manolo that makes the story resonate. The boy's love is "that of a disciple for a master in the arts of fishing," but also "the love of a son for an adopted father." Santiago, meanwhile, calls the boy "son," and his love is especially poignant because Manolo was all he had after his wife died—though he stoically accepts that loneliness is part of old age.

In reviewing *The Old Man and the Sea*, literary rival William Faulkner wrote, "Time may show it to be the best single piece of any of us" because "this time, he wrote about pity." Everything about Santiago evokes pity—even the "benevolent" skin cancer he developed from a lifetime working in the sun. But like the scars on his hands that came from working handlines rather than the kind of rod and reel sport fishermen use, his cancer is a badge of honor. Santiago's positive attitude, wisdom, skills, and experience elevate what could have been a merely sad and pitiable character to one that's admirable. Santiago has learned how to read the sky and the activity of birds, and he knows "many tricks"—like eating turtle eggs for strength and drinking shark liver oil for his eyesight. He knows how to let the current do a third of the work, how to bait a hook and fish the bait at precise depths, and how to keep his lines straighter than anyone else. Although he had to sell his bait net and has no money for food or bait, and though his body is worn, the old man's eyes have an "undefeated" look, his spirit still strong. As a result, Santiago has been a memorable if not inspirational character for generations of high school students assigned to read *The Old Man and the Sea*.

Santiago talks to himself while alone at sea because he has no radio to keep him company as the rich do. Unlike all-business fishermen who speak of the sea in derogatory terms, Santiago loves the sea and considers the fish and even the great marlin that tows him far from land over a two-day period "brothers." He apologizes for having to kill the marlin but vows to win the battle or die trying. Santiago says he's not religious, but he talks to God, prays to the Virgin Mary, and promises to say ten Hail Marys and make a pilgrimage to the shrine of the Virgin of Cobre if he lands the fish. Yet true inspiration comes from New York Yankees all-star center fielder Joe DiMaggio, whom he reveres for playing baseball to perfection despite a nagging bone spur. DiMaggio's father was a fisherman, and if DiMaggio can triumph despite injury, Santiago believes he can too, even with the clawlike left hand that has plagued him since birth. The boy refers to Santiago's "great record" of eighty-seven previous fishless days—an ironic "strikeout" record compared to DiMaggio's record fifty-six-game hitting streak.

Santiago tells the boy he knows he did not leave him because he "doubted." It was the boy's parents who lacked faith, he says, introducing a religious element that will be substantiated near the novel's end when Santiago sees the first of the sharks and cries out as if a nail had been driven through his hand into wood. Later, when Santiago shoulders his mast and weakly carries it uphill, it's hard not to think of Christ carrying his cross up skull-shaped Golgotha hill.

When *The Old Man and the Sea* was first published in complete form in the September 1, 1952, issue of *Life*, the magazine sold 5.3 million copies in just two days, and when it was published in book form it remained on the best seller list for twenty-six weeks. "It is often highbrow practice to find symbolism in Hemingway's work," wrote the *Life* editors, who nevertheless couldn't resist playing the symbolism game. "Perhaps the old man is Hemingway himself, the great fish is this great story and the sharks are the critics," they wrote. Hemingway's 1950 novel *Across the River and into the Trees*—his first since *For Whom the Bell Tolls* (1940)—was so widely panned by critics that some were saying Hemingway was washed up. *The Old Man and the Sea* ended his writing drought. It won the Pulitzer Prize and was the only book mentioned by the Swedish Academy when it announced Hemingway as the recipient of the Nobel Prize "for his mastery of the art of narrative, most recently demonstrated in *The Old Man and the Sea*."

When *The Old Man and the Sea* was adapted for film in 1958, Hemingway thought Spencer Tracy too white and too paunchy to play Santiago, and he hated that the studio used a rubber fish for some of the scenes. Hemingway, who had been living in Cuba near the fishing village of Cojímar since 1940 and spent three decades fishing the Gulf Stream, was a Hall of Fame member and former vice president of the International Game Fish Association. Santiago was a composite inspired by two first mates who worked aboard Hemingway's *Pilar*: Carlos Gutierrez, whom Hemingway praised as the best marlin fisherman in the Gulf, and Gregorio Fuentes, to whom Hemingway would will his beloved boat. Santiago's story was an expansion of one he heard from Gutierrez that he detailed in the April 1936 *Esquire*, though in the "real" story the handline fisherman was picked up after two days, exhausted and crying as sharks still circled his boat. In *The Old Man and the Sea*, which Hemingway originally thought to title *The Dignity of Man*, Santiago remains quietly, stoically heroic to the end.

Hemingway gave his Nobel Prize medal to Cuba's Shrine of the Virgin of Cobre; when the author died in 1961, the Cojímar fishermen commissioned a bust of Hemingway made from their scrap metal. As with Santiago and the boy, it was a love that went both ways.

Bibliography

The Old Man and the Sea (1952)

Works Cited

Baker, Carlos. "The Boy and the Lions." In *Ernest Hemingway's* The Old Man and the Sea: *Modern Critical Interpretations*, edited by Harold Bloom, 7–12. Philadelphia: Chelsea House, 1999.
Bloom, Harold, ed. *Ernest Hemingway's* The Old Man and the Sea: *Modern Critical Interpretations*. Philadelphia: Chelsea House, 1999.

Brenner, Gerry. *The Old Man and the Sea: Story of a Common Man.* Twayne's Masterwork
   Studies No. 80. New York: Twayne, 1991.

Crow, Johnathan. "William Faulkner's Review of Hemingway's *The Old Man and the Sea*
   (1952)." Open Culture (online). Posted July 8, 2014. Accessed July 24, 2018. http://www
   .openculture.com/2014/07/faulkners-review-of-ernest-hemingways-the-old-man-and
   -the-sea.html.

Grimes, Larry, and Bickford Sylvester, eds. *Hemingway, Cuba, and the Cuban Works.* Kent,
   OH: Kent State University Press, 2014.

Hendrickson, Paul. *Hemingway's Boat: Everything He Loved in Life, and Lost, 1934–1961.* New
   York: Knopf, 2011.

"IGFA Hall of Fame Inductees: Ernest Hemingway." International Game Fish Association. June 25, 2018. Accessed August 16, 2018. https://www.igfa.org/Museum/HOF
   -Hemingway.aspx.

—JP

EBENEZER SCROOGE

First Appearance: *A Christmas Carol*
Date of First Appearance: 1843
Author: Charles Dickens (1812–1870)

It's all HUMBUG, I tell you, HUMBUG!

Charles Dickens's classic novella *A Christmas Carol* is arguably the most famous
Yuletide story next to the biblical one about the birth of Christ. Among its many
possible interpretations, we might read this secular version as a moral tale mirroring the Christian call for sinners to redeem themselves in the face of the loom-
ing grave and eternal judgment. Everyone loves a good redemption story, and
Ebenezer Scrooge certainly gives us one here with the help of visiting appari-
tions. Whether they be hallucination, dreamscape, or spirit-guides heavenly or
otherworldly, these uninvited nocturnal visitations provide the right powers of
persuasion, leading Scrooge to discover a humane vision of life he had lost somewhere along the way. His journey sets a standard for the value of soul-searching,
personal transformation, and a sort of earthly resurrection. Scrooge discovers the
promise that while breath exists there is the chance to change one's ways and, in
the bargain, enjoy a good holiday turkey dinner with family and friends.

Ebenezer Scrooge has a long way to go before he gets to that happy celebration,
however. He is as bleak and bitter as the English winter and as far from a sunny
disposition as the season's solstice is from its summer counterpart. Dickens describes his physical appearance, in fact, arising from the coldness that lies within
and affecting Scrooge's personality so that "he carried his own low temperature
always about with him." Whatever has led Ebenezer to his current status as the
most enthusiastic of penny-pinchers, he sets the bar so high that his last name has
become a noun, now in lowercase letters, synonymous with "miser." His act of refusing to spare one extra cent for even the most wretchedly poor starving child on
London's streets would be insufferable at any time of year, but when juxtaposed
against the holiday of especially heightened generosity and goodwill toward men,

women and children included, the contrast becomes even harsher. Scrooge is as unsympathetic as it gets, and severe coercive forces will be necessary before he absorbs what his dead partner Jacob Marley has learned in death and imparts to him from beyond the grave—that "mankind should have been my business!"

Dickens places *A Christmas Carol* in nineteenth-century London, where the Industrial Revolution's economics and working conditions, especially for children, were a humanitarian catastrophe for the impoverished masses. To build on his political critique and heighten allegorical intent, Dickens uses narrative shorthand with such blatant symbols as the emaciated children "Ignorance" and "Want" that the Ghost of Christmas Present reveals hidden under his robes. Coupled with that image, Scrooge has a newly gained awareness of his employee Bob Cratchit's crippled child, Tiny Tim, who the Ghost of Christmas Future informs him will die for lack of good nutrition and health care. With the addition of a few more serious blows Scrooge receives along the way, including his forecasted death and failure to be mourned, Mr. "Bah! Humbug!" wakes up from his three midnight journeys a new man now changing his tune about Christmas and his former abhorrent response to pleas for charity.

Beyond *A Christmas Carol*'s religious implications, psychologists, sociologists, and historians want to get in on the analytical discussion about what eats at Scrooge's Christmas pudding. One critic notes that the Dickens classic is "heavy on the Freudian sauce," of id, ego, and superego representing his childhood as a source of trauma, the present as a dose of reality, and the future as a cry for moral conscience. Scrooge can also be judged from the perspectives of utilitarianism, egalitarianism, Marxism, socialism, and other political and philosophical "isms" all based on the indictment of poverty and power the money-laden "haves" hold over the impoverished "have-nots," emphasizing the former's ability to use this leverage for good or for ill. Charles Darwin's *On the Origin of Species* (1859), or the less politically correct extended title "*. . . by Means of Natural Selection, or the Preservation of Favoured Races in the Struggle for Life*," was not published until a bit more than a decade after *A Christmas Carol* (1843), but Dickens's work might also be viewed as a precursor to anti-Darwinian referendums against the concept of survival of the fittest at the expense of the weak, upon whose backs nature has put a symbolic impersonal "X" marking their inevitable demise. The Scrooge we first meet will happily see the poor kicked to the eternal curb and indeed even encourage them to rush to it, but Dickens says, "Not so fast."

Somewhere along *A Christmas Carol*'s journey as a grim adult morality tale or a case study about the inner psyche of holiday depression and the need for love, family, acceptance, and the milk of human kindness, Ebenezer Scrooge's story has taken on popular cultural wings and shifted from a dirge to the cheery veneer of a musical, cartoon, television/film cult classic caricaturizing its iconic protagonist. Dickens's tutorial for how to be one's best self through three easy ghost-visitation workshops becomes a children's entertainment piece with a *Mr. Rogers' Neighborhood*–type lesson tucked in at the end, and the range of possible variations boggles the mind. Fill in the blank: _____'s *A Christmas Carol* with any number of happy remakes: Mickey Mouse, Muppets, Bugs Bunny, Looney Tunes, Sesame Street, Smurfs, Flintstones, Jetsons, Mr. Magoo, and Barbie, and you have an abbreviated list of the children's versions. Add to those a sci-fi Klingon rendition, feminist and black feminist versions with female Ebenezers, fringe theater with eight actors and a lightbulb (what's up with that?), six actors and a fiddler, and Dickens's great-great-grandson playing twenty-six different roles, and you have *A Christmas Carol* smorgasbord.

Any transformative character like Ebenezer Scrooge not only inspires creative adaptations, it fosters derivative versions as well. Hollywood's ever-popular Christmas classic *It's a Wonderful Life*, though based on a book called *The Greatest Gift*, can thematically trace its ancestry further back to Dickens's classic tale. And there is the ever-popular Dr. Seuss's rhymed-verse children's story *How the Grinch Stole Christmas*. Scrooge becomes a cave-dwelling green animal of unknown origins suffering from a heart "two sizes too small." Like the Scrooge of old, the Grinch sees the error of his ways, demonstrates generosity, and joins his newfound friends for a Christmas meal of roast beast to boot. All ends well when everyone eats well!

A Christmas Carol has never been out of print or out of fashion since its 1843 debut. The ever-popular work has been translated into many languages, and as we've seen, Dickens's classic runs the gamut of genres it could be shaped, adapted, transformed, or just plain shoved into to stay fresh enough for each successive generation to make its annual pilgrimage to both old and new versions of the film, play, or fireside reading. Ebenezer Scrooge is a success story as soul-searching reform narratives go, and Dickens leaves us with this symbolic and ultimately joyful Christmas carol, with the story's last line, "God bless us, everyone!" Christmas remains a blessed event filled with Dickensian carolers, good cheer, and our sinner's dramatic reversal proving redemption is possible for even such an abominable creature as Mr. Ebenezer Scrooge.

Bibliography

A Christmas Carol (1843)

Work Cited

Batuman, Elif. "The Ghosts of Christmas: Was Scrooge the First Psychotherapy Patient?" *New Yorker*, December 24, 2015.

—GS

SETHE

First Appearance: *Beloved*
Date of First Appearance: 1987
Author: Toni Morrison (1931–)

No matter how much I wanted to. I couldn't lay down nowhere in peace, back then. Now I can. I can sleep like the drowned, have mercy. She come back to me, my daughter, and she is mine.

Matricide is a common theme in literature. In Greek mythology, Orestes kills his mother Clytemnestra, while Shakespeare's Hamlet and Coriolanus struggle, with very different consequences, with the impulse to free themselves from the overbearing influence of the women who bore them. That's not to mention Norman Bates in Robert Bloch's pulp novel *Psycho* (1959), the inspiration for the Alfred Hitchcock film, who not only kills his mother but assumes her identity to punish himself for it (while still managing to put the blame on poor Mrs. Bates).

Filicide—and in particular, mothers who murder their daughters—is far rarer, the infrequency suggesting the act is so taboo as to be nearly unimaginable. Yet Sethe, the central character in Toni Morrison's landmark *Beloved*, has committed just such an atrocity. The question that haunts the novel is whether madness drives her to it, or whether, amid the oppression and inhumanity of American slavery, slitting her daughter's throat is the most rational way of sparing her child from suffering bondage.

In the 1970s Morrison discovered the inspiration for Sethe in the story of the runaway slave Margaret Garner while editing a collection of lost African American history. In 1856 Garner had escaped from Kentucky to Ohio but was quickly cornered. Under the 1850 Fugitive Slave Act, both she and her family were required to be returned to their Southern master. Rather than allow her four children to suffer this fate, Garner attempted to kill them, succeeding only before she was subdued in slitting the throat of her two-year-old daughter. The incident sparked a legal battle that became a rallying cry for abolitionists, inspiring poems by Frances Harper and Elizabeth Barrett Browning and later a painting called *The Modern Medea* by Thomas Satterwhite Noble. Condemned back to slavery, Garner died of typhoid only two years later and was long forgotten when Morrison learned of her actions. The novelist wasn't interested in a courtroom drama, however, or even historical fiction. Instead, Morrison cast the tragedy as a gothic tale that mourns not only the violence of slavery but the trauma African Americans have been forced to repress throughout their history in America. *Beloved* is a ghost story, but what haunts is not just one mother's guilt; the national silence that prevents America from reckoning with its legacy of oppression causes deep anguish as well. While Sethe is only one central character in this richly poetic meditation on what Morrison calls the "unspeakable things unspoken" for too long in American history, her suffering as a mother calls special attention to the burdens on African American women to sacrifice themselves in the name of family, even when it means bearing the scars of a past that continues to wound them in the present.

Beloved opens in 1873 describing the torture a ghost full of "baby venom" has inflicted on Sethe and her surviving daughter, Denver, at their home at 124 Bluestone Road in Cincinnati since they escaped north nearly twenty years earlier. Mirrors are constantly shattered, mysterious handprints appear in cake frosting, and pots of chickpeas are toppled. Sethe's sons, Howard and Buglar, ran away long ago, and the only caring presence in the women's lives, Sethe's mother-in-law, Baby Suggs, died around the Civil War's end. Sethe has effectively given up on life, trapping her and Denver in lonely, homebound alienation, until Sethe's long-lost brother-in-law, Paul D, appears. His presence rekindles repressed memories from the Kentucky plantation where Sethe was raised, Sweet Home, that emerge over the course of the novel. Paul D confronts the evil spirit and, thinking he has banished it, moves into 124, assuring Sethe that as a family they can heal each other.

Their happiness is short-lived, however. Returning home from a carnival, they discover a young woman on their doorstop. She calls herself Beloved and seems to be the reincarnated ghost of Sethe's murdered daughter. Manipulative and needy, Beloved begins to suck the life out of all three characters. She seduces Paul D, who eventually abandons Sethe when she confesses she killed her daughter. Although Denver grows attached to Beloved, she soon recognizes the presence of this mysterious guest is killing her mother. Sethe wants so desperately for Beloved to understand why she was forced to murder her that she wastes away attending to the girl's every demand. Beloved incarnates what Morrison calls "rememory," a pain so inescapable it becomes personified in human form in the physical world. To save her mother, Denver must recruit the local community of women who once shunned Sethe and rid 124 of this ghost.

Before the women can confront the vengeful spirit, though, Sethe lapses into the memory of the girl's murder. She imagines that Denver's employer, Mr. Bodwin, is the vicious overseer, known as "Schoolteacher," who cornered her in the woodshed of 124 only twenty-eight days into her freedom and forced her to her desperate act. Instead of reenacting the murder of her child, though, Sethe attacks the man with an ice pick. By the time the crowd can pull her back, Beloved has disappeared for good. The novel ends with the newly returned Paul D comforting Sethe, assuring her she need not to die of grief. When Sethe laments that Beloved was her "best thing," Paul D consoles her that her life has meaning outside of motherhood: "You your own best thing," he tells her.

Morrison is uncompromising on the abuses Sethe has survived. Schoolteacher whipped her so brutally her back is scarred in the shape of a chokecherry tree. His sons held her down and stole her breast milk, and even the undertaker forced her to have sex with him so the infant Beloved might have a grave. Beyond these physical abuses, the novel focuses on the psychological grief inflicted on slave mothers who were doubly damaged, first by slavery denying them the right to succor their children through maternal bonding and then by communities that judged them harshly when they failed to heroically overcome their bondage to save their children.

Although Morrison has written several other classic novels—including *The Bluest Eye* (1970) and *Song of Solomon* (1977)—*Beloved* is widely considered her greatest accomplishment. It's often cited as the most important American novel of the later twentieth century and was a major contribution to her winning the 1993 Nobel Prize in Literature. Jonathan Demme's 1998 movie adaptation, starring Oprah Winfrey as Sethe, is faithful to the plot but comes nowhere near attempting Morrison's virtuoso experiments with language and magical realism, sacrificing its complex literary qualities in favor of accessibility. Morrison returned to the inspiration for Sethe in 2005 when she wrote the libretto for *Margaret Garner*, which makes moving use of the African American spiritual tradition. Still, Sethe exists most compellingly in this novel, a mother who must forgive herself for a crime that was in reality the greatest act of love she could show her child, an act whose horror must be properly blamed on the institution of slavery that drove her to it.

Bibliography

Beloved (1987)

—KC

TRISTRAM SHANDY

First Appearance: *The Life and Opinions of Tristram Shandy, Gentleman*
Date of First Appearance: 1759
Author: Laurence Sterne (1713–1768)

I am, that I have begun the history of myself in the way I have done; and that I am able to go on tracing every thing in it, as Horace says, ab ovo.

Eighteenth-century novels—the first prose fictions to go by that name—offer no shortage of memorable characters. There's the resilient shipwreck survivor of Daniel Defoe's *Robinson Crusoe* (1719) and the durable con-woman heroine of that same author's *Moll Flanders* (1722); the adventurer Lemuel Gulliver of Jonathan Swift's satire *Gulliver's Travels* (1726); Alain-René Lesage's hardworking valet Gil Blas (1715–1735); the virginal Clarissa Harlowe and her odious rapist, Robert Lovelace, in Samuel Richardson's didactic *Clarissa, or The History of a Young Lady* (1748); Clarissa's unapologetically promiscuous polar opposite, Fanny Hill, in John Cleland's oft-banned *Memoirs of a Woman of Pleasure* (1748–1749); Fanny's equally lusty male counterpart Tom Jones, the hero of Henry Fielding's epony-mous 1749 novel; Voltaire's disillusioned philosopher Candide (1759); Goethe's prototypically sensitive young artist Werther in *The Sorrows of Young Werther* (1779); and the Machiavellian Marquise de Merteuil and Vicomte de Valmont in Pierre Choderlos de Laclos's frequently adapted *Les Liaisons dangereuses* (1782). That's in addition to lesser-known Roderick Randoms, Peregrine Pickles, Humphry Clinkers, and Joseph Andrewses.

Pound for pound, though, the quirkiest of these Enlightenment-era heroes has to be Tristram Shandy, a narrator so garrulous and digressive that after nine vol-umes of his *Life and Opinions* published between 1759 and 1767 he barely makes a dent in the life story he promises to tell. The creation of the Anglican clergyman Laurence Sterne, Shandy is a comedic tour de force whose endless opining and whimsical observations parody presumptions about knowledge, time, literary form, and language. His name derives from a word meaning "crack-brained" or "half-crazy," which certainly seems fitting, but his plea to readers to "let me go on, and tell my story my own way" is a deliberate protest against the conventions of rationalism and order that insist that tales must have a beginning, middle, and end. Such is the rambling nature of *Tristram Shandy* that more than one critic has called it literature's greatest shaggy-dog story. Yet for all the sense that the book is one long (perhaps *overly* long) joke, an epic of chatterboxing, its experiments in not getting to the point have influenced avant-garde authors for nearly three centuries.

Most of the stories Tristram defers his autobiography to tell concern his ec-centric family and their life at their dilapidated estate in the English countryside. (The real-life "Shandy Hall" in Coxwold, North Yorkshire, where Sterne wrote installments of the novel, is a well-preserved tourist attraction.) Tristram's father, Walter, is a retired "*Turkey* merchant"—a purveyor of Middle Eastern goods—whose idea of parenting involves compiling a "Trista-*paedia*" rather than teaching his son substantive skills. Walter's passion for philosophy and erudition leaves precious little room for affection or even human interest. As a result, the boy is drawn to his uncle Toby, who after a groin wound in the 1695 battle of Namur spends his time building elaborate scale models of military fortresses with his speechifying sidekick, Colonel Trim. There's also the eminently scientific Dr. Slop, who campaigns against what he considers the bugaboo of midwifery, and Parson Yorick, whose *"gaieté de coeur"* opposes the high seriousness of men like Walter. Each of these men has a certain "hobby-horse" or dominant personality trait he tends to ride—a "humor," in eighteenth-century parlance—and Tristram's overriding message is that all can peacefully coexist with a little tolerance and patience for each other's idiosyncrasies, a sign of the novel's overall tone of acceptance and bonhomie. In this colorful world, only Tristram's mother, Elizabeth, a paragon of common sense, gets short shrift; her main job is to stay out of the way of the men's endless dithering.

For all the novel's oddball characters, Tristram's most important relationship is with the reader. Writing to him is like a conversation, and the audience is expected to provide half the entertainment. By one critic's count, Tristram addresses "Dear Sir" and "Dear Lady" some 350 times. At points flattering us, at others badgering us, he insists we commit to a level of imaginative participation that elevates interpretation into collaborative act every bit as crucial to the story as its plot and style. For readers who like action, Tristram can come off as interminably fussy and buttonholing. "Nothing odd will do long," grumbled Samuel Johnson about Tristram's volubility, though the fame Sterne enjoyed from the novel suggests otherwise.

Beyond his effusiveness, the narrator indulges in some outright typographical gimmickry. When he can't conjure up a proper picture of the Widow Wadman whom Uncle Toby courts, Tristram provides a blank spot in the text to draw our own image. When Parson Yorick dies, he juxtaposes two instances of the inevitable Shakespeare citation ("Alas, Poor Yorick!") against a page shrouded in black, as if pausing the narrative for a moment of silence. Volume 3, meanwhile, includes a single marbled page with a colorful design that Tristram calls "the motley emblem of my work," as sort of proto-Rorschach test to gauge what shape the reader sees the novel's chaotic form taking. That's not to mention the satirically excessive use of asterisks and dashes to cover up obscenities, or the chapter in volume 6 in which he charts the plot of preceding volumes with a series of squiggles that illustrate just how circuitous his narrating is. At all points Tristram Shandy intently reminds us that *Tristram Shandy* is a book we hold in our hands.

If the self-reflexive tricks were all that made Sterne's alter ego memorable, though, it's doubtful he would appeal beyond readers who like literary games and puzzles. Tristram is also an endearingly hapless character, one whose mishaps foreshadow the humiliations suffered by such modern-day put-upon schmoes as Philip Roth's Alexander Portnoy. Tristram dates his life not from his birth, for example, but from his conception, when his distracted mother interrupted his father's concerted effort to impregnate her by asking if he remembered to wind their bedroom clock. Because of the interruption, Tristram's humors are thrown all out of whack. Then, at the moment of birth (which Tristram doesn't get around to until volume 3), Dr. Slop mangles his nose delivering him with a pair of forceps, ruining him in the eyes of Walter, who believes a man's success in life depends on the shapely size of his schnoz. Even Tristram's name is a bungle: Walter wants him christened Trismegistus after the occult philosopher Hermes Trismegistus, but the maid, Susannah, mistakes it for a name much closer to Tristan, which means "sorrow." Then there's the small matter of the accident that befalls the narrator as a toddler—as Tristram pees out an open window, the sash drops, inadvertently circumcising him.

As such slapstick suggests, *Tristram Shandy* revels in penis humor. Sterne even ends on a pun, declaring his novel "a COCK and a BULL" story. Those concerned about gender equality can rest assured there's an equal number of vagina jokes. The genitalia references may not be as explicit as in *Portnoy's Complaint*, but they're just as numerous. Eighteenth-century novels have a reputation for bawdiness, but Sterne took it to extremes, though playfully, and without a hint of malice. Tristram Shandy himself may be prematurely clipped, but his geniality and fellow feeling—not to mention his inventiveness—are not.

Bibliography

The Life and Opinions of Tristram Shandy, Gentleman (9 volumes, 1759–1767)

Work Cited

Wagoner, Mary S. "Satire of the Reader in *Tristram Shandy*." *Texas Studies in Literature and Language* 8, no. 3 (Autumn 1966): 337–44.

—KC

SHANE

First Appearance: "Rider from Nowhere" in *Argosy*
Date of First Appearance: July–October 1946
Author: Jack Schaefer (1907–1991)

There's no going back from a killing, Bob. Right or wrong, the brand sticks and there's no going back.

In reviewing the 1953 film adaptation, legendary critic Pauline Kael called Shane, Jack Schaefer's western hero, "Galahad on the range." The equally legendary Roger Ebert thought so too. "There is a little of the samurai in him, and the medieval knight," Ebert wrote. "He has a code. And yet—there's *something else* suggested by his behavior, his personality, his whole tone." There's a darker side to Shane, one buried in his past that threatens to surface in the present. As a shopkeeper observes after Shane walks away from trouble, Shane wasn't afraid of the young gunslinger. "He was afraid of himself."

Shane is a complex character—even more so in the *Argosy* magazine installments ("Rider from Nowhere," 1946) and 1949 novel that established him as one of the great western heroes, despite appearing in an imperfect first book that was nonetheless voted #3 on their all-time greatest list by the Western Writers of America. With *Shane*, Schaefer perfected a prototype that first emerged in Owen Wister's *The Virginian* (1902) and surfaced with variation in John Ford's film *Stagecoach* (1939), solidifying the now-familiar conventions of the western hero. On the American frontier, where justice is dispensed at the end of a gun barrel or rope, the western hero knows the unwritten rules and abides by them. Skilled at fighting, shooting, horsemanship, and all things manly, he is the quintessential man among men whose "code" reinforces his superior position: Strong and soft spoken, he's slow to anger, cool under fire, and more duty bound than the common citizen or the most stoic settler. In the lawless West, such a hero has a heightened sense of personal morality and his code requires him to act, even when action could result in a quick trip to the cemetery. Yet, while he typically "saves" society, the western hero is never fully accepted by the town or settlers he helps, and he often has to ride out of town as suddenly as he entered. Shane is all that and more. Though he became the recognizable model for most of the western heroes to follow, he was also proof that a western hero could be multidimensional.

Shane's "specialness" is immediately apparent. As he rides into the lives of the homesteading Starrett family, the novel's narrator, eleven-year-old Bob Starrett, notices two cowhands staring at Shane "with a curious intentness" as he passes. Shane had symbolically taken the fork in the road that led to the homesteaders and the town they built, not the road that led to cattle baron Luke Fletcher at a time when Fletcher was trying to steal or buy up all the land. As "self-sufficient as the mountains," Shane sits tall in the saddle and has a quiet power with eyes that "missed nothing"—though in his easiness there was a "suggestion of tension." While pulp fictions and Hollywood westerns conditioned Americans to think "good guys" wear white and "bad guys" wear black, Shane is decked out in all dark colors, with a dark silk bandana and hat.

Though he says, "Call me Shane," that probably isn't even his real name. Yet he's invited to stay on as a hired hand because all three family members are instantly drawn to him. It may take five men to beat him in a brawl, but Shane can relate to the boy because, as Joe Starrett notices, "There's still a lot of kid in you." Shane fascinates the boy so much that young Bob (called Joey in the film version) follows him everywhere, sometimes secretly, so he can see and presumably emulate his every move. Through the eyes of a boy who now wants to grow up to be like Shane rather than his father, Shane becomes even more heroic. Marian, meanwhile, "never saw a man like him before . . . so nice and polite and sort of gentle" but also "mysterious. But more than that. Dangerous." He is uniquely gentle, but also uniquely dangerous—two opposing characteristics that she finds attractive, especially when there is no sheriff and the nearest marshal is 100 miles away. Later in the novel, the rancher Fletcher will threaten Joe by suggesting that he and his hired guns will take over the ranch and have their way with Mrs. Starrett if he doesn't sell. But Shane is no threat and Joe trusts him implicitly, even when he sees how fond both his wife and Bob have become of the man. "He's dangerous all right. But not to us, my dear. . . . In fact, I don't think you ever had a safer man in your house."

Never has a drifter with an air of mystery and danger been so welcome, and Shane rewards Joe's trust. When Marian flirts with him and asks him about hats he's seen women wear elsewhere, and when she deliberately starts to wear her own hat the way Shane describes, Shane, who knows everything, knows that he could "have" this woman anytime he wants. But they both respect and in fact love Joe so much that they would never act on it.

Shane, who no longer carries a gun but hides it in his saddle roll, bonds with all three family members—earning a place in Joe's heart when he tackles a large stump that Joe had been wanting to remove. Together, all day long, the men chop away with their axes, a gargantuan effort, finally getting the best of the stump and giving Shane some sense of how hard farming can be. Later he prevents a cultivator salesman from cheating Joe, and, predictably, he stands up to two of Fletcher's men who try to run him off. Ultimately, he knocks Joe unconscious to keep him from a showdown with Fletcher—sacrificing himself for the family he's grown to love. And yet, like any self-respecting western hero, he reaches for his gun and acts only when forced to do so.

The Western Writers of America voted George Stevens's 1953 adaptation the #1 western film, with Alan Ladd able to capture Shane's warm and gentle, mysterious and guarded, and dangerous sides—something a pre-*Kung Fu* David Carradine was unable to do in a 1966 television series that lasted only seventeen episodes. In fact, all western heroes since Shane have fallen short in replicating the hero's gentle and sensitive side—something that also set him apart from other men in the West. Joe has it to *some* degree, and maybe that's why he's able to recognize that core trait in Shane. But Shane does something Joe would never do: He picks a petunia out of Marian's garden and sticks it in his hatband, and he's as comfortable talking about women's hats with Marian as he is describing the stock show for Joe or taking Joey into town to buy him a new jackknife and later showing him how to handle a clunky old pistol that a shopkeeper gave the boy. Shane can tell what each of the family members is thinking and feeling, and he isn't afraid to relate to them and give them a part of himself. That unique capacity balances his dangerous nature in a way that we haven't quite seen in western heroes who came before him, or after.

Bibliography

Shane (1949)

Works Cited

Ebert, Roger. "*Shane*." Review of *Shane*, by Jack Schaefer. RogerEbert.com. September 3, 2000. https://www.rogerebert.com/reviews/great-movie-shane-1953.

Kael, Pauline. "*Shane*: Review." *Kiss Kiss Bang Bang*. Boston: Atlantic Monthly Press, 1968.

Nava, James. "The Best Western Novels of the 20th Century from the Western Writers of America." JamesNava.com. August 18, 2011. http://www.jamesnava.com/18/08/2011/the-best-western-novels-of-the-20th-century-from-the-western-writers-of%c2%a0america/.

"25 Best Western Novels: A List of the 25 Best Western Novels as Chosen by the Western Writers of America." Trivia-Library.com. https://www.trivia-library.com/b/25-best-western-novels.htm.

—JP

ÁNTONIA SHIMERDA

First Appearance: *My Ántonia*
Date of First Appearance: 1918
Author: Willa Cather (1873–1947)

Things will be easy for you. But they will be hard for us.

When envisioning the West of the 1800s, two stock male characters come to mind: the rugged pioneer/cattle rancher and the western gunslingers. Women are background characters marginalized as wives whose bonnet-covered heads peep out from under the tarp of a covered wagon or as prostitutes who hang out behind the swinging doors of dusty saloons. With the exception of Laura Ingalls Wilder's family-centered *Little House* series, wives and daughters don't factor much in the culture of western stories. Willa Cather interrupts the paradigm with her prairie novel trilogy *Oh Pioneers!* (1913), *The Song of the Lark* (1915), and *My Ántonia* (1918), the most acclaimed of the three featuring women in the American West. This Nebraska-centered work tells the story of an immigrant family, the Shimerdas, and their oldest daughter Ántonia, who demonstrates remarkable grit, fortitude, and grace as she quietly but stoically carves out a life and a lifetime on the windswept frontier plains with prairie grass as far as the eye can see. She and her family represent the ideal behind the Statue of Liberty's famed poem "New Colossus," openly embracing "the homeless, tempest-tossed," whose desire for a better life led them to America. What lies unsaid behind this hope is a stern reality that the life they can expect to lead on a new continent will most certainly be a harsh one. Cather's novel reveals this hardship up close and in a personal way, and for Ántonia, the heroic fortitude with which she faces the challenges makes her one of the remarkable women in literature.

Jim Burden is Ántonia's childhood friend, in some ways a foil to her own experience, and he pays Ántonia tribute by telling her story. She and Jim arrive in Nebraska the same day—her family choosing to orphan themselves in a new land with an unbounded hope to find prosperity there, and he an actual orphan sent to live with his grandparents after his parents' death. Jim's and Ántonia's paths meld for a few short but formative school years, divide for much of their adulthood, and briefly come back together again years later. Jim says of her, "More than any other person we remembered, this girl seemed to mean to us the country, the conditions, the whole adventure of our childhood," and it is Jim's memories of Ántonia and the exigencies of her life that shape his telling of the story and our sense of her both as an individual and as a representative character.

Ántonia remains on a farm in Nebraska essentially living the life she had first begun in America, and Jim becomes a successful New York City lawyer working for the lucrative railroad companies. Their circumstances suggest the strong American divide represented by his urban intellectual life and her vastly contrasted agrarian existence. Jim marries but remains childless; Ántonia bears nearly a dozen children, including her first child born out of wedlock because her fiancé leaves her to shoulder the responsibility alone. In typical fashion, Ántonia not only makes the best out of the hard life she has been dealt, she thrives in it.

Jim understands that this is the Ántonia he is likely to find when he returns to Nebraska, and as a coda at the end of this story, he says of her, "She was a battered woman now, not a lovely girl; but she still had that something which fires the imagination, could still stop one's breath for a moment by a look or gesture that somehow revealed the meaning in common things." She herself was a common thing in the world's eyes, but she possessed an inner beauty that bespoke the fire within her that had made her so compelling. Going beyond the bedrock quality of her personality and the innate power she possessed, Jim would raise his vision of Ántonia to a mythopoetic level by saying, "She was a rich mine of life, like the founders of early races."

Famed critical curmudgeon of the 1920s H. L. Mencken, who provided biting criticism about everything, also praised Ántonia and her pioneer experience when he wrote (quoted in the *American Conservative*), "What Miss Cather tries to reveal is the true romance that lies even there—the grim tragedy at the heart of all that dull, cow-like existence—the fineness that lies deeply buried." Ántonia embodies that life which Mencken sees "as real as real can be—and withal moving, arresting, beautiful with strange and charming beauty." Widely respected biographer Hermione Lee shares Mencken's opinion and sees Cather's Ántonia as "the standard-bearer . . . for vanished American values" and Cather "as a kind of Midwestern Robert Frost" who also centered his work around the hired hand, the work of the fields, the value of the common laborer. Ántonia shows quiet endurance as she tills the land and manages the man's work of the farm, and she serves as a symbol of so many unsung prairie women who helped settle the West as surely as the men did.

If there is one strong criticism about Cather's writing in *My Ántonia*, it is that she romanticizes Ántonia's experience. A *Los Angeles Review of Books* essay sees the novel as "more dewy nostalgia than an accurate depiction of life on the frontier," and goes on to say that Cather's poetic descriptions are more like "romantic oil painting in prose" than a true picture about the depth of misery many pioneer families endured: the isolation of the geography, the sod huts that were cold and muddy hovels, the harshness of weather conditions, the lack of food, and the shear backbreaking work of eking out the barest subsistence from the land. Much of this hardship exists in the pages of *My Ántonia* and is borne by her, but perhaps not as grimly conveyed as some feel it should have been. Cather does include the suicide of Ántonia's father, who could not endure the dramatic loss of his former life as a musician and well-respected community member in his homeland of Bohemia, so at least in some portion his fate speaks to the desolation and failure of hope from which many immigrants were unable to recover.

Cather presents Ántonia, however, as a buoyant and memorable character who rises above misery and comes to represent the many unsung female settlers, especially the immigrant ones, who, like Ántonia, were often left to do this without men in a country that was foreign and often inhospitable. In the end, she shares an enduring relationship with the land and its bounty, and she becomes a symbol of its vast and rugged beauty. Jim realizes that through it all Antonia "has not lost the fire of life." No finer tribute could be paid.

Bibliography

My Ántonia (1918)

Works Cited

Birzer, Bradley J. "*My Ántonia* at 100." *American Conservative*, August 29, 2018.
Lee, Hermione. "Willa Cather: A Hidden Voice." *New York Review of Books*, July 11, 2013.
Slayton, Robert A. "*My Ántonia* Revisited." *Los Angeles Review of Books*, October 25, 2017.

—GS

LONG JOHN SILVER

First Appearance: *Treasure Island, or The Mutiny of the Hispaniola*
Date of First Appearance: 1883
Author: Robert Louis Stevenson (1850–1894)

Take a cutlass, him that dares, and I'll see the color of his inside, crutch and all, before that pipe's empty.

In pop culture, pirates are as popular as dinosaurs—*more* popular, if you consider that there's no international "Talk like a Dinosaur Day" as there's been to celebrate piratespeak since 1995. And a number of clichés associated with the public's romantic fascination with pirates can be traced to Long John Silver—like the wooden peg leg, the parrot on his shoulder that cries, "Pieces of eight! Pieces of eight!" and the sea shanty he leads his crew in singing: "Yo-ho-ho and a bottle of rum." When BBC News named Long John Silver the #1 fictional pirate, it called him "the daddy of them all. The man who set the benchmark for piracy as a fashion statement."

All pirate stories since Silver's adventure seem to involve a map, and *Treasure Island* not only featured one, it began with one. Scottish writer Robert Louis Stevenson wrote in the introduction to the 1894 American edition of his collected works that once he spent a great deal of time confined, for health reasons, in a house where he passed the time with a "school-boy" home for the holidays. To amuse the lad, he explained, "I made the map of an island; it was elaborately and (I thought) beautifully colored," with detailed harbors, inlets, shoals, swamps, and other topographical features. He called it "Treasure Island," and as he "pored upon" the map "the future characters of the book began to appear there visibly among imaginary woods." Years later, Stevenson confessed with mixed horror and embarrassment that he had unwittingly plagiarized the opening chapters of his coming-of-age adventure story from Washington Irving's "Treasure Seekers," which he said he hadn't read "for nearly twenty years." But the character that makes his novel come alive is a bona fide original.

Stevenson said as he stared at that map he had an idea for John Silver "to take an admired friend of mine" and "deprive him of all his finer qualities and higher graces of temperament, and to leave him with nothing but his strength, his courage, his quickness, and his magnificent geniality." The inspiration for Silver was

William Ernest Henley, a poet-journalist friend whose leg was amputated at age nineteen and who walked with a wooden leg and crutches. "No doubt the parrot once belonged to Robinson Crusoe," Stevenson conceded, but as he explained to Henley, "It was the sight of your maimed strength and masterfulness that begot John Silver"—the central character in a novel he was then calling *The Sea Cook or Treasure Island: A Story for Boys*. Henley responded by sending him a copy of *A General History of the Robberies and Murders of the Notorious Pirates*, a 1724 collection of pirate biographies inspired by newspaper stories, thinking he might find it a useful reference. What stands out now is that every one of the pirates in that book was captain of his ship—not a ship's cook mutineer, as Silver was, making Silver a dramatic departure from the typical pirate of the day.

First appearing in seventeen installments in *Young Folks* magazine as *Treasure Island, or The Mutiny of the Hispaniola* (1881–1882), *Treasure Island* was published in book form by Cassell and Co. in 1883, and it became an instant sensation. Years later Stevenson admitted he was "not a little proud of John Silver also, and to this day rather admire that smooth and formidable adventurer." The adventure begins when three pirates visit an inn owned by young Jim Hawkins's family, with one of them giving narrator Hawkins a map. After seeing it, the local lord, Squire Trelawney, is inspired to go on an adventure to find the treasure, with Hawkins as his cabin boy. Before they sail, Squire sends Jim to take a message to John Silver, who hired on as ship's cook and volunteered to find a crew for the Squire and his captain. Jim finds Silver at the "sign of the 'Spyglass'" near the docks: "His leg was cut off close by the hip, and under the shoulder he carried a crutch, which he managed with wonderful dexterity, hopping upon it like a bird. He was very tall and strong, with a face as big as a ham—plain and pale, but intelligent and smiling" and "whistling as he moved about among the tables."

What makes Silver a great character is that he's unique, he's complex, and he's dynamic. Melville's Captain Ahab also had a peg leg, but he didn't think (or wasn't confident enough in his disability) to have a "line or two rigged up to help him across the widest spaces" of the ship's deck during rough weather. In a world where men seem either smart or strong, Silver is both. Other pirates spend their loot and die penniless, but Silver invests in a public house run by his wife when he's at sea. Instead of burying his pirate booty, he deposits it in a number of bank accounts. And while other pirates seem mired in a life of high-seas crime, Silver intends to "retire" after he recovers Captain Flint's treasure. As the coxswain, or steersman, tells Jim, "He had good schooling in his young days, and can speak like a book when so minded; and brave—a lion's nothing alongside of Long John! I seen him grapple four, and knock their heads together—him unarmed." But Silver also "had a way of talking to each, and doing everybody some particular service," the coxswain says. "To me he was unweariedly kind; and always glad to see me in the galley, which he kept as clean as a new pin."

Climbing onto the side of the ship Silver was "agile as a monkey," but as Jim would later witness on Treasure Island, Silver was also quick as a snake if someone got in his way. Fighting an ex-shipmate, Silver "twice buried his knife up to the hilt in that defenseless body." Through Jim's eyes we see many facets of Silver's complicated personality: kindly fellow, charmer, brawler, smart but firm leader, resourceful survivalist, ruthless killer, brilliant schemer, mentor, and unlikely ally. One of the most chilling moments occurs when Jim learns that Silver and the men he recruited are Flint's old crew, plotting to mutiny and murder all officers onboard. Yet, Jim and Silver form a cautious bond built on some degree of fondness or admiration. Jim, whose father died at the beginning of the novel, clearly sees traces of a father figure in Silver, and their ambivalent relationship plus Silver's richly imagined character notches him quite a few cutlass cuts above the typical fictional character.

Treasure Island has inspired more than fifty film and television adaptations (including animated and sci-fi versions), with Robert Newton's performance in film and on a TV series named for his character solidifying Silver's image for contemporary audiences. Silver inspired not just a handful of prequels and sequels from other authors, but also numerous stage and radio productions, poems, and comic books. In music, Jefferson Airplane released an album titled *Long John Silver*, but in all of pop culture Silver might ironically be known to more people worldwide because of a fast-food seafood restaurant chain that bears his name. As Silver would bellow, "Shiver my timbers!"

Bibliography

Treasure Island (1883)

Works Cited

Mehew, Ernest. *Selected Letters of Robert Louis Stevenson.* New Haven, CT: Yale University Press, 1997.
Stevenson, Robert Louis. *The Novels and Tales of Robert Louis Stevenson: Vol. II, Treasure Island.* New York: Charles Scribner's Sons, 1897.
Watson, Greig. "The Top 10 Fictional Pirates." BBC News. May 24, 2007. http://news.bbc .co.uk/2/hi/entertainment/6663451.stm.

—JP

LENNIE SMALL

First Appearance: *Of Mice and Men*
Date of First Appearance: 1937
Author: John Steinbeck (1902–1968)

An' rabbits. An' I'd take care of 'em. Tell how I'd do that, George.

John Steinbeck's *Of Mice and Men* is frequently taught in America's high schools because it's a brief and pretty straightforward account of two drifters trying to find work during the Great Depression. The fable-like tale published in 1937 is mostly memorable for a character named Lennie Small, who's been warmly embraced by pop culture, thanks, in large part, to Warner Bros. Animation Studios.

In the novel, George Milton is a small, intelligent man with strong features. He travels with and looks out for his companion, Lennie, "a huge man, shapeless of face, with large, pale eyes, with wide, sloping shoulders" who "walked heavily, dragging his feet a little, the way a bear drags his paws." Although Lennie is sweet and gentle, he's also a giant who doesn't know his own strength. Developmentally disabled, Lennie has the intellect and emotional level of a child—an instinctual person who's often described in animalistic terms, whether it's those large paws or the way he drops to drink from a green pool of water that he and George come upon, gulping and "snorting into the water like a horse." As he makes rings in the water with his fingers he beams and says, "Look, George, look what I done."

There are, of course, a lot of huge and intellectually challenged characters in literature, but none with Lennie's distinguishing characteristic: Lennie is obsessed with stroking soft things. He especially likes to pet velvet and fur, and he often asks George to recite the story of their personal American dream: to find a place of their own so they can "live off the fatta the lan'." And, of course, the part of the story Lennie likes best is when George tells him they're going to have rabbits he can tend.

George often catches Lennie with a field mouse he's captured and accidentally killed. "I could pet it with my thumb while we walked along," Lennie pleads, when George takes the dead mouse and throws it into the brush. "I wasn't doin' nothin' bad with it, George, just strokin' it," Lennie says. But the message is clear: That trouble "up north" they had when Lennie tried to touch a girl's soft dress and she pulled away, screaming, and him grabbing on tighter? It's something that could happen again. Only next time, there might not be an irrigation ditch they can hide in, submerged, until the local vigilantes give up the search.

Less than ten years after *Of Mice and Men* was published, Warner Bros. started producing cartoons alluding to Lennie and George. In "Lonesome Lenny" (1946), a big overgrown pampered dog says, "I wish I had a little friend . . . just for me to pet and play with." Then he reaches into a fur pocket and pulls out a skeletal mouse. "I had a little friend once, but he don't move no more." In "Hoppy Go Lucky" (1952), Lennie and George are cats, and the Lennie character says, "Goodie goodie, George, let's go in and get me a mouse to have for my very own. I will hug him and hug him and pet him and pet him." Then, to the audience: "George is my friend." Those familiar with *Of Mice and Men* took delight in the cartoons, which steered clear of the tragic end that astute readers could anticipate in the novella. Warner Bros. played it for laughs again in 1961 with "The Abominable Snow Rabbit," which featured an Abominable Snowman doing the Lennie thing: "Just what I always wanted. My own little furry Rabbit. I will name him George, and I will hug him and pet him and squeeze him."

Steinbeck told the *New York Times* that Lennie was based on a real person he worked alongside—someone who was eventually institutionalized. "He didn't kill a girl. He killed a ranch foreman. Got sore because the boss had fired his pal and stuck a pitchfork right through his stomach." Steinbeck's Lennie is more pure and simple than that, and there's a backstory to explain the way he is. As George tells people, Lennie was kicked in the head by a mule when he was little—which may or may not be true—and Lennie's aunt Clara took care of him since he was a baby. When she died, "Lennie just come along with me out workin'. Got kinda used to each other after a little while."

Lennie fascinates because he's an emotionally unstable, destructive power that could be released at any moment. When he tells one of the ranch hands about the rabbits George promised him and is told that feral cats might go after the rabbits, Lennie darkens. "You jus' let 'em try to get the rabbits. I'll break their God damn necks." Yet, he's not a bad or naturally violent person. As much of an innocent as Frankenstein's monster, he simply can't help his visceral reaction to certain things. When the boss's son, a small man with a small-dog complex, picks a fight with Lennie, Lennie just stands there and takes a beating to the face without fighting back . . . until George says, "Get 'im, Lennie" and the next thing you know Curley's hand is crushed and the men are taking him to the hospital. "You told me to, George," Lennie says. "I didn't wanta. I didn't wanta hurt him. I can still tend the rabbits, George? I didn't mean no harm." We see that with a puppy that George gets him, thinking it's bigger than a mouse and might be able to stand up to Lennie's "petting." But that doesn't end well either. "He was so little. I was jus' playin' with him . . . an' he made like he's gonna bite me . . . an' . . . an' I done it. An' . . . an' I made like I was gonna smack him. Then he was dead."

When Curley's wife catches Lennie alone in the barn and wants to talk with him, we finally see a side of him that we haven't seen before. After he confesses that he likes to pet nice soft things with his fingers, she responds, "Well, who don't?" That makes Lenny feel validated. "You bet, by God," he cries happily. George might be his best friend and caretaker, but here, finally, is a woman who not only understands his love of soft things but tells him it's not sick or wrong. Unfortunately, she invites him to touch her soft hair, and things escalate quickly after he keeps holding on. Soon he's saying, "I done a bad thing. I done another bad thing." But just as Lennie can't help himself, readers can't help but be fascinated by him. He's become so much a part of pop culture that, in addition to those Looney Tunes cartoons, Hollywood has produced five film adaptations and two made-for-TV movies. In the sixties, the top-rated TV western *Bonanza* even featured two episodes featuring a Lennie character.

"You're nuts," Curley's wife tells Lennie. "But you're a kinda nice fella. Jus' like a big baby" . . . with the kind of power that can maim and kill, but guarantee literary immortality.

Bibliography

Of Mice and Men (1937)

Work Cited

"Mice, Men, and Mr. Steinbeck." *New York Times*, December 5, 1937.

—JP

SONNY

First Appearance: "Sonny's Blues" in *Partisan Review*
Date of First Appearance: Summer 1957
Author: James Baldwin (1924–1987)

You walk these streets, black and funky and cold, and there's not really a living ass to talk to, and there's nothing shaking, and there's no way of getting it out—that storm inside. You can't talk it and you can't make love with it, and when you finally try to get with it and play it, you realize nobody's listening. So you've got to listen. You got to find a way to listen.

As a rule, Cain and Abel stories usually don't end well, but James Baldwin's oft-anthologized "Sonny's Blues" turns the theme of sibling opposites on its fratricidal head to make an important statement about African American endurance. If not exactly optimistic, the story nevertheless finds value in human suffering. First published in *Partisan Review* and collected in Baldwin's lone short-story collection, *Going to Meet the Man* (1965), "Sonny's Blues" draws together several important themes found throughout the author's work: the importance of music—jazz and the blues, specifically—to black American identity; the tension between the individual and the surrounding community that offers comfort at the cost of conformity; the influence of religion as a medium and of Harlem as a setting for channeling the rage that comes with being black in America; and the durability of family ties. As the story's Abel figure, the fallen brother Sonny offers one of the great portraits of a black survivor in African American literature. He's a man who finds redemption by embracing both the thing he chased—art—and the thing he most sought to evade—his very own Cain, the story's narrator.

The story begins with the narrator discovering from the newspaper that the long-estranged Sonny has been arrested for selling and using heroin. The news shocks him—although his brother had a reputation as wild, he wasn't self-destructive, at least not in the way that the narrator, a teacher, has seen Harlem boys become as they bang their heads against "the low ceiling of their actual possibilities" as black men. He sees that rage when confronted by a friend of Sonny's who wants to know what the narrator plans to do to help his brother. For both men, Sonny's fall seems to undermine the possibility that any black man can elude despair, but only the friend seems to accept that he could have helped Sonny avoid his addiction, something the narrator isn't prepared yet to admit.

Only after his daughter, Grace, dies of polio does the brother write Sonny in prison. The response isn't bitter or accusatory, which makes the narrator feel even worse. When Sonny is released, the narrator takes him in and ponders their long, fractured history together. He can't figure out how he escaped into a career while his brother, so much more talented, succumbed to addiction. The answer, as the story reveals, is that Sonny is much more aware of his suffering than the narrator is his own. The older sibling has done everything his culture has told him a black man must to succeed and rise above the poverty he grew up in—he's a professional, a devoted father, and a loyal husband. But that success comes at a cost. In living up to his duty, he has resented other black men like Sonny who didn't follow his same path. That resentment distanced him from his empathy until he could fall out of contact with his brother for long stretches of their lives, failing the promise the narrator made his dying mother that he would take care of Sonny. The narrator remembers in particular how unsympathetic he was when his brother announced his intention to become a musician. Even though he let Sonny live with his wife's parents to pursue his dream, he was angry that his brother skipped school to immerse himself in the Greenwich Village jazz scene. Even after Sonny did a stint in the navy and became an adult, the brothers argued, in part because the narrator didn't feel Sonny appreciated all the sacrifices he'd made for him and all the opportunities he'd offered.

Not until Sonny is released and offers his own explanation for his heroin addiction does the narrator come to grips with his vanity and self-congratulation. Suffering, Sonny insists, is inevitable, but so is trying *not* to suffer. Heroin was his effort to escape suffering, just as assimilating into the American dream is the narrator's. But drugs took Sonny away from the true medium through which he expresses his pain productively: music. It's the medium he intends to return to, too, when he invites the narrator to attend a club to watch him play the piano. The narrator is hesitant for Sonny to return to an environment so fraught with temptations to escape in self-destructive ways; the older brother has fought the urge all afternoon to check Sonny's room for signs of relapse. Yet he understands both Sonny's and his own need for the key thing that allows people to cope with suffering: They need to acknowledge the pain, to listen to it.

From the way Sonny talks about his pain, it's clear that he's come through the experience of addiction and prison more self-aware. Yet the most moving scene in "Sonny's Blues" dramatizes how tentative and fragile self-awareness is, and how difficult expressing suffering can be. When Sonny takes the stage, the narrator first finds his playing "troubled," as if he can't find the groove this first time at the piano in more than a year. Yet the first song is cathartic for the musician; he relives all of his suffering in his flustered effort to find his confidence and regain his talent. By the second song—the blues standard "Am I Blue," best known from Billie Holiday's 1947 rendition—Sonny finds his footing as the other musicians listen to each other, creating community through their collaboration. Suffering in isolation, Baldwin says, is crippling, but expressing one's pain in a communal form gives us a powerful but safe platform for memorializing those wounds—and for helping others pay tribute to their own anguish by giving them the opportunity to listen.

Scenes of African Americans finding purpose in grief through the blues are a common fixture in black literature, from Langston Hughes through Toni Morrison and beyond. What makes Baldwin's description of the form so powerful—and what makes Sonny, ultimately, such a great character—is the way the story's final scene takes him from his initial fumbling on that first song to the beauty he achieves on the second. It's a surprising process; from the way Sonny adeptly describes suffering in his conversation with his brother, we expect him to be able to perform masterfully the first time out. But Baldwin wants us to see that suffering is a process of searching each time we confront it, and only by grappling with the pain—something the narrator has avoided doing—can we render grief into beauty. In the end, the narrator summarizes what he has heard in his brother's performance, and how it benefits both of them: "While the tale of how we suffer, and how we are delighted, and how we may triumph is never new, it always must be heard. There isn't any other tale to tell, it's the only light we've got in all this darkness."

Bibliography

Going to Meet the Man (1965)

—KC

JULIEN SOREL

First Appearance: *Le Rouge et le Noir* (*The Red and the Black*)
Date of First Appearance: 1830
Author: Stendhal (Marie-Henri Beyle) (1783–1842)

My God! being happy—being loved, is that all it comes to?

How a character dies in literature is often an ironic commentary on how he or she lived. Emma Bovary eats arsenic and gives up the ghost in gruesome, excruciating contrast to the heightened passion she recklessly pursues; Captain Ahab's neck is snapped in a fluke instant and his body dragged to the depths in a tangled harpoon line before he can go mano a mano with the white whale that chomped off his leg; the mentally handicapped Lennie Small in John Steinbeck's *Of Mice and Men* must be killed by his best friend to protect him from inflicting on others the murderous strength he doesn't know he possesses.

Julien Sorel, the hero of Stendhal's *The Red and the Black*, meanwhile, is fiction's most famous victim of the guillotine, that gory symbol of revolution run amuck. Among historical figures, Louis XVI and Marie Antoinette hold that dubious distinction, but Julien's state-sanctioned decapitation has little connection to the right or wrong of regicide. *The Red and the Black*, rather, is a case study in social climbing, its hero both a testament to and a caution against an all-consuming ambition to rise through the ranks to attain prominence and wealth. The sheer speed with which a guillotine can lop a head from a body rebukes the conniving with which he pursues his aspirations. And yet Julien meets his maker not for his devious scheming, but for committing a rash act of revenge against a former lover. His crime suggests that for Stendhal consciousness can't control the passions, and that the head and heart are divided long before the blade makes that separation irrevocable.

The Red and the Black is the first great psychological novel in Western literature, depicting Julien's motives with complexity while exploring how frequently his impulses contradict his intentions. The guillotine isn't just a metaphor for the brain/body gulf, though. It also has social import. Stendhal wrote the novel at the tail end of the Bourbon Restoration, the post-Napoleonic period when the monarchy returned to France and the aristocracy retightened the class striations that the French Revolution eliminated—violently—in the name of meritocracy. As a devotee of Napoleon, Julien yearns to be a hero, but he recognizes that men born into poverty like himself can no longer seize military power through their superior intelligence and bravery as the emperor had. His only chance for advancement is through the clergy, although he has little interest in spiritual matters. The guillotine in this sense represents the power of the haves to keep the have-nots in place. Indicting the jury of "indignant bourgeois" judging his crime, Julien defiantly declares, "I see before me men who . . . will seek to punish in me and to discourage forever that class of young men who, born in an inferior station and in a sense burdened with poverty, have the good fortune to secure a sound education, and the audacity to mingle with what the pride of rich people calls society." He effectively goads his betters into executing him, proving they are more worried about maintaining their elite status than justice.

Julien is no martyr for egalitarianism, though. Throughout most of the novel he is driven by pride and vanity, and he is an unabashed opportunist. Because Stendhal's intruding narrator treats him with ambivalence, he's an antihero—possibly the first charismatic one in nineteenth-century literature, preceding such dark (and more gothic) figures as Emily Brontë's Heathcliff from *Wuthering Heights* or her sister Charlotte's Mr. Rochester in *Jane Eyre*. When we first meet him in the fictional village of Verrières, Julien is the abused son of a peasant carpenter, beaten for his intellectualism and fondness for reading over labor. When the local abbot finds him a job tutoring the mayor's children, Julien recognizes how to mold that scholarly aspect of his personality to win favor. Women are particularly attracted to him; he soon begins an affair with his employer's wife, Madame de Rênal, that ends only when the chambermaid infatuated with him, Elisa, gossips to the village. Julien is forced to leave town, eventually making his way to Paris as the secretary of a diplomat, the Marquis de la Mole. Because Julien is self-absorbed, he doesn't realize the marquis involves him in a plot that will benefit the same conservative forces (known as the legitimists) who would deny him opportunities to ascend in high society.

Throughout the novel, seduction is a metaphor for the machinations it takes to wield social power. In Paris Julien pursues an affair with Mathilde de la Mole, his employer's daughter. She finds her father's right-hand man physically irresistible but socially embarrassing, aware that her social circle will mock her for sleeping with a man of a lower social station. Only through an elaborate game of emotional manipulation that involves plagiarized love letters does Julien make Mathilde fall in love with him, even though she is soon to be engaged to a duke. When Mathilde reveals she is pregnant with Julien's child, the marquis agrees to bestow her daughter's lowly lover with a title and property under the fiction that he is actually the long-lost heir to an aristocratic line. Julien's shot at legitimacy is ruined, however, when a letter from Madame de Rênal arrives, outing him as a rake who takes advantage of women. In the novel's most dramatic moment, Julien is overcome with rage for what this long-lost lover has cost him, and he shoots her while she prays at Mass. Although Madame de Rênal survives and petitions to save Julien's life (as does Mathilde), the "peasant in revolt" insists on accepting the punishment for his crime, turning his execution into a protest against the hypocrisy and materialism of the ruling class.

Stendhal drew many of the details of Julien's crime of passion from the story of Antoine Berthet, a former seminary student who in 1827 became a tabloid sensation for attempting to murder his former employer's wife at church for ruining his career prospects. Political events rapidly overtook the writing: By the time the novel was published, the July Revolution of 1830 replaced the Bourbons with the more liberal House of Orléans, somewhat muddling the author's criticism of the aristocracy's amorality as resulting directly from its ultraconservatism. Nevertheless, Julien epitomizes the cultural ambivalence toward ambition. On one hand, he serves as a protest against the barriers imposed on people who can't ply their talents because they're not born into the right class. On the other, he epitomizes the corruption of those talents when people choose opportunism and deceit over idealism, no matter if society gives them few other options. Julien is more than a victim, but he's never quite a villain, which is why readers can't decide whether to mourn or condemn him.

In the end, the only certainty in *The Red and the Black* is a grammatical observation Julien makes when picturing his death: "It is curious, the verb 'to guillotine' cannot be conjugated in all its tenses: one can say, I will be guillotined . . . but one does not say: I have been guillotined."

Bibliography

The Red and the Black (1830)

—KC

WILLIE STARK

First Appearance: *All the King's Men*
Date of First Appearance: 1946
Author: Robert Penn Warren (1905–1989)

I could run this state and ten more like it with you howling on every street corner like a hound with a sore tail.

As this book goes to press, a billionaire sits in the Oval Office largely due to the support of undereducated low-income voters he beguiled with his charismatic personality and populist message, so the essence of Willie Stark will seem familiar even to those who haven't read *All the King's Men*. In fact, the opening chapter of Robert Penn Warren's Pulitzer Prize–winning 1946 novel reads like a textbook study for anyone entering politics—though the author insists in his introduction to the Modern Library edition that it's foremost a novel about a man.

In that first chapter, Stark, whom the narrator calls "the Boss," rolls into a small town with his entourage and walks into a crowded drugstore. He waits in the background until someone recognizes him, and as excitement builds he keeps his head slightly bowed, the picture of aw-shucks humility. Then he fixates on one person who doesn't seem thrilled and approaches him to have a quiet conversation. It turns out that the man's son is in jail awaiting trial because of a fight: "Hit wuz fahr and squahr, but he had a lettle bad luck. He stobbed the feller and he died." The Boss is sympathetic—"tough tiddies"—then addresses the crowd, insisting he's there for personal reasons. "I'm not a politician today," he declares.

But when his attention is drawn to a picture of himself over the soda fountain, he seizes the moment: "I was porely [*sic*] when they took it. I was like I'd had the cholera morbus. Get in there busting some sense into that Legislature, and it leaves a man worse'n the summer complaint." Soon the crowd is praising him for "busting heads" and cheering him on, calling for a speech. And still insisting he's not there as a politician, head still bowed, the Boss walks "straight across the street and across the patch of grass roots and up the steps of the courthouse," where he turns and finally gives the speech he said he wasn't going to give, being sure to mention "The Good Book." Then, walking back to his car, parting the crowd as if it were the Red Sea, he quietly instructs one of his aides to hire a good but not "headline-grabbing" attorney to fix the problem of the man's son. And by "fix," his people understand that it's to be done by whatever means necessary.

Readers' first impression of Willie Stark is a powerful one because it instantly conveys the man's charisma as well as his cool and clever calculation. Stark knows how to work a crowd, and he knows the mythic power of a single story or display of kindness. He knows how to speak to a crowd, too, as readers notice when they see him in different situations, whether it's a one-on-one with a political rival or an impromptu halftime talk when his State boys are taking a beating. It's a well-known cliché that politics is a dirty business, and Stark is the quintessential politician in literature—a slice of American life that also cuts to the heart of what makes America tick. He surrounds himself with yes-men, has an affair with his secretary, seeks revenge on those who embarrassed or tried to derail him, becomes obsessed with a project that can stand as a monument to him long after he's gone, and gets his way by threatening people, paying them off, or digging up dirt—though, as Stark tells the former newspaperman he hired to be one of his aides, "You don't ever have to frame anybody, because the truth is always sufficient."

When the novel was first published, it was a given that Stark's character was based on former Louisiana governor and U.S. senator Huey Long, who, a *New York Times* reviewer wrote, "destroyed the democratic structure of an American State while shouting his championship of the common man." The reviewer also admired Penn Warren's creation: "Willie Stark as a man and a politician is superbly well realized."

Though he bears a striking resemblance to Long and though the title alludes to Long's "Every Man a King" slogan as much as it does the Humpty Dumpty nursery rhyme ("All the King's horses and all the King's men / couldn't put Humpty together again"), Stark isn't just a thinly disguised roman à clef version of the Louisiana politician. He's not just the Citizen Kane of literature. Stark is a standout among fictional characters because he is, as Penn Warren intended, a common man too, but uncommonly described. Readers see him when he's not in the spotlight and witness emotions that range from speechless stupefaction to angry rants. He comes to life in part because Penn Warren spent time one summer in a small Louisiana town where he observed everyone and "like a good number of the population whiled away the afternoons by going to the local murder trials."

The narrator, who had been with Stark for many years, recalls the first time he met the man: "Fate comes walking through the door, and it is five feet eleven inches tall and heavyish in the chest and shortish in the leg." Wearing a too-long "seven-fifty seersucker suit," black shoes in need of polish, and a stiff high-collar shirt "like a Sunday school superintendent," Stark sports "a blue-striped tie which you know his wife gave him last Christmas and which he has kept in tissue paper with the holly card ('Merry Xmas to my Darling Willie from your Loving Wife')," with a sweat-stained gray felt hat. In those early days, Willie was urged to run for office by the Democratic machine—but only, unbeknownst to him, so that he would split the vote and another candidate might win. It crushed him, but made him only more determined to win the next time. He does, and soon turns from an idealistic naïf who in school had been a "bookworm" and a "teacher's pet" to a ruthless governor who runs the state like a dictator and runs enough afoul of people that someone tries to assassinate him. But streaks of his early goodness shine through—enough to where readers believe it when he finally sees the light. After his football-star son lies unconscious and in danger of dying, he tells his wife he's decided to name the medical center after Tom instead of himself. She responds, "Oh, Willie, don't you see? Those things don't matter." As he sinks into his chair, silent, readers suspect that he realizes he's always been conflicted between the drive to do good things for people and the intoxicating allure of power that makes such things possible—a tragic flaw worthy of a Shakespearean hero.

Stark is such a meaty character that Broderick Crawford won Best Actor for portraying him in the 1949 film adaptation, which also won for Best Picture, while Sean Penn played Stark in a less successful 2006 film. But in 1981, composer Carlisle Floyd's three-act opera *Willie Stark* created a small controversy because it popularized opera using elements of Broadway, blurring the line between high and low art in what was no doubt a tribute to Stark's grassroots style. And Stark himself is an interestingly blurred line.

Bibliography

All the King's Men (1946)

Works Cited

Penn Warren, Robert. *All the King's Men: An HBJ Modern Classic.* New York: Harcourt Brace Jovanovich, 1974.

———. Interview by Eugene Walter and Ralph Ellison. "Robert Penn Warren, The Art of Fiction No. 18." *Paris Review* 16 (Spring–Summer 1957). https://www.theparisreview .org/interviews/4868/robert-penn-warren-the-art-of-fiction-no-18-robert-penn-warren.

Prescott, Orville. "Books of the Times: *All the King's Men.*" *New York Times*, August 19, 1946. https://archive.nytimes.com/www.nytimes.com/books/97/03/09/reviews/warren -booksoftimes.html.

—JP

T

DAENERYS TARGARYEN

First Appearance: *A Game of Thrones: Book One of A Song of Ice and Fire*
Date of First Appearance: 1996
Author: George R. R. Martin (1948–)

It seems to me that a queen who trusts no one is as foolish as a queen who trusts everyone.

Daenerys Targaryen has more names and titles than anyone in this book, among them the First of Her Name, Queen of Meereen, Queen of the Andals and the Rhoynar and the First Men, Lord of the Seven Kingdoms, Protector of the Realm, Khaleesi of the Great Grass Sea, Daenerys Stormborn, Princess of Dragonstone, the Unburnt, the Mother of Dragons, and the Breaker of Chains. But "Dany" (as she's called, for short) lives up to all of them.

Slender and diminutive with pale skin, light silver-gold hair, and amethyst eyes, Daenerys has a beauty that beguiles men. But by any measure she's an extraordinary character: unique, complex, and larger than life, with a tremendous growth arc. She also carries thematic weight—the character with a vision of the future who asks the titular question, "What is the song of ice and fire?" Daenerys became such a fan favorite that when her point-of-view chapters were conspicuously absent from the fourth volume of the epic fantasy series, author George R. R. Martin felt compelled to explain in an afterword and provide a "teaser" chapter from the fifth volume, *A Dance with Dragons*.

Without the dragons, Daenerys would still be a strong character, but with them? It's hard to forget the powerful image of a fourteen-year-old girl, still grieving over a miscarriage and uncertain of her future, as she places three petrified, centuries-old dragon eggs by the head, heart, and loins of her dead husband. Then, after lighting the funeral bier and watching it burn, she enters the fire and astounds all who watch by emerging naked and unburned, two hatchling dragons suckling at her breasts and a third draped over her shoulder. She would go on to feed them charred horsemeat, snake, whatever is available, and ride the largest of the three when they grow old enough. They would become her children—also her persuaders and scourges.

Because Daenerys's mother dies giving birth to her the same night a storm destroys the remaining ships of her slain brother and father, the "Mad" King Aerys

II, she becomes known as "Daenerys Stormborn." As anyone who's read the *Song of Ice and Fire* books can attest, the nickname fits. This calm-by-demeanor young woman tends to be at the center of storms that are usually not of her own making—one reason why her charismatic character is so popular that it made Emilia Clarke a star on the HBO-TV adaptation *Game of Thrones.*

When we first meet Daenerys, she's a timid girl of thirteen living in exile and homeless poverty in Essos with her brother, Viserys, who has abused her so much she's careful not to "wake the dragon" inside him. As easy as it was for him to sell the family crown, Viserys conspires with the Magister they meet in the Free City of Pentos to sell Dany as a bride for the powerful Khal Drogo, leader of the primitive horse-riding Dothraki. In exchange, Viserys seeks the Dothraki's help recapturing his crown and the kingdom to which he is now heir.

Though she first thinks of the Dothraki as "beasts in human skins," Daenerys proves to be adaptable—living proof of Nietzsche's maxim that what doesn't kill us makes us stronger. Among her wedding gifts are three petrified dragon eggs from the Magister and a silver horse from Drogo. Both give her a sense of power— one spiritual, and the other physical. When she masters riding, "for the first time in hours she forgot to be afraid. Or perhaps it was the first time ever."

Readers witness Dany's growth from a girl who is ridden from behind "relentlessly" every night by her husband, to a young woman who becomes assertive enough to ride *him,* deriving strength from embracing the lifestyle of her new people. Always perceptive, Daenerys quickly learns when to listen, when to speak, and how to wield her power. When her brother refuses to accept her position of honor as khaleesi, she orders his horse taken so that he must walk behind the column back to the khalasar—a humiliation from which he will never recover. Not long afterward his temper and foolishness will earn Viserys the crown he called for, as Drogo pours molten gold over his head. Yet, watching him die, Dany is curiously calm and thinks, "He was no dragon. Fire cannot kill a dragon."

Daenerys has many character-defining moments, as when her husband lay dying and most of the Dothraki warriors had left to follow another. Daenerys tells the group of slaves left behind, "I free you. Take off your collars." One of the few remaining warriors declares it would shame him "to be a bloodrider to a woman," but his shame vanishes when Daenerys emerges from her husband's crematory fire unscathed. Daenerys has a strong sense of empathy, and she frees slaves in every city she conquers, even telling her warriors they can no longer violently rape the women captives. "If your warriors would mount these women, let them take them gently and keep them for wives." When a warrior scoffs, "Does the horse breed with sheep?" she snaps, "The dragon feeds on horse and sheep alike." And when she approaches Meereen with her army of 20,000 plus 60,000 freed slaves, her advance riders remove the slave children the masters of the city had crucified every mile of the approach. But she tells them, "I will see every one, and count them, and look upon their faces. And I will remember." When she takes the city, she tells the masters if they turn over 163 leaders she will spare the rest. "I am the blood of the dragon," she says. "They are not strong," she tells herself, "so I must be their strength. I must show no fear, no weakness, no doubt."

As a teenage female leader, Daenerys must work constantly to command the respect of men, many of whom want to sleep with her. Even her relationship with

Ser Jorah Mormont, her knight-errant adviser, is complicated. Sometimes, she observes, Jorah thinks of her as a child, and other times as a woman he would like to bed. But she remains levelheaded and in charge, steering their relationship to the "friend zone" where they can still be intimate in their confidences. Another complication arises when Daenerys quickly learns that if she leaves one city to conquer another, the "masters" will try to regain power and enslave or kill those who had been freed. Then there is the matter of her goal: to reclaim the Iron Throne of the Seven Kingdoms, which means building an army and obtaining ships to transport them. Dany proves to be a shrewd bargainer, whether she's haggling over a brass platter in the marketplace or negotiating with heads of state for vessels. But the surprising problem she must deal with is the growing aggression of her dragons, which have gone from helping themselves to farmers' sheep to killing a farmer's daughter. She loves them, she needs them as a symbol of her power, and, lacking the numbers of her enemies, she must weaponize them. It frightens her to lose control, but, of course, that fascinates readers as much as the character herself.

Bibliography

A Game of Thrones: Book One of a Song of Ice and Fire (1996)
A Clash of Kings: Book Two of a Song of Ice and Fire (1999)
A Storm of Swords: Book Three of a Song of Ice and Fire (2000)
A Dance with Dragons: Book Five of a Song of Ice and Fire (2011)

Work Cited

Martin, George R. R. *A Feast for Crows: Book Four of a Song of Ice and Fire.* New York: Bantam Books, 2005.

—JP

TARZAN

First Appearance: *Tarzan of the Apes* in the *All-Story* magazine
Date of First Appearance: October 1912
Author: Edgar Rice Burroughs (1875–1950)

To me the only pleasure in the hunt is the knowledge that the hunted thing has power to harm me as much as I have to harm him.

Is there anyone on the planet who hasn't heard of Tarzan or tried to imitate his distinctive, chest-beating jungle call?

In 1912, Arizona became the forty-eighth state, the unsinkable *Titanic* sank, and Edgar Rice Burroughs's primitive hero, Tarzan of the Apes, first appeared in the October issue of the *All-Story*, a fifteen-cent pulp magazine. Instantly, fans clamored for more. Burroughs wrote his editor, "About a score of readers have threatened my life unless I promised a sequel to Tarzan. Shall I?" The answer was yes, but the *All-Story* turned down the second installment, and five book publishers subsequently rejected the idea of an expanded version. Talk about misguided. The sequel was renamed *The Return of Tarzan* and published by Street and Smith. A mere two years later, when *Tarzan of the Apes* became the first of many to be published in book form by A. C. McClurg, the loin-clothed Ape Man became a true publishing phenomenon.

As Burroughs described him, Tarzan was a "brute" with "great muscles," the son of a British lord raised, since birth, by great apes deep in the jungle and far from civilization—a throwback to the Romantic notion of the noble savage who lived far from the complications and corruptions of society. Tarzan was also the fictional embodiment of the nature versus nurture debate, and the public's appetite for more Ape Man adventures led Burroughs to write twenty-three additional Tarzan books, most of which were first published in pulp magazines of the day. "As a boy I loved the story of Romulus and Remus, who founded Rome, and I loved, too, the boy Mowgli in Kipling's *Jungle Books*. I suppose Tarzan was the result of those early loves," Burroughs said in a 1938 interview.

In *Tarzan of the Apes*, Lord and Lady Greystoke—originally Bloomstoke in the magazine version—are traveling aboard a ship that's overtaken by mutineers. They're put ashore by the leader and given provisions. Marooned, the Greystokes build a treetop shelter and soon encounter an even more formidable foe: the great apes that inhabit the jungle. One night, "a little son was born in the tiny cabin beside the primeval forest, while a leopard screamed before the door, and the deep notes of a lion's roar sounded from beyond the ridge." A year later, Lady Greystoke would pass away and Lord Greystoke would be killed the very next day by the great ape Kerchak. But their baby would be adopted by Kala, one of the gorilla females, as a substitute for her own baby that had been killed; "hunger closed the gap between them, and the son of an English lord and an English lady nursed at the breast of Kala, the great ape."

By the age of ten Tarzan was "an excellent climber," and the other apes "often marveled at his superior cunning." In no time at all, he learned to use his hands "to swing from branch to branch after the manner of his giant mother, and as he grew older he spent hour upon hour daily speeding through the tree tops with his brothers and sisters," Burroughs wrote. "Though but ten years old he was fully as strong as the average man of thirty, and far more agile than the most practiced athlete ever becomes. And day by day his strength was increasing."

More than two decades before Superman would debut in DC Comics as the world's first superhero, Tarzan was depicted as a hero with superhuman qualities. No wonder audiences loved him! He could do it all—even teaching himself to read using books he found in the ruins of his parents' house so he could converse fluently with humans. Add a degree of exoticism that only a simple loincloth and a jungle home can provide, along with a wildness that appeals to every woman's "bad boy" fantasy as he and Jane become attracted to each other, and it's easy to see how audiences would respond to his naïve purity and dangerous, brute strength. He was a classic underdog, too, taking on large groups of enemies, many with guns, while armed with only a knife and bow and arrows. And he made it look easy.

In the first book, Tarzan avenges the death of his "stepmother" by an African tribe, rescues white explorers from cannibals, and fights the lioness Sabor, shooting three arrows into her and using his knife to finish the job. "With swelling breast, he placed a foot upon the body of his powerful enemy, and throwing back his fine young head, roared out the awful challenge of the victorious bull ape" and the "forest echoed to the savage and triumphant paean."

So was born the famous Tarzan yell—one imitated by comedian Carol Burnett on television and by children everywhere who watched former Olympic swimmer Johnny Weissmuller perfect the cry in twelve Tarzan movies for MGM and RKO Pictures, making Weissmuller the definitive and most popular Tarzan in motion pictures.

Hollywood had taken an early interest, with Elmo Lincoln playing the Ape Man in four silent films from 1918 to 1921. James Pierce took over for a 1927 remake, and Frank Merrill wore the loincloth in two films before Weissmuller would make the role his own, starting with *Tarzan the Ape Man* (1932) and ending with *Tarzan and the Mermaids* (1948). Lex Barker played the part for five films, beginning with *Tarzan's Magic Fountain* (1949), but for some fans it just wasn't the same—nor was it when Gordon Scott took over in *Tarzan's Hidden Jungle* (1955), or when Denny Miller tried a 1959 reboot before Scott returned for a time and then Jock Mahoney took over. But the character was bigger than the star. It's worth noting that Tarzan was prominently a part of the public consciousness for close to six decades, with either a new book or film coming out every year.

At a time when World War I had taken a devastating toll, Burroughs's first Tarzan novels must have felt like comfortable escapism, and the public's love affair with the Ape Man continued through a second world war, the Korean War, and even the first part of the Vietnam War, as evidenced by numerous fanzines that celebrated the Ape Man. But Burroughs was also a savvy businessman. As an article in the *Chronicle of Higher Education* observed, "Having incorporated himself in 1923 (the year after *Ulysses* and 'The Waste Land'), Burroughs is truly the father of the secondary-product market." In addition to several dozen licensed films, a long-running syndicated comic strip, and a series of comic books that broadened the audience for Tarzan, Burroughs approved countless product tie-ins. Over time, the character has appeared on such diverse products as lunch boxes, bread bags, gasoline signs, vitamins, watches, luggage, snow globes, pocketknives, and gum trading cards. His name was even attached to a Russian assault vest.

Thanks also to numerous TV shows, films, parodies, and a revival the character experienced in 1999 when Disney animated the Tarzan legend for the big screen, Burroughs's character—whose name derived from a language the author invented for his fictional tribe of anthropoid apes and meant "white-skin"—remains popular and forever a part of America's pop-culture heritage.

Bibliography

Tarzan of the Apes (1912)
The Return of Tarzan (1915)
The Beasts of Tarzan (1916)
The Son of Tarzan (1917)
Tarzan and the Jewels of Opar (1918)
Jungle Tales of Tarzan (1919)
Tarzan the Untamed (1920)
Tarzan the Terrible (1921)
Tarzan and the Golden Lion (1923)

Tarzan and the Ant Men (1924)
Tarzan, Lord of the Jungle (1928)
Tarzan and the Lost Empire (1929)
Tarzan at the Earth's Core (1930)
Tarzan the Invincible (1931)
Tarzan Triumphant (1932)
Tarzan and the City of Gold (1933)
Tarzan and the Lion Man (1934)
Tarzan and the Leopard Men (1935)
Tarzan's Quest (1936)
Tarzan and the Forbidden City (1938)
Tarzan the Magnificent (1939)
Tarzan and the Foreign Legion (1947)
Tarzan and the Madman (published posthumously, 1964)
Tarzan and the Castaways (published posthumously, 1965)
The Tarzan Twins (children's book, 1927)
Tarzan and the Tarzan Twins (children's book, 1936)

Works Cited

Poole, Oliver. "Romance Isn't Dead: An Interview with the Author of *Tarzan*." *Writer's Markets and Methods*, March 1938. Accessed August 24, 2018. http://www.erbzine.com/mag0/0063.html.

Porges, Irwin. *Edgar Rice Burroughs: The Man Who Created Tarzan*. Provo, UT: Brigham Young University Press, 1975.

Vernon, Alex. "Should We Take Tarzan Seriously? (After All, Edgar Rice Burroughs Didn't)." *Chronicle of Higher Education* 55, no. 6 (October 3, 2008).

—JP

OLIVER TWIST

First Appearance: *Oliver Twist, or The Parish Boy's Progress* in *Bentley's Miscellany*
Date of First Appearance: 1837–1839
Author: Charles Dickens (1812–1870) under the pseudonym "Boz"

Some people are nobody's enemies but their own.

Oliver Twist is the most famous of Charles Dickens's literary orphans and the first child protagonist in an English novel, but he is joined by scores of other abject children Dickens creates, first to illustrate and illuminate the strife of London's poverty-stricken street urchins, and secondly, as a means of critiquing the British institutions' failure to protect these most vulnerable citizens. Recognizing the deep emotional sympathy these youths evoke, other novelists in the nineteenth century would follow suit, both in England and in the broad range of countries English literature reached, but Oliver remains the iconic poster child for orphans, and he is the one who first comes to mind for most readers.

Oliver's circumstances are certainly dire. He is born to an unwed mother who promptly dies as soon as she gives birth, and with no family in sight and no legitimate name, one is assigned to him. The first name "Oliver" has no apparent significance, but "twist" was a slang term for the noose which was made of wound rope and twisted about the necks of people to be hanged. At one point, Oliver is even nicknamed "young gallows" to underscore his likely future. From the circumstances of his beginning, society dooms him to be a throwaway child already condemned to a life of misery, but likely a short-lived one if that offers any comfort. Oliver spends his infancy as a ward in an unloving group foster home, and then at the age of nine he becomes one of hundreds of children sent to workhouses called parishes that serve as orphanages and are the chief abusers of child labor. There he and the other children are seriously overtasked and underfed, and early in the novel Oliver loses a lottery that forces him to utter one of the novel's more memorable and action-generating lines: "Please, sir. I want some more." His pleas not only provide him no extra food, they get him sent away as a rented assistant to an undertaker where conditions are different but equally bad. After narrowly escaping from there, Oliver must fend for himself in a series of events that become increasingly grim through most of the novel's central action and culminate in Oliver's near death before his fortunate rescue.

Dickens himself had endured a similar workhouse as an eleven-year-old after his father became unemployed and was eventually put into debtor's prison. The experience obviously deeply impacted young Charles's sense of injustice and the dreadful conditions into which a child could so quickly be thrust, but out of these circumstances were born Oliver and the Artful Dodger in *Oliver Twist*; Pip and Estella in *Great Expectations*; David Copperfield, Charles Darnay, and Sydney Carton in *A Tale of Two Cities*; Martin Chuzzlewit in *The Life and Times of Martin Chuzzlewit*; Nell Trent in *The Old Curiosity Shop*; and Esther Summerson and several others in *Bleak House*. Like Dickens, most of his orphans learn to survive by making the best of what they have, and eventually good fortune shines on them.

Through Oliver's early journey, and even in the dire circumstances to follow after he is taken in by a pickpocket gang in London's most unsavory part of the city, he remains an incorruptibly good child for no apparent reason, or at least no circumstantial one. This group's intent is to use him as another set of hands that can be trained for thievery, and as Oliver finally grasps the situation in which he finds himself, "he prayed Heaven to spare him from such deeds, and rather to will that he should die at once, than be reserved for crimes so fearful and appalling." Oliver is simply too good for his own good, and though almost unbelievably so, he remains uncorrupted.

Dickens writes his usual compelling story with *Oliver Twist*, and his young protagonist's ordeal provides an opportunity to contemplate the nature of humanity and the social influences that shape moral consciousness. Is Oliver innately good and therefore not corrupted by the evil around him, or are others innately bad and unable to reform even if they are placed in the best of circumstances? Or, if given enough time and impetus, is everyone capable of being forced or coerced into behaving differently from what seems to be their natural inclinations? Dickens answers that question at least partially in *Oliver Twist*'s 1841 third edition preface by explaining that he "wished to show, in little Oliver, the principle of

Good surviving through every adverse circumstance, and triumphing at last." But if innate personality is Dickens's intent, he would seem to undercut his social criticism that the system is at fault and its failure has created or at least exacerbated these dire cases of abandoned children living lives of misery and often turning to a life of crime simply to survive. And is it survival, or do they refashion their morals after a time? The general reading audience may not care about the political or sociological nature of the question, but they do care about the beautifully spirited boy born into misery and continuing to live in the squalor that surrounds him while still resisting it. That is just simply too heartbreaking.

If we hadn't already read Oliver Twist's story in the book by the same name and fallen in love with his gentle spirit and innate goodness, we likely experienced him in one of the several movies over the last half century or the BBC's 2007 miniseries re-creating this masterful tale. Arguably, the most memorable of these versions is the 1968 film *Oliver!* arising out of the stage musical drama five years earlier. The movie features the almost effeminately faced and angelically voiced Mark Lester. He's joined by a remarkable group of supporting characters, including the scene-stealing Artful Dodger, a spirited and plucky orphan and a prime example of Dickens's talent with characterization. *Oliver!* convincingly portrays the violence and soul-crushing conditions these outcasts must endure, and Lester's singing of "Where Is Love" from the dark, prison-like cellar complete with window bars could not have more perfectly rendered these abysmal conditions under which Dickens's most endearing lost children are forced to live.

Dickens continued to call out the British government for its failure to protect its poorest citizens, and in an 1866 letter to the Association for the Improvement of Workhouse Infirmaries, quoted in 2012, he wrote, "My knowledge of the general condition of the sick poor in workhouses is not of yesterday, nor are my efforts, in my vocation, to call merciful attention to it." He closed by asking, "Do me the kindness to set me down for £20," but one suspects that his literature did far more to advance the cause than a well-worded letter and financial contribution. The fact that we are led back to *Oliver Twist* and to the other similar works to engage again and again with these exquisitely drawn figures would seem to confirm such a hypothesis.

Bibliography

Oliver Twist, or The Parish Boy's Progress (1838)

Work Cited

Richardson, Ruth. "Charles Dickens, *The Lancet*, and *Oliver Twist*." *Perspectives: The Art of Medicine* 379, no. 9814 (February 4, 2012).

—GS

V

JEAN VALJEAN

First Appearance: *Les Misérables*
Date of First Appearance: 1862
Author: Victor Hugo (1802–1885)

Does human nature thus change utterly and from top to bottom? Can the man created good by God be rendered wicked by man? Can the soul be completely made over by fate, and become evil, fate being evil?

Just as every Abbott needs a Costello and every Rachel a Ross, some of literature's greatest characters really can't be appreciated apart from whoever's yang to their yin. The archetypal rivalries in Western folklore—such as Chauntecleer, the cock, and the fox in Chaucer's *The Nun's Priest's Tale* (ca. 1390), part of his *Canterbury Tales*—require a protagonist and an antagonist. Sometimes these opposites are doppelgängers or doubles, such as Leggatt and the naïve ship captain narrating Joseph Conrad's *The Secret Sharer* (1910). Sometimes they're flip sides of the same personality, as in Robert Louis Stevenson's *Strange Case of Dr. Jekyll and Mr. Hyde* (1886). Often the bad guys prove more interesting than their goody-two-shoes counterparts: In one of the great breaches between art and theology, John Milton in *Paradise Lost* made the fallen angel Lucifer more charismatic than he made God.

One instance where the bad guy *isn't* more captivating is Victor Hugo's epic novel of the French underclass, *Les Misérables*. Amid long digressive chapters on the history of Paris, Hugo's 1,500-page, seventeen-years-in-the-making magnum opus tells the story of the prison escapee Jean Valjean and his relentless pursuer, Inspector Javert. The duo embodies opposing attitudes toward crime and punishment, redemption and persecution, and self-sacrifice and self-destructive obsession. While Javert's fixation with capturing his elusive quarry is his undoing, Valjean isn't so unerringly good he walks on clouds. He grapples with bitterness and jealousy and the necessity of showing mercy even when it's not always been shown to him. Being good is a struggle, Hugo says, and for Jean Valjean the struggle is real.

His story begins in 1795—although the book is not arranged chronologically—when, during a harsh winter, he steals a loaf of bread to feed his extended family.

Sent to prison, Valjean attempts escape several times, stretching his sentence to nineteen years. When he's released after the Battle of Waterloo in 1815, he travels to the small town of Dinge seeking shelter but is refused because he's forced to carry a yellow passport, the stigma of his convict status. Only the kindly Bishop Myriel takes him in, but the hardened Valjean steals his silverware and even toys with killing him. Yet when the police capture the thief, the bishop pretends he gifted the items to him, insisting that with his lie and his forgiveness he has purchased the convict's soul and dedicated it to God. Jean Valjean is now obligated to become a good man.

Which is exactly what he does. Adopting the name Madeleine, Valjean travels to the town of Montreuil-sur-Mer where he becomes wealthy by transforming the local manufacturing base. He uses his money for charity and soon rises to the position of town mayor. His first encounter with his nemesis occurs while saving an old man named Fauchelevent from a wrecked wagon with his almost super-human strength; Javert, witnessing the rescue, remembers a similar feat when he worked as a guard at the prison where Valjean was incarcerated. Later, Valjean inadvertently humiliates Javert when he orders the police to free the prostitute Fantine. In revenge, Javert reveals his identity to the Paris police, only to discover another man has been imprisoned under Valjean's name. When Javert reveals this to the man he knows as M. Madeleine, Valjean suffers a bout of guilt. In a masterful chapter called "A Tempest in a Skull," he struggles with whether the good he'll do in the outside world compensates for an innocent man, Champmathieu, being punished in his name, and he concludes he must turn himself in.

The four books of *Les Misérables* that follow are structured around a series of ever-improbable but unfailingly moral cat-and-mouse pursuits. Time after time, Valjean barely eludes Javert. Readers will be forgiven if they quickly lose count of just how many times he escapes prison, or how many aliases he assumes (in addition to M. Madeleine, he goes by Ultime Fauchelevent, M. Leblanc, and Urbain Fabre). What is constant, however, is Valjean's devotion to mercy and justice. He rescues Fantine's daughter, Cosette, from an abusive family of innkeepers, taking her to Paris where they live as father and daughter. Cosette falls in love with Marius Pontmercy, causing her surrogate father deep jealousy he must overcome.

In the lead-up to novel's most famous scene, Valjean joins the June Rebellion, the short-lived antimonarchical uprising of 1832, in which some 3,000 insurgents barricaded the eastern and central portions of Paris to protest poverty and a cholera outbreak under King Louis-Philippe I. When members of the revolutionary Friends of the ABC are slaughtered on the barricades, Valjean saves the wounded Marius's life by carrying him, just as Christ carried his cross, through the city's intricate sewers—the "intestine of the leviathan," as Hugo calls the tunnels of streaming waste. The filth covering Valjean when he emerges challenges society to see beyond the poor's raggedy exterior to the valiant heart underneath, but the dirt and excrement are really only ironic counterpoints to the hero's ever-changing aliases and disguises. Because the law has declared him a criminal, Valjean must cloak himself to let the goodness in him out.

However iconic the sewer tableau, a slightly earlier scene on the barricades illustrates Valjean's humanity even better. When the Friends of the ABC capture Javert working as a spy, its leader, Enjolras, grants Valjean's professed wish to kill his pursuer. Only Valjean doesn't execute the man, even though it would end his constant fear of being captured. In a secluded courtyard, he sets a shocked Javert free, refusing to take his life. The scene is the ultimate demonstration of mercy over revenge. Valjean must soon make a more poignant, personal sacrifice, however. When he reveals his true identity to Marius after the latter's recovery, Cosette's beau shuns him, convinced that convicted criminals are incapable of good. (He doesn't know who carried him out of those sewers.) Only when Valjean's health fails and he lies dying of heartbreak do the young people recognize their error and receive the old man's message: "Love each other well and always. There is nothing else but that in the world: love for each other."

If Valjean represents humanity at its most noble, Javert stands for something darker and more complex than evil—he represents a fanatical devotion to duty. He believes laws must be followed regardless of circumstance. His uncompromising inflexibility arises from a deep sense of shame: Javert was himself born in prison to a Gypsy fortune-teller, and he grew up despising the "wretched ones" as symbols of social disorder and decay.

Throughout *Les Misérables*, Javert appears on Valjean's heels as a stark insistence that a man's past will always follow him, no matter how completely he reinvents himself or what good he does. Yet Valjean's refusal to take the inspector's life on the barricades upends his belief system—Javert can't fathom why a "malefactor" would show mercy to the authority empowered to punish him. After Valjean's journey through the sewers, the policeman apprehends his quarry one final time, granting the hero's wish to see Cosette before he's hauled off again to prison. Only when Valjean goes to turn himself in after the visit, he discovers Javert has disappeared. In a chapter called "Javert Derailed," Hugo explores the psychological crumbling of a man who discovers his moral code, unlike Valjean's, is skewed. In following the letter of the law, Javert has acted immorally, a paradox he can't rationalize. Unable to abide the contradiction, he hurls himself into the Seine and drowns.

Les Misérables has been endlessly adapted, most notably in the 1985 musical popularly known as *Les Mis*, which ran on Broadway for 6,680 performances over sixteen years (1986–2003), was adapted into a blockbuster 2012 film, and continues to be staged by both international tour companies and regional theaters. Jean Valjean remains iconic for a very simple reason: Despite the 150-plus years since Hugo published his masterwork, we still need to be reminded that charity and mercy are rehabilitative forces in society, and that law and order are only rules, not ideals.

Bibliography

Les Misérables (1862)

—KC

W

OSCAR WAO

First Appearance: "The Brief Wondrous Life of Oscar Wao" in the *New Yorker*
Date of First Appearance: December 25, 2000
Author: Junot Díaz (1968–)

Even his own mother found his preoccupations nutty. Go outside and play! she commanded at least once a day. Portate como un muchacho normal.

He's sweet, fat, and sexually frustrated, but the two essential characteristics of the hero of Junot Díaz's Pulitzer Prize–winning 2007 novel are that Oscar de Léon is of Dominican heritage and that he's an unabashed nerd.

First introduced in a *New Yorker* story in 2000 and expanded seven years later into a bildungsroman with a heartbreaking ending, Oscar speaks for the millions of hyphenated Americans who experience life as hybrids. Multicultural characters since the 1970s have dramatized the promises and perils of living with one foot in an ethic immigrant background and the other in American popular culture. Yet perhaps no novel since Saul Bellow's *The Adventures of Augie March* (1953) captures that divide with such gusto or with such nimble, accessible experimentation as Díaz's tale of a New Jersey boy who grapples with the *fukú americanus*—a Dominican folk curse known as "the Doom of the New World"—while poring over *Fantastic Four* comic books. In many ways, Oscar's life is unexceptional. He reads and writes, pines to fall in love, and suffers severe depression. But in other ways his story is tragically remarkable, including his ultimate fate. It's that unsettling combination, which underscores the theme that first-generation Americans are exiles wherever they go, that etches Oscar so vividly in readers' memories.

At its core, *The Brief Wondrous Life of Oscar Wao* is a critique of Dominican masculinity. As a child, Oscar is well on his way to exuding the idealized machismo of his culture. He's a preschool lover boy, rubbing up against girls and trying to kiss them, his neighborhood's very own "little Porfirio Rubirosa," the polo-playing Dominican playboy-celebrity rumored to be well endowed and romantically linked to Marilyn Monroe and other Hollywood actresses.

Yet his lothario reputation and his luck with women end the day Maritza Chacón breaks up with him, and he cries: Oscar is all of seven years old. Teased as overly sensitive, he retreats into sci-fi novels, ballooning up to between 245 and 260 pounds by his sophomore year of high school at Don Bosco Tech in Paterson, New Jersey. He earns the nickname "Oscar Wao" when one Halloween he dresses up as the iconic sci-fi character Doctor Who and the narrator decides he looks more like "that fat homo Oscar Wilde."

Oscar's lack of masculinity stands in contrast to that of the narrator, who doesn't reveal his name—Yunior—until 200 pages into the novel. Yunior exerts his masculinity by calling women "bitch" and cheating on girlfriends; he is a self-described expert on "playerly wisdom" dedicated to helping Oscar up his game. He can't fathom why Oscar befriends Jenni Munoz but doesn't attempt to "mack" on her. When Oscar discovers Jenni in bed with a boy, he reacts violently and becomes a pariah at college. Depressed, he attempts suicide by leaping off a New Brunswick train track, but he lands on tilled loam instead of on cement, breaking both of his legs and separating his shoulder.

Despite Oscar's haplessness, Yunior discovers through his friend's sensitivity a road map out of his own self-destructive hypermasculinity. Following Oscar's example, he even becomes a writer. But Yunior isn't the novel's only contrast to Oscar. Díaz also tells the story of Dominican dictator Rafael Trujillo, whose brutal regime from the 1930s to his assassination in 1961 was driven by the same destructive machismo Yunior will renounce. Among Trujillo's many victims is Dr. Abelard, Oscar's grandfather, who is tortured to madness for refusing to give his daughter over to the dictator. Díaz spends equal time detailing machismo's negative effects on Dominican women. In a long flashback to her youth, Oscar's mother, Beli, Dr. Abelard's youngest daughter, is beaten so viciously by a lover known as the Gangster—who just happens to be Trujillo's brother-in-law—that she loses the baby of his she carries. Later, after Beli immigrates to New Jersey and gives birth to her children—Oscar's father is out of the picture—it's implied that her daughter, Lola, is raped at eight by a neighbor. While Lola's relationship with her mother is contentious, she also has to deal with domineering men, from her early boyfriend Aldo to Yunior himself, who cheats on her. To fight back against sexist culture, she shaves her head and takes charge of her sexual agency: When a politician in Santo Domingo pursues her, she only agrees to sleep with him if he pays her $2,000. A survivor—she tells her story in a chapter called "Wildwood" in a voice every bit as galvanizing as Yunior's—Lola eventually finds a compatible relationship with Cuban Ruben and gives birth to a daughter, Isis.

Oscar's story is not so happy, even though Díaz celebrates his adolescent love of popular culture. By one critic's count the novel contains more than 200 references to movies, books, comics, and games, from *Planet of the Apes* to Run Run Shaw kung fu movies. The most extended reference is to J. R. R. Tolkien's *The Lord of the Rings*. In his obsession with sci-fi/fantasy novels, Oscar imagines himself becoming a "Dominican Tolkien." Pop culture provides a framework for understanding the world: Oscar frequently compares Trujillo to Sauron, the villain of *Rings*, and the Dominican Republic itself to Mordor, Tolkien's alternative universe.

Oscar's relationship to his cultural heritage is more ambiguous. After college, he travels with Beli and Lola to the DR, where he falls in love with a prostitute named Ybón Pimentel. Her jealous boyfriend, a police captain, takes Oscar into the sugar-cane fields and beats him into a coma. After recovering in the States, Oscar tricks

Yunior into lending him money and returns to pursue Ybón even more ardently. This time when the captain's goons take him into the cane fields, they execute him.

Why must Oscar die? His innocence and sweetness, Yunior suggests, are the *zafa*, or counterspell, that lifts the *fukú* that has haunted his family since Dr. Abelard defied Trujillo, offering Isis a life free from the toxic masculinity of the past. In the novel's final lines, Yunior recounts Oscar's final letter home, in which the innocent young man describes how he finally lost his virginity to Ybón, and how the "little intimacies" of affection overpowered him with joy. "So this is what everybody's always talking about!" Oscar writes. "The beauty! The beauty!"—a refutation of Kurtz's dying words in Joseph Conrad's 1899 exploration of evil, *Heart of Darkness*: "The horror! The horror!"

When it was published, *The Brief Wondrous Life of Oscar Wao* was hailed for its exuberant polyglot style, which mixes Spanglish, slang, and playful footnotes. But while that voice belongs to Yunior (and to Lola in her section), it's Oscar who stays with readers. His good-natured nerdiness, his belief in daydreams and superheroes, his loneliness, and above all his yearning for love all make him a new kind of man—one who doesn't have to prove he is one.

Bibliography

The Brief Wondrous Life of Oscar Wao (2007)

—KC

CARRIE WHITE

First Appearance: *Carrie*
Date of First Appearance: 1974
Author: Stephen King (1947–)

She did not know if her gift had come from the lord of light or of darkness, and now, finally finding that she did not care which, she was overcome with an almost indescribable relief.

She was the first Stephen King character introduced to the public and remains his most famous. Thanks to her 1976 movie adaptation, the blood-drenched image of her, so memorably embodied by Sissy Spacek, is iconic. She's also survived far worse abuse than any she suffers in the novel that bears her name: A pointless 1999 movie sequel featuring a half sister nobody knew she had, an overly long 2002 television pilot for a series that never came to fruition, and a redundant 2013 remake all kept her name alive in the popular culture but came nowhere near generating the gory suspense of King's 1974 novel or of the original Brian De Palma–directed film. That's not even mentioning a notorious 1988 Broadway flop she inspired that closed after only six performances and lost investors $7 million.

However lackluster, none of these attempts to build a franchise around *Carrie*, the book that launched King's prolific career, has dinted the originality of Carrietta White of Chamberlain, Maine. The teenager who levels her high school and hometown with her paranormal powers after years of bullying offered a very different image of adolescence than readers were used to in the 1970s; in doing so, Carrie set the template for modern horror heroines to come. Interestingly, she might never have become an unforgettable character if not for another woman—the author's wife, Tabitha. One night in the early 1970s, Mrs. King fished three crumpled pages out of the wastebasket in the trailer she shared with her struggling writer husband and convinced him that a story about a telekinetic teenager was worth pursuing.

Carrie resonates first and foremost because it exposes high school for the Hobbesian, dog-eat-dog world that it is. Teenagers are relentlessly cruel to each other, and parents, teachers, and administrators are either too corrupt or too beaten down to bring some humanity to a system that rewards prom kings and queens for their good looks and popularity. Like *Lord of the Flies*, King shows how youth survive by marauding in packs, singling out and viciously sacrificing the weakest and most isolated. The novel famously begins with a brutal scene in which female students heckle and haze Carrie when she gets her first period in the locker-room shower. Led by the snobby Chris Hargensen, the girls chant "Plug it *up*, plug it *up*!" while pelting her with tampons. Raised by a fundamentalist mother, Carrie has no idea what menstruation is; she's so innocent she thinks sanitary napkins are for blotting lipstick. King's treatment of women's cycles was unnervingly frank for the mid-1970s, a far cry from more sensitive taboo breakers like Judy Blume's *Are You There God? It's Me, Margaret* (1970) that sought to expunge the cultural shame associated with menses.

The menorrhea scene is really just a prelude to *Carrie*'s other memorably bloody moment, though. When the school suspends Chris for harassing Carrie, she and her lunkhead boyfriend, Billy Nolan, hatch a plot with other members of her gang, the Mortimer Snerds, to vote the girl homecoming queen and then dump a bucket of pig's blood on her from the rafters just as she is crowned. Carrie's peers burst out laughing when the blood hits its target, but the kids have no idea of the ire they've just unleashed. Shortly before the party Carrie learned how to harness her telekinetic talents while fending off an attack from her repressive mother, who preaches that prom is a Satanic temptation. The girl now takes malicious glee in flexing her fury. The gym doors swing shut, gouts of fire rip through the school, and by the end of the night Carries destroys both it and most of Chamberlain, killing nearly 600 people in the process.

Despite its title, *Carrie* isn't a first-person novel. In fact, only about a fifth of the book is told from Carrie's perspective (and only then through limited omniscience and interior monologue). Instead, King weaves in and out of eyewitness accounts from various school administrators, city officials, and bystanders, along with scenes of the girl's tormentors and the one person in Chamberlain who shows her any compassion, Sue Snell. He even has great fun incorporating parodies of Associated Press dispatches, *Esquire* articles, quickie cash-in paperbacks on the incident, and academic tomes with leaden subtitles, all of them examining the scientific merit of telekinesis in hopes of discovering a rational explanation for Carrie's rampage. King even includes transcripts from a blue-ribbon panel called the White Commission that tries to cover up the paranormal truth so the surviving citizenry can go on with life—a takeoff on the Warren Commission that conspiracy theorists like to say whitewashed the Kennedy assassination, an event that would fascinate the author for the next forty years, culminating in his 2011 novel *11/22/63*.

For all the alienation and abuse she suffers, though, Carrie is no Holden Caulfield. She's not a saintly spokesman for adolescent idealism or a symbol of sensitivity. At first King doesn't even seem particularly sympathetic to her— twice he refers to her as "bovine." In her early scenes Carrie barely exists on the page beyond some fleeting thoughts and a few muttered monosyllables; she only truly comes alive when she emerges from her introversion and passivity to seize control of the supernatural powers she's been unconsciously exerting since childhood. In this way, the plot is essentially an allegory of coming of age, with the relish the girl feels at putting her powers to dark use an ironic inversion of the pressure society places on young women to control their emotions and avoid appearing hysterical. What readers lose in empathy for Carrie as she tosses teachers and classmates around like rag dolls and electrocutes others by bursting open water pipes and electrical outlets they gain in an understanding of the chilling lure of revenge fantasies for teenagers. Especially for audiences in the post-Columbine age, when incidents of alienated students slaughtering peers and staff with high-powered assault weapons in their high school halls have become mind-numbingly routine, Carrie's desire to "teach them a lesson" and "get all of them—every last one" is a case study in why young people lash out in nihilistic violence.

King was among the first horror writers to give voice to this internal thirst to make tormentors pay in blood. Before *Carrie*, evil youth tended to be viewed externally through adult eyes, as in William March's *The Bad Seed* (1954), William Peter Blatty's *The Exorcist* (1971), or even David Seltzer's later *The Omen* (1976), often to emphasize the inability of grown-ups to reconcile children's destructive compulsions with their supposed innocence. Carrie is the first of many abused and castigated protagonists to come from King who want to believe that their suffering justifies them turning into raging monsters. Yet part of what makes this debut so great is how he dramatizes the flip side of that justification by depicting Carrie as both victim and villain and exposing the way her persecution feeds her solipsism. "Why couldn't you just leave me alone?" Carrie asks Sue Snell as she lies dying from the knife her mother buries in her shoulder in their climactic confrontation.

What teenager hasn't wanted to believe the solution to her problems was "Leave me alone"?

Bibliography

Carrie (1974)

—KC

WINNIE-THE-POOH

First Appearance: "A Children's Story by A. A. Milne" in *London Evening News*
Date of First Appearance: December 24, 1925
Author: A. A. Milne (1882–1956)

I always get to where I'm going by walking away from where I have been.

Winnie-the-Pooh is an affable, anthropomorphized teddy bear known worldwide for his simple but on-point maxims about life, especially the value of friendship. Most who love him are aware of the general backstory that Pooh is a creation of author A. A. Milne from one of his son Christopher Robin's favorite stuffed animals, and that his friends—Tigger, Piglet, Eeyore, Rabbit, Owl, Kanga, and Roo— were also fellow plush creatures populating his son's nursery. True to his nature as a bear, Winnie likes to roam the Hundred Acre Woods adjacent to the House at Pooh Corner, and he loves honey. He lives simply in carpe diem fashion and serves as the center of an endearing menagerie and a participant in the escapades that proliferate around them.

Milne's creation first appeared by name in a Christmas Eve story published in the *London Evening News*, but he became widely known and loved after the 1926 publication of *Winnie-the-Pooh*. Pooh appears at the beginning of the tale, bear paw firmly grasped in Christopher Robin's hand as he is dragged down the stairs with his stuffed head hitting each tread along the way. His poor furry noggin receives instant empathy, and love for his cheery disposition grows as the stories about his adventures and the crazy plots to steal honey unfold. Beyond Pooh's exquisite adorableness, the book's episodic structure lends itself beautifully to the flux of bedtime storytelling needs with each vignette a self-contained unit perfect for bopping in and out of the action. And as additional enhancement to Pooh's success, he and his animal friends have a nonperishable shelf life as long as there are children to entertain, educate, and put to sleep.

Pooh Bear, as he is affectionately called, has many worthy bite-size lessons to teach in the two volumes he appears in. He utters phrases like, "Sometimes the smallest things take up the most room in your heart," or "Any day spent with you is my favorite day, " and "A day without a friend is like a pot without a single drop of honey left inside." Who wouldn't fall in love with these kisses and rainbows? We might say Pooh is a furry philosophical forefather to the beloved Fred Rogers, who in his long-running television show *Mr. Rogers' Neighborhood* offered up similar soft-spoken pearls of wisdom and also had a cadre of friends with whom he interacted. And Pooh has become a vital part of the Disney stable of characters, one of the gentlest of the lot, whose stories have no scary witches or evil lurking in this forest, just a lovable bear spewing cheerful thoughts to his friends.

Winnie-the-Pooh also has a second and more adult-centered backstory beyond creation simply as Christopher Robin's playmate. All but a handful of studied readers would be shocked to know that the lovable bear is a by-product of military conflict. Milne fought in World War I's Battle of the Somme, and he came

away from this experience both severely wounded and psychologically traumatized, experiencing what we now call post-traumatic stress disorder. Upon his
return, he moved away from the city and near the forest that would become the
fictional Hundred Acre Woods. As cowriter Frank Cottrell-Boyce of the recent
film about the grown boy, *Goodbye Christopher Robin*, has noted in *Smithsonian*
magazine, "The woods are part of the software of the English psyche, and Milne
captures it better than anyone." Winnie-the-Pooh and his friends became a way
to connect father and son and to make the world a pleasant place where problems
are worked out and each episode ends amicably. *Pooh*'s illustrator, E. H. Shepard,
was also a war veteran, and both men seemed to find solace in creating the pleasant stories and illustrations of the mischievous but joy-filled scenes.

U.S. Army veteran Eric Milzarski supports the PTSD assessment and believes
"the stories were a way for Milne to explain his own post-traumatic stress to his
six-year-old son," with Pooh as the guide and each of Pooh's friends representing
an element of trauma singled out in order to bring these personality stresses to a
manageable level. Piglet might be read as paranoid, Eeyore is depressed, Tigger
is impulsive, Rabbit demonstrates perfectionist-driven aggression, Owl suffers
memory loss, and Kanga and Roo are overprotective. This analysis offers a vi-
able reading, and multiple articles from clinical and psychological angles provide
similar discussion of the story's innate value for understanding personality characteristics, especially those that might arise from trauma.

The chosen name of "Winnie" also has a war connection. A Canadian soldier
named Colebourn purchased a bear cub being sold because its mother had been
killed by a hunter, and when he was shipped to England in preparation for
military deployment, Colebourn somehow was able to bring the cub along. But
bears don't belong at the battlefront, and putting him in a zoo was the only logical solution for a growing cub named "Winnipeg" after the soldier's hometown.
In visiting the London Zoo with his father, Christopher Milne came to love the
gentle bear called Winnie, and the name had more ring to it than his own teddy's
more proper-toned "Edward" moniker. The "Pooh" tag came from a response
Christopher used when swans failed to avail themselves of the bread he offered
pond-side. The two words were melded, and the rest, as they say, is history.

Winnie-the-Pooh has an interesting Asian connection as well. He inadvertently
became the object of Chinese dissidence when his image was used to mock
President Xi Jinping, "who is a little sensitive" to photos of himself walking with
Barack Obama that have been reconfigured to represent Pooh and Tigger. Social
media sites suddenly began to list "content is illegal" notifications when Pooh's
name was searched, and, as obvious victim of censorship, the latest film has failed
to gain access in China. The Pooh-poohing continues, though Winnie has connected to Asian culture through the book *The Tao of Pooh*. His quiet wisdom apparently follows Taoist philosophies, and he has maintained his perfect Zen-like
demeanor for nearly a century and still seems to be steady as he goes.

The unfortunate side of the *Winnie-the-Pooh* saga is that the fame that accompanied it became a burden and eventually brought sadness both to A. A. Milne and
to his son Christopher Robin, who didn't remain a boy forever except in the pages
of the book. Fame has its devils, which is too bad for the real-life humans forever

attached to the fictional world of Pooh Corner. But for the rest of us, Pooh is, and can always be, pure joy.

Bibliography

When We Were Very Young, poetry collection featuring one pre-Winnie poem called "Teddy Bear" (1924)
Winnie-the-Pooh (1926)
Now We Are Six, poetry collection featuring several poems about Winnie-the-Pooh (1927)
The House on Pooh Corner (1928)

Works Cited

Desta, Yohana. "Winnie-the-Pooh Is Reportedly Too Controversial for *Goodbye Christopher Robin* to Play in China." *Vanity Fair*, August 3, 2018.
Hoff, Benjamin. *The Tao of Pooh*. New York: Penguin, 1982.
Milzarski, Eric. "*Winnie the Pooh* Was Created by a Vet Explaining War to His Boy." We Are the Mighty. August 1, 2018. https://www.wearethemighty.com/christopher-robin -milne-winnie-ptsd.
Sauer, Patrick. "How Winnie-the-Pooh Became a Household Name: The True Story behind the New Movie, *Goodbye Christopher Robin*." *Smithsonian*, November 6, 2017.

—GS

Y

JOHN YOSSARIAN

First Appearance: *Catch-22*
Date of First Appearance: 1961
Author: Joseph Heller (1923–1999)

The enemy is anybody who's going to get you killed, no matter which side he's on.

Alan Arkin couldn't capture his personality in a 1970 film, and Richard Dreyfuss couldn't do it in a 1973 pilot that failed to get off the ground. Whether Christopher Abbott can make him come alive in an upcoming TV miniseries remains to be seen, but the Vegas odds can't be good. Yossarian is an elusive character.

One of literature's great antiheroes, U.S. Army Air Forces bombardier Capt. John Yossarian is a quirkier, crazier, craftier, and more complex version of Herman Melville's *Bartleby, the Scrivener*, who confounded his employer with an "I would prefer not to" response to every directive. In Joseph Heller's 1961 classic World War II novel, Yossarian takes passive resistance to epic heights.

Yossarian agrees that the U.S. infantry deserves air support, "but not necessarily by me." Though he never actually refuses to fly missions, to avoid enemy fire he drops his bombs farther and farther from the target each time. Yossarian flies forty-four missions and the men like him because, unlike a bombardier who flies straight to the target and puts everyone at risk, Yossarian always takes extreme evasive action—so much so that his formation can hardly keep up with him. Like Orr, the man he shares a tent with, Yossarian tries to figure out ways to get out of fighting, not because he's unpatriotic or afraid, but because his sense of self-preservation is so acute. "They're trying to kill me," he complains, unswayed by the argument that it's all part of war. He may think of himself as a coward, but his "unwillingness to entrust the evasive action out of the target area to anybody else" shows that his self-preservationist concerns extend to his men. Readers witness him tending to a wounded crewman after their plane is hit and trying to strangle a crewman who's too flippant about the man's injury. Once he even goes against his instincts and takes six planes on a second pass of their target, resulting in a successful bombing run but the loss of a plane and its crew. And when the military brass decide to give him a medal, he shows up in formation *nude* to accept it.

No flag-waver, Yossarian drinks and swears and says things like "Fuck my superiors" because he realizes that "most of my superiors were not superior." He is annoyed by "a fair-haired boy from Iowa who believed in God, Motherhood and the American Way of Life, without ever thinking about any of them," and at the officer's club that he takes pride in *not* helping to build, he wants to "machine-gun" people at the bar for singing "sentimental old favorites that nobody else tired of." Instead, he stomps a Ping-Pong ball that rolls toward him. "That Yossarian," two officers chuckle.

When we meet him, Yossarian is goldbricking in the hospital, where he and other officers are forced to censor enlisted men's letters home. Instead of redacting sensitive information, Yossarian subverts the process by declaring "death to all modifiers" one day, axing the articles the next, and censoring everything in one letter except "Dear Mary" while adding a love postscript at the bottom from the chaplain. Instead of using his own name, he signs his censored letters "Washington Irving," and that same irreverence leads him to approach a general at the officer's club while drunk and ask if he's heard about the new 340 mm Lepage gun that the Germans have—Lepage being a brand of glue.

If it were up to Yossarian, he would spend the rest of the war in the hospital, though it too was "a dangerous place" because "people died there." Yossarian makes frequent trips there because he's maintained a fairly constant 101-degree fever and has everything that would indicate jaundice—except for having no yellow skin and conveniently forgetting to tell doctors that his liver pain actually subsided. "Why must we wait for symptoms? Can't we at least do a biopsy?" he asks. "Or anything that's accessible and simple?" Add to that a growing paranoia that two private detectives are following him for some reason, and Yossarian seems crazy. But maybe, compared to the other officers and enlisted men stationed with him on the fictional Mediterranean island of Pianosa, he's the sanest of them all.

Sanity is the main theme of Heller's comic novel, where bureaucracy is ridiculously circuitous and everything seems to be some form of a Catch-22 (a term Heller coined). As the squadron's doctor explains to Yossarian, who had declared he was going to go insane in order to avoid flying more missions, "Anyone who wants to get out of combat duty isn't really crazy." Yossarian "was moved very deeply by the absolute simplicity of this clause of Catch-22 and let out a respectful whistle." Everything in the novel has the same catch, as an old Italian woman explains when MPs round up the homeless whores Yossarian had been sheltering in an apartment: "Catch-22 says they have a right to do anything they can't stop them from doing."

Yossarian may be an antihero, but he's really quite moral, in his own antiauthoritarian way. When he questions targeting a village and the colonel asks why, he responds, "It's cruel, that's why." In Rome, though the other flyboys don't care what age the "whores" are, Yossarian tries to help a twelve-year-old girl. "You've got daughters . . . don't you know what I'm talking about?" When his superiors coerce him into posing as the dying son of parents who have traveled across the world to see him, he pretends to be their son but insists his name is Yossarian. When an airman plots to kill Colonel Cathcart for constantly raising the number of missions they have to fly, Yossarian refuses to take part, though he too is opposed to that numbers racket. And when the mess officer asks him to go in on a "surefire plan for cheating the federal government," Yossarian declines. "That's what I like about you," Milo responds. "You're honest!"

Catch-22 never appeared on the *New York Times* Best Seller List, but it has sold more than 10 million copies. The book was originally called *Catch-18*, but then someone at Simon & Schuster read in *Publisher's Weekly* that Leon Uris was coming out with a book titled *Mila 18* the same year, and they decided to change the title. Heller worked two hours a day and produced a page of polished prose per day over seven years. But the sequel was thirty-three years in the making. When *Closing Time* finally appeared in 1994, a reviewer for the *New York Times* acknowledged that *Catch-22* had become "an enduring part of the lexicon" and "helped change America's view of war." In *Closing Time*, he wrote, "Yossarian, the cynical bombardier who spent World War II trying to get out of flying any more missions, has married twice, worked as a teacher, an advertising executive and a failed screenwriter, and finally became a business and public relations consultant." He even ends up working for Milo's military-industrial company. In other words, Yossarian becomes unfortunately more establishment and less funny than he was in *Catch-22*—which remains his ticket to literary immortality.

Bibliography

Catch-22 (1961)
Closing Time (1994)

Works Cited

"Joseph Heller Interview with Bill Boggs." BillBoggsTV, YouTube video, 9:03. Posted May 3, 2012, by BillBoggsTV. https://www.youtube.com/watch?v=P0eiqJ_TQE8.
Lyall, Sarah. "In 'Catch-22' Sequel, Heller Brings Back Yossarian, Milo, et al." *New York Times*, February 16, 1994. https://www.nytimes.com/1994/02/16/books/in-catch-22-sequel-heller-brings-back-yossarian-milo-et-al.html.

—JP

Z

YURI ZHIVAGO

First Appearance: *Dr. Zhivago*
Date of First Appearance: 1957
Author: Boris Pasternak (1890–1960)

I don't like people who have never fallen or stumbled. Their virtue is lifeless and of little value. Life hasn't revealed its beauty to them.

A grand but doomed love affair set against the backdrop of war. What could make for a more majestic historical romance than *Dr. Zhivago*, Boris Pasternak's novel set in the decades surrounding the 1917 Bolshevik Revolution? An aristocratic family loses its money, political power shifts, and a young poet/intellectual/physician is forced into war and ultimately pressed to make choices between his country or his personal freedom, his wife and family or the woman he comes to deeply love. These are the building blocks out of which epic novels and films are made, and for most who haven't trudged through the hundreds of pages filled with detailed battle descriptions and countless scores of difficult-to-remember Russian names, the 1965 three-and-a-half-hour blockbuster film supplies the gist of the story with sweeping cinematic beauty and close-up romance. Omar Sharif and Julie Christie, relative Hollywood newcomers at the time, will forever provide the mind's eye images for Yuri Zhivago and Lara Antipova, establishing Pasternak's story as a classic on the screen as well as in print.

Pasternak immediately locks in sympathy for his protagonist, the young Yuri Zhivago, as the novel opens with his beloved mother's funeral, and we quickly learn that his industrialist father, once wealthy but now financially depleted, had earlier left them to make their own way in the world. Yuri's parents are relics of an old-world order quickly crumbling, and he must learn to navigate in a new one. His sensitive spirit leads him to literature, poetry, philosophy, and medicine. His interests are intellectual and artistic, and his philosophical penchant will eventually swing toward a rejection of Russia's heavy-handed political dogma. At first encouraged by a war that he had supported because its ideology seemed welcoming, he later becomes disillusioned with the new regime, though forced into involvement in its wars. He will in some way participate in and be greatly affected by almost steady military skirmishes and major battles dogging him for many years to follow. Yuri will eventually leave Moscow to seek a private life away from political centers, and through this experience, he comes to value the individual over support for a distinctly Communist-style state. He will follow his heart and his own mind instead of genuflection before the collective government-sanctioned head, and he adopts this dangerous stance of freedom without disavowing his love of Mother Russia.

The scope of *Dr. Zhivago* is broad, but the story behind the novel provides even more intrigue and mirrors in actual time the political crisis that fills its pages. Yuri's intellectual and philosophical contemplations present an ideological battleground landing on the dangerous counterrevolutionary side of Russian politics. What happens as a result of this conflict also presages, and to a great extent creates, the trouble that will by association be heaped upon Pasternak as *Dr. Zhivago*'s creator. This epic, which would come to be called one of the great pieces of Russian literature on par with works of Chekhov, Tolstoy, and Turgenev, was instrumental in earning its author the 1958 Nobel Prize in Literature—oddly enough, for a book its country of origin refused to print and that had been secretly distributed through an Italian press, Dutch involvement, and covert activity from the United States' Central Intelligence Agency. The CIA saw an opportunity to weaponize the novel as an anti-Russian missive, writing that "this book has great propaganda value," and that it provided "the opportunity to make Soviet citizens wonder what is wrong with their government, when a fine literary work by the man acknowledged to be the greatest living Russian writer is not even available in his own country in his own language for his own people to read." The fact that *Dr. Zhivago* was banned made it all the more desired, and an estimated 10 million copies were sold or secretly disseminated to eager readers behind the Iron Curtain.

Pulling out even one select passage in the book makes this easier to understand. Yuri summarizes his thoughts about the Russian conflict by saying, "Revolutions are made by fanatical men of action with one-track minds, men who are narrowminded to the point of genius. They overturn the old order in a few hours or days . . . but for decades thereafter, for centuries, the spirit of narrowness which led to the upheaval is worshipped as holy." Pasternak knew the danger of such words and told the Italian publisher when secretly turning over the manuscript to him, "You are hereby invited to my execution." Such antigovernment rhetoric as he had written not only caused him to become a persona non grata, he was vilified and scrutinized so that he feared personal danger in his homeland. While some demanded that he be exiled, Pasternak was determined to remain in Russia and instead turned down the Nobel Prize, writing to Khrushchev that "leaving the motherland will equal death for me. I am tied to Russia by birth, by life and work." Staying in his beloved country turned out to be the hard part, however.

Pasternak had previously written Yuri Zhivago's history with the same choice to stay rather than join his family in exile. Yuri retreats from the city's politics and eventually abandons his marriage, though his nature resists such betrayal for quite some time. Juxtaposed against the backdrop of war, he falls deeply in love with Lara Antipova, a woman of past acquaintance who is now a nurse. Both are separated from their families with Lara's husband dead and Yuri's wife and son in exile, and their affair serves as the antidote for loneliness, though they too are eventually separated by the consequences of war and politics. At the novel's end Yuri Zhivago dies of a heart attack, symbolically appropriate, as he searches the Moscow streets thinking he has glimpsed Lara in front of him in a crowd. Pasternak would also die early, two years after turning down the Nobel Prize, and the tragedy of his own lost love, the story serving as inspiration for *Dr. Zhivago*'s Lara, and the loss of his country's official support most certainly hastened his death.

Yuri Zhivago's dream from his youth had been to write "a book of impressions of life in which he would conceal, like sticks of dynamite, the most striking things he had so far seen." That is certainly what his creator does as well. *Dr. Zhivago* is a beautifully written novel, and it serves beyond its literary value as an example of why books sometimes can be seen as dangerous and worth fighting and maybe dying for. At the end of the novel, Pasternak includes several poems, and in one through Hamlet's voice, he quips, "The stir is over . . . / I strain to make the far-off echo yield / A cue to the events that may come in my day . . . / The order of the acts has been schemed and plotted / And nothing can avert the final curtain's fall / I stand alone." Pasternak, like others before him and others to follow, felt that the value found in freedom to speak what one believed was worth the sacrifice, and he was willing to make himself a sacrificial lamb. While it is unfortunate that most readers and filmgoers did not understand or appreciate the consequences Pasternak accepted for literature's sake, perhaps we can.

Bibliography

Dr. Zhivago (1957)

Work Cited

Flood, Alison. "CIA Used *Dr. Zhivago* as a Literary Weapon during the Cold War." *Guardian*, April 9, 2014.

—GS

Appendix:
Top Ten Character List

James Plath: For my top ten, I gravitated toward unique, richly imagined characters that have been embraced by pop culture in substantial or significant ways and are known even by people who haven't read the novels.

1. Don Quixote
2. Sherlock Holmes
3. Hester Prynne
4. Jay Gatsby
5. Alice in Wonderland
6. Harry Potter
7. Dracula
8. Ebenezer Scrooge
9. James Bond
10. Jane Eyre

Gail Sinclair: I saw these characters as memorable for the quality of their spirit or the depth of their angst. They uplifted or haunted me long after I left them in the pages of their books, and the top three were characters/books I wish I had created.

1. Hester Prynne
2. Atticus Finch
3. Jay Gatsby
4. Huckleberry Finn
5. Captain Ahab
6. Frankenstein's Creature
7. Jane Eyre
8. Don Quixote
9. Tess Durbeyfield
10. Ebenezer Scrooge

Kirk Curnutt: I'm drawn to characters who are either fallen angels or aspirational figures. Whether they're on the way up or down, I like people who are broken beyond repair, no matter if they know it or not.

1. Hester Prynne
2. Humbert Humbert

3. Ma Joad
4. Lily Bart
5. Emma Bovary
6. Philip Marlowe
7. Jay Gatsby
8. Sethe
9. Captain Ahab
10. Ántonia Shimerda

Index

About the Authors

James Plath is the R. Forrest Colwell endowed chair and professor of English at Illinois Wesleyan University, where he has taught American literature, journalism, creative writing, and film since 1988. As president of the John Updike Society, he's devoted much of his time to turning the John Updike Childhood Home in Shillington, Pennsylvania, into a museum. A former Fulbright scholar (Barbados, 1995), he is the author of two poetry chapbooks and author/editor of *Conversations with John Updike* (1994), *Remembering Ernest Hemingway* (1999), *Historic Photos of Ernest Hemingway* (2009), *Critical Insights: Raymond Carver* (2013), *Critical Insights Film: Casablanca* (2016), and *John Updike's Pennsylvania Interviews* (2016).

Gail Sinclair is executive director and scholar in residence of the Winter Park Institute at Rollins College. She has served for nearly a decade as vice president of the Ernest Hemingway Foundation and Society and on the board of directors for the F. Scott Fitzgerald Society. Her publications include essays in *Ernest Hemingway in Context* (2013), *F. Scott Fitzgerald in Context* (2013), *Edith Wharton in Context* (2012), *Approaches to Teaching Fitzgerald's* The Great Gatsby (2009), *Teaching Hemingway's* A Farewell to Arms (2008), and *Hemingway's Women: Female Critics and the Female Voice* (2002). She is the coeditor (with Steve Paul and Steven Trout) of *War + Ink: New Perspectives on Ernest Hemingway's Early Life and Writings* (2014) and *Key West Hemingway: A Reassessment* (2009, coedited with Kirk Curnutt).

Kirk Curnutt is professor and chair of English at Troy University. A resident since 1993 of Zelda Fitzgerald's hometown of Montgomery, Alabama, he is a passionate devotee of all things F. Scott Fitzgerald, serving as executive director of the F. Scott Fitzgerald Society, as managing editor of its annual *F. Scott Fitzgerald Review*, and as a board member of the Scott and Zelda Fitzgerald Museum. He is also a trustee of the Ernest Hemingway Foundation and Society. He has published on figures as diverse as Gertrude Stein and the Beach Boys' Brian Wilson. Curnutt is the author of fifteen volumes of criticism and fiction, including, most recently, *Key West Hemingway* (2009, coedited with Gail Sinclair), the pocket biography *William Faulkner* (2017), *American Literature in Transition, 1970–1980* (2017), and *Reading Hemingway's* To Have and Have Not (2015).

CPSIA information can be obtained
at www.ICGtesting.com
Printed in the USA
LVHW061048070719
623148LV00023B/301/P